In Moin Mir we have a prodigious talent. The new Amin Maalouf.

**WILLIAM DALRYMPLE**

In *Travels With Plotinus* Moin Mir takes us on an enthralling journey in the footsteps of the elusive 3rd century CE philosopher regarded as the founding father of neo Platonism. From the streets of Old Rome, to the banks of the Nile, from Athens to Alexandria to the island of Patmos, Mir describes with brio his whirlwind intellectual quest for the meaning of Plotinus's central concept of 'The One'.

**ANDREA DI ROBILANT**

Retracing the footsteps of Plotinus, the ancient Greek philosopher whose dream was to reach India and study the Upanishads, Moin Mir takes us on a meditative, poetic and evocative journey in search of Oneness and Unity. Nearly 1800 years separate the author from his subject, but surely this would have been immaterial had they met.

**ALBA ARIKHA**

In his celebrated novel *The Lost Fragrance of Infinity* Moin Mir retraces the steps of a group of Sufi travellers on their Westward journey from India to Spain and in the process brings to life the richness and beauty of one of the great spiritual traditions of mankind. In his new work *Travels With Plotinus* the author embarks on an Eastward journey, together with one of the founding fathers of that very tradition: Plotinus, the Alexandrian philosopher who had hoped to visit India but never reached it. Now Moin Mir has come to take him there. A voyage like no other awaits.

**STEFAN SPERL**
EMERITUS PROFESSOR IN ARABIC AND MIDDLE EASTERN STUDIES
SOAS, UNIVERSITY OF LONDON

It's not only Moin Mir's quite astounding depth of knowledge but his magical, mystical, compassionate and deeply moving observations that make this book very much more than a 'just read' travelogue.

**NASEERUDDIN SHAH**

# Moin Mir

# travels

# with

# plotinus

## A Journey in Search of Unity

UNICORN

First published in India, 2024

This edition published in 2025
by Unicorn, an imprint of Unicorn Publishing Group
Charleston Studio
Meadow Business Centre
Lewes
BN8 5RW
United Kingdom
www.unicornpublishing.org

*Credit for Insert Images*: Antonio Monfreda: Page 3 (below); Princess Vittoria Alliata and Eric: Page 9 (below, right); Nico and Ritsa Eliou: Page 14 (above); Silka Rittson-Thomas: Pages 12 (above, right), 15 (below, left); Alamy: Pages 4 (above, left); 5 (below, right); 14 (below, right); 15 (below, right); 16; Shutter stock: Page 8 (above).

The copyright for all other images rests with the author.

ISBN 978-1-916846-63-0

10 9 8 7 6 5 4 3 2 1

Printed in India

Make voyages! Attempt them... there's nothing
else.... The violets in the mountains
have broken the rocks.
*Tennessee Williams*


A traveller without observation is a
bird without wings.
*Saadi*


Don't tell me how educated you are,
tell me how much you have travelled.
*Mohammad*

DEDICATED TO

My Grandfather
Mir Khairat Ali Khan

# CONTENTS

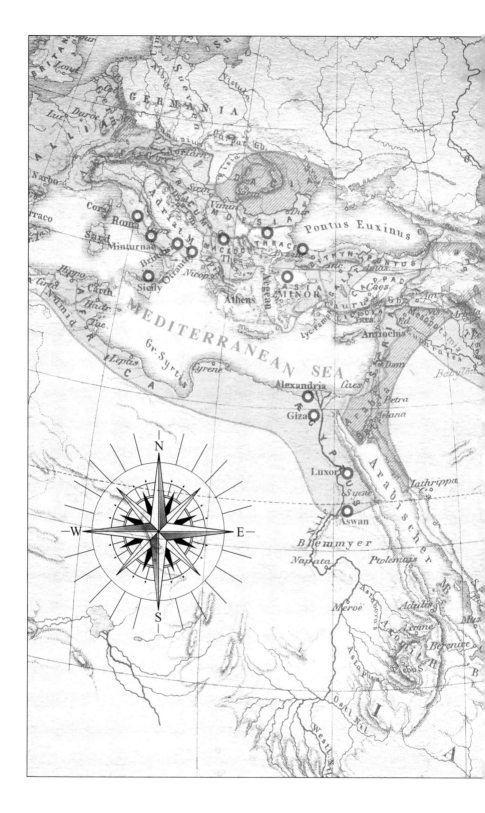

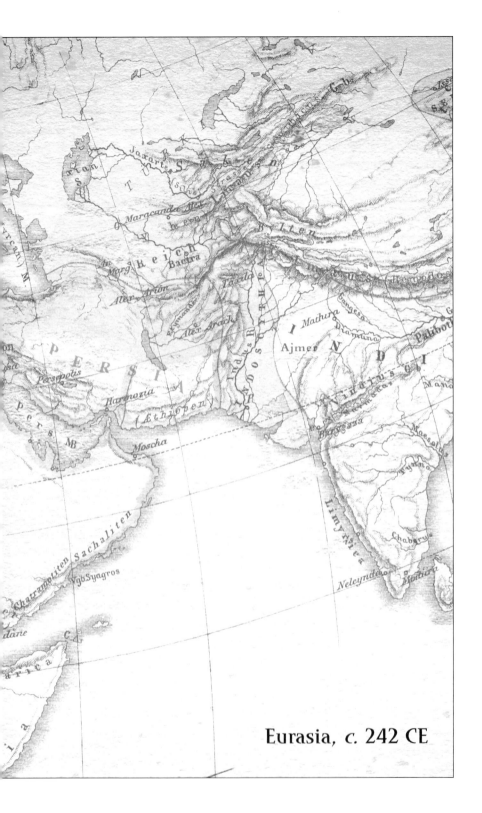

Eurasia, *c.* 242 CE

# ACKNOWLEDGEMENTS

While travelling in the footsteps of Plotinus I had the good fortune of meeting some exceptional human beings. From the simplest farmers and refugees ravaged by war to aristocrats and princesses. From innocent boatmen drifting on the Nile to the destitute that line the streets in Ajmer, and from patient potters and artists in Greece to thinkers and writers in Rome. All of them opened their hearts to me and spoke with beauty, passion, love and sometimes with fear. Without these cherished experiences and conversations, you would not be holding this book in your hand. I thank them all. The names of Fuad and Narek Shogolu have been changed so that no harm befalls them.

I thank the ethereal beauty of our planet which I encountered on my travels, particularly in the isolated parts of Greece, the warm breeze and rustle of the olive branches in Sicily and the formless but beguiling charm of the Nile in Egypt.

This book would not have been possible if *The Enneads*, which had been written in Greek, would not have been translated and edited into English by Prof. Lloyd Gerson. Exemplary commentaries by J. Bussanich and Pao-Shen Ho helped me to better understand Plotinus' philosophy. Prof. Stefan Sperl's lectures on Plotinus and his brilliant book *Faces of the Infinite* were enlightening and so was *The Philosophy of the Upanishads* by Paul Deussen and its English rendering by Rev. A.S. Geden. Edward Gibbon's *The History of the Decline and Fall of the Roman Empire* and Anthony Sattin's *The Pharaoh's Shadow: Travels in Ancient and Modern Egypt* were immensely helpful. The lectures by Myles Burnyeat and Bryan Magee on Plato's Theory of Forms were informative. I have referred to and quoted from all the above works of scholarship and many more which are part of the bibliography and notes section. I thank Aphrodite Gonou for her time in Athens and for her introduction to the artist Nikomachi Karakostanoglou Boutari. I am grateful to the wonderful photographer Antonio Monfreda. Both of us were in Rome on the day of the murmuration of the starlings; while my phone ran out of battery and I failed to take a picture, it was Antonio who was successful and has been most kind to share his picture of the starlings that has been reproduced in this book. Some of Silka Rittson-Thomas' beautiful pictures of Patmos have been reproduced in the book. I thank my wife Leonie and my younger daughter Zohaa for their patience, immeasurable endurance, and encouragement. My older daughter Aara's occasional enquiry about the progress of the manuscript kept me alert.

## Important Dates

Abraham: Approx. 2006 BCE
Upanishads: Approx. 1,000 – 500 BCE
Hermetica: Approx. 1,000 – 500 BCE
Socrates: 470 BCE – 399 BCE
Plato: 424 BCE – 347 BCE. He studied philosophy under Socrates and is considered the architect of ancient Greek philosophical thought.
Aristotle: 384 BCE – 322 BCE. He studied under Plato and went on to become arguably the greatest philosopher to have lived. He also taught Alexander.
Plotinus: 204 CE – 270 CE. Studied Plato, Aristotle and Hermetica in Alexandria and wrote *The Enneads* in Rome.
Mohammad: 570 CE – 632 CE

## Plotinus' Travels

232 CE: Plotinus begins the study of philosophy under Ammonius Saccas in Alexandria after having travelled extensively in Egypt trying to find an inspiring teacher.
242 CE: Plotinus leaves Egypt to join Gordian III's army with the hope of reaching Persia and eventually India.
246/247 CE: Plotinus returns to Rome. Later, he visits Sicily for a short while.
269-270 CE: Plotinus leaves Rome for a country estate near Minturnae.

## Other Reference Dates

332 BCE: Alexander conquers Egypt.

326 BCE: Alexander defeats Porus in a battle near the river Jhelum, India.

323 BCE: Death of Alexander.

47 BCE: Julius Caesar conquers Egypt.

30-350 CE: Kushans rule most of North India, Afghanistan, and parts of Central Asia.

330 CE: Emperor Constantine shifts capital from Rome to Byzantium and renames it Constantinople. Also known as 'Nova Roma' or 'New Rome'.

641 CE: Arab conquest of Egypt.

827 CE: Arab conquest of Sicily.

1453 CE: Ottoman conquest of Constantinople.

In 242 CE, Plotinus, a philosopher who was travelling from Rome to India, tugged at the reins of his horse while breaking his journey in Byzantium. He looked heavenwards for inspiration and after several moments of silence uttered the words:

Intellect is free because of the Good (the One).[1]

Around Plotinus burnt the campfires of a Roman army on the march. He looked closely at those fires. Having just declared that intellect was free because of 'The One' he spoke again:

The intellect though did somehow dare to stand away from the One.[2]

# PROLOGUE

1,780 years later, on 26 February 2022, a group of Catholic monks racing through the narrow streets of Trastevere in Rome headed towards the Apostolic Palace – the residence of the Pope in the Vatican. Under Michelangelo's looming fresco 'The Creation of Adam', the monks walked swiftly, accompanied only by the sound of their footsteps. In the fresco that watched over them, God created man as a reflection of himself and gifted him intellect. There is a certain arrogance in man as he nonchalantly looks at his creator. The creator though seems utterly in love with his creation and seems to be surging towards him ready to give it all. But God doesn't quite touch man, thus, not giving it all away. On the way to their meeting with the Pope, some of the monks must have glanced upwards for inspiration, for what they were going to discuss was something that could change the very fabric of humanity forever. The subject: Artificial Intelligence (AI), its ramifications on humankind, and its use for good and evil.

More than a millennium and a half after the death of Plotinus, one of the greatest philosophers to have walked the earth, I am travelling in his footsteps. On the same date when the Pope was meeting with the monks in Rome, I am in Byzantium, later known as Constantinople and New Rome; now known as Istanbul. But Byzantium is the name by which Plotinus would have recognised it while breaking his journey here on his way to India. My hands caress what remains of the foundations of an ancient Greek wall, quite possibly the Baths of Zeuxippus built over a temple of Zeus. These are the same walls that Plotinus would have touched, and the remnants of the ancient Roman road, the Via Egnatia that I am walking down would have disappeared under the hooves of his horse which he had hoped would carry him to India. To my west lies Rome and to my east Anatolia, Persia, and India. Seduced by Plotinus' philosophy of 'The One' (unity), I have been travelling in his footsteps, reading his work, fulfilling his dream of reaching India, and marvelling at his restless mind.

The beauty of unity is irrefutable, and as Plotinus says, it has bestowed a gift on us – the intellect. It is the free will of intellect, though, that uses unity evidently for intellectual evolution, as in the case of man's greatest astronomical achievement: the Mars landing in February 2021. This was only possible when Swati Mohan, Allen Chen, and Ken

Farley – scientists of Indian, Chinese, and American origin came together as part of NASA's team to land a rover aptly named Perseverance on the surface of Mars. For all its social challenges, a country that has a name beginning with the word 'United' made this monumental human achievement possible. Alarmingly though, unity can also be used by intellect to wreck destruction as Vladimir Putin does by identifying Ukrainians and Russians as 'one' people and unleashing war and human suffering.[3]

The rugged rust-coloured walls of Byzantium overlook the sparkling cobalt waters of the Golden Horn. I feel the restlessness of the waves within me quite like what Plotinus must have felt standing here in the third century. The wind picks up. To the right are the misty blue mountains of Anatolia towards which Plotinus would have nudged his horse. The mountains draw me in. I will travel more for I have been set in motion by the Plotinian thought to learn and unlearn. Delving into our basic instincts of good and evil, I will continue to journey in his footsteps through lands that echo with his philosophy. In those lands, I will stand dazzled by the power of oneness and the stealth of intellect.

# INTRODUCTION

**Rome 242 CE**

Emperor Gordian III flings open the doors of the temple of Janus signalling war as a crescendo of trumpets erupt in the air. The mighty Roman army is going to war with Persia. But one man, given neither to lance or sword, but to letters and thought, has embedded himself in the legions. Travelling with the army brings relative safety and assured provisions. He nurtures a secret dream – one of reaching India. Plotinus, an already renowned philosopher having studied Aristotle and Plato in Alexandria and Rome, now has an unquenchable thirst to drink from the fountains of knowledge in India. That faraway land which lies beyond Persia and beyond the flowing Indus has to offer the most mouth-watering prospect for any philosopher – the study of the Upanishads. In time, history would mark Plotinus as one of the greatest thinkers, but today as he watches emperor Gordian III approaching, he can only hope that the Persian campaign would end in victory, thus unlocking the road to India.

The Roman Empire is imploding with the loss of territories in Mesopotamia which must be regained. Under its audacious emperor Shapur I, Persia has stretched its borders and taken key towns in Mesopotamia that were part of the Roman Empire. The Persian advance must be checked. In response to the war trumpets, famed legions pour into the streets of Rome. Catching the first rays of the sun, armour plates of stalwart warriors glisten on robust chests. Crimson helmet tails of commanders ascend and descend in brilliant unison, and the nervous hooves of their majestic steeds exude a thunderous clamour whilst clashing against the stone road. Passing the Colosseum where in peace times gladiatorial contests between man and beast had entertained citizenry, the legions ride the straight path dotted with olive trees passing the marble pillared Forum of Augustus and the temple of Mars, finally making their way to the Pantheon – the temple of all gods. Here, emperor Gordian III standing on the porch between imposing pillars addresses his troops amidst wild cheering crowds.

After a rousing speech by the emperor, the army winds its way out of the city gates like a serpentine and into the pine-tree-lined hills. The borderlands with Persia are a long way away, and the legions will have to chart their course through the untamed woodlands of southern Italy from where they will board ships which will carry them across the dancing waves of the Adriatic and into the Roman colonies of Macedonia and Thrace, after which they will enter Asia Minor via Byzantium. From there the sweeping lands of Anatolia with its flowing rivers, rugged mountains, gorges, and ravines will open to them. Beyond these lands they will meet the Persian army. Amidst a sea of fluttering war banners and sparkling sabres, Plotinus sees his dream of reaching India becoming a reality.

Born in Egypt into a Greek family in 204 CE, Plotinus, aged thirty-nine and at the peak of his intellectual powers, can feel the excitement running through his veins. An adventure awaits him of which there can be no predicted end. Would he return once he had been enchanted by the charms and philosophical depth of India? What would life be in that distant land whose frontiers had barely been penetrated by Alexander the Great? But Plotinus' dream to reach India would not come true. It would be shattered in Ctesiphon (modern-day Iraq), and he would be forced to return to Rome.

In time, Plotinus, who spoke and wrote in Greek, would go on to dictate to Porphyry (his devoted student) his most profound teachings which would eventually be compiled as *The Enneads*. The origins of the title are in the Greek word Ennea, meaning 'nine'. An Ennea is a 'niner' because each Ennea is composed of nine treatises. *The Enneads* would eventually become the unimpeachable philosophical landmark in the study of metaphysics, the One creator, the concept of unity, the origin of intellect, soul, 'othering', beauty and happiness, origins of mathematics, and the study of the most delicious question of all time – how can we unite with God?

Porphyry describes Plotinus as such:

When he spoke his intellect was manifest even in the way it lit up his face. He was handsome to look at, but even more beautiful in those moments. He exuded kindliness; his face looked gentle but also intellectually rigorous when he was questioned.... A number of men and women of the highest social order (in Rome) brought their offspring to him when they were about to die. They would entrust them to him along with what remained of their property, treating his protection as sacred and god like.... He was, to those who had any dealings with him, kind and accessible. For this reason although he lived for 26 whole years in Rome, and acted as arbitrator in many cases of personal dispute, he never made a single enemy in his public life.... He certainly could not stand talking about his race, his parents or his original homeland and disliked the idea of being painted or sculpted that when Amelius asked him to allow an image to be made he said "Isn't it enough that I have to carry around the image that nature has clothed me with?"[4]

The most impactful theory that Plotinus established in *The Enneads* is that '*it is from "The One" that all beings are beings*'. According to Plotinus 'The One' is indivisible, and in his writings, he often addresses 'The One' as 'The Good', 'Unity', 'Simple', 'First Principle' and 'It'. All five are synonyms for 'The One'. He believed 'The One' generates intellect, the activation of which brings about substance. The intellect then generates soul and being. The intellect also causes multiplicity. But for multiplicity to exist something singular and simple must be in existence prior to it and that is 'The One'. The intellect and soul from the moment they come into existence are injected with a desire by 'The One' to know their originator and they succumb to this desire placing them in a constant quest to reunite with 'The One'.

Plotinus' thought has striking similarities with *Brahman* (the One – the absolute reality) in the Upanishads and the *Atman* (the individual soul that seeks union with *Brahman*). Around 350 years after Plotinus, a man would emerge from the silent sand dunes of Arabia, his heart ablaze with poetic expressions of 'The One' – his name was Mohammad. The philosophical concept of *Tawheed* in Islam where 'The One' is proclaimed as the Absolute and the Creator of the universe resonates deeply with Plotinian thought. And 1,700 years later, modern scientists would accept a theory called the

'Big Bang singularity' – a moment of creation that originated from singularity giving birth to space, time, and the universe.

One can imagine Plotinus crouched over his stone desk in Rome surrounded by flickering candles lamenting never having reached India, desiring only solitude while reciting to Porphyry the most exquisite poetry.

> My soul is still in even stronger labour. Perhaps she is now at the point when she must bring forth, having reached the fullness of her birth-pangs in her eager longing for the One. But we must sing another charm to her, if we can find one anywhere to allay her pangs.... Intellect in love, when it goes out of its mind "drunk with the nectar", simplified into happiness.[5]

Plotinus must have paused, giving his student time to reflect. More words were then uttered by the ageing philosopher in a whisper, for he was about to declare a mystical vision.

> The soul in her natural state is in love with God and wants to be united with It; it is like the noble love of a girl for her noble father... in this way the Soul also loves the One - the Good, moved by it to love from the beginning.... So we must ascend again to the Good, which every soul desires. Anyone who has seen It knows what I mean when I say that It (the One) is beautiful... alone, simple, single and pure form on which all depends and to which all look: For the One is cause of life and mind and being... the knowledge or touching of the Good is the greatest thing and Plato says "it is the greatest study".[6]

As Rome lay shrouded under a blanket of slumber, Porphyry's heart was aglow with enlightenment, and one can imagine him making his way through the deserted mid-night streets of Rome reciting those words he had so diligently penned down for his teacher.

With these words Plotinus championed the following: There is 'One' creator, and He is the first cause of all beings that are in motion. This core principle is incontestably inspired by Aristotle's famous presentation of God as an Unmoved First Mover, as an originator of all processes who Himself stands outside all change. In Aristotle's words, *'There is something that always moves the things in motion and the First Mover is itself Unmoved.'*[7]

Plotinus emphasises that intellect and soul once generated by 'The One' in turn desire 'The One', and based on his claim of visual contact, 'The One' is beautiful, accessible, and immanent in man. Access was possible through ascetic ways which could make man ascend towards 'The One' and finally unite with Him. To do this, man would have to shed all that he knew, which had alienated him from 'The One'. In ancient Greek this final union with 'The One' is termed *Henosis*. Eight hundred years after Plotinus, Sufi mystics – practitioners of mystical Islam – would call this union with 'The One': *visaal-e-ilahi*. Through time, this seeking for final union would have such an impact on writers that even W. Somerset Maugham would find it irresistible, exploring it through a mystical protagonist in his novel *The Razor's Edge*.

Plotinus travelled extensively whilst tilling his mind, chiselling his thoughts, and refining his teachings about 'The One'. Immensely secretive about his childhood and youth in Egypt, he didn't reveal much even to his closest friends and confidants. But we do know that he had a searching mind as a young man growing up in Roman Egypt. This mind that craved the study of philosophy took him to all parts of Egypt in search of an inspiring teacher. He eventually found that teacher in Ammonius Saccas who lived in Alexandria. Ammonius Saccas introduced Plotinus to ancient Greek and Indian thought, triggering a curiosity in him to learn in India. After spending years studying in Alexandria, Plotinus decided to venture to India which led him to join the army of Gordian III on its way to Persia.

And so 1,780 years after his failed attempt at reaching India, I decided to travel in his footsteps to fulfil his dream of reading the Upanishads in India and to understand the relevance of Plotinian philosophy for our times. From the mighty Roman Colosseum to the tranquil waters of the Yamuna. From Egypt where the muezzins' call to prayer resounds alongside the unfading glory of the pyramids, to the olive groves of Sicily where silence is only interspersed by the sweet song of the lark. From the rubble they call the Berlin Wall that once stood as the dark symbol of division, to the wall of 'oneness' in Delphi. And from the abandoned ruins of Aristotle's academy in Athens where dancing crimson poppies still whisper the master's words, to the lonely forgotten mountain caves on a remote Greek island. Through these lands my feet and mind tread and feast on the fertile intellectual fields that Plotinus had cultivated with a resplendent love and heightened allure for 'Unity'. I observe art and architecture, understand language and poetry all of which have the spark to stir the soul with a profound question – for if we are made as a 'Unity' and as a reflection of 'the Good', 'the One', then why aren't we simply that? The answer lies in the free will of intellect. During my travels from the autumn months of 2021 till the autumn of 2022 I observed this 'free will', its remarkable ability for compassion and astonishing appetite, and greed for power and self-enrichment. I absorbed Plotinus' teachings by focusing on 'The One's' most relatable yet elusive definition: 'The Good' and 'Simple', and how humankind has grappled with itself to rise as 'one' and bring the 'simplest good' into our lives – with astounding success, and dismal failure. My wanderings are a response to a summon from the past with a hope that they may become a pointer to the future.

# 1

# THE ENCHANTED FOREST

**Autumn 2021**

Just before twilight, the fabled rose-pink clouds over Rome drift past the dome of St. Peter's Basilica. The great baroque dome that has dominated the Roman skyline since the Renaissance rises above the Sycamore trees that line the Tiber on both sides. Drooping branches of the tall trees bow low as if paying homage to the river and the sacred dome. The Tiber flows unrestrained under the arched stone bridge of Ponte Sisto, its waters reflecting the soft rose-coloured sky in a glazed sheen. Floating on these waters are pale leaves that the Sycamores have shed, signalling autumn. The branches cast their last soft shadows on the pale apricot walls of Roman homes. I watch this serene setting crouching over the Ponte Sisto bridge. A lone starling flies in and takes its place at the edge of the bridge. For a while she is still. Then restlessness seems to overcome her. I notice how curious she is about her surroundings, most of which I think are intelligible to her. But soon she ruffles her sea green plumes and sings. It is a sweet song. Pleasing to the ear, it heightens the experience of a serene Roman autumn.

Then, most extraordinarily, within seconds, the lofty branches of the Sycamore trees are filled with starlings flying in and responding to the originator's call. The lone bird song now has an orchestrated rhythm quite incredibly being conducted by my companion on the bridge. A few idle strollers on the bridge also stop to listen, and we nod to each other in acknowledgement of the natural symphonic beauty we are being treated to. Soon, the desire for flight, the ultimate demonstration of freedom and ascension, seduces her, and she's gone. Moved by love for her and her song, like a moth to a flame, thousands of starlings abandon the trees and follow her in flight. My eyes try to track her, but she has become one with them and they with her and are seen as one whirling band of birds. The band ripples like velvet into stunning shapes as the birds soar and descend and soar again, responding to their originator. They whirl with gay abandon as dusk descends. Eventually, turning their attention to divinity, they circle around the dome of St. Peter's Basilica and vanish. I saw a thousand, yet I saw one. Called the murmuration of starlings, this is a phenomenon yet unexplained in entirety. What makes the birds fly in such unifying beauty is unknown. What is known though, is that they fly together without differentiating amongst one another, be it variation in size or colours of plume or beak. They fly with mathematical precision, and in response to a single originating call of love. Some believe this flight of unified beauty protects them from large predators who can only see an enormous swirling band that changes shape regularly rather than a small vulnerable starling. It is because they fly as one that they produce such a beautiful sight and thrive as a species. Plotinus must have encountered this wondrous murmuration of the

Roman starlings and I can't help but think how he might have responded.

I'm in Rome – the eternal city. Tomorrow evening, I drive to Brindisi following the Via Appia, the ancient Roman stone road that was built by emperors to connect Rome with its southern province of Puglia. It is from Otranto and Brindisi, two ports in Puglia that overlooked Albania and Greece, that Roman armies boarded ships and sailed across the Adriatic to either protect the empire's frontiers or expand them. From one of these ports lying in the bottom heel of Italy, Gordian III's army boarded ships to cross the Adriatic.

Having arrived late in the afternoon from London, I took a taxi straight from Fiumicino airport to a studio apartment I booked on Airbnb in Trastevere. It is small but cosy with a large wall stacked with books including ancient Roman history. The owner is obviously interested in the subject. I wonder if he has read *The Enneads* as I put down my suitcase. A quick scan of the bookshelves and the answer is – no. I pull out my copy, a large hardback edition, and place it on a reading desk for me to get back to. A loft with a bed, above which a low hanging ceiling of wooden beams completes the typical 'Roman apartment for rent' look. After a quick survey of my temporary dwelling, I grabbed my notebook and rushed out to catch the tempting autumn light on the Ponte Sisto bridge.

Having soaked in the 'starling moment' and with only a few hours of light remaining, I decide to walk down the bridge and go past the Jewish quarter, making my way towards Vicolo de Catinari. The charcoal-coloured cobbled streets of Rome cling to the ground in an appealing harmony. As the sun drops Rome is preparing for the night, and the gleaming cobbles reflect the light emanating from street side restaurants and wine bars. Amidst the hum of carefree Rome, two brass plaques on the cobbles glisten with distinction. They catch my eye. I stop and lean over to take a closer look. One of the brass plaques reads 'Qui Abitava Benedetto Dell Ariccia Nato 1874 Deportato Auschwitz Assassinato 30.6.1944'. A startling reminder of the Holocaust under Mussolini, and how this person had been deported and killed in Auschwitz. How different we are to the starlings.

But what I'm most keen to do this evening is begin my journey by walking in the footsteps of Plotinus through ancient Roman streets. Google maps are great, but there's nothing quite like a phone call to an old friend who could hopefully point me in the right direction. And so, standing in Piazza Farnese in front of the fabulous Church of Santa Brigida, out comes the mobile and my fingers push the buttons for Leopoldo di Mottola. Leopoldo is one of those friends who carries the title of 'eternal' quite like the city he lives in. Tall, large, generous, with soft brown eyes, and blessed with a baritone which if he had used for a *Godfather* audition, Marlon Brando would have been shown the door. Leopoldo is of Neapolitan origin but has made Rome his home since many years. He answers the phone.

'When did you get in?'

'This afternoon and off to Brindisi tomorrow, and then to India.'

'Let's get dinner tonight... Nino's, close to the Spanish Steps... 8:30... I'll book,' Leopoldo's baritone surges through the phone.

'Great. Just very quickly, I want to begin my journey by walking in the footsteps of Plotinus... quite literally.'

'The Forum... begin there,' Leopoldo roars and hangs up.

Scribbling notes into my notepad, I make my way. I'm soon confronted with crowded streets, speeding Vespas darting past me, Italian taxi drivers manoeuvring traffic lights with roguish efficiency, and waiters on footpaths desperately trying to grab your attention to sell a greasy mozzarella pizza.

After fifteen minutes of walking down Via di Monte Caprino and Via di S. Teodoro, my eyes are tiring of nineteenth-century architecture and crave the splendour of ancient Rome. I let out a deep sigh. But then almost out of nowhere, the corner of my eye catches a glimpse. Like an elusive siren she lures me in, persuading me to turn into hidden alleys and nooks, and then like a flash of lightning ancient Rome reveals herself.

Overwhelming my senses, she lays herself bare as the Roman Forum – a spectacle of temples, soaring roofless pillars, and a myriad of primordial ruined walls which are a blend of stone and moss-covered terra-cotta brick dating back to seventh century BCE, all of which are glistening like an open treasure chest drenched in the fabled light of a Roman sunset. The Palatine Hill, a maze of haunting rust-coloured brick walls and alleys, runs like a never-ending river. As soon as I lay my eyes on these uninhabited gorgeous pathways of the past with yawning curved enclosures and silent crevices, the noise from the present fades and is replaced by the sound of distant history. Large smooth grey-black stones laid out in perfection mark the streets of ancient Rome. On both sides of this street are elegant pine trees. Their slender trunks rise high, and on their delicate branches like clouds coming to rest are the lush pine. I tread the stony path knowing well that I'm now walking in the philosophers' footsteps.

Making my way through these twisting alleyways I encounter ruined homes; one such could have belonged to Plotinus. The once magnificent temple of Jupiter and the more recently restored temple of Vesta bear testimony to Rome's sponge-like qualities in absorbing Greek influence, be it worship or architecture, for Jupiter was inspired by Zeus, and Vesta the goddess of home and hearth from the Greek word Hestia. More Greek influence is to come as I pass the mighty yet lonely columns of the temple of Castor and Pollux. The temple of Saturn then presents itself in the form of eight roofless columns with wild vegetation sprouting out of their summits. I continue my walk and arrive at a place Plotinus must have enjoyed visiting – the Rostra. This was an honoured and elevated platform from where orators, nobles and thinkers including Plotinus delivered their lectures. Although Plotinus steered away from politics, from the Rostra he spoke passionately about metaphysics, the intellect, and his theory of 'The One'. Not far was the spot where the temple of Janus stood – the pagan god who presided over the beginning and end of conflict. Much revered in ancient Rome, the temple doors of Janus were always shut and opened only to declare war.

At the edge of my view is the towering Colosseum. Its muscular spherical walls, jagged edges and numerous arches absorb the last of twilight and respond by turning an ochre colour. I can visualise Plotinus as the one to have disregarded materialism draped in his simple robes admonishing the Colosseum as a 'mere image of something more intelligible'. In Plotinus' time, the streets leading up to the Colosseum must have been choked with people dressed in robes and open strapped sandals bursting through the sturdy arches to witness giant-sized gladiators clashing sabres and shields in a bloody battle for survival. The carnal roar for blood still reverberates in these streets that lead up to the Colosseum. Chariots of important senators must have hurtled past, their wheels kicking up dust clouds, attracting the scorn of strolling commoners. At the far end of the Forum is a large open space, possibly a local market in Plotinus' time, with rustic shops that sold everything from Indian spices to Egyptian cotton fabric. These shops must have been brimming with bargain seekers and shrewd merchants. But today these criss-crossing roads lie silent, juxtaposed against modern Rome with its cars, cafes and restaurants serving everything from chocolate biscotti to pasta. Time has passed much quicker than I would have imagined. I leave the Forum making my way under the Arch of Titus, a gorgeous architectural gem built in 70 CE to commemorate Rome's victory in Judea. Satisfied that I have begun my travels with footsteps well entrenched in the pathways walked by Plotinus, I make my way to see my friend.

I enter Nino's charming wood-panelled surroundings and ask for a table booked under Leopoldo's name. The restaurant seems to be teeming with people, a sign that the spirit of Rome is fighting back from the ravaging it received at the hands of Covid a year ago. Leopoldo hasn't arrived, which gives me just enough time to chat with the waiter who gives me a brief introduction about the restaurant. Seeing my initial interest, he takes it as a sign to wax lyrical about how the owner, a Tuscany born restaurateur, is obsessed with creating and serving simple Italian cuisine. Leopoldo strides in just when I'm beginning to feel the first strains of a dragging conversation.

Being embraced by Leopoldo is like being ensconced in a warm overcoat.

'So, you are on a journey in the footsteps of Plotino?' He asks as our eyes chart the menu, and after having spoken about our kids and all that's familial.

'Yes... beginning here in the city he lived for twenty-six years and where he taught,' I reply.

'Why?' He asks, pointing to artichokes on the menu and signalling for two to the waiter. I had earlier given my consent for that starter.

'Well... we live in divisive times, and I'm trying to work with his teachings. I'm trying to use Plotinian thought as a lens to understand if "unity" is really used for "good".'

'That's a lot of thinking,' he says, glancing at the waiter who brings in the artichokes doused generously in fragrant olive oil.

'Not really, it is just observance of form, thought, and action.'

I decide to take the line of questioning into another space.

'What is it like to be living in Rome today? How do you see this multiplicity of cultures – pagan, Greek, Roman, and Christian – all coming together?' I probe further, knowing well that Leopoldo is Catholic.

'It is all in me... and I'm in it,' is his response, emphasising on 'it', and looking at me slurping on the tail end of a spaghetti that I am determined not to lose in the tomato sauce. I had earlier devoured the artichoke which had barely satiated my galloping appetite – a result of all the walking. Leopoldo signalled for his main course.

'But what is that "it" that you are "in"?' I ask, trying to get deeper.

'That "it" has come about through the ages. Every brick contributes to the DNA of Rome; every stone and pillar has added a new dimension... sure, bloody wars, human misery and carnage were an integral part of the Roman Empire as it expanded and contracted through time, but Rome constantly absorbed from the Greeks and Egyptians, be it philosophy, art, or politics. For years Rome violently persecuted early Christians and tried to extinguish the faith. But with time it came to accept it and flourished with its ascendance. Today, after more than seventy-five years of peace following the Second World War, I see all these as one. It belongs to me and I to it – a marvel.'

'So, it is peace that has brought about a sense of admiration, acceptance, and love for this multi-layered Roman identity?' I ask.

'Yes, and maturity of mind, which comes with time,' is Leopoldo's response. I leave my friend to his main course which he is relishing and decide not to probe any further. Our conversation meanders on its own and we discuss everything from olive oil, how to identify the perfect sun kissed Tuscan pomodoro, and, of course, wine and cheese. Supper is done, and with leonine grace my host makes his way out of the restaurant acknowledged by waiters and staff for his generosity – a hefty tip.

Leopoldo drives me home.

'Could I drop you here?' He asks, peering at me with his soft brown eyes. 'Your apartment is not far, just a short walk, and mine is to the left.'

'Sure, but what is this?' We are parked adjacent to another ruined site surrounded by supermarkets, pharmacies, restaurants, and modern apartment blocks.

'Ah, well, I knew you'd like this one... it is *Largo di Torre Argentina*, where Julius Caesar was assassinated. The Roman Senate. Enjoy it! And tomorrow visit the Pantheon.'

'I've visited the Pantheon before,' I say, getting out of the car and fixing my gaze on the ruins of the senate.

'Visit it again. The Pantheon will speak to you in the same language as Plotino... go and feel it in your bones,' Leopoldo says, waving with one hand and turning the steering wheel with the other.

I wave goodbye and walk up to the ruins of the senate. Illuminated in the dark are the lemon eyes of stray cats that have made these ruins their home. Some are lounging in the arches and others move in stealth, on the prowl for small prey. Massive, lonely pillars stand roofless at the spot where one of history's greatest figures fell. Stone steps peer out of the night, yearning to tell me a timeless tale. In 44 BCE a man ascended these steps with a desire to possess all power, until other men driven by desire to divide power struck him down. The silence of the night and an autumn chill brings bare the deadliness of intellect. Ambition, a product of intellect, had gotten the better of Caesar, and it had also gotten the better of the person he trusted most, the man who struck last – Brutus. 'Et tu, Brute' became a legendary Shakespearean testimony to betrayal, and it still echoes in a whisper amongst these lonely pillars. The effects of Brutus' 'unkindest cut of them all' plays out with glacial ruthlessness even in the politics of today.

Crouching over the ruined site that lies tranquil in the still night, I ponder over the questions it conceals – would Caesar have met his fate had he not chosen to break away from the senate driven by individual ambition? Dearly loved by his people, would he have contributed to their greater glory had he abandoned personal ambition and instead worked with the senate as one? After all, in Mark Antony's passionate speech while burying Caesar, he was hailed as a man who wept with the poor and granted them his private walks and orchards. As the senators and Brutus struck, were they not overtaken by personal jealousy concealed under the cloak of a greater political motive to unite Romans as one people and not be subservient to a dictator? We will never know. But what was true is that intellect had fuelled suspicion, greed, and discord – the same intellect which, according to Plotinus, could be filled with love and create soul. The 'thought' that brought down Julius Caesar would be debated, and its reverberations felt for centuries in Rome. Plotinus, who lived in this city 290 years after, must not have been unaffected by these reverberations.

I walk on. Descending mist softens the lights from lamp posts which have been standing as silent sentinels on the

Ponte Sisto bridge. The night, the gently gliding mist over the Tiber, and mellow lights presents a dream-like view. I walk over the bridge to cross into Trastevere. In these hazy surroundings, the bridge is playing host to a variety of novice musicians in their early twenties.

'Where are you from?' I ask, leaning against the bridge and glancing at the flowing Tiber.

'Tibet… and she's American,' says the flautist pointing at his drummer colleague who gives me a nod.

For a few minutes, I listen to their sweet music, a seamless marriage of flute and drums. Some people passing by drop coins which are greeted with an acknowledging smile by the Tibetan-American duo. Other musicians are waiting at the other end of the bridge but aren't playing. The Tibetan flautist takes a break.

'How does it work between you musicians? Is there a rivalry of sorts? How do you manage your time on the bridge?' I ask.

'There's no rivalry amongst amateurs. We are a fraternity and support each other,' says the flautist with a slight laugh.

'It just flows you know…,' adds the American lady drummer. 'When we are done, they'll come in and we'll rejoice in their success. It is for the love of music maan… just enjoy it,' she goes on, and then begins wrapping up her drums.

The musicians on the other side of the bridge take this as a sign to come over and take their place. They hug each other.

'Good night,' says the American lady drummer.

'Good night,' I smile, and walk over to Piazza Trilussa which is on the opposite side of the bridge. Piazza Trilussa, with its overflowing marble fountain and a reclining pine tree, has become the watering hole for the young who spend swathes of time in the grip of unbridled youthful joy, song, music, drink, and romance. A man of African origin is speaking fluent Italian with his Asian-looking companion, united through language and the unique fabric of Rome. My route takes me through a maze of narrow streets embellished with graffiti and erupting with dimly lit street side wine bars. I turn the keys to my apartment block, walk up the stairs, and turn in another key to the apartment door.

Placing my notebook on the desk and kicking off my sneakers, I switch on the desk lamp, pick up *The Enneads*, and settle in to read in silence. The view outside my window is a faint red silhouette of the curved dome of St. Peter's Basilica against an ink blue midnight sky. I can still hear a gentle distant tune by the musicians on the Ponte Sisto bridge. In these peaceful surroundings, my mind drifts to the ruins of the Roman senate as I read:

> Just as one who looks up to the heaven and sees the light of the stars thinks of their creator and seeks Him, so the one who has contemplated the intelligible universe gazed into it and wondered at it must seek its creator (the One) as well... and how He generated such a son as Intellect, a beautiful boy who has become plenitude from himself... But beginning as one (the intellect) it did not remain as it began, but unwittingly became many as it weighed down and unrolled itself in its desire to possess everything – how much better it would have been for it not to desire this, for it became the second.[8]

This teaching of Plotinus comes home to rest. 'The One' (The Good) created a beautiful boy called 'Intellect'. As an image of 'The One', the boy too was one and good. But then the boy grew and descended into multiplicity of thought. That multiplicity of thought was greed and ambition. This very desire to *possess everything* makes intellect strive for power. In bloody political theatres is where it then plays out its deadly game. This is what happened in 44 BCE when Caesar fell. Shakespeare would further investigate this multi-faceted dark side of intellect in Macbeth. Tormented by three metaphorical witches - greed, jealousy, and treachery - Macbeth would become the ultimate tragedy.

I take *The Enneads* up to the loft and read it in bed, reflecting on my encounter with the young musicians. I can still hear their faint sweet melody. Theirs was an uncomplicated fresh intellect that generated generosity and a sense of fraternity.

I turn the pages.

> But what sort of person should the man be who is to be led on this upward path? Surely one who as Plato says "...a human child who is going to be a philosopher, musician or a lover..."[9]

I scramble for my notes that are spread all over my bed and pick up a commentary on Plotinus by J. Bussanich.

> Intellect beginning as one did not remain as it began.

Here, Plotinus is suggesting that in the first ontological moment of procession the inchoate (young) intellect is a unity from which, as the following lines make clear, it falls away.[10]

> Intellect was unable to hold the power which it received from "the One" and broke it up and made the one power it received into many, that it might be able so to bear it part by part... not being able to think the whole as one.[11]

I can now relate to what I have experienced today with Plotinian thought. The young intellect generated by 'the Good' ('the One') is one, not multiple. Initially the young intellect looks with love and unity towards 'the One'. But with progression it multiplies and can't hold the power given to it by the One. And so, it divides that power, becomes multiple, and views things as many and different and not as a unity.

Young (inchoate) intellect was what I saw on the bridge where it manifested itself in the youth who had united as a fraternity of musicians. The unabashed joy of young intellect in the musicians did not see any difference between them; it was pure, simple, beautiful, selfless, and radiated love. It is the young who are true reflections of 'the Good'. Compared with the 'progressed intellect' of politicians which turns into greed and divisiveness, young intellect is the song of the divine. My last fading thought before sleep overtakes consciousness and *The Enneads* gently drops from my hand is of the Ponte Sisto bridge – a bridge of unity that brings people together.

The next day, the sun has climbed with force into the blue sky, bringing with it a crisp, clear day. Scurrying out of my bed loft, I take a quick shower, clutch my notebook and dash out. I'm aware that I must make the most of the remaining day before I leave for Brindisi. I breakfast at Caffe Settimiano, a tiny Italian bakery which has the most delicious pastry on offer and is owned by a cheerful moustached baker with glasses straight out of the seventies.

I plant myself on a chair outside the cafe that opens into the cobbled street overlooking Porta Settimiana – a stone arched gateway, the foundations of which were laid by emperor Aurelius in the third century. Today, it is the gateway to Trastevere. I decide to spend a few hours observing. I feel like the noble Ponte Sisto bridge which observes the flowing Tiber. It doesn't judge the Tiber's forceful and at times languid flow, nor does it judge its clarity or at times the residue of the world that it carries. It brings people together.

That's all it does. And so, like the bridge, I observe the world go by while making my way through a cream croissant and an English breakfast tea. This part of Rome is heaving with students studying at the John Cabot University – an American institution. A few American teenage girls sit next to me. They laugh, their conversation flowing between discussing their plans for the day and sending beguiling looks in the direction of a curly-haired Italian student who is perched on another table. Other students not far away are reading Alessandro Manzoni's classic love story *The Betrothed* in amateurish Italian, interspersed with giggles. Around the corner under the Porta Settimiana arch, a writer dabs his pen on his chin, lost in thought, as the arched gateway casts its generous shadow over him, shielding him from the sun, almost nudging him to include it in his story.

I pay for breakfast and make my way to the Pantheon. It is easy to imagine Gordian III's army in which Plotinus had embedded himself marching towards the Pantheon. Approaching this great symbol of Rome from Via Della Palombella, the original structure looks like a gigantic, cylindrical, mud-brick mound. As the Pantheon slowly presents itself to the eager eye, the magnitude of the dome dwarfs one completely. It is astonishingly large. Dedicated to the seven gods of the planets, Pantheon means 'all the Gods'. Initially constructed by Marcus Agrippa as a temple to Roman gods that had been inspired by Greek gods, around 40 BCE, a triangular facade was added to it by emperor Hadrian in 126 CE. Honouring Agrippa's efforts, Hadrian chose not to inscribe his name but retain the original inscription of Agrippa.

In front of the Pantheon rises the Egyptian obelisk originally built by Rameses II in honour of the Egyptian God Ra and brought to Rome in ancient times. The obelisk stood in homage to Isis, the Egyptian goddess of healing and magic, in a temple southeast of the Pantheon. The obelisk was put astride a fountain, at the base of which dolphins and gargoyles with gaping mouths spew out cascading water. Since 609 CE, the Pantheon has been a Catholic Church – the Basilica di Santa Maria. Today, soaking up the magnificent sunshine, the Pantheon is nothing short of an architectural masterpiece that demonstrates the unity of layered history – a unique language that is exceptionally rare in buildings of antiquity. I climb onto the porch where Gordian III had given his rousing speech and pass the Egyptian pillars. Inside the Pantheon, under the might of the dome, I stand speechless. Right in the centre of the lofty dome is a circular opening called the oculus – or the eye. I gaze at it wide-eyed in silence. And then something happens. At the stroke of noon, the sun, as if stirred by man's intoxicated love for the divine, pours itself through the oculus in one voluminous dazzling beam of light, illuminating the interiors with a warm luminosity that seduces the soul. All diversity seems to be accepted by this beam of light, and yet it also sweeps it away and brings it into its own where only that light exists. My eyes follow the light. As it spreads it reveals ancient pagan walls marrying into pillars and they in turn enmesh with paintings of the Madonna and child, which in turn merge into the tomb of Rafael, the fifteenth-century artist who had pleaded to be buried here. This phenomenon of autumn light is the light of life – bringing every aspect of the Pantheon alive in seamless oneness.

I leave the interiors of the Pantheon weak-kneed and rush down the steps from the porch. Walking out into the square that faces it, I take my place from where I can get one final view. I stand behind the fountain commissioned by Pope Clement XI, on top of which stands the Egyptian obelisk. From this point, the view is a comprehensive one.

Plotinus must have stood close to where I am amidst a roaring army, looking at Gordian III delivering his speech from the porch.

Dimensions of history merge into one structure with ease. Greek, Roman, Egyptian, and Christian celebrate each other with vigour and striking harmony. Such was the magnetic lure of this monument that in 1548 a link was established with the arts when the Congregation of the Virtuous was founded in the Pantheon. This later grew into the Pontifical Academy of Fine Arts which held exhibitions in the Pantheon's porch till the end of the nineteenth century, displaying the works of old masters including Rafael, Caravaggio, and Bernini.

Man's hand has created a dance of diversity within one; the Pantheon is that dance, and yet it is one. According to Plotinus, 'desire of vision is sight', and the desire of intellect is to see 'The One'. It is my choice to see it as many or one, many in one, or nothing but one. I see it as the latter.

Today's Rome carries its multi-layered history with immense pride. Its pagan past, its majestic days of empire, and today as the pulsating heart of Western Christendom. With all of this within it, Rome rises, embracing it all in one grand sweep that has triggered an all-inclusive romance with unity. This is a romance that has polished the very soul of Rome – its essence in many ways is this deeply cultivated sensorial belief that it is 'one eternal city'. Here, the Vatican romances the Colosseum. The Pantheon celebrates the Egyptian obelisk gifted by Cleopatra, and the Temple of Mars beguiles the Church of Santa Maria of Trastevere. All of them are interlocked in love for a single city. Rome has developed a unique intellect generated by the immanence of the One within it – a collective wisdom accumulated over time. Indeed, the Holocaust stands as a stark reminder, piercing one's heart, but once again it is the magnanimity of Rome's intellect that reminds itself of its darkest days through those names engraved in brass. Much can be learnt from her current existence. The simplicity and ease with which today's Rome lives through centuries is apparent to anyone with a fertile mind. I realise that a day and a half will not be enough to understand the city or Plotinus' love for her. I will need to return.

I haven't realised it, but I've spent the entire afternoon in admiration of the Pantheon. I stroll into a cafe, order a Mozzarella tomato sandwich for lunch, and dial a local cab service to take me to the car rental service. Getting behind the wheel I will make my way to Brindisi driving along the Via Appia. A message flashes on my screen: 'Driver Honey Singh will be with you in 2 minutes.' Maybe it is a Plotinian intervention to send me an Indian taxi driver. Soon a car turns into Piazza Della Rotonda and stops right in front of me. A sturdy Sikh steps out of the taxi and opens the rear door.

'No luggage, sir?'

'I'd like to stop by my apartment and pick up my bags.'

'Sure,' he shuts the door.

As Honey Singh manoeuvres his way out of Piazza Della Rotonda, I turn and take one last look at the Pantheon. This was from where Plotinus rode out on horseback. My ride towards the same direction is a Toyota Hybrid.

'Where are you originally from, Honey Singh?' I ask, knowing the answer well, and biting into my sandwich.

'India, sir... but specifically, from Alwar, Rajasthan,' Honey Singh answers with iridescent eyes that I catch in his rear-view mirror.

'You've been here long?'

'Twenty-five years, sir.'

'Quite unusual to see Indian taxi drivers in Rome... In London and New York, yes... but Rome!'

'Yes, not many of us here. I came out in 1998 and stayed... married an Italian girl and have two kids now.' Honey Singh was obviously quite eager to give me information. 'And you, sir, where are you from? Iran, Pakistan, or India?'

It is my name that must have got him presenting the first two countries as options.

'From London... but yes, originally from India. And you visit India with your Italian wife and kids?' I turn the questioning back to him.

'Yes, yes... once every few years,' says Honey Singh, with an unmissable Indian nod.

'Like it here?'

'Love it... its home.'

'Have you encountered any racism?' I ask a more probing question.

'No, ... you know us Indians, we work hard and get on with things.'

His radio crackles through and Honey Singh from Alwar responds in fluent Italian. I presume it is about his next journey.

We arrive at the car rental. Honey Singh swivels out of his seat and unloads my luggage.

'Will you take card payment, Honey Singh?'

'Oh no, Sir, only cash.'

'Gosh, I don't have any,' words stutter out as I plunge into my wallet.

'*Koi nai*, sir.' Instantly I know the tone. 'Don't worry... pay when you come back to Rome.'

'How do you know I'll be back?' I say, utterly embarrassed.

'I know, sir... anyone who visits the Pantheon will return... don't worry.'

'Oh c'mon, Honey Singh... I'll go to an ATM and come back with cash... just wait a minute.'

'No sir, I have to rush for another pick up... you go now

and pay me when you are back.' A large smile beams across his face.

'Honey Singh, give me your number and bank details and I'll wire you the money.' My tone gets even gentler.

'Here is my card sir... now goodbye... safe travels.'

Honey Singh drives away smiling and waving, leaving me with a lingering taste of India even before I get there.

I get behind the wheel of my tiny Fiat 500, type Brindisi into the Sat Nav, and wait for a few seconds. A beautiful map of Italy appears on my screen with a slim orange line connecting Rome to Brindisi in the heel of Italy. A six-hour journey through Campania, briefly into the Apennine Mountain range and into the province of Puglia. But with an overnight stopover I hope to make somewhere in the countryside, my journey will be more than the estimated six hours. Then, thinking of Plotinus nudging his horse, I press my foot against the accelerator. Passing the Circus Maximus where the remnants of the Via Appia are still visible, I turn south. After an hour's drive the first signs of rural Italy appear, and Rome disappears in my rear-view mirror. After another hour, suddenly along the fringes of the modern European highway appears a flimsy sign with 'Via Appia Antica' written on it. I swirl in. Before my eyes, stretching out into the far distance under the shade of tall pine trees is the black stone road on which the army of Gordian III marched out. I step out of the car just so that I can feel the ancient stones under my feet. The Via Appia lies in silence today, listening not to marching legions and the grinding wheels of mighty chariots but to an orchestra of bird song. As far as the eye can see the Via Appia continues – a slender trail of mysteries. It whispers through its stones, enticing the keen ear with a thousand tales from the past. But the tale that I'm following – one of a philosopher and an emperor – urges me to keep moving.

Most of Campania is fertile wine and olive country, dotted with little ruins, viaducts, broken walls, and old wells dating back to the Roman Empire. As the sun vanishes behind the branches of orange trees, I find myself driving along the coast of the Tyrrhenian Sea, a part of the Mediterranean. Bidding farewell to a descending sun, plunging cliffs with hugging stone houses turn a mellow saffron. With light disappearing fast I drive into the small town of Paestum looking for a place to spend the night. Nestled in the foothills of the Apennine Mountain range, Paestum is renowned for its Greek temples devoted to Athena, the goddess of wisdom, and Hera, sister, and wife of Zeus, which were later adopted by the Romans and became temples to Neptune and Poseidon. This region was known as Magna Graecia or Greater Greece for it was here the Greeks settled from the eighth century BCE and doused the region with their Hellenistic civilisation.

I drive into Via Tavernelle. A square shaped stone house at the edge of an avenue of olive trees catches my eye. It seems like a basic bed and breakfast. Outwardly charming but narrow and cramped inside, the stone homestay doesn't have a reception. Standing outside the small door, a tall Italian woman who barely speaks any English nods and obliges me with a room. The garden walls of the house are ancient. Some of the stone has come from the adjacent temple complex, and just for that I decide to stay. My room has a small window from which I peer out. A cloud has descended and gently floats under the summit of a hill. A string of lights dangling from orange trees in the next-door farm signals nightfall. The outline of the robust pillars of the temple of Athena peer back at me as if to say that even after millennia they are still revered in Italy. While Athena is no longer worshipped, the temple has found renewed appreciation and is treasured by Italians as an architectural gem – an 'unothered', integral part of their cherished history. Curled up in bed in my narrow room I wait for sleep, gazing at the silk-like outline of the temple of wisdom as it grapples with surrounding darkness. The sound of rain on the wooden roof doesn't help. It pours all night.

Having paid for my lodgings the next morning, a crisp autumn freshness greets me as I drive out into the wet streets. A few hours later, my little car is climbing into the Apennine mountains. Winding roads raise me to mountain peaks where ancient villages wrapped in mist rest in quiet obscurity. The road then plunges south, gifting me with generous views on both sides of lush never-ending deciduous forests rich with black pine, birch, chestnut trees, beech, silver fir, and coniferous pine, teeming with wild boar and deer. These forests that have draped the Apennine mountains for millions of years speak the language of an untamed wild beauty. One mountain though stands bare. Stripped of its wonderful, tapestried coat, it seems to weep. Touched by man's hand, it has been deforested, revealing its bare dry skin. It stands in startled sorrow, quite like a leopard would, having lost its gorgeous hide to a greedy poacher.

Passing the town of Taranto signals my entry into the province of Puglia and almost immediately I re-join the Via Appia. The scenery changes dramatically here. Being the southern heel of Italy, Puglia has a north Saharan climate. Arid fields and date palms are reminders of its closeness to North Africa.

Abandoned roofless eighteenth-century farmhouses speak of faded prosperity. As if defying the ruthlessness of time some walls of dilapidated palazzos cling on in futility to their once lustrous Pompeian red paint, while around them olive trees resembling scarecrows have turned purple and have succumbed to a dreaded disease – one which has destroyed twenty million olive trees in Puglia alone.

Xylella – the dreaded bacteria being the culprit. Passing the town of Bari, I drive down the coast and eventually enter Brindisi. The harbour town has modern ships, tankers and cruises arriving and departing from it almost every hour, and a tall column just before the harbour marks the end of the Via Appia. A few cafes by the harbour are crowded with gossiping locals.

But the closeness to the third-century Roman colonies of Albania and Greece which are just across the Adriatic and into which Gordian III and Plotinus crossed can only be felt in Otranto – another port just forty-five minutes away. It is in Otranto that I finally step out of my car and walk down its harbour. A palm tree crowns the roof of a fawn-coloured building which marks the last and easternmost point of Italy. The surging waters of the Adriatic are choppy. Standing at the edge of this sea where I am today, Plotinus, like the waves of the Adriatic, would have felt a great surge of excitement. From here, Gordian III and Plotinus would have boarded ships making their way East. Looking into the distance Plotinus must have felt the ancient philosophy of the Upanishads calling out to him. How eagerly he must have listened to the warm winds from the East. India with all its intellectual richness was opening its arms to him.

Tomorrow, I will fly back to Rome where a flight awaits to carry me to India.

### Ajmer, Rajasthan, India 5:00 am

In the silence of an early morning, six men rush towards an enormous iron cauldron resting thirty feet high on medieval stones erected as a tall mound. Smoke still emanates from the firewood under the cauldron, but the flames have been extinguished a few minutes ago. Through the night a mixture of rice, sugar, milk, almonds, raisins, saffron and rose petals have been cooking over the wood fire. Peering into the cauldron from the top of the medieval stones are a few men who have stood vigil all night, stirring this aromatic mixture with long wooden ladles. Under the blanket of darkness, the six men that have just arrived pad themselves head to toe with home-made cloth gear that although untidy and quite peculiar, seems to have an extraordinary purpose. With great enthusiasm carrying wooden ladders they climb the medieval steps and reach the top. By this time a heaving crowd of 200 dishevelled beggars, pot-smoking bearded tramps, orphans, poverty-stricken children with salivating mouths, destitute women – some in bright lemon saris (most of whom are Hindus distinguished by the bindis on their foreheads), a number of Muslim women and some Sikh men conspicuous by their turbans, have gathered below the cauldron that promises much.

The six men lower the ladders into the cauldron and letting out a cry of 'Ya Garib Nawaz', lower themselves into the bubbling hot mixture. A thunderous response comes from the crowd gathered below as they acknowledge the bravery of the men – 'Ya Garib Nawaz', the crowd roars back. Quite literally they call out to the saint in whose name this *degh* (meal) is being prepared (Garib Nawaz in Urdu means 'benefactor of the poor'). Meanwhile, the six men clad in coarse cloth as protection are now deep within the cauldron. They dip pots into the mixture which has now become a delicious unity – a combination of all the ingredients. The men slowly send the pots up to a few chosen men who are waiting for them. These men then empty the pots into smaller earthen bowls and send it into the crowd. On receiving their share, the colour of this unified dessert is revealed to them – a delicious deep orange mingled with the fragrance of smoking firewood and roses. Hunger pangs don't discriminate, and this very basic desire to eat erupts in one and all, changing the scene within minutes. The clamour to get their share of the dessert is uncontrollable, and as the crowd surges forward it takes everyone with it in a burst of universal energy. Orphans abandoned by fate dive into their share, Hindus, Muslims, and Sikhs take it with cupped hands as a mark of respect, and the unkempt beggars eat only after they've turned their faces heavenwards and murmured *shukr* (thanks). Here, collective intellect has united to bring hope and a simple unified mixture satiates the hunger of hundreds. It takes nearly two hours to distribute the dessert equally amongst all, and not one leaves hungry. All of them will live to fight another day. In this part of the world, to survive a day is to have lived a lifetime.

I have been watching this scene standing right next to the cauldron thirty feet high thanks to Shabbir Chishti. Shabbir's family have been *khadims* (servers to the shrine) at this great symbol of 'oneness' for the past 800 years. He considers it a privilege and takes it seriously. From where I'm standing to my right, a few feet away a pearl-like marble dome rises in beautiful symmetry. Beyond the dome are mountains, and on top of the dome in the shape of a crown is a golden ornament. Under the dome though, in contrast to the golden ornament, lies a man who lived a life of simplicity, and since his death more than 800 years ago he has been known by the title *Sultan-ul-Hind Garib Nawaz* (Sultan of India – benefactor of the poor). Such was the radiance of 'good' emanating from the shrine that struck by it, Lord Curzon, viceroy of India (1899–1905) is known to have remarked, 'I have seen a grave in India that rules India.' The man who sleeps silently in that grave is Moinuddin Chishti, a Sufi mystic who arrived in India in 1192 CE from

Iran. Given to Sufism, the mystical side of Islam, to *tassawuf* or deep contemplation on existence, and the pursuit of final union with the creator (*visaal-e-ilahi*), his ascetic ways attracted the attention of the poor and the powerful. Steering away from the powerful, it was for the poor that he set up a small kitchen that would feed the malnourished. Taking a cue from the mystic, Mughal emperors Akbar and Jahangir donated large iron cauldrons in the sixteenth century. I am standing next to one of them.

Shabbir and I step down and make our way through a network of twisting alleys dotted with rose sellers. A fragrance erupts as we walk – a spectacular mix of rose and freshly made *attar* perfume. Crouching, we walk through a few marble arches and reach the *Jannati Darwaza* (doorway to heaven) – a large silver door that opens only on the *Urs* when the saint's passing is celebrated as his union with God. We enter the inner sanctum through another door. Before me is the large tomb, draped in a velvet green *chadar*. Just above the tomb, suspended from the inner dome hangs a thick cascading rose cluster which seems to gently kiss the forehead of the saint. A few men enter the inner sanctum with tall, scented candles which they hold up on their heads. I feel an indescribable serenity as I stand, hands folded, before the tomb. After a few moments I make my way out and sit on the marble floor, lured in by the qawwals who have settled in not too far from me. As they adjust their harmoniums and ring out a few rehearsal tunes, from the corner of my eye I see a magnificent Hindu sadhu approaching the tomb. Dressed in saffron robes, with a vertical red *tika* that divides his forehead perfectly, he folds his hand in front of the tomb in reverence. Then he sits at a distance and tucks into the dessert.

The qawwals fiddle with their musical instruments, getting into the mood while doing a few recitals of verses written by Amir Khusrau, the thirteenth-century literary genius. Khusrau's craftsmanship of verse and expressions of love and devotion remains a benchmark in sub-continental poetry. But Khusrau didn't confine himself to poetry – his mastery over Sanskrit and Persian saw him write prose, riddles, folk songs, and literary puns that provoked, refined, and embellished intellectual thought at royal courts and at Sufi shrines. Born in India into a Persian-speaking Turk family, in his creative mind the differences between the local language of Braj and his forebears' languages of Persian and Turkish blurred when he picked up his pen. He plucked words like young buds which he then grafted into a linguistic tree of unity and beauty. The words that flowed from his pen came from a state of mind where the distinctions of language dissolved completely, giving birth to Hindawi – a new poetic expression that brought forth the sensitivity and splendour of Sufi thought like no other. The philosophical texture of a country lies in its language, one that sings to the heart. Khusrau's language is that. In Khusrau's own words: 'I am a Hindustani Turk. I compose verses in Hindawi with the fluency of running water.'[12]

Against the sound of drumbeats pausing at the end of each verse and then booming at the beginning of the next, the qawwals sing the most dazzling of Khusrau's verses:

*Zehaal e miskeen, makun tagahful* (Persian)
*Tora e nainan banaye batiya* (Braj)
*Ke taab a hijran, na daaram ay jaan* (Persian)
*Na leho kaahe lagaye chatiyan* (Braj)

------------ one verse------------

Don't overlook my poor state
By blandishing your eyes and weaving tales

27

My patience has over brimmed
Why do you not take me closer to your chest?

The qawwals continue...

My intellect has grown ripe in the fire of age... no longer do I
entertain greed or avarice
Though my value may be less than yours
Yet if our veins were to be cut open, our blood will come out
the same colour[13]

Shabbir nudges me gently and points out a woman who's risen from the crowd and is shaking uncontrollably. Hands raised high in the air, she flings her neck back and forth with great vigour. She's in a trance also known as *Haal*. It is quite an extraordinary sight and takes five hardy women to eventually overcome her and lead her away from the shrine. It is close to mid-day now, and after listening to the qawwals, Shabbir and I make our way to the main arched gateway. On getting there a sea of humanity opens before us. Covid restrictions have been lifted and as far as the eye can see, human heads are bobbing trying to get to the entrance and make their way in. This is the famous Ajmer Bazaar with shops lined across the street and teeming with thousands upon thousands. This is the same street on which for centuries Mughal emperors and beggars have walked barefoot in devotion.

As a mark of respect one can only enter the precincts bare-foot, and Shabbir yells across to the shoe keeper to bring our shoes that we had left with him a few hours ago. Within seconds the shoes appear, and within seconds Shabbir is yelling again – this time at a rickshaw puller. By now the crowd is so large, it seems almost impossible to reach Shabbir, who is in an animated discussion with the rickshaw puller. He gestures frantically to me to elbow my way to him. I make it.

'Get in,' says Shabbir. With the crowd rising like a wave and threatening to take us with it, I obey immediately.

I somehow manage to squeeze into the rickshaw with Shabbir. Our crouched bodies under the curved canopy feel as if we've been squeezed into a jelly jar.

'Chalo,' yells Shabbir, and the man starts pulling with all his might muscling his way through the throng. He is an old man with hollow cheeks and sunken eyes. Lean but determined in his strides he pulls away, letting out a deep throated cough. I feel great sorrow looking at him, slogging like a mule.

'Let's get off and walk, Shabbir... this is torturous for him,' I say, pointing at the rickshaw puller.

'No, Moin Miyan... we'll never make it through the crowds, and besides, this is his daily business, I will pay him handsomely. You see they need the money... look around.'

'Miyan' is a term of respect used for Muslim men in this part of the world. I look around. Lining the sides of the street are cripples, blind men, and young widows with squealing hungry infants in their arms. Peering from under the canopy my sympathetic look catches the eye of one such woman who, infant in hand, springs to her feet and chases our slow-moving rickshaw. Within seconds she is by my side begging, pleading, and sending prayers my way for a happy life. With one hand she holds her head scarf, with the other her squealing child, and with her feet she matches the pace of the rickshaw, telling me a sad tale of widowhood and abandonment. What if she trips and falls into this avalanche of people? What will happen to her child? I am swarmed with these thoughts and consider lunging for my wallet and giving her some money just so that she'd stop chasing us and return to safety. Shabbir spots that and nods frantically, signalling that I shouldn't for fear of being mobbed by another bunch of ill-fated widows.

She doesn't give up and keeps chasing and sending prayers my way. Then suddenly out of nowhere, I hear a loud slap descending on the back of our rickshaw puller. A uniformed young man probably the age of the rickshaw puller's son comes face to face with him, hurling abuses. Apparently, no rickshaws are allowed beyond a point, and our rickshaw puller has violated that order. The uniformed young man doesn't hold back, and short of slapping the old man across the face spits out everything that would intimidate even the strongest. His last bit of intimidation being a threat of puncturing the tyres which would leave the old man no choice but to return home with the additional cost of repair, which I'm sure he couldn't afford. Abused and threatened, our rickshaw driver pleads to be forgiven. Shabbir and I disembark and apologise on behalf of the old man who stands head lowered with hands folded, coughing away. With an admonishing wave of his hand, the uniformed young man surprisingly disappears after warning us not to use a rickshaw on our journey towards the end of the bazaar. Luckily the rickshaw has brought us close to the exit.

Shabbir pays the rickshaw puller his dues and I give some cash to the woman who's been chasing us. We make our way to the final exit – the Delhi Darwaza. Similar but younger than the arched gateway of Settimiana in Rome with its chipped blue tile work, this medieval stone archway built by emperor Akbar in 1571 is desperately clinging onto its past glory.

Before we sit in a taxi that has been waiting for us, I cast one last look at the surroundings. Almost all the shops begin with 'Garib Nawaz'. It is as if the saint is the provider for every enterprise, be it bangle sellers, food stalls, and even cycle repair shops.

'Without his blessings, none of these shops or the poor would survive,' says Shabbir, who has taken notice of my gaze. In many ways he is right. The saint's aura is such that millions live with it and of it.

Honking away the taxi makes its way out. We are off to a remote hill on which there is a tiny cave not frequented by many because of its isolation, but to the people of Ajmer its importance is immense. This is the cave where the Sufi mystic spent most nights in meditation. Known as the Chilla, it is a fair distance from his last resting place. We climb the hill and soon enough reach the entrance. The cave has low hanging whitewashed rocks that add to the mystical setting. Beyond the cave and the hill are the waters of Anna Sagar Lake that is shrouded in many legends – one such legend being that the lake dried up and poured itself in entirety into the mystic's bowl when he wasn't permitted to use its waters for ablutions. Walking into the cave, I'm struck by its narrowness. A few cloth prayer hangings float from the rocks, and at the bottom some henna paste is spread across the whitewashed stones as a mark of respect. But what is fascinating are the tear drop shapes that the overhanging stones have taken. They are supposedly the tears wept by the cave on the passing of the mystic. Here in complete seclusion Moinuddin Chishti is said to have lived out his last moments. When his body was eventually discovered a verse was found written across his forehead in illuminated light:

God's lover, has vanquished himself in God's love.

His last teaching to his student Qutbuddin Bakhtiar before his death in 1236 CE was simple yet profound:

Love all and hate none.

Bring out the latent powers of your being and reveal the full magnificence of your immortal self.

Be surcharged with peace and joy and scatter them wherever you are and wherever you go.

Be a blazing fire of Truth; be a beauteous blossom of love; and be a soothing balm of peace.

With your light dispel the darkness of ignorance; dissolve the clouds of discord and war, and spread goodwill, and harmony among people.

Never go to the courts of kings, but never refuse to bless and help the needy and the poor, the widow, and the orphan, if they come to your door.

Be present in every moment!

Getting to Ajmer straight from Rome gives one a completely different perspective of life. Having landed in Delhi, I drove straight to Ajmer from the capital's international airport with the hope of flinging myself into a historical and philosophical time capsule that would ring true with Plotinus' thoughts. The unceasing deluge of people from every direction, the never-ending chaos in Ajmer's bazaar, and the utter harshness of life mixed with a mystical acceptance of co-existence in every form makes this visit to Ajmer a meaningful juxtaposition to Rome. The completely contrasting effects both these cities have had on me in forty-eighty hours is astounding, and I feel a relentless pounding on my heightened senses.

I've spent a night at Shabbir's home and will spend another before I drive back to Delhi tomorrow morning. Shabbir's home, like so many in the narrow lanes of Ajmer, has been a *musafir khana* or guest house for centuries. His forebears have looked after visiting pilgrims with basic amenities of clean drinking water, thin mattresses, and three plain meals. As Ajmer's significance as a pilgrimage site grew, particularly with the attention the Mughal emperors gave it, families that looked after the mystic's tomb took it upon themselves to attend to the needs of the pilgrims. They live hand to mouth, do not have a modern education, and survive on the remittances given to them by visiting pilgrims. Quite like a Tekke or Sufi lodge one would encounter in Anatolia, these homes are just about adequate to get by for a couple of nights. Sharing bathrooms with two other families, bathing with lukewarm water from an earthen container, befriending a solitary mosquito that will unleash a buzz with relentless precision in one's ear at night, and sleeping on a mattress laid out on the floor are the four minor challenges that one must be prepared for.

Having returned to Shabbir's home, I enter my spartan room and lay down on the floor awaiting dinner that Shabbir's wife is preparing. Shabbir's great-great grandfather and my ancestor had established a bond during one of my ancestor's visits to Ajmer, and since then this generational bond has gotten stronger. In many ways, living at Shabbir's *musafir khana* is a step taken towards medieval Ajmer. Every so often a baying goat will trot past the house, a lone minstrel singing the praises of Moinuddin Chishti will lumber past on his mule, and on many occasions the waft of simmering dal being cooked over a wood fire will infiltrate your room, all this interspersed with the sound of open drains streaming down the narrow lane.

Shabbir walks in carrying a large *qaab* (plate) and places it on the floor. I rise and take a look. Hot *chappatis*, yellow dal, and fresh ladyfingers cooked with onions, prepared by his wife who has been blowing and fanning the flames of the charcoal *chula* since the last hour. Over dinner I approach a sensitive topic.

'Shabbir, the Hindu-Muslim tension, do you feel it?'

'Anyone who feels it should come with me to the tomb

and then to where the *degh* is distributed... that tension will vanish.'

'So, you don't feel it?'

'Well, what you feel is up to you.'

*He's living in denial*, I whisper to myself. For a few moments we eat in silence. Shabbir is in his early forties; he has three children and a wife he must provide for. In addition to this is the fact that the *musafir khana* is a joint property his grandfather left behind, which means his brother and his children are squeezed in as well. The brother is a feeble cripple and doesn't shoulder the workload with Shabbir, and so I think maybe Shabbir's diplomatic answers are best taken the way they are.

But then he speaks.

'You know, the next room is rented out to a Hindu family who have been coming here even before our great-great grandfathers met.'

Shabbir offers me some of the dessert from this morning's *degh* that had been distributed. We eat in silence while I think: *'The One' will always attract intellect to bring with it the perceived many, mingling them into one – be it faith, language, or dessert.*

Shabbir rises, clears the tray, and disappears. I recline on my wafer-thin mattress which hugs the cold stone floor. With dread I await my solitary whirring friend who will soon be heard with uncomfortable intimacy near my ear. My last thoughts are with the woman chasing our rickshaw with an infant in her arms. Khusrau's verse comes to mind:

> Though my value may be less than yours
>     Yet if our veins were to be cut open, our blood will come out the same colour.

## The Road to Delhi

Had Gordian III made it through Persia it is possible he would have tried to enter India either through Rajasthan or through the Khyber Pass on his way to Delhi and beyond. Through these lands, Plotinus and Gordian III would have encountered the rump of a declining Kushan Empire. Would Gordian have been tempted to meet the Kushans in battle or strike a pre-emptive truce, we will never know. What we can say for sure is that at the frontiers of India, a restless Plotinus in his quest to discover the Upanishads would have found a way of disappearing into India's vast lands. The Kushans under Kanishka (r. 127–150 CE), their mightiest emperor, had been the indisputable overlords ruling over North India, Afghanistan, Bactria (which included Uzbekistan, parts of Tajikistan and Turkmenistan), and chunks of southern China. A syncretic empire, the Kushans traced their origins to the Yuezhi tribe which roamed the steppes of Central Asia and the grasslands of southern China. Eventually they united and then displaced the Sakas from the Eurasian Steppes in the first century BCE. As Kushan influence grew and spread southwards they encountered Zoroastrian, Buddhist and particularly Greek influence across Central Asia and modern Afghanistan. Alexander's withdrawal from Indian frontiers in 326 BCE and his subsequent death on his way back to Macedonia resulted in the division of his empire controlled by various Greek generals. Selecus I Nicator was one such general that got Alexander's West Asian territories, which he and his successors later expanded right up to the Mauryan borders of India. Later, other Greek kingdoms like the Greco-Bactrians also thrived in the region.

By the time the Kushans were rising, the Greek kingdoms of Bactria had lost power, but their cultural influence was still profoundly felt in language, art, and administration, and the Kushans absorbed this prevalent Greek influence into their way of life along with Zoroastrian, Buddhist, and Hindu influences. Greek alphabets were used to describe kingship and authority which Heraios, the first Kushan king, did with unabashed ease, calling himself 'tyrant' in Greek and having it inscribed on his coins. Greek subsequently became the main language of the Kushans. Another Kushan king, Vima Kadphises (r. 113–127 CE), is thought to have accepted Hinduism, particularly Shaivism, as he expanded his kingdom past Mathura. Given not just to expanding his boundaries, Vima Kadphises encouraged trade with Europe, in particular Rome and Greece, resulting in a large amount of gold coins minted in his time. Some scholars attribute this influx of gold into India to a vibrant trading relationship with Rome that flourished under Vima's personal supervision. Vima's son, the most illustrious and famous of Kushans, Kanishka, is even known to have sent ambassadors to the court of Roman emperor Trajan (98–117 CE). Kanishka became a devout Buddhist and built one of the most magnificent stupas dedicated to Buddha in Peshawar, a city that became his frontier capital. Although he became a Buddhist, he kept alive the syncretic values of his empire by issuing coins with the imageries of Greek, Iranian, Indian, and Sumero-Elamite (Mesopotamian-Iranian) divinities on them. Politically astute and administratively practical, he made Mathura a city that lies 150 kms south of Delhi his second capital to oversee his ever-expanding empire. Kanishka replaced Greek, once the lingua franca and administrative language of his empire, with Bactrian, which had a very strong Greek influence in it.

But like all empires, the Kushans rose and declined and by 242 CE they had lost swathes of territory in Bactria while struggling to hold onto Northern India. Gordian III's army could well have faced either the weakened forces of Kanishka II (r. 225–246 CE) or his son Vasishka (r. 247–267 CE) depending on the time Gordian would have spent in Persia celebrating his victory amid fair Persian maidens and brimming wine cups.

As Gordian and Plotinus would have approached, they would have witnessed Greek influence in the region. They would have encountered villages in which a hybrid Sanskritized-Greek, Bactrian-Greek, Prakrit-Greek or even pure Greek was still spoken, and with Plotinus' proficiency in Greek he would have engaged in conversations with some locals. Buddhism had spread across these lands too owing to the propulsion it received from King Ashoka (304–232 BCE) and would surely have aroused curiosity in Plotinus. Gordian, a brave nineteen-year-old, could easily have slipped into an Alexandrian self-comparison. Leading his elite fighting force – the Praetorian Guard – into Indian lands, Gordian would have felt the Roman gods were smiling on him. For the Kushans these would have been fragile times. How different would world history have been had the two armies met with the lurking possibility of Caesar's flag flying over Mathura. Plotinus' thoughts though would have been focussed on splintering off from the Roman army, getting his hands on ancient Indian scriptures and finding a kind Indian hermit who would teach him under an ancient banyan tree rooted on the banks of the shimmering waters of the Yamuna. His heart pulsating stronger with every step his horse took, having waited years to reach India, at the age of 39, it is plausible that Plotinus' mind could have fallen prey to confused thoughts – the possibility of disappearing into the Indian forests, severing ties with the army, seeking an audience with the reigning Kushan king, and the wondrous ponderings of a life as a hermit in India.

My taxi has long passed the arid mountains that surround Ajmer and we have broken into the plains. Village after village bear the marks of Rajput life. Bright red turbans with multiple coils rest on chiselled faces. The ornament of those faces are the handsomely curled moustaches. Women in elegantly wrapped saris and some with translucent face covering *ghunghats* make their way into the fields which are dotted with little white temples, some dedicated to Lord Shiva and others to Lord Ram. After seven hours of driving interspersed with lunch and sugary tea breaks, we enter Delhi well past twilight. I've booked myself into Scarlette, a tiny bed and breakfast. Every ounce of energy has exited my body and the last few days are a blur, but there is a great excitement that grips me as I settle into bed. Tomorrow I will read from my copy of *The Philosophy of the Upanishads* by Paul Deussen and *The Enneads* near the Topra Pillar – a silent sky-seeking column that Plotinus would have encountered had he realised his dream of reading philosophy in India.

Between 1000 BCE to 500 BCE, a few ascetics and hermits given to thought regularly left their mud huts in simple villages and made their way into dense forests that draped the plains around the river Ganges. Seeking further isolation, many trekked northwards. Here, the Himalayas, the mightiest of mountain ranges, with circulating clouds around its summits and icy glaciers hung over the forests. Under the snowy mountains, by the flowing Ganges and in the mysterious forests, these hermits lost themselves to thought and philosophy. From this epoch of over 500 years of introspection, curiosity, and silence, in regular intervals emerged the Vedas. Taught orally over time, this spiritual canon was finally funnelled into a book of secrets. A secret of trying to know Him. A secret that urged a deeper understanding of the individual soul to understand the Creator. Such was the magnificence of that secret, and such was the ineffability of Him, that it could only be passed down from teacher to student through 'secret sittings' that occurred in the quiet jungles. The Vedanta (End of Vedas), also known as the Upanishads, is that secret, and is the final realisation of the Indian doctrine of the universe.[14] The crux of Upanishadic thought revolves around two aspects: Brahman and Atman. Brahman, the unknown is the First Principle so far as it is comprehended in the universe, creator, sustainer and which brings back into itself all worlds. Brahman is the object of inquiry. Atman is Brahman as it is known in the inner self of man.

Under ageing banyan and eucalyptus trees while soaking up the cool Himalayan breeze, bearded old sages whispered this secret to their pupils. Lost in deep contemplation the poetic words that left their lips were so astounding that it took the students days to recover from the impact. But as they let go of all they knew, their hearts sparkled with enlightenment.

Not by speech, not by thought,
Not by sight is He comprehended;
'He is! by this word is he comprehended,
And in no other way.

As the spider ejects and retracts the thread,
As from the well-kindled fire the sparks, essentially akin to it,
leap forth a thousandfold,
So, from the imperishable, the varied living creatures come forth,
And return into It again

With these verses Brahman is simply understood by existence (He is!), and the first cause of all beings unto which all beings will return.

He is God in all the regions of the Universe
Is present in men and Omnipresent
To this God be honour, be honour!

The One enters into the maternal womb, incorporating himself in bodily form,
Into a plant moves, each according to his works or knowledge.[15]

The Upanishads open its arms to Plotinus' theory of 'The One' being immanent in all beings and embraces *The Enneads* as a voice testifying to truth. From my spot under a neem tree overlooking the Topra Pillar, I have been reading from *The Philosophy of the Upanishads* and fulfilling Plotinus' dream. This lesser known and neglected archaeological site becomes the ideal setting to immerse oneself in the teachings of the sacred text. The Topra Pillar was built in the third century BCE and gets its name from the village where it originally stood. Not far from Delhi, this pillar was erected by king Ashoka for the people in his realm to understand the Buddhist Dhamma of kindness and piety towards all living creatures. From Topra this pillar was moved by Firuz Shah, the thirteenth-century king of Delhi, closer to the city as a reminder of the values of Dhamma.

Looking at the pillar, *The Enneads* and the *The Philosophy of the Upanishads*, a realisation dawns that all three are symbols of truth. After a few moments some Tibetan Buddhist monks dressed in crimson robes and with shaved heads walk towards the pillar. Quite conspicuous, they stand before the pillar with hands folded for a few minutes, and then leave. I pick up *The Philosophy of the Upanishads*

I have been carrying with me. Hoping that Plotinus is close by, overhearing, I read.

> As unity we must regard Him
> Imperishable, unchanging
> Eternal, not becoming, not ageing
> Exalted above space, the great self
> Not born and does not die
> Springs not from any, nor becomes any

> 'Who could bring him forth?' This saying shows Him to be causeless

> In the beginning there is only 'that one' (tad ekam) shut in by a shell.
> There is no second outside of Him, no other distinct from Him, there is no plurality at all...
> Brahman! It is Thou and no other, who holdest in thy embrace all that has come to be

> ... thy neighbour is in truth thy very self and what separates you from him is mere illusion.[16]

The power of oneness in these verses brings forth my inadequacies. It was the visual difference of the Buddhist monks that made me see them differently – their crimson robes and their gestures. Likewise in Ajmer, it was my visual senses that differentiated between attires and communities – but if pure unity was my state of mind, this difference would have dissolved. Sight has differentiated them and injected the mind with that difference. Then intellect stepped in to define those differences as separate faiths. With time, travel, and introspection, I hope there will be a 'disintegration of difference' in my mind.

In Plotinus' words:

But how is that One the principle of all things? Is it because as principle It keeps them in being, making each one of them exist? Yes. But how did It do so? By possessing them beforehand. But it has been said that in this way it will be multiplicity. But the One had them in such a way as not to be distinct: They are distinguished on the second level, in the rational form (through intellect).[17]

Scribbling away in my notepad, underlining sentences, relishing this delicious juggle between the Upanishads and *The Enneads*, a silence seems to descend as I return to reading *The Philosophy of the Upanishads*.

The light, as one, penetrates into space,
And yet adapts itself to every form,
So the inmost self of all beings dwells
Enwrapped in every form, and yet remains outside[18]

How often have we encountered this and yet not seen it with the eyes of unity? Every school going child has been shown the simple prism experiment where a single ray of light spears through the prism and emerges as a band of varied colours. The single ray stands outside yet connected with the colours which too is a single band of united colours. Prior to entering the prism that single ray of light held all the colours within it – without distinguishing.

I shut my eyes. The wind carries with it the smell of freshly cut wild grass that surrounds this historical site. The scent of the wild grass is raw and real. Inhaling deeply, I fill my lungs with it. Momentarily this tranquillity is broken by curious children who rush towards the site but are led away by uninterested parents, allowing peace and quiet to come into residence once again. I continue fulfilling Plotinus' dream.

> He who holds that Loftiest and Deepest,
> For him the fetters of the heart break asunder,
> For him all doubts are solved
> And his works become nothingness.[19]

Yet to reach this state of nothingness I will have to go forth, travel, learn, and then unlearn.

The Upanishads were taught and recited in secrecy. They were not meant for the uninitiated. The secrecy of the Upanishads and its mastery was both treasured and guarded by the hermits and ascetics. It was such an enigmatic phenomenon which needed careful understanding that they wrapped it in rules and warnings:

> This (the mixed drink, mantha, and its ritual) shall be communicated to no one except the son or the pupil.[20]

I begin to realise why Plotinus' mind must have thirsted for this nectar, how eager he must have been to reach India and find a master, and how utterly rudderless one can be without philosophical guidance. In the isolation of jungles, students guided by their masters immersed themselves in meditation through poetic ecstasy and physical devotion (yoga) to Brahman. Some reached that point of culmination where the soul is no different to the universe and the universe no different to Brahman the originator, where the union of soul and Brahman takes place, and the soul cries out:

> When all the passion vanishes that finds a home in the human heart

Then he who is mortal becomes immortal
Here he has already attained to Brahman[21]

With Brahman penetrating every living soul, be it man, animal or plant, and all souls eventually merging back with Brahman, everything is one undivided unity set in motion, but only to be brought back to rest within Brahman. With time, the profound impact the Upanishads had on shaping the intellectual tapestry of India would be a phenomenon by itself. So deeply entrenched would its core value of unity be that people of this land would attain a respect and adulation for all beings. As a result, a humility began taking root in India's characteristic spirit that manifested itself in kindness and a spiritual acceptance of all emotions, be it joy, tribulation, pain, and death. Humility also fostered an innate quality to look for the good in man, beast, and plant ringing through in familial life, mannerisms, art, sculpture, and literature. These manifestations of humility play out in this land even after three millenniums when children touch the feet of their parents for morning blessings, when the powerful greet each other with folded hands, when yoga instructors end their classes only after they have shut their eyes and folded their hands in gratitude, and when the Vedas and the Upanishads are still at the epicentre of daily worship. All these and more make India the longest living civilisation on earth.

This sense of humility pervades across Sufi shrines, Buddhist monasteries, and even Sikh gurudwaras that soaked up this elemental ethos of Indian philosophy, as I witnessed this morning on my way to the Topra Pillar. The Bangla Sahib Gurudwara was easily accessible from my bed and breakfast, and so I decided to peep in. An elegant lady adjusting her Gucci sunglasses stood behind a window collecting dirty slippers from beggars, cleaners, and construction workers, and when my turn came, she collected mine too with her bare hands. Evidently from an affluent background she said she voluntarily does this once a month as 'Seva' or service, which she believes is a great human equaliser. All these manifestations stem from the point when the intellect understands and uses the power of unity for good. The most admired modern symbols being Mahatma Gandhi and Vallabhbhai Patel. Gandhi's epic struggle to eradicate the pernicious effects of untouchability from Indian society came from the strength of simplicity – be it his outward manifestation, his simple living in an ashram, or the radiance that sprung from within entrenched in the power of unity. His belief in oneness was so strong that he strived tirelessly till the very end against untouchability. It was when his intellect mobilised this power of oneness that an empire, crumbled. Riding on the might and power of Gandhi's simplicity, a new free India emerged.

In 1947, Vallabhbhai Patel worked ceaselessly to unify the fragmented princely states that dotted India's landscape and successfully merged them into what is today known as the Indian Republic. More recently, in Gujarat, India built the tallest statue in the world and dedicated it to him, calling it 'The Statue of Unity'. A few years after Patel's monumental effort of merging the princely states into one nation came the Constitution of India granting 'equal status' to all Indians. Philosophically, the Constitution professes an inclusiveness that doesn't differentiate on religion and caste. India aspired to be a true reflection of Brahman – a unity which without discriminating, holds everything within it, as one. Since then, India has economically surged forward with its enormous 'middle class' becoming the juicy pasture ground for capitalism and materialism – intellect's deadly spears hurled at the heart of humility.

But, if in 245 CE Plotinus had succeeded in his journey and reached where I am, he would be looking into the forest that had once surrounded these areas, a few scraggy remnants of which are still visible. A thatched hut on the outskirts of the forest could well have been the dwelling of a hermit – a master of the Upanishads. Gingerly, Plotinus would have walked up to this bare-chested hermit with a flowing snowy beard sitting under a tree and gently asked if he could become his disciple. Communication might have happened in Sanskritized-Greek. Struck by Plotinus' humility and passion to learn, the bearded sage would have led him into the forest, both vanishing from sight.

A few prancing monkeys have descended on the ruined fortress, and some have summited the pillar. Plotinus would have been utterly bewildered by monkey sightings in the Indian jungles. Some of them look at me with curiosity perched high up on neem trees. For the next few weeks, I will rest in Delhi and let Plotinus disappear into his enchanted forest and merge with the wondrous mind of the hermit. We will meet him in Egypt next, his birthplace, and from where the desire to know 'The One' first sprang within him.

# 2

## THE MIGHT OF TAWHEED

Travelling to Egypt inadvertently fills one with thoughts of Pharaonic wonder. It is the indelible mark that Egypt has left on the mind. Even if one is visiting it for the first or the tenth time, the images the mind conjures will most likely be of pre-biblical civilisation – a time when man elevated man to God-like stature. And to feed that imagined loftiness, man challenged every notion of knowledge he possessed to make stone speak a timeless language to honour kings as ultimate symbols of divinity – a language that reverberates hauntingly in the silent Valley of Kings, around the final stone that forms the peak of a pyramid and in the temple complexes of Luxor, Aswan, and Abu Simbel that rise gloriously on the banks of the Nile. These thoughts and images came to my mind too even though I was sitting in the modern comfort of an economy class seat in Qatar Airways, trying to avoid documentaries promoting the tiny oil rich kingdom. Instead, I spent time refining my notes, reading *The Enneads*, peering out of the window looking at the Red Sea which had once parted in response to a Prophet's moving call for refuge, and tracking the flight map into Egyptian airspace.

Eventually touching down at five in the evening, disembarking, and making my way to customs, I receive a message on my phone from the hotel: 'Your driver Bassam will be waiting to take you to customs for your Visa'. In all my travels, I've never encountered a situation where a hotel driver gets you a visa upon arrival. As I descend the escalator, I spot a silver-haired, spectacled, portly man of reasonable height dressed in a black suit, black tie and black Ray-Bans, holding up a large cardboard sign with my name scribbled on it. He resembles a funeral carriage driver or an Arab mafioso and doesn't fill me with confidence.

'Bassbort,' he mumbles softly, extending his palm as I approach him. Arabic does not have P as an alphabet, so the pronounced switch to B is conspicuous.

'I need a visa,' I say.

'Yes, yes I get you visa... Bassbort, blease.'

I hand it over to him hesitatingly, thinking about the times when one is repeatedly warned never to hand over a passport in an Arab country to someone you don't know. It is a horrible sinking feeling, but his outstretched hand and flick of the fingers demanding the 'Bassbort' has an obeying effect on me. He takes my trolley too.

'Follow me.'

We make our way to an open counter with a lonely custom officer on duty.

The driver presents my passport.

'Twenty-five dollars, blease,' says the custom officer.

I rummage through my wallet and pull out the exact amount.

He glues on a visa sticker with the proud Egyptian falcon on it and hands it back.

'Ahlan... Welcome... Enjoy Egypt.'

'Shukran,' I say with a smile and relief in my tone, now assured that the driver isn't a fraud.

We collect my luggage and head out towards the taxi.

Cairo is a twenty-five million strong city, and we get straight into it, the driver navigating the ghastly traffic with skill that has quite evidently been acquired over the years. Cars, motorcycles, trucks, cycles, rickshaws, and pedestrians jostle for space as if their life depended on it. Neither vehicle nor human is prepared to cede an inch. While the vehicles vomit exhaust and dark grey fumes, the ones controlling them spit out Arabic abuse at each other. The wild incessant barrage of honking that explodes because of stubborn palms pressed against horns can rupture eardrums. We drive over flyovers under which are sprawling shops selling everything from leather goods to cheap T-shirts. Stuck on one such flyover surrounded by what seems an unending, monstrosity of concrete construction, I am eye level with flashing neon billboards. Some urge you to increase your propensity for a heart attack by giving into a sugar blast of Coca-Cola; other billboards have taken the form of gigantic cut-outs of Mohamed Salah, the Egyptian and Liverpool footballer endorsing Coca-Cola's bitterest foe – Pepsi. The deadliest of capitalist rivalries is playing out in Plotinus' motherland, a corporate clash that has filled coffers with cash and graves with corpses. I wonder what the gentle, kind-hearted philosopher would have thought about all this. Soon, a suffocating blanket of smog begins its ghostly descent. It sits on the Cairo traffic with the heaviness of an ancient grinding stone going about its deadly business in silence. Having thought of the magic of ancient Egypt since the last few days and particularly with unceasing anticipation building on the flight, the immediate encounter with Cairo leaves me disappointed.

Cairo is not a city that Plotinus would have encountered. It came into existence much later only after the Arab conquest in the seventh century CE and was known as Al-Qahira – City Victorious. The surrounding areas around Cairo including Giza, Saqqara, and Memphis which date back to Pharaonic times are where the philosopher was sure to have travelled. We finally drive into the hotel, which is in Zamalek, a residential area of central Cairo. Tipping the driver, which is completely justifiable keeping in mind the fortitude required to get behind a steering wheel in Cairo, I bolt out of the taxi. On entering the reception area of the hotel (not worth mentioning by name) the sparkling granite, gaudy golden interiors, garish spotlighting, and nostril piercing sharp perfume from some of the resident guests is nauseating. I wait for my turn to check in which takes twenty minutes. Finally, I turn the key to my room, lay down my suitcase, and lower myself into a hot bath. Refreshed, I return to the room and begin unpacking. Although my room is on the fifteenth floor, I can still hear the distant hum of traffic.

I walk towards the large single window and part the curtains. The view presents itself. Night has fallen over Cairo and I see a carpet of city lights below me shimmering on the darkened waters of the Nile. Neon signs, traffic lights, streetlights, and signals battle each other in the smog. I take in a deep breath and exhale a dispirited sigh. While I was aware of being greeted by Cairo's unrelenting grind, it is only when one witnesses the glaring grotesqueness of modern construction holding sway over an ancient land that one realises how distant one is from ancient Egypt. Unlike Rome, Cairo doesn't tug at the heart instantly. There is a sadness I feel in thinking that I can't connect with the philosopher and his teachings in these surroundings. I stand facing the window and look out into the distance for a few minutes. From the corner of my eye, I see a glaring blue neon sign. 'Omar Khayyam Casino – Belly dancing night'. A most outrageous tribute that an uninformed mind could pay to one of history's greatest minds. I glance over to the bedside table where I had placed *The Enneads* but can't get myself to read it. I order room service, have a chicken tahini, and turn in for the night. Tomorrow, I visit the pyramids. There I hope to hear Plotinus' voice.

I wake to an overcast smoggy morning. Egyptian winter can be quite deceiving as I quickly find out having chosen to breakfast in the hotel garden. A cup of English breakfast, a cosy sweater, and some warm crisp toast with butter and blackberry jam always helps in reviving dampening spirits originating from the previous evening. Breakfast done; I make my way to reception. Waiting for me is Ahmad, my guide that I had requested the hotel to arrange. It is impossible to get past the logistics at the pyramids on one's own, and so a guide is important. Ahmad is short, bald, and has a trimmed well-kept beard which he is running his left palm over. It is evident he takes great pride in nurturing his facial hair considering its retreat from his smooth head.

'Ahlan Mizder Mir... I am your guide Ahmad,' he says, smiling and taking his right hand to his chest. Quite possibly Covid protocol. The importance being given to the virus is waning thankfully, yet Ahmad's reluctance to shake my hand must be respected.

'Shukran Ahmad,' I respond. There is an ease about Ahmad, and I sense he won't be one of those annoying guides who spin rollicking yarns.

'Blease, this way...,' he points towards the taxi waiting for us. We get in and to my relief burst out of the hotel.

I pull out my notes, commentaries, and books while seated in the back of the car. The Cairo traffic becomes a blur and Ahmad's voice a faint murmur as I attempt to imagine Plotinus' Egyptian times. I plunge into my notes to get a feel for it. The exact birthplace of Plotinus is debated between Asyut and Lycopolis. Extremely secretive about his childhood and his youthful years in Egypt, one can be quite sure that a seeking mind like his must have visited the great Pharaonic sites of Ancient Egypt. What is also certain is that he was interested in Hermetic philosophy which originated in Egypt between 1,000–500 BCE, the same time as the Upanishads. Ammonius Saccas, Plotinus' teacher, had studied it and had imparted its philosophical learnings to his student, influences of which can be seen in *The Enneads*.

Hermetic philosophy came together as one thought in the book *Hermetica* through an amalgamation of Hellenized teachings of the Greek God Hermes and the Egyptian God Thoth. There were many anonymous contributors to the *Hermetica*. The Greeks considered Hermes a protector from thieves and bandits and revered him as the herald of Gods. Thoth, the Egyptian God, was on the other hand the overlord of the moon, wisdom, science, and writing. When the Greeks conquered Egypt under the banner of Alexander in 332 BCE, so overwhelmed were they by the Egyptian religious practices that they chose to absorb them into their own. They took the virtues of Thoth and married them with those of their equivalent – Hermes. The resulting philosophy was termed 'Hermeticism'. In the philosophical *Hermetica*, the ultimate reality is referred to by names such as 'Atum', the complete one, 'God', 'The Creator', 'The All', and 'The One'. As creator he was the progenitor of all deities, the world, and the universe. Thus, God creates itself and is both transcendent and immanent as the created cosmos.

From his birth in 204 CE till he left Egypt in 242 CE, Plotinus imbibed the multi-layered enmeshed teachings of ancient Egypt and Greek philosophy. But the Egypt Plotinus grew up in was witnessing great political turmoil. Rome under Julius Caesar had conquered Egypt in 47 BCE, but by Plotinus' time Rome's grip on Egypt was slowly weakening and rebellions were everywhere. Plotinus experienced this crisis first hand, and it must have been one of the reasons for his constant travels within Egypt seeking safety and security.

I emerge from my thoughts and notes because there is a sudden silence. I look out of the window. We are approaching Saqqara. The first signs of what Egypt must have looked like in Plotinus' times emerge. Small patches of traditionally irrigated fields spring out of what seems a vast never-ending desert. This brings about a contrast of colours – green against satin brown. In the distance I catch a faint glimmer of the flowing Nile. Clusters of tall date palms sway in the wind. Smog has given way, and a lone falcon glides in a miraculously clear blue sky. A band of farmers with wrinkled windswept faces dressed in jellabiyas and mounted on their donkeys guide their trotting beasts with purposeful ease. And then I see it. There is a remoteness to the Step Pyramid of Djoser in Saqqara as it stands at a distance from its more famous cousins in Giza. Proud, yet humble. Weather beaten, yet majestic. Silent, yet whispering. I look at it, taking in its full-frontal view for some time. The thought of 2670 BCE (its year of construction) makes me feel so remote from it, yet when I see this layered architectural tribute to king and divinity in front of me the connection is instant because till not long ago the concept of 'divine right to rule' existed in large parts of the world. I feel as if my mind is racing back in time, and yet my eyes have frozen on its image in the present. This mental and visual tussle produces something quite extraordinary – the mind that is thirsting for ancient visuals injects into vision historic elements, from camels and horses to bare chested labouring men working in breath-taking cohesion chiselling and raising stone to unimaginable heights. A pharaoh's chariot stands close by, mounted on which he supervises this ode to himself, a representative of the gods.

But what must Plotinus have seen philosophically? I ask myself. I am drawn to taking a closer look at this oldest colossal structure of Egypt. The barren landscape surrounding it is dotted with other smaller pyramids, some just rubble, others mere rocky curves still desperately grasping onto their triangular proportions. Now so close to the pyramid, I can see every stone that had gone into making it one single structure. Layer upon layer of riddled limestone in horizontal blocks rise vertically against the backdrop of a cobalt sky. The dull cream-like effect gives the pyramid a lunar lustre. I slowly walk around the pyramid observing the harmony of multiple stones as they rise and unite in this steep embrace. I walk away to get another view from a distance and am presented with sweeping uninterrupted views of silent white sands, wispy clouds, and two Bedouin horsemen dressed in deep blue jellabiyas with face-covering headgear. Lowering myself into a sand dune, feeling my hips sink into it, I fix my gaze at the pyramid again. From here it looks simple – a triangle. Aristotle's most profound question springs to mind: *What is it to be that thing?* The master's answer to his own question: *Unity.* The Step Pyramid of Djosar is that unity. For without unity a stone wouldn't exist, and neither would the pyramid. The triangular form before me is a simple structure that holds within it the unity of stones from the lowest to the highest, layered one upon another becoming indistinguishable to the mind and sight as they rise as one.

A gentle breeze picks up and the white sands stir as I open *The Enneads* and some commentaries to read:

The last and lowest things, therefore, are in the last of those before them and these are in those prior to them, and one thing is in another up to the First, which is the Principle.... The One, therefore is said to "encompass all things".[22]

I read on.

It is by the One that all beings (including stone) are beings... For what could anything be if it was not one? For if things are deprived of the one, which is predicated of them, they are not those things.[23]

Plotinus urges us to believe that while the One stands alone, simple, absolute and powerfully productive, elements of It have transcended into everything, including man, sand, stone, animal, and plant – what has come to be known as the Great Chain of Being, a cascade of hierarchical emanations through which the One passes ever diminishing shares of itself down to the lowest manifestations of existence (stone).[24]

I gaze at the satin like sand dune I'm sitting on. Each grain is a unity in itself; billions come together and become indistinguishable as a dune. A unity within unity. Afternoon has given way to early evening. A chill is descending, making me draw out my shawl from my rucksack. I wrap it around me. I look towards the pyramid again soaking up its volume. Its stillness though conceals another story. Another version of the pyramid's 'coming into existence'. A darker version. One which doesn't get told very often.

I stay with Plotinus' thought of 'The One' (the Good) generating intellect which turned in desire towards 'The One' but couldn't understand 'The One' as a whole and so *unwittingly* broke its understanding down into multiples. Some of those multiples were greed, ego, and ambition. Driven by uncontrollable desire to *possess everything,* intellect itself fell into a state of greed and self-love. Does this in some way reflect what stands before me as a pyramid today? A riddle wrapped inside an enigma. If 'The One' is immanent in all beings as Plotinus writes, then its presence in Pharaoh Djoser must have attracted the pharaoh's intellect towards it. As a tribute to 'The One' which he saw as divinity within himself, the pharaoh decided to build himself this pyramid. The progressing intellect in the pharaoh took over and manifested itself as greed and ego, luring him to believe he is divine. Sucked in by his ego, this pyramid became for the pharaoh an ode to himself as a God. Consumed entirely by this self-love, the pharaoh inflicted great suffering on the people brought in to build the pyramid. This took the pharaoh away from the simplicity and the good that was within him. Lashing whips, bloodied backs, torn soles, and hurling corpses is what went into building this symbol of pharaonic divinity.

The Egyptian winds still resonate with Plotinus' cautionary words: *The intellect did somehow dare to stand away from 'the One' (the Good)*. The intellect became many, adding facets to it that stand away from 'the good', and from here on according to Plotinus the descent of the soul begins. The pyramid isn't simple anymore.

My thoughts are interrupted by the faint neighing of Arabian stallions. I look across the sumptuous sand dunes and see the silhouettes of two Bedouins approaching in a steady gallop against a sinking sun. I realise now that I have been in Saqqara since mid-day. Five hours have drifted by lost in thought, walking, reclining on sand dunes, reading, and making notes. I've even been downright rude to Ahmad. His voice has been a faded mutter through these hours, and I've admonished him for pursuing me. It is as if I had faded into the past and am only now returning to the present. Ahmad's gentle voice comes through.

'Mizder Mir, we must leave now... you know, after a while it will be night.'

'Ahmad, I'm so sorry... I was so rude.'

'No, don't worry... You haven't even had lunch... I brought you some, but you told me to....'

'Gosh Ahmad, please forgive me... I'm so ashamed of what I said.'

'Mizder Mir you are my guest; you don't have to abologise... Come now... I have a treat for you.'

'Treat?'

'Yes, you see those riders?'

'Yes.'

'They are Bedouins... they will give us their horses and we will ride to Giza.'

'Ahmad!'

'Yes yes... that's how we grew up.'

'But....'

'No buts... this is my treat... you ride, don't you?'

'Well... it's been a very long time....'

'Ah don't worry... I am with you.'

Sand flying, the sturdy riders gallop in and dismount in one neat swing.

'Shukran ya Habibi,' says Ahmad as he smoothly mounts one of the stallions.

I rush for my rucksack and books that were scattered on the sand. Putting the notes and books back into the rucksack, I approach my horse. Seeing my hesitation, Ahmad speaks again.

'Your horse's name is Khalid... named after the famous Arab general Khalid bin Walid.... Just put your foot in the strap and mount.'

The Bedouin rush to help. He signals for my rucksack. I look at Ahmad, who gives a nodding approval while swivelling his reins. The Bedouin attaches the rucksack to the saddle, then comes around and helps me mount.

'Salam,' yells Ahmad, nudging his steed forward.

I do the same.

'Maasalam,' comes the response from the Bedouins who wave us goodbye.

A gentle trot and we are well into the desert.

'Ahmad, this is a real treat, thank you.'

'Well, Mizder Mir, you know nowadays one can't ride freely into the desert... things are not as they used to be because of kidnappings....'

Ahmad sees the shadow of apprehension descend on my face.

'Don't worry, Mizder Mir, what I meant was... it is unsafe for foreigners riding on their own... but with me by your side, there's no broblem.' There is sincerity in his voice.

'By car, with traffic jams, from here to Giza will take you half an hour... on horseback it is fifty minutes, but you will feel the real Egypt... now enjoy yourself.'

He doesn't say the name, but the fear of the outlawed Muslim Brotherhood and their extremist ways is what he means. I initially feel an unease, but as the trotting grows to a steady gallop all fears and apprehensions disappear. The last time I rode was twelve years ago in Hyde Park at a measured pace with helmet, riding boots, and body protection. This is the complete opposite. Keeping a steady pace with Ahmad, the unbroken view till the eyes can see are sand dunes taking the shape of melting gold as the sun drops into them. The mane of my horse flies in free spirit as the last of our shadows spread across the silent Sahara.

'Do Bedouins still live an ancient life?' I ask, manoeuvring the reins and looking at Ahmad riding next to me.

'Yes, in the vast uninhabited Sinai desert,' he replies with a grand biblical hand gesture.

'Are they free to do so?'

'Of course... some things remain untouched by time.' Ahmad has a smile on his face.

There is an inexplicable sense of freedom and a seamless integration into history when riding a black stallion named Khalid in the wilderness of an untamed desert, with only the soft smothering thud of hooves on sand and a crisp breeze in one's face. Then as the sun hastens its descent, in the distance at the edge of the view from the sand emerges the head of a pharaoh immediately followed by the body of a lion, the Sphinx, and around it like triangular pointers to the divine - the pyramids of Giza. We gallop on towards them.

Guided by Ahmad we swivel our reins to a point from where we can witness the final gasp of the sun as it lights up the pyramids. It feels like the edge of the horizon. Beyond the pyramids the first signs of modern Cairo are barely visible, but where we are and all around us is antiquity. And this is where I want to be. Moments later, by a will that couldn't be fathomed, the pyramids of Giza changed colour; as if celebrating being drenched in the last shower of sunlight, some turned a dull gold, others a matt silver.

'Do you want to get closer?' asks Ahmad, not taking his eyes off the pyramids.

'No... sometimes being at a distance gives you a perspective like none other,' I reply, keeping my eyes glued to the pyramids. In silence we sit, soaking in the view.

Releasing a pleasing sigh, Ahmad speaks again. 'I see this most evenings and haven't tired of it.' Hesitatingly he continues, 'Would you like to come to my home for an Egyptian dinner?'

I turn my face from the dull glow of the pyramids and look at him. There is a genuineness to the invitation. Sensing I might refuse, or he has spoken out of turn, he quickly adds, 'Or maybe you'd like to go back to the hotel?'

'I wouldn't want to have dinner anywhere else but at yours, Ahmad, thank you.' By doing so I quickly ambush the unpleasant thought of having to dine at the 'Omar Khayyam Casino' over a belly dancing performance designed for salivating, wife-escaping investment bankers out on a team building corporate event.

'Very well. Follow me, then... Yalla.' Ahmad nudges his stallion into a gallop.

'Where do you live?' I ask, catching up with him.

'Opposite the Sphinx... we'll light a fire in my courtyard and have some olives, fava, and bread.'

'Wine?' I inquire.

'Haraam... Ya Shaikh!' Comes the immediate response.

I laugh and nod in respect. We ride under the stars which have now made a shy appearance in the deep purple sky.

Ahmad's house, as he said, is opposite the Sphinx, surrounded by a cluster of restaurants and old souvenir shops. The courtyard overlooking the Sphinx is carpeted with traditional crimson rugs, hexagon shaped small Syrian wooden tables, and a Shisha prepared for guests. It is clear to me that I am not the first guest. Olives and tea are brought out by Ahmad as I begin enjoying the Shisha.

'Do you have children, Ahmad?' I ask curiously.

'Of course, two girls... both go to English secondary school, you know.'

'Oh, well done.'

'My wife won't be joining us... you know,' says Ahmad, implying that she wouldn't join an all-male gathering.

'Sure... I understand.'

Cosying by the fire that Ahmad worked hard to light and subsequently sustain, I wonder about those Bedouins and their antiquated lives in the isolated Sinai desert.

'Those Bedouin, Ahmad... tell me more about their customs.'

'Well... most of them live in the Sinai desert where only howling winds are heard... they are still herders and shepherds living off camel milk, goat meat and other livestock... they have a barter system in their remote settings and don't use money.'

'Really, even now?' I say, drawing in from the Shisha.

'Don't be surprised, Mizder Mir, this is Egypt, and ancient customs still live on.'

'Yes, but time...,' I say, blowing out smoke and having my sentence interrupted.

'Time hasn't touched them.... Quite like the women of Luxor,' he says, throwing in some more wood to keep the fire going.

'What do you mean?'

Ahmad comes closer, quickly looks around, and whispers, 'Some women who want to get pregnant still pray to the ancient Egyptian gods,' all the while Ahmad keeps a watchful eye on his housekeeper who brings out fava and bread.

I had read about this practice in Anthony Sattin's book *The Pharaoh's Shadow*, but I was hearing it for the first time from an Egyptian.

'Aren't they Muslim?' I ask, putting down my Shisha and lowering my voice into a whisper.

'They are... of course, they are, but you know, these are old customs in our blood, and although it's secretive, they do pray to the ancient gods,' he says in his whispering tone.

'Can I see this custom playing out?'

'Very difficult... you know illegal and all that thing... but...'

'But what?' I say, dipping some bread in the fava and placing it in my mouth.

'Maybe if you get a brave guide in Luxor... he could show you.'

I nod.

Dinner is delicious.

Ahmad walks me to the taxi, and I hand over a tip for which he is grateful.

'Maasalam,' he says, bringing his hand to his chest.

'Maasalam, Ahmad. Shukran.'

The taxi makes its way out of the narrow street.

Egypt, with its multi-layered history, presents a wanderer like me with a chance to experience the country as a philosophical whole. When one travels through a land where millennia have painted many splendored historical tapestries, the opportunity to immerse oneself in the whole is utterly seductive. The next afternoon I drive to the Cairo Museum where a deluge of multi-coloured mummies dating as far back as 2000 BCE lie in silence. I lock eyes with Tutankhamun who ruled Egypt from 1332–1323 BCE. The spectacular opulence of Tutankhamun's golden face mask endowed with haunting kohl-lined eyes holds me in a hypnotic gaze. But only for a few transient moments. Some distance from him, lost in an eternal yearning to reunite with its master, is his resplendent golden throne. But there is a distance between the two. Never shall they meet. Even with all the symbols of power and wealth bedecking both king and throne, they stand cast away by time as nothing more than a relic of the past upon which masses come to lay a momentary gaze. As if struck down by time for having an audacious intellect (Tutankhamun meant 'Living image of God Amun'), the king's shrivelled mummy was discovered in the Valley of the Kings in 1922. His tomb had been adorned with treasure that he would take into his after life with the gods. But this 'living image of God' – a brittle collective of bone and teeth – didn't carry his treasures with him. Both mask of king and throne, symbols of power, intellect, and God-like virtue are only objects that bring momentary fantasy to the eye. Progression and regression of the body are symbols of time. Advancement and retreat of skin, body, mind and thought that form a human and then the eventual decomposition of it all is an everlasting truth. What is left is only polished gleaming metal for us to either live in a false acceptance of man's eternal glory or to understand his complete failure in attempting divinity.

I head back to my hotel room. I lie in bed and watch the Cairo smog descend through translucent curtains that are spread across the window. For hours I lie still and tranquil listening to Jo Stafford's 1952 hit 'You belong to me', the most affecting strain delivered with a longing and deep nostalgia – 'See the Pyramids along the Nile, watch the sun rise on the tropic isle, just remember darling, all the while, you belong to me...'. It is as if time itself has sung this song for everything that lives or lived, including Pharaoh Tutankhamun.

As the evening drifts into night and the Nile shimmers, reflecting the streetlights, I lumber out of bed and pour myself a steaming bath into which I willingly sink. I let every pore of my body and every strand of hair absorb a simple, colourless, formless liquid which is a unity of two elements – it is called water. The force that forged this unity didn't differentiate between the two elements. The emergence of this 'unity' led to life 3.8 billion years ago. Almost 70 per cent of our planet and our individual bodies are this unity. We are because of its oneness. Accessible to sight, touch and thought as one substance, yet inaccessible to physical grasp, without this unity every comprehensible form of life will perish. Our blue planet will cease to exist. Utterly simple without it no pharaoh or peasant would have walked this earth. Constantly giving, replenishing, refreshing, quenching, cleansing, and nourishing, this unity never takes, only gives. Such is its power of oneness that it doesn't differentiate when sustaining life, and such is its simple beauty that it doesn't need any additions. Surging across this planet, its oneness is the essence of growth – from the first wiggling living cell which was single, and which became a mammal, and from a coarse seed that became a majestic oak with dense foliage. In natural surroundings it flows as mountain streams, rivers, seas, and oceans, and when harnessed intellectually for good it flows in fields as canals. It also flows into this bathtub re-energising me and sweeping away fatigue. But intellect has also diluted its simplicity. The result – contaminated livers, veins flowing with sugary blood, and disease riddled intestines. I only realise, I've been languishing in this steamy bath for more than an hour when the phone rings and I grab it with my fingers that have become wrinkly because of the long period of soaking.

'Hello'

'Mizder Mir, you had requested an authentic Egyptian dinner?' It's the hotel reception.

'Oh yes….'

'We had booked you a table at Abou El Sid for 10 pm….'

I look at the watch.

'Gosh, it's close to midnight! I'm so sorry.'

'No broblem, Mizder Mir… they can wait for you for another half an hour.'

'Of course… of course… I'm on my way.'

Rushing out of the bath, dripping, I lunge for some clothes in the cupboard, put on whatever I can, grab *The Enneads*, my notebook and pen, and run out of the door. A few minutes' walk from the hotel and I arrive at the restaurant's arched door with geometric designs on it. Pushing it open, the dimly lit interiors seem cosy and welcoming. Dull green walls, Mediterranean tiles, and rust-coloured multiple arches complete the 'authentic Egyptian look'. The restaurant has a charming tale of its origins. Abou El Sid was a kind-hearted, generous but poor farmer from Cairo who loved to cook for others. Abou El Sid's dishes were richly influenced by the regions and people that surrounded him. Soon his culinary skills and delicious dishes got the attention of the Ottoman Sultan who ruled Egypt in the sixteenth century. Abou El Sid invited the sultan who was so taken in by the explosion of flavours in his mouth that he made the poor farmer a captive in his palace, forcing him to cook only for him. After many years of struggle Abou El Sid, who wanted to feed common people and not royalty, escaped with his cookbook. But while escaping, he lost his cookbook. Centuries later this cookbook of 'authentic Egyptian recipes' was unearthed, and this restaurant came into existence. Self-admittedly, the restaurant has imbibed Palestinian, Turkish, Syrian, and Levant flavours and styles, including tahina sauce, pigeon and rice, molakheya with rabbit, and humus; all of which have unified on this menu as 'Egyptian cuisine'.

I order a vegetarian tajine, and after having enjoyed it spend some time reading *The Enneads*. It is an hour past midnight. The restaurant is empty except for one couple cuddling up under the dimly lit portrait of a bulky, distinctly Egyptian noble wearing a crimson Fez cap popularised during the Ottoman influence in Cairo and which the Egyptians made their own. The dim lighting makes it difficult to read. I hear the hushed footsteps of a waiter who brings a glass of fresh water and a beautiful carved candle lamp. Placing it on the table with a smile, he hesitatingly says, 'Sir, it's nearly 1 am... we will close by 2 am.... I hope you don't mind?'

'No, not at all.... In fact, I'm happy to leave,' I say getting up.

'No, no, please carry on,' he says with sleepy eyes, '... but at 2...'

'Of course.'

I turn the pages of *The Enneads*.

> No doubt we should not speak of seeing; but we cannot help talking in dualities, seen and seer, instead of boldly the achievement of unity. In this seeing, we neither hold an object nor trace distinction; there is no two.[25]

I raise my eyes and look at the water in the glass glowing under the candle lamp. Water's unity – incontestable, and the two elements that constitute it are indistinguishable to sight.

> The man is changed, no longer himself nor self-belonging; he is merged with the One, sunken into it: one with it: centre coincides with centre, for on this higher plane things that touch at all are one; only in separation is there duality; by our holding away, the One is set outside. This is why the vision baffles telling; if we have seen something thus detached we have failed of the One which is to be known only as one with ourselves.[26] ... He (man) has become the Unity, nothing within him or without inducing any diversity; no movement now, no passion, no outlooking desire, once this ascent is achieved; reasoning is in abeyance.[27]

Plotinus would like me to think that duality is in sight. While mind and soul have the capability of not distinguishing, it is sight and other senses that differentiate. For Plotinus, such are unity's all-accepting, all-inclusive virtues that multiplicity and difference are reduced to being merely an image that is the product of sight, and which has no importance. Sight stands marginalised and reduced in status while mind is elevated, provided it thinks of everything as one.

... for to be a god is to be integral with the Supreme; what stands away is man still multiple, or beast.[28]

Sound of the dim lights being switched off and cutlery being lifted off tables interrupts my reading. It is past 2 am and I have overstayed my welcome. My departure from the restaurant goes unnoticed. I step into the silent lanes of Cairo. In the distance is a main road and some traffic is visible through the smog. A city of twenty-five million won't give into slumber in entirety. A broken cement pavement under a looping flyover finds my cautious steps. I don't feel the urge to sleep or to return to the hotel. My phone glows with Google maps as I push in Sayyida Zainab district. It is a one hour walk but I feel an inexplicable need to get there by foot.

The district is named after the granddaughter of a man who in 610 CE dazzled the Arabian deserts with the light of truth. Orphaned at the age of six, he grew up imbibing a tenderness of heart and a gentle demeanour. In his youth, like Plotinus, he was known for his righteousness and truthful nature. Mohammad attracted people who went to him to iron out their differences. Such was the soul soothing truth that sparkled in his simple words that they called him Al-Amin (the trustworthy). But he was surrounded by corruption and distrust that an unenlightened society gives birth to. Disillusioned with social strife erupting from a society riven by divisions, Arab tribalism, and where the air chilled with the blood-curdling screams of girl child infanticide, Mohammad climbed Jabal-al-Noor – a lone arid mountain on the outskirts of Mecca. This muscle tearing climb to the summit would also become the ascent of his soul. An ascension which would change the world forever.

Just below the summit of Jabal-al-Noor, he confined himself to a cave called Hira. Night after night he spent in silent contemplation. Then one night, in darkness, activated thought ceased. Intellect raised reason. Further on, intellect didn't reason. Mind and soul churned. Working backwards from the soul that was within, he reached universal intellect – a state of love and desire for the originator. From there he reached deeper, further, and the further he went, the closer he felt to the originator. Then, as if his soul and intellect had been choked out of him into a state of surrender, they succumbed and became pure love. At this stage with soul and intellect making the ultimate surrender to the originator, he heard:

> Read! In the name of thy Lord and Cherisher
> Who created man out of a mere clot of congealed blood
> Proclaim! And thy Lord is Most Bountiful
> He Who taught the use of the Pen
> Taught man that which he knew not
> Nay, but man doth transgress all bounds,
> In that he looketh upon himself as self-sufficient,
> Verily to thy Lord is the return of all.[29]

That single clot of blood was nothing but unity, brought together by a force that was single – the First Principle. The Pen is intellect, and its use for doing good has been taught. Trembling in fear, drenched in sweat, gasping for breath, struck by the beauty and velocity of what he had heard, he burst out of the mouth of the cave and hurled himself down the mountain, racing down its face in an uncontrollable dash to his humble dwelling. Heart racing, nerves pulsating, he broke open the door and flung himself in the arms of his wife, Khadija. Wrapped in a shawl, he repeated what he had heard – the first revelation, which in time would glow as a philosophical jewel: the Quran. Islam had arrived.

In this faith – the ultimate surrender to the One – there are no races, there are no sects, and there is no clergy. Simply because as a reflection of 'The One' there can be no distinction in humankind. Early Muslims even rejected 'kingship', viewing it as the megalomania of a single human driven by the urge to subjugate and a desire to be seen as divine. For them there simply wasn't anyone worth bowing to except the One God. In time, they would have leaders called Caliphs who were meant to guide and lead for the good, but these leaders were never deified. Like Plotinus, the founder of Islam concerned about being deified insisted that no portrait or sculpture be made of him, instead he urged his followers to focus on the main tenets of the faith – Unity of the Supreme Creator, charity, self-discipline through fasting, and equality of humankind.

A few years after the passing of the founder of Islam, his grandson would refuse to give into political greed, factionalism, and the fragmentation of his grandfather's faith of unity. His rival to the Caliphate had ambitions of self-enrichment and desired power to satisfy his insatiable craving for self-adulation. He enticed the populace of Arabia and Iraq with money and lucrative positions, causing a rift in the young, morally endowed Muslim community the Prophet had left behind. In a one-sided clash at Karbala, Iraq in 680 CE, the Prophet's grandson's head would be severed by forces of division. His decapitated, dismembered body – head buried in Cairo, body in Iraq – would become a chilling metaphoric reminder of what intellect could do if it chose the path of division. Soon after, Islam itself would plunge into a turbulent schism – Shia and Sunni. But the grandson's soul resplendent in beauty became a symbol of unity, love, and compassion – a soul that is revered even today as Imam Hussain. Sayyida Zainab was his sister who came to Cairo and lies buried in the district that bears her name, towards which I am now walking.

I have been walking along the banks of the Nile. In the quiet night, the only other sound accompanying my footsteps are the river's rushing waters lapping against the banks as if it was their last sigh. Some anchored boats bob in a languid sideways movement. A handful of optimistic fishermen are preparing nets for an early morning foray in the river's abundant waters. The walk takes me past a variety of Arab sounding street names – Al Khalig, Al Borg, Al Andalus, and to the Qasr al Nil bridge which I cross, taking me to the famous Tahrir Square where Egyptians had mobilised starting December 2010, giving rise to the Arab Spring. Now drowned in silence, Tahrir square seems to have forgotten what brought it out of obscurity and placed it on the world map. Taking a break, I sit in the square on a bench under a streetlamp sipping water and arranging my notes. Some policemen parked in their jeeps around the square look at me quite obviously wondering what I'm doing at 3 am. Much to my surprise, none of them come to question me.

From Tahrir square I turn right passing the American University and another host of Arab sounding street names, and finally reach Sayyida Zainab district. A little further away is the Ibn Tulun Mosque built in 879 CE by Ahmad ibn Tulun. I walk towards it and inspect its gorgeous honey-coloured walls that seem to be responding to the faint crimson lining of dawn. I take another break outside the mosque and watch the early murmurings of life that are slowly emerging out of slumber. A man rides his donkey whose visible breath makes one aware of this winter setting. Laden with jute sacks bursting with wheat the beast trots along, followed immediately by a cart pulled by a mule loaded with sugarcane. A few moments later, a rag picker dressed in a ripped jellabiya appears from a dark lane. He immediately goes about his business of picking rubbish from the streets.

A pull from within makes me enter the mosque. I climb the stone steps and walk in gingerly. A mighty quadrangle opens up. On all four sides of the quadrangle are lofty symmetrical arches running like a canopy of infinite curves. There is a heavenly ordained simplicity to this symmetry – a hallmark of uncluttered Islamic architecture. Right in the heart of the quadrangle is a dome under which in the quiet pre-dawn setting, only the sound of water and a few pigeons can be heard. Framed in one of the arches as a perfect view is a darkened silhouette of a minaret with inviting stairs curling up its sides. So inviting, I can't resist. I rush towards it and climb right up. The view that presents itself from the top of the minaret is heart-stopping. Old Cairo's mud houses lie below. In clear sight is the Nile and in a distance against the dark blue sky are the silhouettes of minarets topped with curling crescents of other mosques, including the Rifai Mosque and the Hassan Mosque. I am alone in these surroundings. The winter air has a freshness and I inhale deeply. I feel the first signs of a stillness of mind and desertion of thought. Just then, from the opposite minaret a deep base laden baritone that has an unrivalled rawness the likes of which I haven't heard, breaks the silence with a smoothness I have never experienced before.

The *azaan* – first delivered by a freed black slave named Bilal, chosen by the founder of Islam to do so, and for me to fall in love with 1,400 years later:

'God is Great... God is Great'
'God is Great... God is Great'   *an echo in the arches*

*Silence*

'I bear witness... there are no Gods... but One God'
'I bear witness... there are no Gods... but One God'
'I bear witness... Mohammad is the messenger of God'
'I bear witness... Mohammad is the messenger of God'

*Silence*

'Come to prayer'
'Come to prayer'

*Silence*

'Come do good'
'Come do good'   *an echo in the arches*

'God is Great... God is Great'
'There are no Gods... but One God'

I look around and the minarets of the surrounding mosques break into an orchestra of *azaans* reverberating over Cairo.

Compelled by man's proclamation of the unity of divinity, divinity obliges by breaking dawn. Darkness retreats. Such is the power in this simple testament to 'the One' that in the distance the waters of the Nile seem to tremble in reverence. The Nile has encountered this might before. In 641 CE, Amr the Arab general who conquered Egypt for Omar, the Caliph of Islam, wrote desperately to him at the behest of the Egyptian people when the river didn't rise. Amongst his complaints was one describing a barbaric pharaonic custom of sacrificing young girls at the banks to please the legendary river. Omar unhesitatingly wrote back with words radiating confidence and faith and commanded the letter be thrown in the river instead of a slain young girl.

In the letter Omar directly addressed the river:

> From Abd-Allah Omar to the Nile of Egypt. If thou flow of thine own accord, flow not; but if it be God, the One, the Mighty, who causeth thee to flow, we implore God, the One, the Mighty, to make thee flow.[30]

No sooner had Omar's letter been dropped, a trembling Nile rose. Its waters surged forth, soaking the banks with a great generosity, and bringing abundance by turning parched lands into lush sugarcane and rice fields. Why wouldn't it rise? For the Nile is nothing but a unity of two elements which were brought together as one by a singular force as a reflection of Itself. Omar's bold call to the Nile echoes in similarity to Aristotelian philosophy where 'the First Principle' is the first cause of all.

Still standing on the minaret, I observe the entrance of the faithful. Some are rubbing sleep from their eyes. I can tell by the multi-coloured jellabiyas that four of them are Egyptians. They line up shoulder to shoulder. Rushing up and taking his place next to them is a black man from Sub-Saharan Africa. Two men, quite possibly Chinese or Central Asian, come and take their place too, rubbing shoulders quite literally with the black Sub-Saharan African standing right next to them. Dressed in jackets and compared to the Egyptians and their immediate neighbour, they seem wealthier. Just before the prayers are to begin, inside rushes the rag picker I had seen outside the mosque. Unhesitatingly, he lines up right next to the wealthy Chinese looking men. Prayers begin.

> 'In the name of God. Most Gracious, Most merciful'
> 'He is God. The One and Only.
> God, the Eternal, Absolute;
> He begetteth not, Nor is He begotten.
> And there is none like unto Him.'[31]

Other verses are uttered in which they plead for refuge in 'the One' from that part of the whispering intellect that injects jealousy (hasad) and mischief.

They bow in unison. Repeatedly they submit to that unseen God. Then, heads lowered, they raise their palms in a final plea. Not once is there a moment of hesitation while standing next to someone who looks different or is at the lowest ebb of material possessions. This is unity in its simplest yet most powerful form like I have never witnessed before. During their prayer they tap into the energy of 'The One', bringing that energy within while becoming one with each other, and in doing so becoming a true reflection of 'The One'. At that moment of prayer, distinction, and difference dissolve. It is pure unity. They are like the Nile.

As they make their way out, I see them give some coins to the destitute who have gathered outside the walls of the mosque. Even the rag picker seems to be giving something to a cripple – a person more ill fortunate than him. The One is immanent. The One is Unity. Unity is acceptance. Acceptance leads to generosity. And like the generous Nile, those men of faith reflect these qualities.

I make my way down the minaret and into the large quadrangle thinking of the philosophical meaning of the declaration of faith which emphasises: *There is only One God and Mohammad is His messenger.* Kenneth Clark, one of the great historians of the twentieth century, summed it up: 'It is the simplest doctrine that has ever gained acceptance and that gave the Prophet's followers an invincible solidarity.' Ever since I was a child, I have repeated this declaration of faith innumerable times. Born into a Muslim family it is the first thing you are made to say, and it was no different for me. But to me what does it mean philosophically? Living in times where 'othering' and divisiveness are rampant, why did this simple declaration have such a profound impact on societies in the past and even today? What is in it that makes it so acceptable? I pace up and down the long corridors of the mosque tossing this declaration of faith in my head, trying to understand its philosophical meaning, and giving it words.

Briefly pausing and looking at the pigeons, sometimes at the curling crescent on the minaret and gazing into the silent arches where the *azaan* echoed with such majesty, it is only after an hour that it dawns on me with crystal clarity. To me in its philosophical essence, the declaration of faith that more than a billion Muslims recite is uncomplicated and effortless: *'There is nothing but Unity'*. I write it down in my notepad. For a while I just look at it. Then I read it again. *'There is nothing but Unity.'* The philosophical meaning comes to rest with me. It makes sense. The Muslims at prayer deny everything but oneness. In its very denial of 'others' (including deities) is the acceptance of unity, which is absolute inclusiveness. Because multiplicity and difference are refuted, the oneness of unity rises and encompasses everything. And because visual difference is dashed, unity in mind does not 'other'. The eye may see multiplicity and difference, but the mind with its fertility to understand everything as one stands elevated over vision. All those men of faith praying in the mosque, belonging to different races, dressed in different attire, and straddling different socio-economic strata, stood in unity in one line, shoulder to shoulder, without being 'othered' or 'othering'. This simple, core unity that sparkles in Islam as a philosophy even today makes it the fastest growing faith in the world – a faith in which no intermediaries are needed between God and human and all humans are equal before Him.

After the splendorous night of revelation (*Lailat-ul-Qadr*) in the lonely cave of Hira and with the progression of his faith, the founder of Islam went on to imbue the philosophical concept of 'One' (*tawheed*) with timeless virtues like love (*wadud*), mercy (*raheem*), originator and initiator (*baari* and *mubdi*). In a move that would stun the world, he would stretch his belief in equality by ensuring women were given rights to initiate divorce and own property in seventh-century tribal Arabia.

Gliding through the clouds, slanting beams of sunlight now bathe the Ibn Tulun Mosque in bountiful splendour, drenching every wall, minaret, and dome in a delicious honey colour. Pigeons have flocked near the water that flows under the central dome while others flutter around the minarets. At a distance under one of the magnificent arches that hang over the silent corridors, a young preacher wearing a red Nike cap has settled in to give a talk on faith. Surrounding him are young students of theology and Islamic philosophy, probably from the Al-Azhar University. I make my way out of the arches. A plaque catches my eye which gives the name of the chief architect of this glorious mosque: Saiid Ibn Kateb Al-Farghany, an orthodox Christian. I turn, take one last look at the honey doused dome, and recite Plotinus' words before walking down the steps:

> Thus the One as containing no otherness is ever present with us; we with It when we put otherness away' when we reach towards the One.[32]

A brief stopover at the Gayer-Anderson Museum which is right next door to the mosque proves to be a reminder that my eyes are craving sleep. Ensconced in the museum's cheerful winter sunbathed rooms are the most stunning artefacts collected by Gayer-Anderson *Pasha*, a doctor who left his family behind in England for the love of Egypt. In many ways, in his heart, he became Egyptian, adopting Egyptian customs and an 'oriental' addition to his name. He lived here between 1935 and 1942. One of the rooms presents an ideal setting to fling oneself on a cushioned settee under intricately carved wooden arches which distil streams of soft sunlight. A sense of happy tiredness descends.

I have a flight to Aswan in the evening. I return to the hotel and give in to drooping eyelids.

The Egypt Air flight from Cairo to Aswan is an hour and a half long. After having slept through the day with my head buried under pillows and only having made it to the airport thanks to my iPhone alarm, I surprisingly found myself rather energised during the flight. Besides making notes of my experiences through the previous day and night and underlining key passages in *The Enneads*, it was the flight path that caught my eye. We were flying into Upper Egypt which lies to the south of the country. The reason it is called Upper Egypt is because compared to Lower Egypt (which is northern Egypt), it is closer to the source of the Nile. The flight seems glued to the Nile's trajectory and follows it like an intoxicated bee chasing the scent of nectar. To the upper right corner of the screen I notice borders demarcating Jordan, Saudi Arabia, Lebanon, and other

Arab countries. Interestingly, there are daily flights from Cairo to Tel Aviv – a brave attempt at encouraging people-to-people contacts.

Having landed in Aswan, collected my bags, and found my driver – all rather smoothly – I make my way to the Old Cataract Hotel. My overenthusiastic driver seems keen to take a slight detour and show me the Aswan Dam which was built across the Nile in the 1960s and was responsible for harnessing the river's tremendous potential for irrigation through increased reservoir storage. My flagging interest in the dam doesn't go unnoticed, and soon the conversation dies a natural death.

Eventually we drive into the Old Cataract Hotel at sunset and almost immediately everything seems to slow down. The hotel is perched on dun-coloured rocks through which the waters of the Nile meander at a gentle pace. The rocks seem to be persuading the Nile to flow unrushed just so that the people of Aswan can admire her. Rising from the rocks are tall, swaying date palm trees. Through their parted branches and dark green leaves pours the soft light of a fading sun. And as if saying farewell, the sun glitters on leaf edges. Between the branches I can see the drifting sail of a felucca as it sails on the river. The Old Cataract and its sunset setting are draped in a mystical magnetism. The hotel was made famous by Agatha Christie who wrote and set her remarkable thriller *Death on the Nile* partly in this hotel. It is not difficult, even to this day, to peer down the rocks and see the stone steps of the hotel leading into the river, all the while imagining David Niven, Peter Ustinov, Bette Davis, and Maggie Smith gingerly walking down to board the cataclysmic boat in which death awaited them.

Following the receptionist to my room I pass never-ending corridors that stretch out before me, gloriously high ceilings from which hang nineteenth-century lamps, gorgeously polished wood panelling, exquisite wooden lifts, and majestic Moorish arches. My room is reasonable in space but vintage in character. While it pleases me to be in the room, I feel a pull to the terrace. I rush back, sink into a large cane chair, and catch the most magnificent sight of the sun's last rays and felucca sails embraced in an ethereal ballet on the Nile. An early dinner of grilled chicken and a bottle of red wine finishes off the perfect evening. I decide to begin early the next day and book a felucca to take me upstream at 7:30 am.

Feeling completely rested after a good night's sleep, unalarmed by creaking wooden floors (quite possibly ghosts from Agatha Christie's characters lurking in the quiet corridors), the next morning I make my way down the stone steps of the terrace to find a man waiting for me. Dressed in a chocolate jellabiya with a white turban, he is a man of swarthy skin. A white jaw-hugging beard with the most dazzling emerald eyes completes the look of the felucca manager.

'Salam Alaikum,' he says, walking up to me.

'Walaikum Salam.'

'Your felucca is right here,' he says, pointing to a stunning delicate boat with the most elegant sail. '...and he is your boatman.'

I look into the boat and see a young man, probably in his early twenties, peering out with a warm smile. He takes his right palm and presses it against his chest.

'Ahlan... my name is Fuad.' He gives me his hand and helps me get into the felucca.

'Mizder Mir, and here is some lunch arranged by the hotel.' A box is handed over to me.

The clarity of the blue Nile is stunning as the felucca carries us upstream. I pull out *The Enneads*, the commentaries, and my notes, and lay them on deck, hoping to read as and when I feel moments of inspired intuition. I recline on the slender deck, lock my arms behind my head, and look at the oscillating triangular sail against the blue sky. These are moments of immense serenity. We drift past jagged rocky islands that jut out of the river begging a passing glance. The lapping of gentle waves against the felucca and of the wind are the sound of ambling aimless time. The smooth lazy sailing takes us past gently rising riverbanks, some of which have patches of green cultivation and others which are sand dunes. A few water buffaloes are enjoying a morning swim while getting a facial from sparrows picking out insects from their nostrils. Fuad, it seems, picks up my state of mind – unstated happiness and calm. He comes over with a carved transparent glass filled with Egyptian tea. The fresh morning brew adds to the happy state of mind, and I sip it with great pleasure. Turning on my side to face the river and the passing sand dunes, I reach out for The Enneads and some commentaries, wondering what Plotinus might have in store for me. The curvaceous flow of the Nile meandering through dunes and pasture lands is a sight unchanged for millennia, and Plotinus through his childhood and youth would have seen exactly what I am witnessing today. I turn the pages of The Enneads.

For we are not cut off from The One or separate, even if the nature of body has intruded and drawn us to itself, but we breathe and are preserved because that Good (the One) has not given Its gifts and then gone away but is always bestowing gifts…. For there must be something simple before all things, and this must be other than all the things which come after it, existing by itself, not mixed, for if It is not to be simple, it could not be the First Principle… but how can one describe the absolute simple? It is enough if the intellect comes into contact with It; but when it has done so, while the contact lasts, it is absolutely impossible, nor has it time to speak, but it is afterwards that it is able to reason about it.[33]

There is nothing but water, wood floating on water, the sun, and Plotinus' words. The felucca changes direction as Fuad swerves it around slowly, bringing it to rest in front of a rising hill. I continue to lie sideways watching the view present itself. On top of the hill is a small, sand-coloured mausoleum which is the last resting place of Aga Khan III. It stands at a distance from the Nile, not too far but not too close either. Against the blue waters, the sandy hill and its enmeshed mausoleum seem to be longing to dissolve into the Nile. I watch the swaying sail and the mausoleum for some time.

Then I hear the most endearing voice emanating from the mausoleum. Hidden behind the walls, unseen, a muezzin probably sitting by the grave of the Aga Khan is reciting a verse from the Quran's most beautiful chapter, Surah-e Rehman (The chapter of Mercy), which speaks of 'the balance' set up by the Creator. The one sentence though delivered by the muezzin with repeated compassion is:

Then which of the favours of your Lord will ye deny?[34]

He repeats this line. At the edge of the felucca Fuad has shut his eyes and is shaking his head gently, mesmerised by the beauty of this Quranic line. After a while he realises the felucca needs his attention and he springs out of his thoughts, scurrying to manage the sail and steer the felucca onto its rightful course. It is past noon and Fuad rightly senses I'm hungry. He brings me my lunch box and goes back to the edge of the felucca. There he sits quietly smiling to himself and peering into the Nile, probably amusing himself with some speeding fish that are darting around the boat. It is a magnificent European lunch – focaccia and rich mozzarella as starter, a delicious cheese and spinach pie as a main course, and tiramisu for pudding. But before I can dive into this Italian meal, I see Fuad rummaging through his pockets. He pulls out three dates and a slice of coarse bread.

'My mother gave me this for lunch... can I have it now? Or would you like me to take the boat further?' he asks.

'Fuad... please have your lunch.'

He flashes a smile, pops a date in his mouth, then looks over into the river. He laughs. Then he turns to the one slice of bread he has, breaks it in half. One half he breaks into smaller and yet smaller pieces. Looking down into the river he sprinkles the tiny breadcrumbs. I follow his trajectory and look down too. Several tiny fish are bobbing up and feeding on the breadcrumbs with dazzling speed. He laughs again.

'Can I feed them too?' I ask.

'Yes, of course.' and he holds out the remaining half of his bread slice towards me.

'Fuad, no.'

I break tiny pieces of the focaccia and lower it into the river. The fish rush towards my side of the felucca and so does a laughing Fuad.

After a while, I decide to settle into lunch and spread out the three courses. I notice Fuad has gone back to the edge of the felucca and has his back turned towards me. But I can see he is eating. I think: *Is he ashamed of his food?*

'Fuad,' I call out. 'Come and join me.'

There is silence.

'Come, please join me,' I re-emphasise.

He walks up.

'I share with you... here, see, take.' He holds his quarter slice of bread and one date in his palm and presents it to me. Then he looks at the date in his hand. Something catches his eye. It is dusty. He assumes I wouldn't like it. 'Oh.' He sighs and rushes to the edge of the boat and lowers his date into the waters of the Nile. After a few seconds he pulls his hand out.

'The great river has cleaned it... Please take,' he insists.

'Fuad, no, please, I would like you to share my food.'

Hesitantly, he sits down. Then cautiously he tastes some of the cheese and spinach pie. He has a little bit more. Then stops. I can tell he hasn't quite liked it. With a smile he says, 'Too much. Too heavy.'

It is clear, the food is too rich for him. Too creamy and heavy. Not simple and delicious like his bread and dates.

'What about the bread? Try the focaccia,' I say.

'OK... I try.'

'Nice?'

'Yes... good bread.'

'Good.'

He opens his palm. The date is presented again.

I take it. A few droplets are still on it. It is delicious with a slight taste of the sweet Nile.

He takes a couple of focaccia slices and goes back to the edge of the felucca. There, he sits down and eats.

After lunch, we sail on.

'Fuad, are you from Aswan?' I ask, reclining on the deck, surrounded by my notes.

'No, I'm from a village not far from Aswan.'

'And your father? Where does he work?'

'In the church... he's a cleaner.'

'Church?'

'Yes, I am Coptic Christian.'

I sense there is a meaningful conversation to be had.

'Is it difficult being Christian in Egypt?'

To my surprise Fuad doesn't hold back.

'Very difficult... They don't like us... they hate us... they want to kill us.'

'Who "they"?' I probe further.

'The Muslim Brotherhood,' he replies.

For a few seconds there is silence. Then he continues.

'They burn down our churches, don't allow us to worship... Aren't we Egyptian?'

It's apparent Fuad wants to speak more.

'They big bully you know... We not many... They not brave,' he says with damp eyes that glisten in the sun.

Such anguish in the voice of a youth who, till a few moments ago, was submerged in the innocent joy of sharing his sparse meal with other inhabitants of his planet. Those moments had brought him happiness and now he was in agony. But he was brave, I thought, to speak so openly to a stranger. All that he was saying was true. The Muslim Brotherhood had wreaked havoc in Egypt. Since 2013, many churches have been torn down. Some reports have estimated the number to be more than fifty. To save face in the international community, the Egyptian government had acted swiftly and decisively hunting down the perpetrators and having some of the churches restored. But confidence amongst the Coptic Christians of Egypt is almost non-existent, and most like Fuad believe their fate hangs by a thread. Christians form ten per cent of the Egyptian population making them vulnerable to majoritarian politics and when a majority 'bullies' a minority, it is cowardice, not bravery.

In the felucca speaking with Fuad, for the first time in my travels I encountered how intellect fosters 'otherness'. In Plotinus' words:

For one must always understand intellect as otherness and sameness if it is going to think. For otherwise it will not distinguish itself from the intelligible by its relation of otherness to itself, and will not contemplate all things if not otherness has occurred to make all things exist... for without otherness there would not even be two.[35]

The Muslim Brotherhood uses the word 'brotherhood' to unite the Muslims of Egypt that form a majority to 'second' the Coptic Christians. As second-class citizens their future is bleak. As the felucca sails on, I ponder: why 'Muslim Brotherhood' and not 'Biradereen-e-Khalq' (Brotherhood of Humankind)? Wouldn't this have been a true manifestation of *Tawheed: One God. One humankind?* Wouldn't this have transcended the boundary of dogmatic religion, taken Islamic theology and married it with the pinnacle of Islamic philosophical thought – 'There is nothing but Unity' – and wouldn't this have unified Egypt in entirety with all-inclusiveness at its core?

The sailing continues under the strong afternoon sun. Although it is winter, by the afternoon Aswan warms up noticeably. Energy reservoirs are quickly depleted when one lies directly under the most gigantic star. Sluggishness and silence have cast a spell on the felucca. Fuad is obviously quite sad. A frown seems to clasp his face with an unrelenting force. Lost in this pensive mood, he is a picture of loneliness. To bring him back to his original state of innocent joy, I rise and spring an idea.

'Fuad, shall we have a swim?'

Instantly he turns to me with lit up eyes and a smile.

'You swim with me?' There is disbelief in his voice.

'Yes of course,' but then I quickly realise what I have proposed. I don't have a change of clothes, we are about fifteen minutes sailing from the hotel, and the water must be freezing... but why not? It'll refresh both of us.

Sweaters off. Jeans dropped. Felucca anchored. Fuad is the first to jump off, splashing and bursting into uncontrollable laughter. I stand at the edge, look down into the Nile, the most wonderful unity – the greatest reflection of 'The One' and the catalyst for life. Plato's words from *Phaedrus* describing the creator leave my lips.

> What is in this place is without colour and without shape and without solidity, a being that really is what it is, the subject of true knowledge, visible only to intelligence, the soul's steersman.

I fling myself in.

The Nile receives me with a freshness that erupts from my toes and submerges every hair follicle. After being initially stunned by its cold vigour, the body slowly adapts. As if inspired by the power that brought about its unity and thus its existence without differentiating between two elements, the Nile doesn't differentiate between a Muslim and a Christian. This moment is the greatest manifestation of *Tawheed*. I feel cleansed of all thoughts. I look at Fuad. He is in ecstasy. His lifted spirits are a testimony to the Nile's ever-gifting virtues. It has washed away his anguish and unease. We float with arms spread out. The river lifts us into weightlessness. Floating, I look up into the cloudless blue sky absorbing as much sky as I can. Time drifts with me staring into the vast blue. Plotinus seems to speak.

> He is lifted on high by a kind of swell and sees suddenly, not seeing how the vision fills his eyes with light and does not make him see something else by it, but the light itself is what

he sees. It (The One) is the ray which generates intellect and does not extinguish Itself in the generation, and that intellect comes to be because this Good exists. For this was not of the kind It is; that would not have come into existence.[36]

In short – if 'the One' wasn't good, the Nile wouldn't have come into existence. I wonder if Plotinus had these thoughts after a swim in the Nile.

After a few minutes, I swim back to the felucca, wipe myself down with my T-shirt, put on the sweater, and urge Fuad to return. He does after a few minutes. Shivering till we reach the steps of the Old Cataract, I climb up the steps, turn around, and wave to Fuad. Unbeknown to him, he has answered Plotinus' question on how to describe 'contact with the absolute simple'.

He will be back tomorrow and we will sail to Philae Temple.

Among the numerous Greek philosophers that mention Philae and its temples are Diodorus Siculus (first century BCE) and Strabo (63 BCE–24 CE). This temple complex has had a profound impact on what it is to be Egyptian. Fuad's brilliant navigation of the Nile through a misty morning is astounding. With limited vision he manoeuvres the felucca with great skill and confidence. The sail responds beautifully to him. As we approach Philae Island, the mist seems to rise from the water resembling a band of soft white sugar. Through this sugary mist emerges Philae like a bastion rising from the water. Its light brown colonnades and pylons are the first to make an impression. Here too, sumptuous date palms burst through the rocks at the edge of the Nile and envelope the temple island. Such is the antiquated setting that one would be forgiven for seeing ancient Egyptian priests dressed in white robes ascending and descending the temple steps. It is no wonder that Philae is considered one of Egypt's most seductive sights.

I rush up the steps rising from the river and make my way into an open space. At the edge of my view are two almost rectangular shaped tall pylons. This is the temple of Isis. Although the cult of Isis at Philae goes back to the seventh century BCE, the earliest remains on the island date from the reign of the last native king of Egypt, Nectanebo I (380–362 BCE). Both pylons boldly carry Egyptian art on their facades. But leading up to these pylons is a colonnade of pillars built in perfect symmetry. Each singular column, though, testifies to its multicultural oneness. While the bottom and middle part of the pillars bear Egyptian artistry, the apex is shaped in Greek Corinthian design with floral manifestations. This can be explained by the Ptolemaic dynasties' great regard for Egyptian civilisation. Ptolemy I was a Greek general in Alexander's army when the Macedonian king conquered Egypt. On Alexander's death, Ptolemy was appointed satrap of Egypt. In time, local Egyptians came to accept Ptolemy as their ruler. Ptolemy responded by flinging himself in what it meant to be Egyptian and adopted the title of Pharaoh Ptolemy I. He dissolved differences by adopting local dress and customs including wearing the nemes – a striped cloth that draped the pharaoh's head and hung over his shoulders with the uraeus cobra at the centre. In time his descendants, the Ptolemaics would add pillars, buildings and art to temples dedicated to Egyptian gods in Philae. In fact, the carvings on the first pylon are reliefs of Ptolemy XII Neos Dionysos looking utterly Egyptian, smiting the enemies of Egypt with a raised club. He is accompanied by Isis. The second pylon has Ptolemy XII making offerings to Horus, the son of Isis. Greek immersion in native Egyptian culture was absolute. Even Cleopatra who summed up everything Egyptian was of Ptolemaic descent. But the Greeks weren't doing this kind of cross-pollinated cultural experimentation for the first time. In fact, Ptolemy was just taking a leaf from Greek kings of the past.

The legendary animosity between Greece and Persia in the fourth and fifth century BCE led to multiple conflicts and wars, yet through that conflict emerged a Greek curiosity about Persian life and culture. Greeks, in particular Arbinas – ruler of Lycia – wore Persian caps, robes, and even had himself depicted in the arts in a typical Persian reclining position while drinking wine on an elevated platform with a curled Persian beard.

But the colonnades of Philae have more to tell. With the Roman conquest of Egypt by Julius Caesar, a new dimension was added. Like the Greeks, the Romans too succumbed to Philae's charm and its main god – Isis. A column has a carving of Roman emperor Tiberius dressed as a pharaoh offering gifts to Isis. The ceiling, which is mostly destroyed, is decorated with stars and flying vultures, while the rear wall has two rows of bas-reliefs of Tiberius and Augustus (Julius Caesar's nephew) making offerings to other Egyptian gods. Many inscriptions and reliefs of later Roman periods, especially the reign of Augustus (r. 30 BCE–14 CE) are noticeable. Emperor Augustus built a temple at the northern end of Philae in 9 BCE, Tiberius and Nero added reliefs and inscriptions, and Hadrian added a gate west of the complex leading to the island of Bigeh. This shows that the new regime of Roman emperors in Egypt maintained and absorbed the temples of Philae into their way of life. By Roman times, Isis had become the greatest of all Egyptian gods worshipped right across the Roman Empire even as far as Britain. Indeed, as late as 550 CE, well after Rome and its empire embraced Christianity, Isis was still being worshipped at Philae until early Christians eventually made the temple's hypostyle hall into a chapel. Having encountered Egyptian influence in the Pantheon in Rome, standing here I get a sense of the genesis of the magnetism of ancient Egypt that sprung from Philae and drenched Rome in its magnificence.

At a distance from this multi-faceted historical jewel stands the Kiosk of Trajan, or the pharaoh's bed. This unfinished cube of pillars built by Roman emperor Trajan (r. 97–117 CE) is at the water's edge. There are parts of the structure, though, that date back to emperor Augustus' time, and although roofless one can't help admiring its compact beauty. Like preceding Roman emperors including Augustus, Tiberius, and Domitian (who particularly loved wearing the pharaonic nemes and uraeus headgear), Trajan too had himself depicted as pharaoh giving gifts to the Egyptian God Hathor in the far away temple of Dendera in Upper Egypt. Standing in the pharaoh's bed, I turn around and get a sweeping view of the temple complex.

To me, Philae is all what Plotinus was himself. As someone of Greek ancestry but born and raised in Egypt and eventually settling in Rome, Plotinus must have considered Philae an extension of himself. His oneness, like Philae, was all inclusive.

I make my way back to where my felucca awaits me. Settling in I watch the giant pylons and colonnades slowly reduce in size as we sail upstream. Pondering over what I have just seen, each column and pylon bear the mark of an amalgamation of cultures with Egypt being the host culture. It is irrefutable that during the early years of Greek-Egyptian interaction and later Roman-Egyptian interaction there was conflict. Severe conflict. Even 'othering'. But what comes surging through is that once those initial differences were put aside, Egypt successfully lured the Greeks and Romans to culturally unite with it. Indeed, political, and social sensitivities must have played an important role in convincing the Greek and Roman emperors to become pharaohs, but what is unimpeachable is the sincerity that sparkles in the image of Ptolemy XII (an Egyptian pharaoh of Greek origin) defending Egypt against its enemies as Isis rises to support him.

I leave for Luxor the next day knowing that I might never see Fuad again. It is a three-hour drive from Aswan to Luxor and we pass the tiniest villages interspersed with cotton and sugarcane fields. Village mud walls overflow with pink, white and orange bougainvillaea, and as the car navigates curling rural streets a few inquisitive children burst through the lanes and chase the vehicle, as if a magician were driving through their village. A few simple mosques made of mud and brick emerge on the fringes of the fields quite conspicuously. Then almost without any warning and without reason, two giant-sized faceless stone statues scaling 18 m rise from the green plains. Dating back to 1350 BCE, these are the images of Pharaoh Amenhotep III and each weigh a thousand tonnes. Sitting well enthroned and surveying his realm from that steep height, the pharaoh looks at ease, but it is the Greek and Roman inscriptions on it that add to the intrigue. The Greeks named the statues Colossi of Memnon after the African king who was allegedly slain by Achilles during the Trojan War, and due to a crack, that appeared in the upper body of the northern statue, the Greeks heard a whistling sound emanating from it at sunrise. They attributed this phenomenon to Memnon's cry while greeting his mother Eos, the goddess of dawn, and she in turn would weep tears of dew for his untimely death. It was only after Roman emperor Septimus Severus (r. 193–211 CE) repaired the statue that the sound was heard no more.

For the next two days I will be staying at the Al Moudira – an oasis of thick palm tree clusters on the west bank of the Nile. It is not in Luxor but some kilometres away in the countryside. Its rural charm enhanced by its isolation and relative inaccessibility make it a chosen retreat for writers, historians, and painters. Run by a Lebanese lady, the hotel's name means 'The Boss'. Zeina Abou Kheir is all that an ideal 'Boss' should be – strong-willed, dedicated, elegant, and sophisticated. Fluent in Arabic, French and English, she is the final word at Al Moudira. Her French husband, Sammy Ketz, has a unique job of floating between Iran, Egypt, and Paris, covering local politics. With its intellectual owners, pale peach walls, curving domes, arches, and wooden Arabesque architecture, Al Moudira is a splendid place to read and write.

In the evening, strolling into the lounge, I'm greeted by the creative diversity staying here. The lounge is a cocoon of sorts; it is not large but instantly cosy dotted with Syrian and Egyptian hexagon-shaped wooden tables. The first to greet me with a sedate yet welcoming smile is Phillip Hewat-Jaboor. As I gather through self-introduction, he is a seventy-five-year-old art dealer from London and, as I discover further, he is also a curious and amateur Egyptologist. In the next few days, he will be heading into the remote Sinai desert. Under warm lamps, he and his partner dressed in a red suit were poring over a game of chess, but both were extraordinarily well-mannered to greet me when I entered the lounge. After a brief chat, I wander over to the bar and order a glass of red wine. Here, I meet an Irish trio of musicians and actors who come every year to Al Moudira to sing carols on Christmas Eve under a resplendent date palm in the main foyer. They do this just for the love of singing at Al Moudira. Not far from them, standing at a distance but soon joining our conversation on what makes a great 'carol singer', is a moustached, spectacled man with a very soft voice. As the evening progresses, he reveals his past life as a British soldier in Afghanistan. Quite the opposite in disposition to a Taliban-hunting British army man, he is erudite and well-read, quoting Persian poets.

Al Moudira also attracts local historians, most of whom are retired teachers who keep their love for the subject alive by spending time with guests and accompanying them to Luxor. It is supposed to be an easy experience, with a possibility of a friendship developing at the end of the day. Strolling through the foyer, I meet one such rather chubby historian sipping sugarcane juice. His name is Bashir, and he invites me to join him for a trip to Luxor the next day, which I find myself accepting almost instantly.

After dinner, Zeina Abou Kheir arrives and gathers us around the palm tree in the main foyer. As evening turns to night the palm tree attracts a flood of sparrows that begin an orchestra of chirping. What initially sounds quite melodious quickly descends into a chirping war and becomes a severe imposition on one's senses. Occasionally an attendant will stroll in and smack his palms into a resounding clap, which disperses the sparrows. Emphatically, Zeina declares that New Year eve celebrations will include a short musical on 'Princess Lola' – the fairy-tale princess who was courted by princes from all over the world but eventually lost her heart to a prince's goat herder. Zeina scans the rooms for volunteers. Some raise their hands, but not enough. Then with determination, she picks the actors with the most charming smile. None can refuse. I gingerly trace my footsteps to the back of the crowd as she goes about her business. A delightful cheer erupts once the final casting is announced. Zeina gives way to the Irish carol singers who gather around a piano and begin their rehearsals under a string of mellow lamps hanging from the palm tree. I listen to them for a while, cheer them on, and retire to my room.

The next morning, seeing me breakfasting alone, a man wearing an elegant fur cap initiates a conversation. His name is Gilles Kepel and he, as I would discover during our conversation, is a French Political Scientist, Arabist, and author of books with titles such as *The Revenge of God: The Resurgence of Islam, Christianity, and Judaism in the Modern World*. He has a way of making his point on controversial topics with a disarming smile which can get you to agree to almost everything he says. Almost, but not everything. But what has caught his eye is the *Diwan of Mirza Ghalib*, arguably the greatest Urdu and Persian poet of the nineteenth century, from which I read a few couplets every morning. The book has been lying on my table and has drawn him in. He tries to wrap his tongue around the name and succeeds soon enough. We chat about Ghalib's poetry and philosophy, and by the end of our chat I hope I've given him a flavour of Urdu poetry steeped in love and kindness that flowed from the pen of a Muslim thinker not too long ago. After a brief conversation and inspection of Ghalib's work, he departs to join his son on another table.

Having breakfasted in the rural setting of date palm clusters intermingled with blooming pink oleander and the fragrance of freshly irrigated soil, I leave to see the temples of Luxor with Bashir. For the next six hours it is a 'temple blitz'. We begin with the gorgeous Madinat Habu which is set against the backdrop of the Theban mountains and was built by Rameses III. Here, the pharaoh built a temple to himself and a smaller one dedicated to the god Amun. Artistic depictions of Rameses victorious in war and presenting prisoners to God Amun and his vulture wife are clearly visible. The original paint work dating back 3,000 years still speaks a language of beauty. Christian blocks forming a chapel peep out as if urging visitors to take notice of them. The next temple we visit is the temple of Hatshepsut (1473–1458 BCE). Vandalised by early Christians, it was made into a monastery. From here we head to the Karnak temples where the artistic optics are overwhelming. Human headed sphinxes, ram headed sphinxes, a colossal statue of Rameses II, a network of cylindrical columns with exquisite engravings, Christian frescos still fresh in pastel blue, a Sufi shrine dedicated to Yusuf Haggag encrusted within the temple, and the sacred lake of Amun Ra all merge into a cultural mosaic evoking a surreal bewilderment.

It is at the sacred lake of Amun Ra that I decide to bring up a sensitive topic. I ask Bashir about the women who still pray to Egyptian gods in the hope of getting pregnant.

'Who told you about this?' His voice becomes agitated, and his face wears a sullen look.

'Well, I've read about it.' I decide not to tell him about my conversation with Ahmad in Giza.

'It is haram ya sheikh,' he replies, and walks towards the lake.

'But does it happen? Can I see it?' I ask, following him.

'You must not speak about it,' comes his abrupt reply.

'So it does happen?'

'Well... sometimes,' he says hesitatingly after I've cornered him for an answer.

'Can I see it?'

'No... no absolutely not.'

Seeing disappointment descend on my face, he responds.

'You see the lake?'

'Yes.'

'There at the far end, sometimes, in the evening or at night....'

'Bashir, do you know any of the ladies who have prayed there? Can I please meet them?'

'No, I don't know anyone... Please, Mizder Mir, this conversation has not happened. If you continue this conversation I get into trouble. Please no more... I think it's best we go back to the hotel now. Tomorrow, we go to Valley of Kings. You will like it there... ok?'

It is past sunset. Almost miraculously, as soon as Bashir has finished his monologue I see a figure moving at the very far end of the lake. I look closer and walk towards the lake. It is too far to tell but I can see a small human shape draped in a black *abayya* from head to toe. Alone, her body suddenly seems to erupt in a strange movement. Then, she looks around like an alarmed deer. Something seems to tell her she's being watched, and she runs away. What I have seen remains inconclusive. The distance was too great.

Bashir has followed me to where I am.

'Sir, we go now... I insist.'

'Ok... ok.'

Back at Al Moudira, night has descended. I decide to go back into the date palm-oleander oasis and read *The Enneads*. Oil lamps hang from some of the branches under which is an inviting cane chair. It is tranquil except for the sound of rushing water running through the network of slender mud canals and the fragrance of moist soil. A few chirping sparrows signal the end of day as they nestle back into the branches. A baying donkey in a nearby field declares his fatigue from all that has passed since dawn. A faint *azaan* from a distant mosque calls the faithful to the night Isha prayers. Planting myself under the oil lamps, I reflect on the day and the extravagance of the art I have witnessed. Art that was made to please kings and gods. Art that would elevate the stature of man and the stature of divinity. In some cases, like the Christian murals at Karnak and the monastery at Hatsheput, art and architecture were created to supersede the previous manifestations of loyalty to the divine, and with an intention to demonstrate the superiority of a new faith. Yet with all these artistic renditions on them, the temples stand today as one.

Through art, though, Plotinus seeks out a method that would take us closer to simplicity on our journey towards the Good. Instead of lavish artistic creations including portraits, he pleads for an awakening undertaken through an inward journey of quiet contemplation of 'the Good' and demonstrable actions.

> What art is there, what method or practise, which will take us up there where we must go? Where that is, that it is to the Good, the First Principle, we can take as agreed and established by many demonstrations; and the demonstrations themselves were a kind of leading up on our way.[37]

Centuries later, unknowingly, Paul Cezanne seemed to have answered Plotinus' question in 1893. The great nineteenth-century French artist initially started as an impressionist, landscape, and portrait painter, and became a rage in Paris. His exhibitions drew large crowds and his art, which was detailed, became a source of great conversation and needed an acquired understanding. But with time Cezanne came to love the stillness of life. He left bustling Paris and withdrew into the country to paint the 'still life'. One day he declared, 'I will astonish Paris with an apple.' Only a simple apple he believed could convey the beauty and struggle of this world. While Paris thronged to see the maestro's 'apples' while sipping wine and eating cheese, Cezanne had communicated so much more than just a delicious fruit lying still. His apple spoke of hunger, pain, starvation, satisfaction, beauty, and temptation – Cezanne's uncomplicated and plain depiction of the fruit that sent man descending from the heavens has the most profound meaning in its unornamented form. Most of the art connoisseurs in Paris didn't understand this still simplicity and had come to expect verve and impressionism from him. After having painted that series, Cezanne himself was moved by its effects. 'The world doesn't understand me, and I don't understand it,' he famously said. But one man would understand the power of simplicity in Cezanne's art. Years later, Picasso would call Cezanne 'the father of us all'.

My thoughts keep wandering to the many-hued architectural delights I encountered today – historical layer upon layer, compressed in one space in Karnak and yet its beauty so striking. Sight has seen the different forms of architecture, but can the mind just admire its sheer 'wholeness'? I shut my eyes for a while just so that my soul can soak it all in. A few minutes later I open my eyes. Right next to the pages of *The Enneads* that I am turning are some oleander flowers. Their fragrance in the Egyptian night adds to the contemplative experience of reading Plotinus. One of the flowers is in full bloom. Its many petals of different shape and form have unified to form a gorgeous oleander. This has taken time. The other is a fledgling bloom just emerging from a bud. Some petals have formed, others are taking shape. On closer inspection with a lowered oil lamp, I can see that there is an internal tussle between the different shaped petals for survival. Coming through the ovule and the receptacle, each petal is jostling for space and nutrition. Some weaker petals might fall away. In time though, each petal will find its space, friction will cease, and they will come together as one, its unified beauty will find adoration and admiration – quite like the Karnak temple that houses the statue of Rameses, a Christian mural, and a Sufi shrine.

Through the oil lamps in the distance, I can see and hear the rehearsals for Christmas and New Year celebrations. The Irish carol singers sing in a rising unison, culminating in a stirring crescendo. I walk up towards the foyer which falls on the way to my room. To everyone's excitement, Zeina Abou Kheir has selected one of the guests as princess Lola. She's a strikingly beautiful northern European and is part of the rehearsal for the musical. Princess Lola arrives on a palanquin and takes her place on a throne. Her kohl-lined green eyes scan the room for prospective lovers. The goatherd riding his beast catches her eye. And from there on, it is Guns N' Roses and paradise city. On that note, I turn the keys to my room.

The next morning Bashir and I find ourselves in the Valley of the Kings. Lying not far from me is the tomb of Ramesses III, the greatest excavation discovery since Tutankhamun. We sit sipping tea in a tent meant for local historians. Some of Bashir's friends have their papers spread open. One of them called Imaad is busy reading. A few seconds later he slams the newspaper on the table in front of him.

'Ah! The mess of the Middle East!' He roars.

I listen in.

'The borders drawn up in the Arab world are the root cause of the problems in the Middle East.... Jordan, Iraq, Lebanon, none of these existed 150 years ago.... We stand a divided lot,' continues Imaad.

'They are just lines. We are Muslims, Arab Muslims, one people,' Bashir interjects.

'Bashir, I want to correct you.' A middle-aged, bearded man decides to enter the conversation. 'I am not an Arab Muslim. I'm an Egyptian Muslim. The Arabs came only in 641 CE. My forebears go back to the time of the pharaohs,' he says, pointing to the tomb of Ramesses III. 'Yes, we accepted Islam, and we speak Arabic, but I'm Egyptian, he emphasises, slapping his thigh with an open palm.

'You see?' Imaad turns to Bashir, 'We are a divided lot'.

The complexities that plague the socio-political problems in the Middle East are vast and multi-layered. Criss-crossed with modern man-made borders, the Middle East has spiralled into a horror chamber of identity led violence. Conflict in the Middle East has led to insurmountable suffering for all. In the Holy Land, innocent Jewish, Christian and Muslim blood flows with chilling ease. With violence spilling over into Lebanon, Syria, Jordan and Egypt, not only did Arabs and Jews kill each other, but so did Shia Muslim and Sunnis, Maronite Christians and Greek Orthodox Christians. In this whirlpool of hatred and under the embers of burnt orchards is the unheard wail of humanity. In the Holy land the soul has fallen. And for the death of humanity and the fallen soul, standing in Egypt today, Plotinus would have cried a river.

This hatred for each other is unfathomable when one thinks of Abraham being the patriarchal Prophet of the One unseen God who is hailed and loved by Jews, Christians, and Muslims alike. Abraham's two sons from his two wives became the fountainheads of Jews and Arabs, thus making them cousins.

Strife, discord, and disunity have the upper hand over inclusiveness in this turbulent region. The bloodshed from all sides is nothing but evil rising from strife.

But can we find solace and hope in philosophy? To me, strife and chaos begin as 'motion', which finds its roots in the opposite of stillness. And if unity is 'all-inclusive stillness' then strife is a means by which intellect can possess, control and dominate through excess. Once it has begun, strife will spread through 'othering' and violence, eventually leading to the destruction of everything it encounters. When collective intellect nurtures strife, in its uncontrollable form it can attack good and sweep humanity aside. This force is evil. It is latent but can be summoned by intellect because of intellect's free will. And once this force is unleashed – law, ethics, morality, and compassion stand trampled by it.

Aristotle believes that love is the cause of good things and strife the cause of bad things. He emphasises that 'Good' is an indestructible principle and that evil is not a principle but comes into existence only because of strife. In his writings Aristotle leaves a philosophical window open for the destruction of strife.

In the Hermetica, which Plato, Aristotle, Ammonius Saccas and Plotinus studied, 'The One' (The Good) keeps an eye over anarchy and disorder and chooses the moment to bring order at Its own will.

> Someone there must be who is the Maker and the Master of all; it could not be that place and limit and measure should be observed by all, if there were not One who has made them. For all order must have been made; And yet, even that which is out of place and out of measure is not without a master. If

there is aught that is in disorder, it is not without one who will bring it to order if there is anything possessed by disorder; for disorder also is subject to the Master, but he has not yet imposed order on it.[38]

That 'will' to finally bring order to strife can only be exercised by 'The One'. It is clear even in Michelangelo's fresco 'Creation of Adam', where God almost touches man with divinity but holds back just that ever so slightly, keeping the final 'will' to Himself. But how would that order come about? Only through the 'goodness' already injected in humankind and only when it rises universally and trounces strife and evil.

In Arabic, 'Strife' is mentioned as *Fitna* and is defined as a state of mind that defies unity and good. It stems from greed and jealousy. For Plotinus, the state of mind which has 'absence of measure' and is 'darkened by matter (materialism)' produces cowardice and a desire for excess. This is evil. And this he likens to the 'eternal descent' of soul.[39]

Fleeting though they maybe, the Holy land and the deeply coveted city of Jerusalem have experienced moments of inclusiveness when violence and division were briefly smothered. The first being when Omar the caliph of Islam took Jerusalem after a bloodless siege in 638 CE. As the Christian inhabitants of Jerusalem trembled in fear, Omar entered the walls of the city leading his camel on which sat his camel guide. Travelling under the desert sun from Medina, Omar decided to alternate riding the camel with his guide. It so happened that when the time came to enter Jerusalem, it was the camel guide's turn to ride the animal and Omar's to lead it. Omar kept his word and entered, leading the camel. Most of the inhabitants thought the camel guide to be the Caliph, only to discover otherwise much later. Omar had successfully sent a signal of Islam's core philosophy of human equality to the Christians of Jerusalem. Later, at the invitation of Patriarch Sophronius, he approached the Church of the Holy Sepulchre – Christianity's most holy site containing the spots where Christ was crucified and that of his tomb.

The Patriarch on receiving Omar invited him to pray in the church but Omar refused, believing that it would endanger the church's status and set a precedent for some Muslims to convert churches into mosques. Instead, Omar chose to pray on the east side of the church where a mosque was later built and stands even today carrying his name as Mosque of Omar. In a decree that permitted freedom of worship and peace towards all inhabitants including the Jewish and Christian population of the city, Omar had won Jerusalem's heart. It seems quite certain that Omar had followed the example of the Prophet of Islam who, after years of being persecuted and banished from Mecca for preaching his faith, re-entered it triumphantly and peacefully, forbidding plunder, loot and revenge killing in 629 CE, thus establishing Islam as a faith of peace.

In 1099 CE, Christianity's holy warriors, the crusaders, took Jerusalem from the Muslims. In complete contrast to Omar's tolerance towards Christians and Jews, the crusaders unleashed a bloodbath, slaughtering tens of thousands of Muslim and Jewish inhabitants. Feebly clashing against the raised sword of fanaticism, the cries of mercy from women and children only found a slashing blade running across their throats. Nearly a hundred years later in 1187 CE the greatest Muslim general Salahuddin, who was a Kurd, and had risen to become sultan of Egypt, Syria, and Iraq, unified an army. Under his command the numbers of men at arms swelled. Yet Salahuddin did not attack Jerusalem, choosing to honour a truce reached with the crusaders. A man of courage and chivalry, his name was taken with respect and admiration even amongst the Christians and Jews. His act of sending his physicians to his rival Baldwin IV, the leper king added to the legend of Salahuddin. It was only when the crusaders broke the truce by attacking an unarmed Muslim caravan and killing his sister that Salahuddin entered the fray giving battle at Hattin and inflicting a crushing defeat on the crusaders. Jerusalem was next. Yet again like in the time of Omar, the Christian inhabitants feared a mass scale slaughter. This time they were convinced it would happen as revenge for the crusader massacre of Muslims a hundred years ago and more recently for the cold-blooded murder of Salahuddin's sister.

But taking a leaf from Omar's entry, Salahuddin entered Jerusalem in peace. Mounted on his black stallion he issued orders that no Christian man, woman or child would be harmed and those who wanted to leave would be given safe passage. Keeping in mind the revered position of Virgin Mary and Christ in the Quran, he ensured the Christian places of worship would be respected, and Jews and Christians would find equal opportunities in this land held sacred by all three faiths. It was a bold attempt at unifying a divided city through tolerance and acceptance, one that Jerusalem has not experienced since. Such was the radiance of Salahuddin's personality that more than 800 years after his death, in 2019, the *Economist* wrote:

> Saladin preserved Christian places of worship including Jerusalem's Church of the Holy Sepulchre and Hospital of the Order of St. John. He ransomed a Christian woman from her kidnappers and generously redistributed his wealth....

Bashir and I have been roaming the Valley of Kings discussing all of this – history and philosophy from pharaohs to Aristotle and Salahuddin. I observe that every so often people walk up to Bashir, take his hand, and kiss it in reverence. He's aware that I've taken notice but doesn't utter a word. It is a sign of respect given to a *Sayyid* (a descendant of the Prophet of Islam). We walk on towards the car park where a taxi awaits me.

'You see, Mizder Mir, we are Muslims who know our faith. Look around Egypt, from Giza to here... the pyramids still stand, the temples still echo of the past.... We are not the Taliban who blew up the Bamiyan Buddhas... *Lakum deen a kum waliad deen*.... Each one's faith to them.... God be with you.'

'And with you, Bashir. Shukran.'

I sit in the taxi and in a few minutes, we are out in the fields driving past a wonderful sight of a farmer guiding his donkey and straddling another with his right leg supporting the sugarcane wobbling on the beast's back. An inexplicable urge to join him takes over, and I get my driver to slow down and ask the farmer if he'd allow me to ride with him. Initially surprised by what I asked for, both driver and farmer help me mount the donkey.

'The donkey's name is Bassam... the one who laughs a lot,' says the driver after consulting with the farmer.

Just like the man who got me my Egyptian visa who barely smiled.

'Sir, are you sure you want to do this? Al Moudira is 10 kilometres away... it will take you more than an hour.'

'Yes, yes.'

'Straight road, sir,' he continues.

'Ok.'

'This donkey will be baying till you reach,' the driver laughs, while the farmer loads up some sugarcane on his donkey.

'It's alright… his namesake didn't laugh much,' I say with confidence.

In Arabic, the taxi driver tells the farmer where I need to go and races off. I don't know Arabic, my newfound farmer acquaintance doesn't know English, but we've established an understanding through my appreciation of his unusually white-coloured donkey with the most exquisite dark brown eyelashes. I'm in the hands of man and beast. The owner of the donkeys is of medium height wearing a light blue jellabiya with wild, fuzzy hair and a shaggy beard. The trotting turns out to be quite rhythmic as we look into swaying bamboo, slim white fern, and sugarcane fields, with the Valley of the Kings looming behind us. We leave behind mud-baked village walls that having absorbed the sun for decades, have a rich sandy colour. We ride past open fields sprouting with cabbage, lettuce, and other fresh vegetables. Every so often my companion while guiding his donkey looks at me with a smile that exposes his rotting teeth and squinting laughing eyes. This is followed by a quick compressing of the palm to his chest, quite possibly a gesture reassuring me that he is an honourable man. Now that I've put myself in his hands, I have no option but to believe it. This is Egypt at its ancient best.

Through signals I receive regular instructions on how to control Bassam. Some are indicated by the farmer squeezing his ankles against the sides of his donkey – it slows down the animal, very similar to riding a horse. And if riding fast is the objective, then it's best to keep one's legs outstretched after nudging him a couple of times. We ride under the mammoth Colossi of Memnon, and while I strain my neck upwards in admiration of the pharaoh, my riding companion doesn't bother. He's too busy guiding his animal with one hand and drawing out a sugarcane shaft with the other. In seconds he ruptures the sugarcane shaft, successfully tearing into it with his decaying teeth and swallowing the delicious juice with one throated slurp. It's a tantalisingly inviting sight. Having done this as a child growing up in India, I do the same, though not as easily as him but with some measure of success. My triumphant slurp gets him nodding and smiling at me with a sense of brotherhood. But as soon as that word enters my mind a suspicion seems to rise within. What I've been hearing of the Muslim Brotherhood and kidnappings suddenly manifests itself as fear. As we trot in the wilderness, evening turns to dusk. But consumed by fear, I can't see the beauty in the setting.

The man riding next to me has done nothing but smile. He has, though, become an object of suspicion. I begin looking for signals that might confirm my doubts and start questioning my decision of abandoning the taxi. How foolish of me. I remember the words of the taxi driver who said, 'it's a straight road ahead' and so every twitch my riding companion makes to the reins of his donkey, I think he's going off in another direction. How easily the mind gives in to doubt. I feel winter's unceasing cuts as the wind slashes across my face. We pass a clutch of mud houses, and a few village children chase us, but he admonishes them with such ferocity and abuse that they disperse faster than they had appeared. A nervousness seems to strangle the evening and I am consumed by the terror of ambush. But just when I think of pulling out my mobile phone and calling Bashir, I see the soft glow of oil lamps in the far distance – Al Moudira. I look at the farmer and almost instantly all fear vanishes as I signal to him to race me to the edge of the fields.

'Yalla,' and I kick Bassam into a swift trot. Then, stretching my legs out, I let my reins go. Bassam lets out a loud bay and surges forward. Before I can tell though, the farmer has shot past me. Barely struggling to keep myself on Bassam, I reach the gates of Al Moudira. Dismounting, I offer the farmer some money which he snatches from my hand in a second.

Pressing his palm to his chest he says:

'Abdallah,' and looking at his donkey he says, 'Phiron'. His name and his donkey's. While his name means servant of God, Phiron is pharaoh. A servant of God has tamed the pharaoh. Nicely done, I think to myself.

Abdallah pulls out a sugarcane shaft, gives it to me which I accept, and before I know it, he's trotting away on Phiron with one leg resting on Bassam. I watch him disappear from my vision.

That evening was the last of 2021.

Tomorrow, I travel to Alexandria where Plotinus found his teacher.

As soon as dawn breaks in 2022, in Egypt and the Western world there is a sense of relaxation towards Covid. At the same time, I receive news that the virus is surging in India. I'm on a red-eye flight to Cairo. Luxor airport is pure pandemonium. Unorganised and chaotic, it is not for the faint hearted. There are no rules. You've got to elbow, shoulder, and even trip your way through the crowds to get on your plane. After disentangling myself from an argument with a fiery Spanish lady over who was first in the security line, I manage to nail down the dodging boarding gate and get to my seat. Landing in Cairo after an hour, I find my taxi with relative ease. Alexandria is a two-hour drive from

Cairo, and after a brief detour into Memphis we are on our way to Alexandria. It was in this city where the blue waters of the Mediterranean embrace the satin sands of the Sahara that Plotinus heard Ammonius Saccas speak sometime in 232 CE. So moved was he that he declared: 'This is the man I was looking for.' Having spent most of his youth travelling in Egypt learning from various teachers, it comes as no surprise that it was in Alexandria that he found his mentor. This was the city that carried the name of its founder with glory. Alexander founded this city so that it could become a melting pot of ideas and intellectual pursuit. It was here that the greatest and most legendary library of ancient times attracted scholars, thinkers, kings, and students to drink from its wine cups of knowledge. Built by Ptolemy II, the library became the centre of learning between 284 BCE to 260 CE, its multiple shelves housing nearly 400,000 scrolls. Plotinus though must have only witnessed the faded grandeur of this bastion of learning, as regular rebellions and diminishing funding in his times brought with it the effects of stagnation.

Rumour had it that Ammonius Saccas was a descendant of the Sakas – a tribe that made their way into northern India from Iran in the second century BCE and eventually landed up ruling parts of Northern India. These origins of Ammonius Saccas were contested but his curiosity to study the Upanishads remains uncontested. The Greek influence in India and the curiosity that the Greeks had for Indian philosophy and culture meant a regular sharing of knowledge and a back and forth of literature. Many scholars in Alexandria had been exposed to Indian philosophy. Ammonius Saccas had made Alexandria his home and taught regularly at the library and by the Mediterranean shore, passing on the curiosity to study the Upanishads to Plotinus.

I make it a point to slip Antony Sattin's *The Pharaoh's Shadow* into my already bursting rucksack of books and notes. Sattin's wonderful book has some interesting clues to find remnants of an ancient city that today lies under the yoke of modernity. I had been warned by many writers not to get my expectations too high. Again, almost as soon as we leave the dreaded Cairo traffic behind, delightful sights of the Nile flowing with a calm serenity emerge. We drive along it quite like all the ancients did and most farmers still do. The ancients, if they weren't sailing on the Nile, must have felt secure staying close to it. It must have given them direction and prevented them from getting lost. The river is the longest in the world and runs through the heart of Egypt. It has been the sole reason why a civilisation flourished for over a millennium. Without it, the sands of the Sahara would have suffocated any embryonic semblance of civilisation. It has fed mind, soul, and stomach, and even today farmers till its banks using the most archaic methods of bull and hull with hope and joy in their hearts. In response, the river metamorphoses its banks into paddy fields and clusters of fruit laden banana trees. I lower my window and inhale the fragrance of these moist fields. Cranes and storks languish in these fields until they unearth prey and instantly take flight. Village children leave their mud houses and play by the river and the elderly gather by its flowing waters discussing village intrigues. Lycopolis, Plotinus' alleged birthplace, is before us, but honouring his decision of dismissing his origins we drive past, and instead I concentrate on reading his work – something he would have preferred me to do. Besides, there isn't much to see in Lycopolis.

When I get to Alexandria, it is midday. The first place I visit is the Alexandria University. The university stands on the ground where the Alexandrian library once stood, and one can imagine Plotinus walking through its pillared corridors. Nothing is left of the ancient library, but just standing on that spot gives me a perspective of the time and space inhabited by the philosophers of that time. Not far is a marketplace which was always there, selling everything from pomegranates to bread, and I stroll in its narrow winding streets. In *The Pharaoh's Shadow*, Sattin mentions that 'Strabo, the Greek geographer who saw Alexandria around the time of Jesus described the city as having two particularly impressive streets 'of greater breadth than the rest, being upwards of a plethron (100) ft wide and these intersect each other at right angles.'[40]

Later in the fifth century, a bishop named Achilles Tatius wrote:

> A range of columns went from one end of it to the other. Advancing down them, I came in time to the place that bears the name of Alexander, and there I could see the other half of the town which was equally beautiful. For just as the colonnades stretched ahead of me, so did other colonnades now appear at right angles to them.[41]

I stand at these intersections picturing the past although none of the columns exist today. Plotinus though would have strolled through this intersection of columns daily. I make my way into a local café. Reading and underlining parts of Sattin's book while sipping tea and enjoying bread and hummus leads me to a mouth-watering question: Which is the exact spot where Alexander the Great was buried? According to Sattin's book, speculation was that he was buried at the central crossroads built by Ptolemy I in 320 BCE, in a building called Soma which was probably a pyramid. Excited, I pay the bill and follow Sattin's footsteps knowing well that these were also the footsteps of Plotinus. Walking along the sea front and following a long busy shopping street which matches the description of the ancient street, I come to the tomb of the prophet Daniel. Suddenly, a line from the passage I'm reading while walking and dodging other humans makes me stop in my tracks, pull out a pencil, and underline 'Perhaps, as has often been suggested, his (Alexander's) tomb was destroyed in one of the many riots which upset the city's balance in the third and fourth centuries.'[42] This line reveals much. Plotinus did witness these riots. These turbulent times sent many intellectuals fleeing for their lives and in search of more conducive environments for learning. But most importantly, could Plotinus have witnessed the destruction of Alexander's tomb? We will never know because when he left Egypt for Rome he never spoke about his past and so being a witness to the destruction of Alexander's tomb could well be a secret that Plotinus concealed from the world right till his very end. The alleged tomb of Prophet Daniel which, according to Sattin, is the tomb of a fourteenth-century Shafei Sheikh who happened to enjoy the same name, became the focus of the final attempt to find Alexander's tomb with the arrival of Heinrich Schliemann in the 1880s. This great antiquity detective arrived in Alexandria after his magnificent discoveries of Troy, and declared after much investigation that this was the spot under which the great Macedonian hero lay. Nothing came of it, because Schliemann was denied permission to excavate the holy site for fear of offending Muslims. I am standing right on top of it.

Late afternoon brings with it an icy chill and an overcast sky that looms menacingly. The noise of trams and traffic begin taking over as rush hour approaches. I pull out a scarf from my rucksack and wrap it around my neck. A shopkeeper in a white jellabiya with a black leather jacket worn on top of it sends a toothy smile my way as if rejoicing in the fact that another foreigner has not taken Egyptian winter seriously. I make my way to the ruins of the temple of Serapis. This temple was built to unite the conquering Greeks with the local Egyptians. Serapis, a uniting God with an Egyptian theology, and a bearded Greek face, was forged during the reign of Ptolemy I. The devotion to Serapis reached its zenith in the time of Ptolemy III (r. 246–222 BCE) when he dedicated a temple to Serapis at Rhakotis hill. Such was the power of unification that stemmed from this temple that the cult grew exponentially, bringing people together and resulting in temples dedicated to this composite God from Athens to India.[43] Today, as I walk amongst the temple ruins looking at the Greek inscriptions that speak of a forgotten time, I'm convinced that Plotinus must have found sparkling rays of inspiration for his theory of 'The One' and 'Unity' while walking in this spectacular temple dedicated to a God whose sole purpose was to unite people.

Overlooking the blue Mediterranean, worshippers at this temple must have seen the arrival of the first Christians by boat who eventually opposed the worship of Serapis, leading to much conflict and riots in the city. With history, religion and beliefs being layered upon Alexandria, there was bound to be friction. But such was the lure of Serapis and his uniting spirit that Roman emperor Hadrian would write in Alexandria in 134 CE: 'Those who worship Serapis are Christians and those who call themselves bishops of Christ are devoted to Serapis'. Quite evidently, to the emperor they amounted to the same thing.[44] In 391 CE though, 120 years after Plotinus' death, rioting mobs would tear down the temple devoted to the God of Unity. The mob that razed it to the ground was debated to be either Roman or Christian – men that refused to see the beauty of unity but chose to believe in superiority of their faith. Today, the mounds of dust and rubble speak with great sorrow – the language of the defeat of the God of Unity.

I leave the temple of Serapeum, walking along the Mediterranean shore towards the Sultan Qaitbay Citadel. The paved pathway lined with trees doesn't take away from the natural sweeping view of the glorious waves, bobbing on which are a string of fishing boats. Against this, as Sattin puts it, 'a chocolate box' fortress rises. Built in the fifteenth century, this fortress found existence when the Mamluk Sultan of Egypt decided to strengthen the city's defences. Within minutes one is treading Egyptian, Greek, Roman, Christian, Arab, Turk, and Napoleonic history on this remarkable shoreline. It leaves me feeling vulnerable to time yet awestruck at the 'oneness' of Alexandria as it stands today. A oneness that today doesn't see the difference but the unity of simply being Alexandrian.

When the Arab general Amr took Alexandria in 641 CE, he wrote to the Caliph Omar about its '4,000 palaces, 4,000 baths and 4,000 theatres'. He must have seen these juxtaposing themselves against the ruins of the Serapeum – a Greco-Egyptian temple, a Coptic church, and a Roman pillar. As Sattin puts it:

> What I saw when I arrived at the Harbour was not the Royal Palace, Cleopatra's playground, or deathbed, but a line of late nineteenth- or eighteenth-century buildings. Even in these it was impossible to miss the hallmark of Alexandria, an unashamed cosmopolitan eclecticism that felt entirely at ease mixing elements from Renaissance Italy with Luis XVI's France, Henry Tudors England with Alexander's Macedonia, and Rameses's Thebes.

Commenting on how faiths pulled aspects from each other, Sattin goes on to write:

Just as Christians converted pagan temples and defaced the images of the old gods to conduct their own services in them – or built over the past as the Church of St. John the Baptist was built over the Serapeum in Alexandria – so Christianity absorbed some of the basic theology and rituals of the pagan cults. It is impossible to know whether this was a conscious act on the part of the early Christians or merely a form of religious osmosis, but the merging of ideas from the old cult to the new certainly occurred. It is epitomised by a fifth- or sixth-century invocation found on a papyrus fragment at Oxyrhynchus: "Hor, Hor, Phor, Eloei, Adonai, Iao, Sabaoth, Michael, Jesus Christ", it reads, calling on pagan, Jewish and Christian divinities. "Help us and this house. Amen."[45]

I stand looking out into the Mediterranean. These shores witnessed the landing of philosophers like Ammonius Saccas, and the great fires that destroyed Julius Caesar's fleet and the ancient library too. Beyond the orange horizon to the right lies Greece – Plotinus' ancestral land, and to the left lies Rome. Winds from these lands must have carried Aristotle and Plato's words to him.

I feel rain drops on my face. A gentle sunset drizzle begins over the orange-blue Mediterranean waves and over the sandy ruins of the temple of Serapis. I watch as the rain drops dissolve on the debris of the defeated God of Unity. Then, as if in defiance of this sight, the *azaan* reverberates over a minaret. The God of Unity lives on.

After spending some weeks in this city built for intellectual stimulation by the Macedonian conqueror, I will leave for Istanbul (known as Byzantium in Plotinus' time) tracing the philosopher's footsteps as he marched along with Gordian III's army across Anatolia.

# 3

# HOUSE OF GREED

Gordian III came to power through great civil strife that engulfed Rome. It began when Maximin, a soldier of Thracian origin, conspired with his legions and usurped power in 235 CE from the then emperor Alexander Severus. Maximin was a brute of a man. Standing close to eight feet tall he allied himself with the military and completely isolated the senate. He did this with the objective of making Rome a military state. He preferred to spend most of his time outside Rome in the countryside which suited his plans of keeping the legions under his control. From the outskirts of Rome, he exerted influence on the senate and the people. Renowned for his enormous physical strength which was built on public displays of great wrestling triumphs including a single-handed victory over sixteen fighters, Maximin thrived on this image of physical invincibility. He gorged on food and drank publicly like a beast and is known to have had the capacity to drink down seven gallons of wine and consume forty pounds of meat in a single day. He could move a loaded wagon and break a horse's leg with a punch. Known as the

The Forum or Forum Romanum was the focal point of the ancient city of Rome.

The oculus, an opening to the sky, in the massive dome of the Pantheon, Rome.

The Pantheon, Rome. With its multilayered history it stands as an architectural unity.

Via Appia Antica – the ancient Roman road. Gordian III's army marched down this road.

Alter of the Mithraic cult in Basilica di San Clemente's bottom pit. In Plotinus' time cult worship continued. Today, it is considered an integral part of Roman heritage.

Interior of the Basilica di San Clemente, Rome. Today it is a functioning chapel.

The mosaic of St. Cyril in the Basilica di San Clemente.

Honey Singh, the driver in Rome.

Holocaust symbols in Rome.

The murmurations of starlings, Rome.

Philae Temple, Egypt. Engraving of Ptolemy XII Neos Dionysos of Greek origin dressed like a pharaoh striking the enemies of Egypt.

Column at Philae Temple, Egypt. Engraving of Roman Emperor Tiberius dressed as a pharaoh making offerings to Egyptian gods.

Ibn Tulun Mosque, Cairo. Commissioned by the ruler Ahmad ibn Tulun in 876 CE, it was designed by a Christian architect.

The bust of Serapis. Imbued with Egyptian theology and a Greek face, Serapis united local Egyptians and the conquering Greeks.

The *degh* in Ajmer. A unified mixture of raisins, rice, sugar and milk. It is served without discrimination to the hungry.

The Step Pyramid of Djoser, Saqqara, Egypt, *c.* 2670 BCE. With six layers or steps, the height of the pyramid is 204 feet.

'The Pharaoh's bed' built by Roman Emperor Trajan. Another example of how Roman emperors saw themselves as pharaohs, thus blurring identities.

Topra Pillar in Delhi, with inscriptions of morals built by Ashoka in the third century BCE. Plotinus would have seen it had he reached India.

Fuad's felucca sails on the Nile.                    Interiors of the Hagia Sophia, Istanbul.

The still life: 'I will astonish Paris with an apple.' Paul Cézanne's apples.

Christian mosaics and Islamic calligraphy in the Hagia Sophia.

Arbinas, the Lycian King (c. 400 BCE) adopted Persian customs including clothes and caps. He is seen here receiving emissaries in a Persian style.

Tomb of Seyit Gazi and Eleanora, Turkey.

Palatine Chapel, Palermo, Sicily was commissioned by Roger II of Sicily in 1132 CE.

The Fatimid stars in the ceiling of the Palatine Chapel, a fabulous example of enmeshed Islamic and Christian architecture.

Interlocking Islamic geometry patterns in
the Palatine Chapel.

Playing street cricket in Sicily.

Palazzo Zisa, built in 1189 CE. The Islamic
muqarnas, niches and arches merge
seamlessly with Christian art.

Writer, translator and journalist, Princess
Vittoria Alliata at Villa Valguarnera, Sicily.

The date and olive orchard at Azienda Agricola Mandranova, Sicily.

The ruined foundations of Aristotle's Academy, Lyceum, Athens.

Ruins of the Berlin Wall. Built in 1961, it stood for division. Its tearing down in 1989 preceded the reunification of Germany.

I have named this 'The wall of Oneness'. In ancient Delphi, the names of freed slaves were engraved on it.

Selinunte, an ancient site of Greek temples in southern Sicily.

The Temple of Apollo, Delphi, Greece.

The ruins of Plato's Academy, Athens.  Cave of the Apocalypse, Patmos.

The Monastery of St. John the Theologian perched on top of a mountain in Patmos, Greece.

The hermitage of Prophet Elias, Patmos.

The walk up to the hermitage of Prophet Elias.

The simple feast of Prophet Elias.

Xara in the Valley of the Good Men, Patmos.

Nico and Ritsa, the patient potters of Patmos.

The ruins of ancient Minturnae along the Via Appia. Plotinus spent his last days in this area.

The bust of Plotinus. It eluded me twice.

The ruins of Velia. Quite possibly the city Plotinus wanted to rebuild as Platonopolis, in honour of Plato.

Looking out towards the Aegean Sea from the Monastery of St. John the Theologian, Patmos.

The bust of Gordian III.

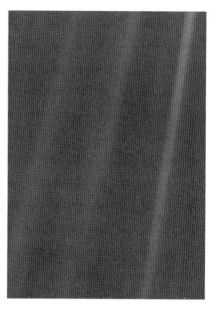

The School of Athens by Raphael. Plato walks with his index finger raised explaining the Theory of Forms to Aristotle who walks next to him.

The Pale Blue Dot – our home.

Swati Mohan and Allen Chen part of the NASA team celebrate the landing of Perseverance on Mars on 18 February 2021.

'tyrant', Maximin also developed a never-ending thirst for cruelty.

When a plot to assassinate him was unearthed, many Roman senators along with 4,000 alleged accomplices were put to death without trial. In no time, all of Rome was infested with spies and informers. At the tyrant's whim, many a Roman noble was chained to a chariot and brought into his presence where the noble's fate was sealed. The ones Maximin loathed the most were sewed alive into rotting carcasses of slaughtered animals or simply clubbed to death. Eventually the senate that had come into being for the better administration of Rome and its citizens gathered the courage to appoint Gordian I as emperor and his son Gordian II as his consul. Rather reluctantly, Gordian I draped himself in the purple cape – a sign of being anointed the new Caesar.[46]

Descending from emperor Trajan, the Gordians had a reputation of being just, kind, and able administrators. But the two Gordians almost immediately moved their court to Carthage in North Africa, not wanting to bear the full brunt of Maximin's wrath that could befall Rome. The shifting sands of power, though, ensured that things changed swiftly as the Gordians found out when a governor of Mauritania chose to attack them. The younger Gordian died in battle, while the father ended his life bringing his thirty-two-day reign to a tragic end. On hearing this news and fearing the terror of Maximin who was lurking outside Rome, the ever-resilient senate swung into action and elected two new emperors – Balbinus and Maximus. But the honourable reputation of the dead Gordians got people out into the streets, and they surrounded the Temple of Jupiter demanding that a third emperor be appointed from the Gordian family. And so, Gordian III, a boy of thirteen who was the grandson of Gordian I, was chosen as Caesar. Amidst cheering crowds, he was invested with ornaments and titles and hailed as the chosen one making him the youngest emperor of the greatest empire in the world.[47]

As Maximin advanced on Rome ready to tear down the city, the senate hatched a plot. Somehow, they got word into Maximin's most trusted legion the Praetorian Guard and tempted them with positions of power in Rome. Historically, the Praetorian Guard had been the elite fighting force and the one the emperor kept closest to him. But even they weren't immune to temptation. Abandoned by his guards Maximin was murdered in his tent along with his son and their heads carried out on spikes. Rome celebrated the death of the tyrant with trumpets and street parties where court jesters and poets enacted the beastly drinking of the slain despot. Calm and stability are what Rome thirsted after and yet it eluded the city, for barely had the death of Maximin been played out that Balbinus and Maximus would meet an even grimmer fate. Both men fell prey to jealousies of each other and failed to unite against the threat of the ever-restless Praetorian Guard. Once again, it was this most trusted of legions that betrayed the two emperors. Some guards who had been loyal to Maximin and others who were tempted by the senate (who wanted to check the rising popularity of the two emperors) stormed into a palace where the two emperors were busy quarrelling. The guards tore the robes from the two emperors' bodies and dragged them naked through the streets of Rome, all the while torturing and beating them. After their last gasps had left them, their brutalised bodies were left in the streets, attracting both pity and scorn from the public. Within a few months, four emperors had been consumed by treachery and the lust for power.[48]

This left the thirteen-year-old Gordian III as the sole remaining emperor. Almost immediately, ministers and senators descended on him – some deftly guiding him philosophically and with morality, and others manipulating and manoeuvring his simplicity to further their ambitions. Gordian III also fell under the influence of eunuchs that surrounded his mother, and for many years the young Caesar remained hidden from public eye, confined only to his tuitions and a victim of palace intrigues. It is only with the advent of Misitheus, a wise minister and a man of letters that Gordian III came into his own. Under Misitheus' guidance the young Caesar imbibed fine qualities of valour, a keen sense for justice and truth, and a nobility that soon became evident in his conduct with other senators. In time he shook off the yoke exerted by the eunuchs and broke free, striding confidently into his youth with a great desire to clean up politics in the senate and expose the courtiers who strove relentlessly to propagate lies for personal ambition. Gordian married Misitheus' daughter and immediately elevated his father-in-law to the powerful post of Prefect of the mercurial Praetorian Guard – a move that illustrated political astuteness and demonstrated an eye for identifying the worthy.[49]

By 242 CE when Gordian III was in his late teens, Rome's greatest external foe raised its head again. The Persians invaded Mesopotamia. For centuries, the Romans and the Persians had played a cat and mouse game in the region where the Tigris and the Euphrates flowed. The territory shifted ever so often between the two empires, each of them laying claim to it. Shapur I, the Persian king of the Sassanian dynasty, was at the peak of his powers, and sensing the civil unrest in Rome invaded the town of Nisibis and prepared to march on Antioch which was deep within Roman territory. On hearing this news Gordian cast aside the luxuries of palace life, assembled one of the largest Roman armies, and set out to meet Shapur I.

Gordian III's army approached Byzantium having followed the ancient Roman road – the Via Egnatia. Starting off as a straight line where the Via Appia ended in Brindisi, the Via Egnatia began from across the Adriatic in Albania and linked Macedonia, Greece, and Thrace to Byzantium. Wading through forests and crushing a fledgling Goth rebellion in Thrace near the coastal town of Dionysopolis on the Black Sea (modern day Balchik in Bulgaria), the army was buoying with confidence as it approached the walls of the city. No one though in the army, including philosophers like Plotinus, would have imagined the fate of Byzantium just eighty-five years later when Constantine I, witnessing the decaying of Roman politics, would shift his capital to Byzantium, declaring it 'Nova Roma' or 'New Rome'. Almost immediately the city would bear the name of its emperor and would be known to the world as Constantinople.

From 330 CE since its founding as Constantinople till its eventual conquest by the Ottoman sultan Mehmed II in 1453, the city was the seat of Roman civilisation, gleaming with architectural masterpieces like the Hagia Sophia, the Basilica Cistern, and the Chora Church, where the most beautiful frescos of the Virgin and Christ clung to walls and domes from where they cast a merciful glance at humankind. From 1453, under the Ottomans, and with a new name – Istanbul – the relentless architectural beauty surging out of this city took the shape of sky searching minarets and sumptuous domes, as the Sulaymaniyah Mosque, the Blue Mosque, and the Top Kapi Palace shimmered on the cobalt waters of the Bosporus. Armenian poets, whirling Sufi dervishes, and solemn Greek Orthodox Easter processions with their haunting choirs, were the cultural fountains that sprang in the city streets right till the last Ottoman sultan was put on a boat and sailed out into exile in 1922 by Mustafa Kemal Ataturk.

But in 242 CE, as Gordian III's army entered Byzantium, the city was considered one of Rome's distant territories built originally by the Greeks in 657 BCE, and one with a prosperous merchant community thanks to its astonishing location. Nothing more, nothing less. In Byzantium and in its surrounding countryside Gordian's army rested a few days before it would commence its journey into Asia Minor, and then towards the Persian borderlands where it would engage in battle. Gordian was considered 'innocent' by his legionaries yet respected for his forthright nature and brave decision to personally lead his army to meet the enemy. Although he carried the title of 'Caesar' and 'Emperor' he was relatively untouched by the cunning required for politics. Philosophical by nature, he is known to have spent much time in conversation with his troops. Leaving his heavily guarded tent he would walk into the evening gatherings of his soldiers, sit by the campfires, break bread with them, and try to understand their lives and needs. Although he was aware of the past treacheries of the Praetorian Guard, his appointment of his father-in-law as its Prefect seems to have given Gordian the freedom and confidence to go out and engage with the legions and try to understand them as humans rather than soldiers. Plotinus observed the young Caesar closely, and these observations could well have inspired his writings on the innocence of youth and 'inchoate (young) intellect' being a simple unity searching for good.

Having flown into Istanbul from Alexandria early in the morning, I checked into Pera Palace Hotel overlooking the Golden Horn. The hotel has a unique history. It has hosted guests travelling on the Orient Express in the nineteenth century and boasts of a special room dedicated to Kemal Ataturk, housing some of his memorabilia. But none of this is enough to hold me back from walking in Plotinus' Byzantium. And so, I spend most of the day by the old walls which have a centuries-old undiminished rugged charm to them. It is through these walls that the Via Egnatia entered Byzantium – more specifically, through the southern gate of the old walls. Below the gate and along the walls one can see the faint remnants of the Via Egnatia.

I trace my steps down where the Via Egnatia comes to an end. Curling away from the walls, the road leads me down towards the vast open space on which stand the Hagia Sophia, the Top Kapi Palace, and the Blue Mosque. But it is the Hagia Sophia that draws me in. As soon as I enter, I sense angels circulating its lofty domes. Built by Justinian I in 527 CE, the Hagia Sophia's 140 columns brought in from Egypt and Ephesus hold the domes aloft with a persevering devotion to the divine. It seems the columns are endowed with a silent resolve to show the world walking under them that it doesn't matter if manmade inscriptions take the shape of Allah or Mohammad, or mosaics of the Madonna and Christ gleam in gold leaf, for they live under the dome in a stunning symphonic harmony. The grand sweep of vastness, the expansive volumes of width and height, the generosity of silence, and dimly lit interiors - all come together in a deeply moving lordly calm. But against the dimly lit interiors my eyes are dazzled by clusters of glowing oil lamps lowered from the ceiling. Lined side by side, these clusters of light resemble a whirling galaxy of stars, each one touched by the light of divinity. The Hagia Sophia for the longest period (900 years) was a Catholic church, and from 1453 until 1935 it was a mosque. In 1935, it was turned into a museum to reflect the secular values of modern Turkey. In 2020, it became a mosque once again.

My first evening in Istanbul coincides with the opening of the Istanbul gallery week. Loitering through art galleries seems a wonderful way of spending the evening. Walking down Istiklal, the main street in the heart of Istanbul and down the slope, I encounter a flood of people standing outside a line-up of galleries with wobbling wine glasses in their hands. In one such noisy corner I spot an old friend – Narek Shogolu. Narek has been one of the leading art advisors in Istanbul and has come to enjoy a wonderful reputation as a 'thinking' art influencer. Emerging from the crowd holding up a bottle of wine and two paper cups, Narek comes straight up, and we embrace.

'Walking the streets of Istanbul, my friend?' asks Narek, handing me a paper cup.

'More like Byzantium,' I reply.

'Yes... yes... that's how it all began here.'

'And how's it going in the art world, Narek? You still representing some of the old hands?'

'Well, they invariably do well... so yes... but it is the young Turks that are specially exciting... fresh... new ideas and hopes....'

Almost instantly, I think of Gordian III and his sense of idealism.

'Many young artists emerging from here?'

'Oh yes....'

'And what are the subjects?' I probe further while enjoying the delicious wine.

'Love, nature, climate change, racial equality... all that needs addressing... pretty good stuff.'

'Well... that's how the young are, bold, beautiful and....'

'And?' Narek asks.

'Simple and good,' I reply with a smile.

Nodding and smiling, he continues sipping wine.

'And political unrest? Social divisions? What about that, Narek?' I ask.

Almost immediately, the colour from Narek's face vanishes. I'm not surprised. Narek is Christian with an Armenian ancestry. His forebears have been living in Istanbul for centuries, but since the last few years the Christian minority in Turkey is leading an uneasy existence. Narek leads me by the arm, and we slowly begin walking away from the crowd.

'It is getting difficult for you here... isn't it, old friend?' I ask as we walk towards Istiklal, and the din from the street parties begins to fade.

Narek remains silent for a while.

Hesitatingly, a few words come from Narek. 'We have to live here... there is no choice... just keep our heads down and stay away from anything controversial.'

'It is that bad?' I ask.

Narek stops walking and faces me. Behind, looming over him, I can see the steeple of the eighteenth-century Church of St. Anthony.

He sighs, shrugs his shoulders. 'It's so suffocating.'

Within a few minutes, the clusters of laughter, drink, joy, and carefree abandon have vanished. The gleam of happiness dulled, replaced by apprehension and lurking fear.

'Religious nationalism is the problem,' Narek continues. 'I feel I'm on thin ice...in my own country'.

'I'm sorry you feel that way Narek.... It seems the secular values Ataturk laid down for this country are fast eroding.'

'Well, Ataturk tried to Europeanise Turkey... he changed the script of the language, he forbade head scarfs, tried to keep religion out of state... He shouldn't have....'

'Keeping religion out of statecraft is a good thing... don't you think?' I ask.

'The more one suppresses religion, at least in these

parts of the world, the more strongly it comes back in a defiant and aggressive way.... He should have let religion be... that's it.... There was no need for "Europeanisation" when more than two thirds of Turkey lies in Asia where everything European is alien.'

'Complex clash of identities, culture, and aspiration,' I reply.

We walk past the Church of St. Anthony. Its charming arches seem to be speaking to Narek, who stops, looks at their magnificence, and releases a sigh of anguish.

'Life has changed so much in these few years,' says Narek.

I let him continue.

'From being free and joyful, I'm constantly looking over my shoulder, watching my words, ensuring I don't say anything controversial... I feel I'm living in a gilded cage....'

'Have you thought of migrating, maybe...?'

He looks around. 'The thought has crossed my mind... but I can't get myself to leave the beauty of this city... just looking at it lifts me from depression.'

'Depression?'

'Yes... it's been a while... I've been on medication... just don't feel good within.'

It is apparent Narek is in a constant battle with himself.

'Go travelling, Narek... it'll do you good.'

'Travelling, workouts, healthy eating... I do everything to feel better... but this incessant fear of losing it all because of who I am gnaws away at my soul.'

After a brief pause, he nervously says, 'I must go back to the gallery opening,' his face suddenly wearing a forced smile.

'Of course, you must.'

'Don't you want to come?'

'I'll just stroll the streets.'

'As you wish, my friend.'

I watch Narek walk down Istiklal and disappear into the night.

Instead of heading back to the hotel, I walk back towards the old walls. A few hawkers are roasting chestnuts. The night sky turns a smoky grey from the charcoal embers as the hawkers vigorously fan the flames. Beyond the walls is the Golden Horn, the waters of which are quiet and still. Resting in these settings Plotinus pondered about 'happiness', and I think of how happiness has retreated from Narek's life.

For Plotinus, Gordian III was the subject of observation – a young ruler who, on many occasions, voiced philosophical eloquence on the unhappy burden of kingship, the lack of joy, and the fear that came with it because of the constantly plotting soldiers. Plotinus' response was such:

> Actions do not by themselves endow one with happiness but one's dispositions make the actions beautiful, and the practically wise person enjoys the fruits of the Good....One's country might, after all be saved thanks to a bad person, and that which is pleasurable in its being saved could be found in the practically wise person even when another did it.... It is the settled state (Inner peace) which produces the happiness and whatever is pleasurable comes through that. To place being happy in actions is to place it in externals rather than in the virtue of the soul.[50]

As I walk past, I caress the ancient walls with my palms. Around these walls, Gordian rested by campfires and tried whole heartedly to create a collaborative and interactive relationship between the men at arms and the ruler – this, he believed, would only benefit Rome, and also be a source of happiness for him. Watching the young Caesar's struggling efforts, Plotinus' beliefs were emboldened that ultimate happiness lay only in the departure of the soul from this menial world and its ascension towards the 'Good'.

> Plato too rightly judged it appropriate that one who intends to be wise and happy should receive his good from the intelligible world above and looking at that, to assimilate himself to that and to live according to that. He should then have this alone as a goal... He must give to this embodied life what it needs
>
> Insofar as he can, he himself being other than it, and not be prevented even from abandoning this life.... So, for him some deeds will contribute to happiness, whereas some are not for the sake of the goal, and generally did not come from him, but from that which is yoked to him, which he will tend to and endure as long as he is able....[51]

Istanbul's chestnut sellers have left, leaving its shoreline deserted. The sloping hills with cypress trees, minarets, and domes are covered in an inky darkness. I think of Narek's words and his lack of happiness which stems from an identity crisis. I also think of Turkey's struggle to straddle East and West. Civilisations that have been marked and distinguished by these two words. Nowhere is it more apparent than on the island of Cyprus not far from where I stand. Cyprus, an island claimed both by the Greeks and the Turks stands divided in half – an island where not just two countries exert pressure but two continents lock horns – Asia and Europe.

It is here by the Bosporus where imagination is kissed by the beauty of geography, that we conjured the East and West and wove fabulous fables of an embracing of the orient, for in the end it is only land and water. Everything and yet nothing.

The next morning, having successfully secured a rental car, I drive out of European Istanbul and head into Anatolia with the objective of cutting across the Turkish heartland to Ceylanpinar, near the Syrian border, where Gordian eventually fought the Persians. Gordian's route through rural Anatolia took him through wild countryside infested with bandits and rebellious raiding parties. Driving south and turning east I pass through mountainous ravines, every so often plunging into flat lands where stocky Turks work their fields which they have tilled since 1071 CE. Rose-cheeked children stand by the roadside selling fresh berries and vegetables straight out of their farms. Some farmers can be seen descending windswept mountains with their cattle and leading the beasts into fertile pasture lands.

The Turks burst into Anatolia in 1071 CE after Alp Arsalan defeated Byzantine emperor Romanos IV at the Battle of Manzikert on the far eastern front of Anatolia. After that victory the Turks gradually pressed on, climaxing with the conquest of Constantinople. As I make my way through the countryside, I get a real sense of how different most of Turkey is to Istanbul. It is conservative and closer to Turkmenistan and Uzbekistan both architecturally and linguistically. Unlike Istanbul, women in headscarves are a prominent sight here. Although Anatolia is dotted with Greek and Roman ruins, today there is nothing 'European' about this land or its people that was once part of the Roman Empire. This is where one realises the merit in Narek's argument. For years the country had obsessed about joining the European Union. But after Turkey was rejected in 2019, the country turned inwards and began looking towards the East both for economic opportunities and in its search for an identity: what did it mean to be a Turk thousands of miles away from the heart of Europe and equally far from the heart of Turkmenistan? My route takes me first into the town of Bursa, which was once the Ottoman capital.

Breaking for lunch, I drive into a kebab diner. I find a table in the corner and sit facing a large window. A cosy fire is burning in the distance. The sound and sight of crackling wood, dancing flames, and crimson Turkish floor cushions along with the aroma of grilled kebabs is relaxing. A few moments later, a gently drifting snowfall outside the large window begins. My eyes follow its silent descent as Beethoven's orchestra seems to accompany its gentle drift. As snowflakes falling like feathers from an angel's broken wing weave a pattern of beauty, the framed view in the window transforms into a picture of pure joy. Charmed by the sheer delight of this sight, my gaze continues, uninterrupted as unmeasured moments pass.

But soon the harshness of life makes its way into the frame, walking into it in the form of frightened refugees. Holding onto tiny cloth bundles, they crouch on the cold floor outside. Exhaustion has sucked out the last ounce of energy from their bodies. Out in the cold, women clutch the young to their breasts, others shiver under their torn shawls, while some men enter the diner. They are met by the owner who nods at them and disappears into the kitchen. I gather some courage and push open the window slightly. An icy wind cuts through.

'Where are you all from?'

Some turn upwards and look at me in bewilderment. Others don't bother. Quite obviously they don't understand me. After a few moments, a young man probably in his mid-twenties speaks up.

'I from Afghanistan.'

'Where are you going?'

'Don't know,' he lowers his head.

'How did you get here?'

'I walk.'

'You walked from Afghanistan?'

He nods his head.

'You run from the Taliban?'

'I Hazara... so Taliban kill us... I run away.'

Hazaras are the Shia minority in Afghanistan that are hounded by the Taliban.

'Your family?'

'No... rocket kill mother and sister.'

'What's your name?'

'Ali.'

'And all these people around you? Where are they from?'

'From Syria,' he says, pointing to the women sitting on the floor holding their infants close.

'And they from China... and those from Burma.'

'China and Burma?'

'Yes... those are Uyghur Muslims and those Rohingya Muslims... you know?'

'Yes, of course.'

'You know, in China, Uyghur Muslims treated very badly and in Burma... Buddhists kill the Rohingya Muslims, the Burma government do nothing, so they run,' Ali says, looking at the Rohingyas.

I look closer at the Rohingyas.

The fear in those eyes is so naked, I grip the tablecloth.

I can almost hear their hearts pounding in dread against their ribs.

After a few seconds of silence, words stumble out of my mouth.

'How did you all get together?'

'In Syria... then Turkey announce they take Syrian and Rohingya refugees... I come with them.'

Just then, the owner walks out of the diner and brings them food. I shut the window but continue looking at the shivering lot. National identities melt away. Those on the other side of the window are simple people – struck down by the madness of discrimination and violence. The frame is now one of human suffering as under winter's unsheathed sword they huddle together and eat.

I drive out of the diner making my way further southeast, taking with me that haunting look of fear in the eyes of the Rohingya Muslims. The rawness of what I saw outside the diner cuts sharply. Fear is latent in all of us, but the chilling ease with which it takes root within us is understood only when one witnesses the swiftness and brutality with which our species turns on one another, stripping each other of the very dignity of existence. This vulnerability is present everywhere, and in everyone. The sinister ease with which hate overtakes every other emotion is deeply disturbing. Hate unmasks the resident fear in the 'other'. Seized by terror, abandoned by dignity, and shuddering in trepidation, the 'other' is left alone to grapple with fear and the unknown.

China's rise as a superpower is entrenched in a singular majoritarian identity – Han Chinese. With this unified strength and on the back of brilliantly organised and structured economic policies, China strides like a colossus in the global economic theatre. With this might, China's 'othering' of its Muslim Uyghur minority continues unabated and unopposed. In a relentless persecution, the Uyghurs are being 'Hanised' in concentration camps. In these camps they are forced to learn the ways of the Han Chinese including language and customs, while witnessing the obliteration of their literature, poetry, and art. China's message of inclusion is clear – the Uyghurs will be brought into the mainstream forcibly and 'Hanised', only then will they be included on its growth path. Fleeing before they are thrust into these camps, some of the Uyghurs successfully make it into the mountainous regions of Turkmenistan from where they begin an arduous walk towards Anatolia. Here in Turkey's heartland a humanitarian catastrophe is unfolding. But what is true is that Turkey has a remarkably humane refugee policy. From Syria, Burma, and China, the helpless pour into this country where they are given residency and where they try to find work with a flickering hope of restoring their dignity.

I drive on, passing through bare orchards which have surrendered their leaves to winter. After a five-hour drive from Bursa I reach the small town of Seyit Gazi. The town did not exist in 242 CE when Plotinus and Gordian made their way through this countryside. Surrounded by rolling hills dotted with cypress trees, Seyit Gazi takes its name from a legend, one of love. I had read about this tiny place which is almost entirely undeveloped and where one can still sense the beauty of Greek antiquity. But the story around which it finds its relevance to today's times dates to the eighth century CE. This was the site of ancient Nacolea which was part of the greater territory of Akroenos. The rocky mountains of Akroenos are magnificent and mighty and were the pride of the realm of the Greco-Roman Lord of Akroenos. Known for his wealth and pride, the Lord of Akroenos wielded enormous influence in Anatolia. The rugged mountains provided protection to his principality, but also hid a secret – a whispered truth of the beauty of his daughter Eleanora. Such was her fabled beauty that the sun, so impressed at her birth, scattered its rays which became her golden tresses. The moon gave its radiance and shape to her face. Rose petals gave their colour to her lips and honey the colour to her skin. Wild gazelles imbued her with their eyes and grace and olive branches bequeathed her their sensual sway. Gifted with a feline walk that felled many a mighty warrior, with her one gaze,

the strongest of them put down their weapons and took
to playing harps.

A hidden treasure, Eleanora was kept away from public
gaze because the effect she had had on men. As the pride
and influence of the Lord of Akroenos grew, he became ever
so belligerent and cruel towards his farmers unleashing
torture and extracting exorbitant taxes. On one occasion
though, his sense of invincibility got the better of him when
he had a farmer flogged who happened to be the tiller of a
bordering prince – a Muslim Arab. Enraged by this, the Arab
prince asked for an apology. The Lord of Akroenos refused
and instead threatened to invade the Arab's territory. This
brought the entire Arabian force into action, which laid
siege to Akroenos in 740 CE. Leading the Arabian charge
was a man called Seyit. Brave, chivalrous and blessed with
exquisite looks, Seyit pushed back the forces of the Lord
of Akroenos. Mounted on his white steed, sabre in hand
cutting through the Greco-Roman legions, Seyit and his
men reached the very doors of the fortress. Struck by panic,
many Greco-Roman soldiers fled into the fortress and word
reached Eleanora of its impending fall. In utter distress she
ran out onto the ramparts of the fort, unveiling her beauty
for all to behold. Standing on the rampart she looked below,
her eyes falling on Seyit. The Muslim general surrounded by
the enemy was fighting on. But Eleanora almost instantly
lost her heart to him. Without a helmet, which he had
probably lost in the heat of battle, Seyit's shoulder-length
hair flew in the wind. His face chiselled by divinity rested
elegantly on a long neck, his brown eyes exuded a fierceness
but also had a softness to them, and his broad shoulders
seemed strong enough to carry the weight of the world.
As men stopped and looked at Eleanora, Seyit carried on
fighting. When he did eventually look up at her, holding his
sword aloft, he remarked, 'God is beautiful. Your beauty

comes from Him. Without his generosity you are nothing.' Eleanora hadn't heard anything as simple and powerful as that. Such was the strength of the brazen truth just uttered from the handsomest of men that she felt the full force of it and took a step back. From then on, she refused to move from that spot.

At sunset when fighting ceased and men went back to their tents, word reached Eleanora of the humane treatment of the Greco-Roman prisoners taken by the Muslim general. Food was shared with them. They weren't chained – they were allowed to pray and even given fresh clothes to wear. Eleanora that very evening wrote to Seyit and had the letter smuggled into his tent. In the letter she pleaded for peace, even expressed her love for him, and desired a future with him. Undeniably, Seyit too had been struck by Eleanora, and he wrote back desiring peace and praising her beauty. But Eleanora's father discovered the secret romance and would have none of it. Instead, he insisted on a night raid on the Muslim camp. Caught unawares, Seyit was stabbed in the back multiple times and his body brought out on spikes towards the fortress. As the mounted body approached the ramparts, the glow from the flaming torches that illuminated it revealed the horror of Seyit's death to Eleanora who had not moved from the rampart. Never having experienced love before her glancing romance with Seyit, Eleanora in full view of both armies plunged a dagger through her heart and fell from the ramparts. As she lay gasping, her last words were a wish – to be buried next to Seyit. Such was the power of love that both armies refused to lift their weapons. Unable to bring themselves to fight, soldiers are known to have wept for days for the slain young love. In death and through love, Seyit and Eleanora had brought peace to Anatolia.

It is late evening when I enter the mausoleum of Seyit Gazi. Under a large dome are two graves. One is exceptionally long, quite possibly exaggerated in length to suit the legend of Seyit as a very tall man. The tomb is covered in a green cloth with Quranic verses embroidered on it. Lying next to him is a smaller grave. This tomb too is simple and modest. At the bottom is a rectangular placard – Eleanora. Under one dome, unified in love, from the obscurity of this remote shrine a profound message of unity through love rises and makes its way out into the world for all to hear.

After a few moments in the shrine, I make my way out towards a Sufi tekke where I will be spending the night. A short Turk greets me outside and cheerfully takes me in to show me my lodgings. A single bed with a large window looking into the cypress tree lined hills of Anatolia suits me just fine. In the centre of the wooden floor is a handmade rug from Uzbekistan distinct with its interwoven crimson and blue fabric. A Bukhari fireplace with freshly inserted wood adds to the cosy rural charm of my small room. I have a quiet dinner of bread and yoghurt served up by the Turk and tuck myself into bed hoping to sleep soundly after all the driving.

A few moments later though I hear excited voices. I make my way out to find a group of youngsters quite possibly in their early twenties crowded around a laptop in the main common room of the tekke. Glued to it they are watching a recording of NASA's landing on Mars which happened in February 2021. It is quite possible that they are seeing it for the first time. I ask them if I can watch it with them and with unhesitating enthusiasm, they allow me to pull up a chair. On the screen is an image of a female Indian scientist. Her name is Swati Mohan. Surrounding her are tense looking scientists with Asian and Caucasian features. In a distinct American accent, Swati begins the countdown for the landing of Perseverance (the name of the rover). The youngsters get closer to the screen which begins showing images of the descending rover. With each passing second the image of Perseverance gets clearer as it breaks through Mars' atmosphere hurtling towards its surface. Swati's voice remains calm as she continues with the countdown. Eventually, there is touchdown. The entire NASA team including Allen Chen and Ken Farley (scientists of Chinese and American origin) leap from their seats, embracing each other, and cheering this monumental human achievement. Perseverance will be controlled from millions of miles away and will roam the surface of Mars, take pictures, collect samples, and even undertake helicopter surveys of this heavenly body. Named after the God of war and destruction, the red planet has finally been harnessed by a great love and passion for exploration, driven by a team from across the world that came together in a common pursuit of knowledge, successfully bringing this planet into our sphere of understanding. What we do with it is entirely up to us. But as of now, the youngsters of remote Seyit Gazi marvel with gaping mouths and joyous smiles, celebrating humankind's phenomenal achievement which was accomplished without any racial barriers, and of which they have taken intellectual ownership.

I spend the night in the Sufi tekke hoping to leave early in the morning and head further east. The next morning after a refreshing cup of crimson Turkish tea and delicious scrambled eggs, I step out into the bitter cold. Frost has crystallised on the streets. As soon as I turn on the ignition and the wipers battle against the frosted windscreen, I hear banging on the window. As the wipers do their work, I look straight ahead and get a clear view of a massive crowd gathered in the middle of the road. Sirens blaring a convoy of police cars shoot past me. I roll down the window and ask the manager of the Sufi tekke (whose been banging at my window) about the commotion.

'It is PKK... Kurdish party....'

'What do you mean?'

'There is too much danger... they attack... anytime... you no go further... too much danger... road closed now.'

'But I must'.

'No... No... police closed road... See.'

Barricades come up in seconds and the police are all over the street. Turkey has been battling the PKK for years. The Kurds have been demanding a separate homeland both in Turkey and in Iraq, unleashing violence with ease and at will. The embattled Turkish forces pummel this stretch all the way till the Syrian and Iraq borders with advanced air firepower, and the Kurds hit back with bomb attacks. The cycle of violence is unceasing. I have no choice and reluctantly, my hands turn the steering wheel towards Istanbul.

Plotinus' hands, though, must have held steady on the reins of his horse which carried him through Anatolia on this cold frosted path. All the while, the philosopher observed Gordian III as they closed in on the Persian camp. With his father-in-law Misitheus as Prefect of the Praetorian Guard guiding him, Gordian felt confident of his expedition. Eventually, in 243 CE the two greatest armies of the third century faced each other. Seeing the enormous size of the Roman army, the Persians initially retreated, and Gordian reoccupied some of the lost territories. But this ignominy was too much for Persian emperor Shapur I, and he finally gave battle at the plains of Resaena. Gordian personally led the Roman charge, and along with Misitheus and Phillip, another general, attacked the Persian army with great fury. The Persians seem to have underestimated the zeal and vigour of the young Caesar, who mounted on his steed cut a heroic picture in the eyes of his soldiers who rallied behind his war cry and fell upon the Persians. Such was the force of the attack that the Persians were completely routed, fleeing the battlefield, leaving behind armour, helmets, swords, lances, and chariots. After the victory at Resaena, Gordian wrote to the senate in Rome announcing his triumph. But true to his character he wrote with humility and grace, attributing the success to the wisdom of his father-in-law and the courage of his soldiers. The senate in Rome was surprised at the magnanimity shown towards the common soldier and viewed this with suspicion. Misitheus was rightly credited by Gordian because it was his efforts that kept the rumour mongers within the Praetorian Guard at bay. Misitheus achieved this by ensuring the troops were well fed and watered during the arduous journey – bacon, barley, wheat, and wine were abundantly supplied along with entertainment and well conducted war games which meant the soldiers didn't have any idle time for hatching conspiracies.[52]

For days the Roman army celebrated their dazzling victory. Hundreds of sheep were slaughtered, and feasts held by campfires. Gordian drank and rejoiced with his troops, as part of his efforts of building an unshakable bond with them. Long nights were filled with poetry, song, and dance. But the sweet taste of victory and accomplishment is always accompanied by two of active intellect's most potent aftereffects – greed and jealousy. A few days after the victory at Resaena, Misitheus burst out of his tent vomiting blood and choking on his outflow. Within a few hours he was dead – poisoned by some of the guards loyal to Phillip. A man who had been a professional thief, Phillip the Arab (as he was known because of his Arabian roots) had a reputation of being a brave and competent soldier. With these abilities he had risen in rank and now desired the ultimate prize – to become emperor and Caesar. This ambition he kept close to his chest and shared it only with a few chosen men. With the loss of his trusted father-in-law and recalling Phillip's courage in battle, Gordian immediately appointed Phillip to Misitheus' position as Prefect of the Praetorian Guard. Phillip now believed that only Gordian stood in his way to becoming Caesar. Slowly, he planted discord in the military ranks and stirred them to revolt at the time of his choosing. At the same time, he weaved a dream for Gordian, one which would make him the greatest Caesar in Roman history. The defeat of the Persians at Resaena meant they were weak, and if Gordian would go deeper into their territory and inflict a final blow on Persia he would stride in the footsteps of Alexander. A victory deep in Persian territory would mean the opening of the floodgates to India – a land where no Caesar had ventured before. Such a dream could come to fruition if only Gordian dared.[53]

At nineteen, Gordian still carried freckles from his childhood. His soulful, sparkling blue eyes had the innocence of youth, yet the curiosity and wonder for this big, undiscovered world. His hair, a light brown with swirls that rested gently on his forehead, were untouched by grey or silver. Facial hair, a sign of masculinity, had only recently begun sprouting around his jaw line, and a deep dimpled cleft on his chin had attracted the admiration of several young females in Rome. Standing tall at over six feet, Gordian was a strapping youth. He had been a good student in Rome and had shown immense potential for poetry and literature. While we do not know if Plotinus taught Gordian, it is a strong possibility that the two exchanged views and thoughts during this expedition. After the death of Misitheus, Gordian descended into great sadness. For days he neither had food nor engaged with the soldiers. A thoughtful withdrawal began taking place and he spent most of his time reading, walking alone, and evaluating his options. He craved to be in the arms of his wife Tranquilina, quite aptly named, for it was with her that he had found moments of peace when the viciousness of Roman politics would drag him down.

Plotinus too spent these days of uncertainty pondering his options of reaching India. Breaking away from the army would compromise his security because along the Euphrates and the Tigris roamed lawless bandits. Even if he managed to dodge them as a lone rider, he would soon run out of food and supplies and starve to death in the Persian desert. The possibility of being captured by the Persian scouts that roamed the borderlands was a genuine one, and being taken for a Roman spy would mean sure death. But then if he did break away from the army he would be heading exactly where he wanted to end up (India) without depending on the result of war. Maybe the Persians would respect a philosopher and let him pass through. At the time of the campaign, Plotinus was thirty-nine. Physically strong, energetic, and mentally agile, he must have found this period of uncertainty utterly frustrating. Should he mount and just ride away, or should he move with the army? This question was tossed a thousand times in his head. Standing at the crossroads of empires and destiny, these times of unease gnawed away at emperor, philosopher, and soldier. It is these moments that change the course of history – the moment when confusion, sadness, ambition, fear, and excitement all come together at once, and just then intellect forces the hand of man to write his own fate. In many ways, the freedom to act and the action itself for good or bad occurs at that moment.

Plotinian words question all of that and fate:

... It is illogical to say that our own parts when moved by
our controlling part are moved by fate –... And in this case
neither will we be ourselves nor will any deed be ours....
Our considered views are the acts of calculative reasoning
belonging to something else. Just as it is not our feet that
kick, but we who kick by means of our feet which our parts
of ourselves. The truth is that each thing must be separate,
and our own actions and acts of thinking must exist; and both
the good and bad actions of each person come from each
individual himself; at least one should not trace back to the
universe the producing of shameful actions.[54]

With these words, Plotinus separates the First Principle
cause (The Good) from the free will of intellect.

On an evening when twilight tussled with light and
darkness quite like the internal turmoil that was consuming
Gordian, Phillip entered the emperor's tent. Only a few
guards were around, and the young emperor was staring
into a wood fire. A few books lay scattered on his desk along
with a map of the Persian Empire. Outside the emperor's
tent, the languid movements of a torpid army could be
heard. Horses trotted past – their hooves kicking up sand
and dirt. Some legions prepared for an early supper and
stood around cauldrons cooking up lamb stew. Many had
abandoned their armour not knowing the direction in
which they would march, and a sense of general lethargy
pervaded the army. Phillip walked up slowly behind
Gordian and whispered into his ear. With each word he
heard, Gordian conjured up an image – the fall of Persia
and Gordian mounted triumphantly as Caesar, emperor,
and Shah in Persepolis, with only India left to conquer. The
whisper worked. Gordian swung the purple cape of Caesar

around his shoulders, stormed out of his tent, and let out a thunderous war cry. The deafening war trumpets rang out almost immediately and the legions breaking camp swung into action, putting on their armour, mounting their steeds, buckling their sabres, falling in line, and marching towards Ctesiphon deep into Persian territory. While Gordian had chosen to conquer, Plotinus too made a choice – that of not breaking away and making his way to India on his own, but instead accompanying the army.

On the plains of Misiche in March 244 CE not far from Ctesiphon (in modern-day Iraq), the Roman army caught sight of the Persian force. It seemed modest and one that could be easily overrun. The Persian army had the Tigris behind it, and so any chance of reinforcements seemed minimal. Gordian and Phillip almost immediately hurled themselves at the Persians. The Roman cavalry charge, like thunder, descended on the Persians with its full might. The fighting was bitter but one sided, in favour of the Romans. Just when victory seemed in sight, the unthinkable happened. Shapur I at the head of an immense body of troops emerged from behind a few sand dunes that separated a slender part of the plains and the flowing Tigris.

All along, the Persian emperor had waited for this moment. Encircled, the Roman army panicked as Shapur and his men launched themselves into battle. Plotinus, who had accompanied the Roman army, was caught in the middle of this killing frenzy.

Legion after legion were decimated by the Persians. Dust clouds rose amidst clashing metal, overturned chariots, and mangled bloody bodies. Watching the collapse of his famed fighting force and realising that impending defeat was irreversible, Gordian led one last thrust into the Persian ranks but fell from his horse and found himself trapped under it. The impact of the fall broke his thigh bone, leaving him struggling in the dirt. From this point on the exact sequence of events is not clear, but what many chroniclers and historians believe and write about is the role that Phillip played. Seizing this opportunity, Phillip rallied his trusted soldiers in the Praetorian Guard who murdered Gordian as he frantically tried to release himself from under his horse. As the young Caesar breathed his last Phillip walked up, ripped off the purple cape, and draped it around himself. He was the new Caesar. Within moments, Phillip sent messengers to Shapur seeking a truce and agreeing to surrender. As fear gripped the remaining Roman soldiers, Shapur rode up surrounded by his legions and addressed Phillip who remained standing in obeisance. Shapur demanded 500,000 dinars as ransom for sparing the life of the new Caesar, and any remaining men in the Roman contingent which included Plotinus. The borders would be sealed, and no one from the Roman contingent would be allowed to cross the Tigris. Phillip agreed to the terms. This humiliating scene would later be sculpted in the Naqsh-e-Rustam stone carvings in Persepolis depicting a horse mounted Shapur arm raised and a subservient Phillip standing below. Misiche would be renamed as Peroz Shapur (Victorious Shapur).

No preceding Roman army had been subjugated and humiliated thus. Under Phillip's instructions though, a horseman sped to Rome carrying the message of his appointment as Caesar by his legions and demanding the senate's approval. In due course, Phillip would receive that much coveted approval. As the beleaguered legions began their ignominious march back to Rome, Plotinus stood on the banks of the Tigris looking at both the armies pulling away. The body of Gordian lay covered in dust as Plotinus approached it. Both Caesar and hermit had been defeated by their choices. Plotinus' poignant words capture that moment.

Let the human being who lives in the world of corporeal goods be beautiful and tall and wealthy and the sort of ruler over people that one can be here, yet he ought not be envied for these things, since he was deceived by them. But the wise person would perhaps not even have these to begin with, though if he did, he will lessen their impact, if indeed he cares for himself.... He will not wish to be inexperienced with pains. If these (pains) do not come to him when he is young, he will wish to learn about them....[55]

As Plotinus looked across the Tigris, he knew that beyond the deserts of Persia were the fertile lands of India. He had come so far, and yet his dream to reach that ancient land lay shattered on the battlefield of Misiche. India had eluded him. Like a mirage it had vanished. He turned the reigns of his horse and followed the flowing purple cape of the new Caesar. Heading back to Rome, the new Caesar, and the hermit both looked for a new beginning.

# 4

# ITALIAN CRICKETERS

248 CE – the thousandth year since the foundation of Rome. It has been a millennium since the legend of Romulus, the abandoned child who had been suckled by a wolf in the forests and who, with time, and on the strength derived from the wolf's milk, grew into a strapping youth and fortified himself with a few shepherds along the banks of the Tiber, thus giving shape to the first formations of what would become the 'eternal' city. It had been a couple of years since Plotinus and Phillip returned to Rome and Phillip seized this opportunity to regale in his new avatar. No sooner than he received the mandate from the senate as the new Caesar, Phillip the Arab declared open the most lavish games since the time of Augustus, celebrating Rome's thousand years and his appointment as Caesar.

The Colosseum roars again. The stunning extravaganza of endless pomp and ostentation is one which Rome hasn't witnessed since decades. Every aspect of the games is astutely shaped to stir nostalgia and reverence for glorious Rome during the times of Julius Caesar, Augustus, Tiberius,

Trajan, and Hadrian. Occult sacrifices are made along the banks of the Tiber for three consecutive nights, while musicians and dancers perform amidst countless flaming torches and lamps that illuminate the Pantheon. Religious hymns in devotion to the gods pierce the sky. Sung while sailing down the Tiber in candlelit boats by a chorus of twenty-seven youths and virgins and their parents from Rome's nobility, the relentless singing beginning at dusk and lasting through the night beseeches the gods for a favourable present, future, and for the infinite glory of Rome.[56]

Flinging themselves into this fever of celebration are people from all parts of the empire. Throngs flow into the Colosseum cheering like men possessed, as man and beast cut open one another's chests in bloody gladiatorial contests. The most exotic animals from hippos to leopards and from lions to rhinoceros fight for survival against gladiators armed with sword and lance. Through days of slaughter and gore more than 1,000 gladiators and an equal number of animals lie dead in the centre of the Colosseum. In the Circus Maximus the crowds thunder as chariots as fast as the wind crash into each other, and riders are trampled in their zeal to emerge triumphant.

But in the pine tree-lined avenues and in secret gatherings where philosophers like Plotinus gathered, it is whispered that this spectacle is a distraction from Phillip's crimes, inaptitude in governance, a morally rotting society, and the defeat at Misiche. In their troubled minds, the thinkers toss the glory of Rome and the empire's future. The empire still extended from the shores of the Atlantic to the Tigris and from Mount Atlas to the Rhine, but the noble aim to make Rome a just state devoted to its people had been lost and replaced with corruption and lethargy. The vigour for social justice had vanished and a lumbering bureaucracy driven by self-enrichment had become the oppressor of the imaginative and industrious.

The spirit of Rome which attracted people from the farthest stretches of the empire was grounded in inclusiveness, where honest endeavour could catapult a man to positions of prosperity. At the height of the Roman Empire, citizenship was granted to people under all its dominions. From Spain to Germany and from Egypt to the borders of Persia, people were Roman. Citizenship grants, demographic growth, and settler and military colonies rapidly increased the number of Roman citizens. This achieved its peak with emperor Caracalla's *Antonine Constitution* in 212 CE, which gave citizenship rights to all free inhabitants of the empire. It is for the most part though not clear to what extent most Roman citizens in antiquity regarded themselves as being Roman. Most likely, local identities were prominent throughout the Roman Empire due to its vast geographical extent, but a Roman identity provided a larger sense of common identity and belonging. Absorbing all into its social tapestry, Rome accepted Goths, Germans, Spaniards, Egyptians, and a gradual process of osmosis where an unconscious assimilation of various ideas, thoughts and sharing of knowledge made it a place where even an Arab could be accepted as Caesar.

By 248 CE though, that magic had dulled. Bribery replaced merit as a requirement for service in the military and in the senate. This led to the appointment of the incompetent in the legions and in statecraft. Managed by the incapable, the economy began to flounder as the price of grain and essentials rose in the street markets. Politicians began discriminating between races and identities to secure their positions of power. Majoritarian politics took hold as politicians and senators began asserting a puritanical Roman identity. Moral degradation had sown the seeds of division, and deep social cracks began to appear in Roman society. Othering gained momentum. Soon the Goths raised a banner of revolt, and like an infectious rampant plague, rebellion spread across the Eastern frontier provinces, including Thrace and the Balkans. With internal strife strangling Rome like a serpent's coil around its prey, the external foes saw an opportunity. The rapacious barbarian hordes smacked their lips and closed in. If unchecked, these rising waves of unrest threatened to reach the very walls of Rome, and so in response to this, Phillip chose Gaius Messius Quintis Decius to quell the rebellions and bring order to the agitated provinces. Decius was a man of vigour, and most importantly had the backing of the senate. In a blistering attack along the Danube, he decimated the rebellious armies and emerged victorious. Such was the effect this victory had on the legions that in the countryside far away from Rome the most eminent of legionaries proclaimed Decius the new Caesar. Power, the ultimate seductress with many a promise for the future, was now ensnaring his imagination. In his mind she had begun exalting him to a position of final authority from where he could look down on other men as grovelling mortals. Like many in the past, Decius succumbed to temptation and accepted his new title.

Feeling the surge of power under his wings, Decius wasted no time and marched on Rome. There had been much unrest in Rome with riots breaking out in the city over the lack of wheat supply from Egypt that had occurred because of the high handedness in which Roman authorities had treated Egyptian merchants. Once held in high regard by Rome's custom officials and considered important citizens, the Egyptian merchants were now being subjected to racism in the form of public taunts and demos to curtail their civil rights. Feeling slighted and discriminated, the Egyptian merchants revolted by short supplying wheat.

The ensuing riots in the streets were bloody and went on for weeks.

Fatigued by the ordeal of bringing order to the streets, Phillip was further tormented when he received news of Decius' betrayal. Almost immediately he set out to meet Decius at the head of a large force. The two men, carrying with them a legacy of betrayal, met in Verona. As the battle raged, it became clear that the momentum was with Decius. Sensing defeat and at the same time sniffing an opportunity to ingratiate themselves with Decius, the legionaries of Phillip turned on him, bringing him down from his horse and plunging their daggers into him. Treachery had caught up with Phillip who, in his last moments, allegedly saw Gordian's ghost standing above him. As Phillip's cremation flames went up, he burnt to the bone by the fury of his own ambition. With these events the Roman Empire stood at the beginning of its end.

Plotinus had been greatly moved by the savagery of war he witnessed in Mesopotamia and by the death of the teenage Gordian III. Having returned to Rome, the unceasing political turmoil, vulgar exhibition of blood and gore in the name of entertainment, moral degradation in Roman society, and the constant betrayals playing out between men scheming to wear Caesar's wreath made him a recluse and a deeper thinker. During these tempestuous times he became a vegetarian, ate frugally only to survive, and spent most of his time in his study and teaching his students. It was in these times that his most devoted student Porphyry entered his circle of influence. Soon through complete dedication to the rigorous study of philosophy, Porphyry elevated himself in Plotinus' eyes. He was eventually selected by Plotinus as the one to whom he would dictate *The Enneads*.

On occasions, Plotinus was known to leave his home and venture to the Rostra in the Forum where he would give lectures to his ever-growing number of students. In many ways his voice of compassion, unity, and goodness attracted people from all walks of life who sought refuge from the anarchy that was befalling Rome and its provinces. Many senators beleaguered and jaded by the wickedness required for Roman politics turned to him for a more philosophical meaning to their existence. Porphyry writes:

> Quite a few senators attended his lectures: Marcellus Orrontius and Sabinillus in particular worked at philosophy. Another senator was Rogantianus who came to reject this life (in politics) to such an extent that he gave up his possessions, dismissed his slaves and resigned his position. He was due to be inducted into the office of Praetor - The Lictors were even there. But he not only refused to go on, he resigned all public office. After he relinquished the management of his own household as well, he would dine and sleep at the houses of various friends and acquaintances, only eating every other day. As a result of his renunciation and abstinence he recovered from his gout which had been so severe that he used to be carried about in a chair; and whereas before he could not stretch out his fingers, he became more agile than craftsmen used to working with their hands. Plotinus took him into his inner circle and was full of praise for him - Eventually adducing him as a good example for philosophers.[57]

Porphyry's adulation for his teacher was such that he conspired with another student to have a portrait made of Plotinus which he could hold onto after his education. Plotinus had refused in the past to sit for portraits, dismissing the importance attached to them, even being embarrassed about having a body. Instead, he urged his students to concentrate on matters related to the soul.

Did he have to consent to leave behind a longer lasting image of this image as if it were something worth looking at? Since he made it clear that, for this reason, he would refuse to sit for a portrait, Amelius got Carterius – the best painter of his generation who happened to be his friend – to come to Plotinus' seminar and meet him (Anyone who wanted was allowed to attend these seminars). Amelius had Carterius concentrate on looking at Plotinus so that, over time, he acquired a clear mental image of him. He then drew a picture of the image thus laid down in his memory. Amelius corrected the sketch to make it as true to life as possible; and in this way the skill of Carterius furnished us with a very close likeness of Plotinus and Plotinus knew nothing about it.[58]

In Rome, although Plotinus kept away from festivals, he made it a point to celebrate 'The Feast of Plato'. Inspired by Plato's *Symposium*, writers, philosophers, and poets were invited by Plotinus over wine to read their latest works. These wine parties, Plotinus ensured, were held in Greek style where everyone was equal, reclining on the floor without any hierarchy. No philosopher, poet or student was greater or lesser than the other reclining next to him. On the floor, drinking the same wine, students were philosophers and philosophers were students. Against the sweet sound of the harp played by female flautists - thought, verse, and drink flowed without any barriers. At one such celebration, teacher-student loyalty is wonderfully presented by Porphyry:

> He never revealed his birthday to anyone since he did not think that anyone should sacrifice or hold a feast for him – although he himself would hold feasts for birthdays of Plato and Socrates. I read a poem called The Holy Marriage at the Feast for Plato, and because a lot of it was expressed

obliquely, in the mystical language of inspiration, someone said, "Porphyry is mad! In everyone's hearing, Plotinus said to me: 'You proved yourself to be at once poet, philosopher and priest'"... Plotinus was so happy with me that in our seminars he would constantly add: "Shoot like this, if you want to illuminate men."[59]

Although Plotinus taught with passion on his return to Rome and his students absorbed all that came from him, he restrained himself from teaching certain 'secrets' that he had learned from Ammonius Saccas. This could well have been inspired from the master-student tradition of the Upanishads where only the chosen student or son could be given the ultimate secrets of revelation. As the Roman Empire suffered setbacks, the city reeked with superstition and suspicion lurked in every corner. Magic and rituals played out in streets, homes, and in intimate gatherings in an exhibition of human weakness. Porphyry's observance of Plotinus' strength in the face of superstition and fear reveals much about the philosopher's character:

Amelius was fond of sacrifices and used to busy himself with rites of the new moon and rites to allay his fears. He once tried to get Plotinus to participate but Plotinus said, "They must come to me, not I to them". We did not know what consideration led him to make such a grand pronouncement, and did not have the nerve to ask him.... Plotinus did have a natural endowment that set him apart.... An Egyptian priest came once to Rome to summon Plotinus' guardian daemon. Plotinus agreed to meet him. The invocation took place at the temple of Isis. When he called upon Plotinus' daemon, a God came rather than a member of the genus of daemons. 'You are blessed since you have a God and are not accompanied by a member of a lower genus' said the

Egyptian.... Among those with pretensions to philosophy was Olympus of Alexandria who hated Plotinus and used magic to attack him, trying to get him star struck. When Olympus realised that the attempt only rebounded he said that the power of Plotinus' soul was so great that he could deflect attacks made against him onto those attacking him. Olympus eventually gave up.[60]

This close bond between Plotinus and Porphyry in times of uncertainty and great upheaval in many ways brought about a philosophical revival in Rome and acted as a healing balm to the city. As has often been the case when disorder fuelled by greed infiltrates society, it is men like Plotinus who have provided solace for mind and soul.

I ensure that Honey Singh collects me from Rome's Fiumicino airport at midday and we make our way to Trastevere. The Istanbul–Rome flight is barely two and a half hours, and I land feeling as fresh as a daisy.

'See, I told you sir, you will return,' Honey Singh says in a confident voice. Today, he is dressed in a suit.

'Yes, indeed, you are right... the Pantheon has pulled me back.'

'Ha ha.'

'How are you, Honey Singh?' I ask, looking at him in his rear-view mirror.

'All well, sir,' and he gives me the Indian nod.

'Your family well?'

'Yes, very well, sir, I will be going home early today.'

'Why?'

'It is my son's birthday.'

'Ah, I see. Any special Indian celebrations planned?'

'No, not really... we live in Rome so... you know the saying... when in Rome... that kind of thing.'

'Of course.'

'You know, sir, my sons and I keep a strand of uncut hair as a mark of respect for Sikhism.' And then he hastily adds, '...we also celebrate Christmas... we are one happy Indo-Italian family.' He laughs.

'Excellent, Honey Singh, that's wonderful.'

I pay Honey Singh for his past and current efforts and make my way to my apartment door that opens straight up from the Piazza di San Calisto. Striding up, I'm pleasantly surprised with how cosy this tiny studio apartment is. With a window opening onto the square and a bed under a high beamed and tiled Roman roof, it's a charmer. It is a fabulous bright day and I head out almost immediately with my notebook and *The Enneads* in hand. Back at the Forum and leaning by the Rostra, romancing the ruins, and gliding over the pages of *The Enneads*, my eyes retrace a passage.

> But if intellect, thinking, and the object of thought are the same, if they become altogether one, they will make themselves disappear in themselves, but if they are distinguished by being the other they will again, not be the Good.[61]

Putting myself to the test, I make my way to the Basilica di San Clemente. Just outside the entrance, a Bangladeshi woman sitting on a suitcase is tuning a small radio. Walking past her I recognise the song playing on the radio. It is a 1980s Hindi film song adapted to the silver screen by Jeetendra – a handsome Indian actor who had gained renown for his dance moves while wooing his love interest. It works, and the woman who is most probably a refugee, swings her head back and forth in the most preposterous manner to the music. I find this sight bizarre as it disrupts Rome's character and atmosphere. Bangladeshi refugees swarm all over Rome. Dozens sleep in singular hovels. They leave their clammy surroundings each morning selling chestnuts, rubber trinkets, and little toys at Piazza Navona and Piazza Farnese. It is a life of struggle, disappointments, and immense homesickness. I rush down the steps of the Basilica with a purpose.

Descending through a chamber of corridors right at the bottom of the structure is a network of mud and stone alleyways. I soon find myself navigating these sombre, dark, second-century streets with the adventurous spirit of a novice explorer wading through frozen sheets of time. With every step I feel like Harrison Ford in *Indiana Jones*. Following the torchlight of my mobile phone, I see the bottom pit where the pagan gods of Rome were worshipped with such devotion that the walls absorbed the chants of the cult of the Mithraes, and 2,000 years later they still seem to whisper them.

The temple and the sturdy Mithraic altar stand as haunting symbols of a vanished occult. A low arched ceiling crowns the altar, on which is the engraved cult figure in flight surging through time and fiendishly descending into the present. Through the dark tunnel I can see stone slabs that stretch out, on which cult worshippers and priests must have sat overlooking the altar, fire, and sacrificial rituals – a dark tale of horrifying screams and chilling pleas for life. These rituals played out during Plotinus' times and his observation of them made him question the need of intermediaries between man and God. Crouching and following the torchlight, I make my way into another corridor. The dampness from the walls mixed with the smell of ageing moss infiltrates my nostrils as I pass a room which was the Mithraic school. By the fourth century CE, though,

Christianity had become the state religion of Rome, and the cult of Mithras was banned and declared illegal for what was considered unholy practice.

Further down, the severe dampness is explained by a fresh spring that has been flowing for the last four millennia. I trace my steps upwards. Emerging into the next level a waft of fresh air comes cascading through and a beam of sunlight manages to break the strangle of darkness. I sense I'm being watched, quite possibly by a tender spirit. Almost out of nowhere, from the darkness in front of me emerges the gaunt face of St. Cyril encrusted against a stunning gold mosaic. His soul-piercing eyes draw me in and hold me with a transfixing yet gentle gaze, which must have been one of the reasons the Slavs listened to his sermons. Utterly mesmerised by his words, they stepped into the Christian faith.

A linguistic genius, St. Cyril invented the Slavic language and along with St. Methodius spread Christ's word in the Balkans. His large tomb is of great spiritual and cultural importance, attracting pilgrims from all parts of the world to pray on the Feast of St. Cyril. A variety of art that makes this building so unique springs forth as I make my way out: stone slabs that have pagan and Christian prayers inscribed on both sides and are easily visible when swivelled, a sarcophagus engraved with the Greek myth of Phaedra and Hippolytus; a series of frescoes depicting Christ descending into hell to save noble souls that had died before his coming; and the Miracle of the Sea of Azov depicting a child saved by St. Clemente from a receding tide. On top of all this stands the Basilica di San Clemente built in the twelfth century. Intellect's homage to the divine manifests itself through pagan, Greek, and Christian Rome as they created art and built architecture layer upon layer, with the objective of distinguishing. I too have done nothing but distinguish. Right from the moment I distinguished the Bangladeshi lady for her national identity, her possible refugee status, and scorned at the music that brought her joy and respite from her hardships, till the moments I disparaged the pagan Mithraic cult from other forms of devotion. Yet, I am in Rome - the eternal city that holds it all within it today. And today, the collective intellect of Rome doesn't other or discriminate. Simply put – all of it is Rome, and Rome is it. Here a catholic priest at the Basilica will take great pride in its rich history and will welcome you to wander and discover pre-catholic worship. Here, in Rome, museums, authorities, and common folk, protect, rejoice in and nurture everything that is pre-Christian, all the while being devoutly catholic.

Tossing Plotinus's words in my mind, *'if they are distinguished by being the other they will again, not be the Good'*, a great sense of disappointment descends on me as I leave the Basilica and make my way into the cobbled streets. That moment when I saw the starlings as one and the Pantheon as a unity has obviously deserted me. How I long to feel that again. Most of the evening is spent in dejection and sipping wine at the Camponeschi wine bar in Piazza Farnese. Overlooking the beautiful, but brooding fountains in the square, while listening to the sound of water overflowing in basins extracted from the third-century Baths of Caracalla, my mind is with Plotinus. How far Plotinus seems. So elusive, so evolved – his state of mind so unfettered and uncluttered by simply accepting and not distinguishing, not othering and not discriminating – his state of mind seems ever so distant and unachievable.

Dinner tonight is with Andrea di Robilant, a wonderful writer who teaches creative writing at the American University in Rome.

The soup is delicious and so seems the evening.

'So, what's the mood in Britain after Brexit?' Andrea asks, peering through his glasses.

'Depends on where you are and who you ask,' I say, eating my delicious pumpkin soup. 'London and Scotland aren't happy, but the rest of England is.'

'The European Union won't be the same again, you know,' Andrea says.

'Of course, it won't... the seeds of disunity have been scattered far and wide.'

'We achieved so much by being united,' Andrea continues.

'True, when I was growing up in India, we were told about how the West united after slaughtering each other through two world wars and innumerable religious differences in the centuries preceding those wars. Europe's golden age was from the 1960s... free trade, common market, common currency, common defence, open borders within the EU... all that is now being tested.'

Andrea sighs listening to my monologue.

I continue: 'South Asia should have become an EU. Imagine driving from Kabul to Kerala without any restrictions.' It is now my turn to sigh.

'But it's not just Brexit, there's Putin pushing his way in from the East now,' says Andrea, rising and clearing our soup bowls. In comes the delicious Ossobuco and I dive right in.

I keep the conversation going by saying, 'And Putin does what he does in the name of a common identity... Ukrainians and Russians are "one" people, he says.'

I press on. 'One identity has so many layers and dimensions to it. There are a vast number of Ukrainians who speak Russian and live in Russia... they marry into each other... Putin uses that fluid sense of belonging to a region and calls them "one people" but then he brings war under the pretext of unifying... so many Ukrainians have disappeared into camps in Russia. No one will know what happened to them. So many innocent Ukrainians have lost their lives.' I finish off gulping my last sip of wine.

Andrea comes over, fills my glass and his, then reclines back in his chair and speaks. 'Well, oneness is simple and complex. Let's look at language. Even Italian as is spoken and understood as a single language finds its "coming together", if you wish, only in the sixteenth century mainly thanks to the eloquence and literary genius of Pietro Bembo and Baldassare Castiglione.'

'Tell me more, Andrea.'

'Well, Pietro Bembo is considered the midwife of the Italian language based on Tuscan. Baldassare Castiglione on the other hand favoured a more flexible language, one which was more open in contrast to Bembo's more rigid and academic language.'

We polish off a bottle of red discussing my travels, after which I make my way back.

The taxi drops me off at Piazza Trilussa and I walk down the cobbled streets. The wine bars are still brimming with lovers and, quite charmingly, a bookshop called 'Almost corner bookshop' is open. A young man of Persian descent by the name of Jahan runs this little gem, which is one of the rare English bookshops in Rome and the only one in Trastevere. I step in and we exchange pleasantries in Farsi. This little bookshop is a den of centuries of wisdom. There is nothing quite like the fragrance of fresh paper as one turns the pages of a beautifully bound book – these familiar fragrances are like clouds of opium in which I have lost myself since childhood. I ask for *The Book of the Courtier* by Baldassare Castiglione. It is promptly served up, and within minutes I am back on the street. At Piazza di San Calisto, I decide not to open the door to my apartment but sit under the streetlamp and flip through some of the pages. Castiglione was born into an aristocratic Italian family in 1478 and received a thorough humanistic education, acquiring a refined appreciation for arts and language. In *The Book of the Courtier*, he sets out to define the essential virtues needed at court through lively imaginary conversations between real life courtiers to the Duke of Urbino, where his speakers discuss qualities of noble behaviour. But most importantly in the book, he discusses what influenced the beauty of the Italian language as we know it.

> This is the manner in which I would have our courtier speak and write; he should choose clear and beautiful words from the speech current in all parts of Italy though I would also praise him for sometimes employing terms, whether French or Spanish that are now accepted here.... Sometimes, to, I would like him to use certain words in a metaphorical sense whenever it is appropriate, putting them to novel use like a gardener grafting a branch onto a healthier trunk, and so increasing their attractiveness and beauty.....Then again, he should not hesitate to coin new words altogether, and to make use of novel figures of speech, taking these over elegantly from the Latin as the Romans once took them from the Greeks. Therefore if among educated men, living today, of good intellect and judgments, some were to take the trouble to write in Italian, in the way I describe, things which were worth reading, we should soon find our language adorned and enriched with fine phrases and figures of speech, and as good a medium for literature.....rich and varied like a delightful garden full of all kinds of flowers and fruits. This phenomenon would be nothing new, since from each of the four languages on which they could draw, the Greeks selected whatever words, expressions, and figures of speech they wished and constructed a new so-called common language; and

subsequently all five of these dialects were known collectively as Greek....[62]

Aristotle's profound thought *'The whole has many parts'* holds true for language, but Plotinus supersedes that thought when he invites us not to distinguish and discriminate within the whole, and therein lies the beauty of seamless, flowing language and architecture. What takes the mind into that state of 'not distinguishing and not discriminating' is love. Baldassare Castiglione's love for Italian saw him weave words into it without discriminating them because of their origin. If I were to stay true to Plotinian thought, then the Basilica di San Clemente should have been seen and thought of simply as a beautiful building devoted to divinity. If we achieve that state of mind then we don't other, and we just celebrate beauty and oneness. Plotinus emphasises that *'Intellect is the movement towards the Good in desire of the Good.'*[63] Subconsciously and consciously, our instinct is to move towards the good and build unity; be it a sparrow with a twig in its beak meant for a nest, knitting a sweater, a potter moulding a pot, baking a cake, even writing a sentence (the book you are holding in your hand began with one alphabet, which became a word, then a sentence, a page and finally a book), or creating a language, accepting customs from another culture, opening up immigration and even the act of procreation. All these are examples of the first instinct of intellect moving it towards unity (the Good). This occurs because everything (including you), are a unity (one), built in the image of 'The One', and unconsciously striving to reunite with 'The One'. While instinctively intellect moves towards the good, as we have seen earlier, it is intellect's free will that makes it *'dare'* to stand away from Good.

I am sitting alone on a bench in Piazza di San Calisto. The sounds of the last hushed footsteps in the square vanishes into the quiet night. The light from the lamppost above me flickers as if it wishes to speak. My thoughts wander and come to rest with the victims of war in Ukraine. This war is the first in Europe since the ethnic Yugoslav wars that spanned the 1990s. Ethnicity and identity led violence is what is playing out between Ukraine and Russia.

*Thy neighbour is in truth thy very self and what separates you from him is mere illusion.*

How distant these meaningful words from the Upanishads seem to the men who have propagated this war. To Plotinus, oneness is acceptance without distinction. How remote this thought seems from one man's vision for that region. In that region the tree of unity is watered by blood and acceptance perceived as weakness. I look up at the flickering light from the lamppost. The flicker resembles the last gasps for life which a father, mother, child, brother, or sister is taking right now on the battlefield. With a last sizzling gasp the light goes off leaving me in darkness. I rise, fumble for my key, manage to find it and turn the key to my apartment.

The next morning, I breakfast outside, sitting in front of the Basilica of Santa Maria in Trastevere. It is a typical Roman square with a stone fountain and a gorgeous cathedral. The cathedral's ethereal beauty is resplendent as the sun's slanting rays illuminate its fading golden frescos. The colour contrast of dull gold against the blue winter sky makes it a wonder that sings with the sweet voice of divinity. As the sun seems to meander and melt in the sky showering the cathedral with its light, the cathedral casts symmetrical shadows on the ground. Sitting in its soothing shadows, its sunlit radiance is so alluring that I can't help being pulled in. I leave my chair and walk towards it. Standing within its interiors, in silence, I feel like an embryo in a womb. My eyes remain glued to a painting of the Madonna looking at her baby boy. Her hands are spread wide. A slight tilt of her face and a slimmest of curls at the edge of her lips form a faint smile as she examines the embodiment of love which she has brought into the world. The peaceful countenance of the painting delicately brings forth the purity of life which emerges from the power of love. It melts my conscious state into pure ecstasy. All I know is that I'm smiling and my soul senses a flash of wholesome happiness – a state of speechless wonder where the soul is a valley of roses and the heart itself a blooming rose. How have I reached here? Love. Plotinian words leave my lips:

> Stricken with poverty having not united with the One, the soul gives birth to love; an emotion that will lead it to "the Good".
>
> And we shall no longer be surprised if that which produces these powerful longings is all together free from even intelligible shape; Since the soul also, when she gets an intense love of the One, puts away all the shape which she has, even whatever shape of the intelligible there maybe in her.[64]
>
> One must believe one has seen, when the soul suddenly takes light... for this is from the One. We must think that It is present whom someone called to his house, It comes and brings light to us... So the unenlightened soul does not have It as God, but when she is enlightened she has what she sought and that is the soul's true end to touch that light and see it by itself, not by another light, but by the light which is also her means of seeing. She must see that light by which she is enlightened for we do not see the sun by another light than its own. How can this happen? Take away everything![65]

Drunk on Plotinus' words, it is only when I step out of the cathedral blinking in the sun that I realise what I didn't notice. A ceremony is playing outside for those who didn't catch it inside. This cathedral in the heart of Italian Rome has hosted a Spanish sermon by a priest from Andalusia. Surrounding him are Peruvian worshippers who celebrate the word of Christ dancing in traditional South American Indian style. And finally, they ask for divine grace by holding out their open palms in Islamic style while the crescendo of a European choir with a haunting beauty rises in the background. While these distinctions played out, I didn't notice them because of that momentary flash of complete sensorial dissolvement.

> We are always before The One: but we do not always look: thus a choir singing set in due order about the conductor, may turn away from that centre to which all should attend: let it but face aright and it sings with beauty, present effectively.[66]

In the chapel it was love for oneness that didn't 'other' me, neither did I as a Muslim other myself. We do not know Plotinus' thoughts on Christianity, although Porphyry is quite dismissive of this new faith that had gathered momentum in Rome by the third century. Porphyry's dismissiveness of Christianity seems utterly naïve when one encounters this passage from Edward Gibbon's classic, *The History of the Decline and Fall of the Roman Empire*:

> While the great body (The Roman Empire) was invaded by open violence or undermined by slow decay, a pure and humble religion gently insinuated itself into the minds of men, grew up in silence and obscurity, derived new vigour from opposition, and finally erected the triumphant banner of the Cross on the ruins of the Capitol... Christianity offered

itself to the world an exclusive zeal for the truth and the unity of God... The church still continued to increase its outward splendour....Christianity was most favourably received by the poor and the simple.[67]

But Christianity's rise was not without turbulence. Rome brutally persecuted Christians in all its provinces – feeding them to lions in the Colosseum, trampling them under chariots, and flogging them in icy winters. The horrifying tortures knew no end. St. Sabina was publicly humiliated and beheaded. St George was torn by an iron-toothed wheel, then flung in a burning lime pit while made to wear red-hot shoes. St. Cecilia was locked in a room of burning steam for three days, almost suffocating to death, before being beheaded. Worst of all was the ghastly disembowelling of St. Erasmus. But torture and repression only seemed to strengthen this fledgling faith, its numbers swelling on the back of unspeakable cruelty. Indeed, Christianity also drew its astonishing success from the corrupt Roman society, and its message of equality and kindness surged through the empire as trampled souls hungry for justice and compassion lapped up its philosophical simplicity. Such was its impact that a Greek Christian queen who would bear a son and inject in him an intellectual curiosity for this faith would rise to become Constantine the Great, the first Roman emperor to convert to Christianity in 330 CE, after whom Byzantium would be renamed Constantinople and go onto become the epicentre of what would be known as the Holy Roman Empire. But the most powerful aspect of this faith that a gentle carpenter in Nazareth had spoken about, and that turned the mightiest empire that once savagely opposed it into its greatest defender, would be a word, a feeling, and an emotion. Love.

Love though, wasn't quite so simple, as Porphyry would find out. It was rumoured that he loved a woman who rejected him. Driven to a state of near madness Porphyry attempted suicide. To calm his nerves, in 268 CE, Plotinus sent his devoted student to Sicily only to follow. In Sicily he developed a passionate love for olive orchards and contemplated living out the rest of his years there. I leave for Sicily tomorrow as I attempt to find an olive farm where I will read *The Enneads* and pen down my thoughts, quite like Plotinus did. I leave Rome driving past the Basilica Di San Nicola in Carcere which also houses the temple of Janus in its bottom pit. Stone and pillars from different times merge – a structure devoted to divinity.

Plotinus' restless spirit and constant urge to move from one place to another allowed him to view the world from different perspectives. His detachment from worldly affairs, and in particular his utter disdain for politics, polished his soul. His hero, Plato, had sailed to Sicily three times in search of inspiration and so it is not surprising that Plotinus did the same. In Sicily he was constantly on the move, reading Plato and Aristotle, riding into tiny villages and speaking with simple farmers, writing in orchards, and observing worldly affairs from a distance. In the third century, the island was an integral part of the Roman Empire. Its gorgeous coastline was a garland of dun-coloured Greek temples overlooking the contrasting emerald waters of the Mediterranean, and its sparsely populated countryside resembled a thick carpet of olive trees. This made it the most idyllic place for a man of Plotinus' disposition. Quiet and serene, it was in Sicily that an abundance of flowers from bright red poppies, yellow broom, and purple pansies erupted in spring and summer covering the countryside in a myriad of colour and where the sun never ceased to shine on its juicy lemon trees and drooping grape trellises. Sicily proved to be the paradise where away from the political churnings of Rome, Porphyry under Plotinus' care seems to have found new heart and a re-energised zest for life.

I arrive in Syracuse just before midday on a day when the sun is shining, and winter has just begun its retreat. I lessen my burden by dropping off my luggage at Livingston, a slender hotel elegantly perched on a cliff. Wandering, aimless walking, and daydreaming, I believe, have been my strongest allies while writing this book, for it is only through these that my observations have heightened. I walk through a few narrow streets where the sun struggles to break through, and the sky can only be seen as a slender trail of blue when gazing upwards. Eventually I end up in Ortigia. Further down, the winding streets give some relief by opening into a square. Here, I'm presented with the most delightful sight. A bunch of young boys, some in their early teenage years and others still bouncing single digits, are immersed in a cricket match. Street cricket in India is a religion. I grew up with it. But here in Sicily it seems utterly bizarre at first, but I soon abandon that thought when on closer inspection I realize that the kids have Bangladeshi origins. An instinct that only people of South Asian origin will understand overtakes me and I find myself rushing to them. Seeing me approach they stop playing and send a cold stare my way. But this too changes in a few seconds when I politely ask if I can have a bowl. Toothy smiles break across their faces and the eldest of them hands me a bat instead of a ball. Communication is difficult because they speak only Italian and a bit of Bengali. A few words in Hindi like 'Chalo' (let's start), 'Ball do' (give me the ball) are understood. But the language spoken with fluency between them is Italian.

The best way is to introduce each other by name, which we do, and Hassan the eldest teenager rushes off to the top of his run up while I take guard in front of makeshift stumps. The field is set, and Hassan's teammates begin a coordinated roar. Hassan's run-up reminds me of Michael Holding, the great West Indian paceman. Hassan delivers a vicious inswinger with such pace that my attempted cover drive resembles an ugly inside edged flick. *By God! He's fast*, I think, as Hassan is already standing at the top of his run up ready to come charging in. The next one is a shorter rib cruncher and I barely manage to fend it off. Hassan has a smile from ear to ear and his teammates can't stop cheering him on. Now I realise why he handed me the bat instead of the ball. I'm determined not to make a fool of myself and focus.

From the corner of my eye, I can see a Bangladeshi couple stepping out of a tiny grocery shop. They join the cheering. My eyes focus on Hassan's wrist. *An outswinger this time*, I think aloud. He's going to mix it up. Before I can blink, Hassan's whippy action delivers an inswinger faster than all the previous deliveries and crashes into the stumps through a yawning gap between bat and pad. I'm a goner. Hassan's teammates rush to him as he punches the air in delight. Even the couple that has stepped out of the grocery store seem to have enjoyed Hassan's moment of triumph. The youngest of them all, barely seven years and who's been hanging from a lamppost watching the proceedings, climbs down, and runs past me with his thumb down. Then he swiftly turns to me and gives me his name – 'Imaan' – and gestures for me to come into the grocery shop. The couple standing outside the shop come over and speak to me in broken Hindi. They are Hassan and Imaan's parents who run the small grocery shop. They invite me in for tea and biscuits. We stand around drinking hot beverages and devouring plates of chocolate biscuits. In broken Hindi the parents reveal that eighteen years ago they initially moved from Chittagong to Sicily as street cleaners, and then as plastic toy sellers in the majestic square of the Cathedral of Syracuse. Every night in the square, the father would throw into the dark sky little illuminated purple parachutes that would slowly descend, all the while hoping that someone would buy one – secretly also hoping that his life, too, would get wings. Only last year did they gather the courage to set up this grocery store. For them, this new venture stemmed from entrepreneurial inspiration. They had Hassan and Imaan in Italy and hope to give them a brighter future. The mother calls out to Hassan and Imaan, who have gone back to fiddle with bat and ball, to remind them that it is time for prayer. The boys obey and return to the shop.

I walk along the shoreline, marvelling at the clarity of the emerald waters as they come to rest on the pebbled coast. Soon I turn into the square of the Cathedral of Syracuse and think about the beauty of what I have just encountered: Bangladeshi boys ensconced within an environment where the Cathedral of Syracuse looms large. The cathedral's square, probably one of the most ornate in all of Sicily, stands on the ruins of a fifth-century BCE Greek temple dedicated to Athena – the goddess of wisdom, inspiration, and courage. Its columns, still visible and relatively untouched, tell the tale of how the Greeks viewed humans and the columns. They identified the human being with the characteristics of the column: strong, orderly, proud, erect, and beautiful. The column symbolised the human being, while the human being symbolised life, the intellect, and the human spirit. The Greeks dedicated their many-columned temples not only to the gods, but also to the idea of the human being. The human being was indeed the measure of all things, even of his gods. And just as each column contributed to the support of the whole structure, so each human contributed his support to the whole community. Hassan and Imaan will one day, I hope, become those columns supporting Italian society.

Back on the Ortigia shoreline, I stumble into a cluster of blue wooden chairs and tables strewn across the edge of the street. A sunset bottle of red wine under the pink sky overlooking the Mediterranean is an ideal way of finishing off the first day in Sicily. The last thoughts for the evening are of the innocence of those boys and from the Upanishads:

> So then after that the Brahman has rejected learning, he abides in childhood.... He sought not after the knowledge of books, which only gives rise to words without end, before whom words and thought recoil, not finding him.[68]

The next morning, I drive out along the coast working my GPS and with the purpose of finding an olive farm from where I can read and write. I detour into the countryside, driving past rolling vineyards. Silent valleys and hills draped in grapes stretch out as far as the eye can see. Intermittently, orange orchards and date palms make an appearance. Sicilian farmers on horseback ride through the narrow avenues inspecting their vineyards with great attention. After a brief stopover in Caltagirone for lunch and a quick visit to the Ceramics Museum where Arab tile influence is showcased with great pride as Sicilian heritage, I drive back towards the coast and make my way northwards passing Gela and Lucata. From here on for miles and miles is quiet olive country drenched in brilliant sunshine.

Azienda Agricola Mandranova is an olive farm in Agrigento. The farm is encrusted halfway on a large rocky hill. Built in the terrace farming style the sloping farm is most inviting, and I'm overjoyed when I'm told I can have a basic farm room for my stay. For the next two days, I decide to partake in spartan meals of olive, bread, and dates, quite like Plotinus did. I have arrived at sunset after a four-hour drive, and I make my way up the hill from where the sweeping views of swaying slender olive branches merge with the Mediterranean. When Porphyry was in Sicily and before Plotinus arrived, the philosopher sent his student some of his works to edit. They included On Providence, On Happiness, and On Love. Leather wrapped, these works were brought by couriers who sailed in fishing boats and arrived at these shores, then made their way into the hills to deliver them to Porphyry. Standing atop hills like these, Porphyry's sad eyes must have looked out into the Mediterranean eagerly awaiting those boats carrying his teacher's words. I make my way into one of the dense olive groves and settle under a tree. The tree I've chosen is ancient. Its thick, twisting, and aged trunk seems to speak a universally understood language of wisdom. I feel as if I am sitting at the feet of a sage. The wind picks up. There is nothing quite as beautiful as the rustle of olive and bamboo branches when a breeze passes through them. Slim and delicate they sway in the wind, emanating the softest of rustles. A fragile dance ensues between branch, leaves, and breeze, each caressing the other with gentleness and love. Porphyry's fragile state of mind was like the olive branches and Plotinus' words, the caressing breeze urging him to understand that true love is for the beauty of the formless. In one of the most dazzling descriptions of love, matter, and the soul's craving for divine beauty, Plotinus with these words lays bare his own sparkling soul:

> In the higher world the Good (The One) itself doesn't need beauty, though beauty needs It. Beauty brings wonder and

shock and pleasure mingled with pain. It even draws those who do not know what is happening away from the Good.[69] The soul only becomes desirable when the Good colours it, giving a kind of grace.[70] What is primarily beautiful, is formless; and beauty is the nature of the Good (The One). Matter (physical form) is furthest away (from The One). If then, that which is love is not matter then we must posit Beauty to be formless. Since the soul sought Beauty, it would exchange nothing in place of Beauty not even the whole universe. Even if other things around the soul was destroyed (riches, power, sciences) the soul could be alone with Beauty.[71]

In the sensible world all those who love, fashion themselves into a likeness of the person they love. In this way the soul loves the Good, because it was moved to love from the beginning. And the soul which has this love is always searching, because it wants to be carried towards the Good. It despises things in the sensible world because it sees that they are flesh and bodies and defiled by their present habitation. Love here is limited.[72] ... The Good (The One) is the principle of beauty. When you are self-gathered in the purity of your being, nothing now remaining that can shatter that inner unity. When you perceive that you have grown to this: now call up your confidence, strike forward yet a step- you need a guide no longer-strain and see. This is the only eye that sees the mighty Beauty.[73]

One can only imagine the impact these words must have had on Porphyry. After a dinner of bread dipped in locally made olive oil, I sleep soundly.

The next day reveals the full splendour of the farm. Sprawling before my eyes are date palms, their branches drooping with bountiful fruit. The view is a festival of riotous colour as each tree trunk rises from the earth. The trunks' brown scaled skin transforms into resplendent green stems and palm leaves shaped like razors, from which emerge sun-loved yellow branches at the end of which are bunches of sun ripened dates, some in a deep velvet red, others in luminous ochre, all of which are set against a light blue Sicilian sky.

Through the branches of this never-ending canopy of trees the sun peeps and disappears like an inquisitive and mischievous child, leaving glowing patterns on the moist soil. Each tree is a unity in its own; the date orchard merges into the olive groves and walking through these lonely avenues of beautiful trees is how I decide to spend most of the morning and afternoon. The formlessness of true beauty that Plotinus wrote about and urged Porphyry to understand takes me to Plato's monumental philosophical achievement, one that influenced not just Aristotle and Plotinus but even Christianity and Islam – the Theory of Forms. 'The theory asserts that in the familiar world all the objects that exist have no real existence at all. All the substance and matter, including planets and human bodies, are merely reflections of a true reality. This true reality exists eternally, is unchanging, and lies behind and completely outside the world of space and time. This true reality is completely inaccessible to sensory apprehension of any kind, but through the use of our intellect we can achieve some measure of communion with that Supreme Reality.'[74]

Initially dismissed as utter madness, it was only with the passage of time that Plato's remarkable work received attention both by philosophers and men driven by science. Plotinus used this theory for the basis of his theory of the One being eternal and, although immanent in everything, standing *beyond being* as we understand being, and emphasising that Its immanence in everything is only a pseudo-reflection of It. But then those reflections or images would be unity too. This means everything is a unity as a reflection of the true unity, including us humans – visually brilliantly attempted by Michelangelo in his 'Creation of Adam' where man is created by God as His image.

As I stroll for hours through the date and olive orchard listening to the sweet song of the Sicilian Blackbird Merlo, while the sun continues to peep and disappear through the branches, Plato's theory comes to life. The date tree has manifested itself to my eye in many perceived realities – trunk, leaves, branches, and fruit. But there is another reality that, as Plato points out, is beyond the comprehension of senses – the root. It lies in a world of its own – underground. There, the root is single, indivisible, is the cause of life, and is invisible to the eye. All that is overground (which is another realm), including branches, leaves, and fruit, are only a reflection of the hidden root. If I were to dig at the base of the trunk, find the root, and observe its functioning and the realm it inhabits, I would find it teeming with another kind of reality. In this world, fungi come together and work as one in brilliant cohesion through a mycorrhizal network connecting individual plant roots together and transfer water, carbon, nitrogen, and other nutrients and minerals between trees, providing nutrition to each tree and healing the soil. Yet, this reality lies hidden from our immediate senses. But most importantly, this 'hidden underground realm' existed much before the date that I am about to pick and pop in my mouth, came into existence overground. In the same way, Plato emphasises that the true meaning to words like justice, beauty, and courage existed long before in another realm before they became latent in soul, which then entered body (matter), which inhabits this empirical world.

After a strolling lunch of delicious dates and olives, I drive out of the farm towards Selinunte – the Greek temple dedicated to Greek goddess Hera, and one that Porphyry loved. Perched on top of an East facing hill that slopes into the Mediterranean, Selinunte to me is a distant and forlorn voice that carries with it Porphyry's great sense of melancholy. For it was in Sicily and quite possibly at Selinunte that Plotinus and Porphyry met each other for the last time. Rome had a new emperor – Gallienus (r. 253–268 CE). The emperor and his wife Salonia revered Plotinus and wanted him back in Rome to teach philosophy with the noble intent that Rome would have philosopher emperors in the future. Plotinus' departure from Sicily must have left an enormous vacuum in Porphyry's life. Standing on the hill watching Plotinus sail away and disappear into the horizon, Porphyry must have felt as if his soul had departed. He would not see the man that healed his wounded heart again.

It is the sheer stillness of Selinunte that resounds with Plotinian philosophy. Quite like the momentary desertion of thought I felt in the Ibn Tulun Mosque, I feel the same abandonment as I walk towards this deserted temple. Only the sound of chirping sparrows accompanies my footsteps which navigate rocks and shrub scattered across the hill. The history of Selinunte vanishes from the realm of activated thought and is replaced by a stillness like its quiet columns. Sitting between these columns soaking up its poignant beauty amidst roaring silence, there is nothing to do but recite from *The Enneads*.

> Keeping quiet, it (mind) busies itself no more, but contemplates having arrived at unity... don't chase after the One but wait quietly as it appears... as the eye awaits the rising sun....[75]

At the edge of the stone steps, a swaying wild lavender attracts a bee. A sign that spring is near. As soon as the bee begins sucking for nectar, it falls silent. Enriched, it flies away. Rustling wild grass and shrubs, the temple's companions since centuries fall silent as the wind drops. The sun on the horizon sinks into the emerald waters, bathing everything in mellow gold with its last gasp. The sky, an infinite divine canvas that had held the sun as a mere flame within it, replaces it with a rising moon. Shaped like a sickle, the moon's slanting beams slowly flood the temple in silver light. It's just me and these moments of spectacular silence. The silence is so profound that in my subconscious I'm faintly aware of entering a semi hypnotic space. I feel the world retreating. Surrounded by matter – stone, shrub, moon, and body – the soul is still. In this stillness, the soul becomes the monastery of solitude. A desire rises for communion with Plato's Supreme Reality which lies behind everything my senses perceive. Then there is more silence. It is only when a sparrow with its last chirp retires for the night in a crevice in the temple that I make my way out. Back at the farm lying in bed with the faint rustle of olive branches, I realise how lucky I have been to have had Selinunte all for myself. Those moments, no small treasure.

The next morning, bidding the farm farewell, I drive further North, continuing to skirt the Sicilian coastline and meandering into the town of Mazara del Vallo. The proximity of Mazara del Vallo to the Tunisian coast is such that on a quiet night, African drumbeats can be heard. It was on the soft sands of Mazara del Vallo that a small band of Muslim Arab soldiers sailing up from Tunisia landed in 827 CE. What brought the Arabs into Sicily was the case of Euphemius – a Byzantine fleet commander who was recalled to Constantinople for eloping with a nun.[76] Rumour had it that Euphemius lavished the poor nun with such incessant lust that she finally gave in. Enraged by the ignominy he suffered, Euphemius rebelled against Constantinople for sacking him and invited the Arabs to help him retake Sicily. Within a few years the Arabs had taken all of Sicily. The

Arab rule between 827–1091 CE left an indelible influence on the island, particularly in Palermo, their capital. The Arabs brought art, architecture, sophisticated administration methods, and terraced farming irrigation techniques that added to the productivity of the land. Thanks to the Arabs, citrus fruit, fig trees, and sugarcane swayed in the Sicilian breeze, and the study of Greek philosophy continued to flourish uninterrupted in village and mountain schools. Courtyard gardens embellished with indigo tiles, delicate fountains, and lined with lemon and tangerine trees lured Arab musicians to string the sweetest notes from their Ouds, and tambourines elevating the atmospheric charm of Sicilian life like never before. Ferocious infighting, though, amongst the Arabs weakened them, and Sicily split into various warring Arab fiefdoms. The Normans saw this as an opportunity, and when invited by Ibn al Timnah the Emir of Syracuse to battle a rival Emir they did so unhesitatingly. By 1091 CE the Normans had replaced the Arabs as the new masters of Sicily.

After years of bloody Norman-Arab conflict with power being the coveted wine cup, the dust of 'othering' settled and the quiet hills of Sicily experienced tranquillity yet again. This is when the most exquisite Norman-Arab culture unfolded under the reign of Roger II (r. 1130–1154 CE) and his grandson Frederick II (r. 1197–1250 CE). Enchanted by the Arab legacy in Sicily both rulers became fluent in Arabic, encouraged Arabic literature, and their courts became flourishing gardens of knowledge where the fragrance of Latin, Greek, and Arab culture mingled freely.[77] Under Roger II, administration and the army continued to be dominated by Arabs, while the navy was dominated by the Greeks. Such was Roger II's love for everything Arabic that on the death of one of his sons he had an elegy composed by the poet Abu al-Daw who found inspiration in Quranic verses:

Does the horror of death snatch him away, deceitfully, unexpectedly. How treacherous death is.

It cast a shadow over the face of the moon,
And just as it reached full illumination its glow was dimmed
Its only natural that tears be shed over him, tears like pearl and coral trickle down the cheek
And their hearts were rent, not the sleeves of their robes, the nightingales chanted 'To God we return as minds and hearts trembled.[78]

Roger's grandson Frederick II displayed similar virtues. An Arab poet in his flowing robes accompanied by Jewish and Roman poets reciting verses in Frederick's multi-arched Islamic style court set amidst the lingering scent of orange blossom would not have been an unfamiliar sight. It was in his court that the Arabic 'muwashahat' poetry inspired the birth of the sonnet. But greed to secure power and the fear of losing it – both emanating from intellect shattered Sicily's fragile tranquillity. On one hand, the Arabs, unable to stomach the imagined ignominy of being ruled by a Christian, revolted, and made a strong attempt to regain dominance over the island under the leadership of a Muslim woman known as Virago of Entella. On the other hand, Pope Innocent IV, fearing the rising popularity of Frederick, declared him the predecessor of the Antichrist, a heretic of Saracen custom and a friend of the Sultan of Babylon. The Pope would soon follow this up by excommunicating Frederick. In 1220 CE, Frederick responded by deporting the already dwindling Muslim population of Sicily to Lucera in Southern Italy. Under the pretext of giving them a safe haven, Frederick put the colony under strict supervision. While they could practise their faith and regale in their culture, they could not play an active part outside the colony. High walls were erected around their colony, and they couldn't venture out. It was sugar-coated imprisonment. In Lucera, having brought with them a love for the arts, the Muslims moulded clay to perfection, producing the most exquisite ceramics. Huddled in a cluster behind high walls, living in constant fear of the unknown, their hands created the most exquisite Arabesque vases, pots, and wall decorations. There seems to be a sense of guilt that Frederick felt, and to show how much he trusted the Muslims of Lucera he appointed 600 of them as his personal bodyguards. But what happened to the Muslims after Frederick is not entirely clear. Some write about a slaughter under the orders of Charles II in 1300 CE, others write about their forceful conversion to Christianity and being sold into slavery, and yet others put it down to a deportation to North Africa.

Verses by Ibn Hamdis, a poet who was forced to leave Sicily albeit prior to Frederick II, speaks of the pain of separation from the island:

> When she approaches at night, I extend my cheek in joy, and I greet her with a kiss on the hand.
> I enjoin my affections to her soul, so that they may cool the burning of a broken heart. She strokes my face with the palm of her hand like an enchantress, and her veil is like a bouquet of sweet scented flowers moistened with dew.
> I recognise her approach by the whiff of her sweet aromas just as a patient recognises a physician among his visitors
> What is it with me that I endure a long estrangement from my homeland?
> Have I been born fated to live in exile?
> Forever shall I squander my resolve in a distant land, for a hope only to be dispersed in faraway place?[79]

I find myself relishing a chicken tagine at a restaurant in a small kasbah in the Arab section of Mazara del Vallo. Nestled by the Mazara River, a clutch of mud and stone houses have sprung up. The origins of these houses are the same as the ones once lived in by the Arabs of Sicily in the time of Frederick II. Almost instantly one is transported to medieval times. Living in them today are Tunisian migrant fishermen who, after more than 800 years, have made a re-appearance. The winding, narrow streets of the Kasbah are embellished with Arabic art and coloured majolica. The tiny wooden doors painted in bright green, magenta, and cobalt, whisper a story about the gentle return of a vanished culture. Walking through these twisting lanes where some Arab men resting against the mud walls spring to their feet on hearing the faint call of a muezzin funnelling through, I wonder if some of them still carry the story of Frederick II in their hearts. A story of a man who loved their culture, but also of one who sent them to their doom.

Onto Palermo. I only manage to get into the city after an unnerving hour, having almost run out of petrol in Corleone – a remote countryside province. For all its beauty, this part of Sicily arouses uneasiness just by its name. True to it, there is a menacing silence that sits in Corleone, and it is no wonder that Francis Ford Coppola chose it as the family name for the protagonist of the greatest mafia film ever made. After whirling around in circles and with my GPS surrendering to the Corleone factor, it is with sheer luck that I managed to roll into a petrol station with only a few drops of fuel left. The unmanned, dilapidated petrol station seemed wrecked by time, and I was only pleased to see it disappear in my rear-view mirror after it served up what it had to.

I arrive in Palermo and make my way to meet my friend, Andrea Lo Bue, who has invited me to spend a few days in his beautiful house. Soft spoken and erudite, Andrea has a great passion for Arab Sicily. I'm given a generous room in his palazzo at the centre of which is a stunning rosewood four-poster bed surrounded by renaissance art hanging from pistachio walls.

After a day spent resting from all the driving, I wander the streets of Palermo, admiring the buildings built by the Spanish Bourbon kings of Sicily between 1734 and 1860. Self-adulation manifests itself in life-size sculptures of kings carved into the facades of buildings, arrogantly surveying us mortals walking below in their sprawling shadows. The next day Andrea informs me of a wonderful invitation to visit a princess for lunch. Having virtually starved myself on the self-inflicted Plotinian diet, I welcome this invitation. We drive out to the nearby town of Bagheria and make our way through narrow winding roads where bougainvillaea overflow above mud walls, hiding elegant baroque homes. A few moments later, a large door swings open and in front of us lies Villa Valguarnera – Sicily's most majestic stately home. With its gold bordered walls, glorious baroque architecture, and sprawling gardens, Villa Valguarnera is a marvel. Red haired and elegant, Vittoria Alliata, the scion of one of Italy's oldest noble families, greets us warmly. But almost immediately, I can sense a deep-seated resilience inhabiting her. As we stroll around her exquisite villa, with wafts of fabulous sea food coming my way, my hunger pangs are only diverted when Vittoria's multi-dimensional personality comes to the fore. Most aristocrats are insufferable bores, consumed only by their fading grandeur, but Vittoria is fantastically different. An accomplished academic having studied Arabic history in Lebanon, she has travelled extensively in Arabia and Iran, driven by a zest to understand the life of Muslim women. But her greatest literary achievement is the translation into Italian of J.R.R. Tolkein's *Lord of the Rings*. Vittoria was also responsible for organising the first seminar in the western world on the teachings of Ibn Al Arabi, the Sufi mystic

The sweeping views from the palace grounds, glittering chandelier grandeur, and a sumptuous lunch including shrimps, caviar, and sea bass which I devour with gluttony all fade in comparison to Vittoria's fabulous tale of survival. The mafia has been targeting her house and ancestral lands for years. Presuming that a single lady in her seventies would be easy picking, the mafia has been relentless in its pursuit of possessing Vittoria's home. Vittoria, though, has dug her heels in and refused to budge from her home. She simply refuses to leave. During an after-lunch walk we climb a hill from where we get a majestic view of her lands. In her mind is a single-minded belief for doing good, as her house hosts charity affairs for the underprivileged and art exhibitions for the unheard and unsung creative people of her region struggling to make a living. Her house and her heritage are her dignity, and that the mafia has failed to snatch them from her bears testimony to her determination. Today, amidst political intrigue and the churning of the mafia, Vittoria stands tall, sparkling with valour.

My last day in Palermo is spent doing what I love doing: walking and searching for places where unity can speak its unique language through architecture. I find it while visiting the Palazzo del Cuba and the Palazzo della Zisa, where Islamic muqarnas designed like honeycombs and Christian frescos merge in unison, transforming the environs into silent cradles meant only for whispering angels. But it is only in the Palatine Chapel that the beauty of unity brought about by the cross-pollination of craftsmanship comes to rest with me. Built in 1132 CE by Roger II, this chapel has been touched by a magician's wand. It was here that the Islamic muqarnas were used for the first time in Europe. As Christ draped in an indigo robe looks down from his elevated position amidst glistening golden arches, Islamic tile work in maroon, emerald green, and white adorn his presence. On the carved wooden ceiling, clusters of four, eight pointed stars typical of Fatimid design come together to form a cross. The mosaics in dull gold, copper, and blue bring alive the magic of enquiring intellect as Roger's gaze, and robes speak of him as a lover of everything Arabic. Such is the aura this place inspires that to the eye and mind, time has tied Christianity and Islam in a unifying love knot, never to be separated. Here in this microcosm of space and time there is only the beauty of unity. According to Aristotle, the whole may have many parts, but here, the 'many' melt away and only the whole remains in its true essence – here, in Plotinus' words, I see 'The Mighty Beauty'. Resting high in the chapel's ceiling, those Fatimid stars to me are Hassan and Imaan, tied in a love knot for Italy. For without the Fatimid stars the Palatine Chapel is incomplete, and I hope in time that without the likes of Hassan and Imaan, Italy would be incomplete, for in the future one of those boys could well become the captain of Italy's fledgling cricket team. Although he spoke about loving the formless, Plotinus would have loved standing here.

I leave Sicily tomorrow having seen the Island's majestic and bloody past. What if Sicily could ask a question of its past rulers, be it Greek, Roman, Byzantine, Arab, Norman or Spanish?

Sicily: Was it only when you gripped power that you accepted the one who lived in my embrace before you?

Roger II: If there hadn't been conquest could the beauty of the Palatine Chapel come to be?

And how would Sicily answer that? Quite possibly, through this poem I write while sitting in a cafe looking at the Palatine Chapel:

> See me as a garland into which thee came
> Roaming my misty forests, yearning for sun kissed harvests and fame
> The love which I returned draping my hills in grape and sugar for thee
> Did that love not suffice? Its beauty did you not see?
> But turned thee away from me and instead built ornate mansions of morality
> Be tranquil now all my kings, for you lie in my garden, thy kingship silent
> My spring waters still sweet, my birdsong still melodious and free

> - M. M

My last thoughts in Sicily are of the *azaan* in the tiny kasbah in Mazara della Vallo which calls the poor Tunisian fishermen to prayer. Will majoritarian politics extinguish it? Its smothering would be the end of something beautiful that is just beginning to flower. For these people with their majolica colours, wall paintings, and street ceramics are not here for conquest, but simply to better their lives and add to the beauty of Sicily. It is an opportunity to embrace. A fortunate situation not stemming from greed of land or power but for dignity. May no wall of distinction 'other' the kasbah, for there was a wall that divided a continent and its people for decades. I will stand before it. In Berlin.

# 5

# WORLD OF WALLS

The sun glistens on a dew drop resting on a scarlet petal. It also glistens on a tear drop gliding down a pale cheek. The woman standing next to me wipes that tear drop, places the scarlet at the bottom of a rubble, and walks away, her pretty feet in simple shoes wobbling on the dirt while her head rests on a man's shoulder. The ugly debris, some mangled rectangular chunks of cement and stone, others small concrete slabs painted with graffiti, is all that is left of the Berlin Wall – a man-made monstrosity which once stood as the defining symbol of division controlling the destiny of millions. A few metres before me is 'Checkpoint Charlie'. I walk towards it and peep in. It is a dingy little white cabin with a single leather chair squeezed in. I am standing before the tiniest gateway ever made to the simplest, yet most profound calling felt by all of humankind – freedom. It is freedom that unites. It is an inexplicable natural urge. Freedom and love are the two guiding principles that bring about unity. Young men, women, and children, driven by freedom's eternal promise of unity, leapt, climbed, crawled, and scratched their way to get to the other side of the wall. Most were shot, many electrocuted, and the survivors that hung like scarecrows from barbed wires were flung in jails. The scarlet that lies at the rubble and the wiped tear is the measure of those times.

With the end of the Second World War in 1945, Germany was divided between the Soviet controlled East and the American controlled West. The wall itself was built in 1961 but its origins were, as Plotinus would put it, in the desire to '*possess everything*' characteristic of the intellect and the '*fall of the soul*'. Both these lurked in a man of dismissive physicality but who was endowed with charisma and enormous vigour. Adolf Hitler's intellect, when it mobilised, united Germany in a way the world has yet to witness. Intellect wormed its way into souls and turned a natural love for one's country into an insecurity. Urging his countrymen to love their nation and at the same time recognise its greatest imagined threat – a prospering minority, Hitler transformed patriotism into a weapon against his own and his neighbours. Wherever he went, mass hysteria gripped men and women who showered him with love. Intellect had enslaved love. With the country united behind him and drenching him in love, he became the scourge of humanity. Gas chambers, firing squads, mass graves, and Auschwitz were the result of Hitler's rampaging intellect that gorged on the frenzied adulation bestowed on him.

The words of Anton Chekov, Russia's greatest playwright, could not have found a better example when he wrote: 'Love, friendship and respect do not unite people as much as a common hatred for something.' As the Soviet Union and United States divided the country into East and West Germany following Hitler's defeat at the hands of a United Allied force, the Berlin Wall became the iron curtain on either side of which lived two political ideologies. And yet when division seemed to have become an accepted norm, after twenty-eight years the German people rose as one and tore down the wall in 1989. Germany reunited as one people and one nation. Today a united Germany is at the forefront of economic growth, prosperity, and, until the end of Angela Merkel's chancellorship, a beacon of compassionate politics, welcoming in more than a million refugees, encouraging the return of Jews (including the orthodox Hassidic Jews that I witnessed on my flight to Berlin), becoming the pivot for the European Union, and in many ways challenging Chekov's words. Plotinus did not visit Germany, but for me to understand the power of oneness, the force of division, and the execution of the free will of intellect that Plotinus spent most of his life exploring, there is no better place than Berlin.

Orhan, my taxi driver, is quite recognisably a Turk.

'Which part of Turkey are you from, Orhan?' I ask.

'Iznik.'

'Ah, where they make the most amazing tiles.'

'Yes, that's right.... You've been?'

'No, not to Iznik, but I have travelled a fair bit in your country.'

'In Germany?'

'No, I meant Turkey.'

'Oh... when you said "your country", I thought you were talking about Germany... I've lived my whole life here.... This is my country you know....'

'No, I don't know... what do you mean?'

'Turks are the largest migrant population of this country and I'm second generation... so this is home.'

'Don't you visit Turkey?'

'Once in five years or so.'

'So, you feel German?'

'No.'

'No? I'm confused.'

'I love Turkish food... German food is so bad.'

'Hah! You're right.'

'But seriously sir, Germany has been good to us... See, it was Ugur Sahin and Ozlem Tureci who invented the Covid vaccine. They are Turks... German Turks. I mean if Germany would not have given them the opportunity to settle here and start their company, where would the world be? They saved the world!'

'Very true, Orhan... very true... their company teamed up with US-based Pfizer to create this brilliant vaccine.... It is all about coming together and doing good stuff!'

'Yes, yes, I agree,' he says, looking at me in the rear-view mirror.

'Do you read about the ongoings in Turkey?' I ask.

'Yes... I don't know why the Hagia Sophia had to be converted into a mosque? So many mosques in Istanbul. There was no need, you know.'

'Hmm.'

'I worry about the impact on us here. We are Muslim Turks in a Christian country; people will look at Turks differently now... as if we are only thinking about religion.'

'Don't worry, Orhan, you have the examples of Ugur Sahin and Ozlem Tureci to hold onto.'

'That's right, sir.' A big smile breaks on his face.

I pay Orhan his dues and make my way into my hotel. I'm in Berlin just for a day and I can sense a heaviness hanging over the city which is easily explained by its violent past. Somewhere close by, as the Russians and the Allied Forces closed in on him, Hitler shot himself in 1945. I banish the thought in favour of the glittering lights of a modern city that have just made an evening appearance. I leave the hotel almost as soon as I've arrived and head off to Paris Bar in Charlottenburg, a restaurant in the 'cool' part of Berlin, for an early supper. Sitting at the bar, I order a glass of German red. This part of Berlin is abuzz with a fantastic variety of restaurants, wine bars, and live music shows.

But one must just observe closely, and the East-West differences come to the fore as I find out overhearing a conversation in English between an Englishman and a German both aged in their mid-thirties. The conversation begins with Brexit. The German regales in his childhood moments when he would cycle through villages and unknowingly cycle into Austrian villages without any border checks. He rejoices in the power of the EU, where even today a European cyclist can, on the strength of the simplest movement of his legs, travel from Berlin to Lisbon without a visa and pick up a job as a waiter or a director of a museum on the Atlantic coast. He is quite obviously doing so to make the Englishman wallow in regret over Brexit. The Englishman quite typically listens and gesticulates only with a raised eyebrow and a shrug, the meaning of which is difficult to decipher. Then, the conversation veers closer to home and the cultural vibe of Berlin. The German who, till a few seconds ago was illustrating the beauty of unity and who is quite obviously from the West part of town, doesn't hesitate for a second in calling the Easterners 'Ossie', which comes from the word 'Osten' meaning East. 'Ossie' is a derogatory term for Berliners with their origins in East Berlin, the once less prosperous part of the city. Quite abrasive in his dislike for the 'Ossie', the West Berliner chugs down his beer, mocks at their unrefined past, and quite unabashedly elevates himself to a station of superiority.

When the wall stood, American controlled West Berlin was the more advanced part of the city. It had access to everything Western from Coca-Cola to rock bands and from being the hub of car manufacturing, including BMW and

Audi, to putting out Olympic champions. On the other hand, Soviet controlled East Berlin was a completely different world where Germans couldn't buy German made cars or even a can of Coca-Cola. They had no voting rights and were subjected to a life of constant state monitoring. This explains the air of superiority a Berliner with origins in the Western part of the city carries with him. There is a casual rudeness to this part of town where it's considered rather hip to not give you a table at the time you've booked or to be quite brazen about your order; but this is the new Berlin. Bold, confident, and the striking opposite of the previous generation which cowed down in 'collective guilt' – an emotion that had sprung from the deeds of the generation that preceded them.

## From the Wall of Division to the Wall of Oneness

Winter has vanished. Framed like Monet's water colours, Europe blooms. Spring, 2022.

Apollo, the handsomest and bravest of all Greek gods, resides in the soaring mountainous ravines of Delphi. Given to music and healing, Apollo looms large over Greek mythology and psyche. Bold and mighty it was he who slew the python, the symbol of whispering cunning. The ancient Greeks considered Delphi the centre of the world – its navel where the oracle resided and interpreted prophesies and beseeched the Gods on behalf of the people. The oracle, though, was lured into temptation and captured by the python. As the ancient Greeks trembled in fear, Apollo challenged the python. Delphi's remote mountains, gorges, and ravines shuddered as God and demon engaged in ferocious battle. Dust clouds as high as the mountains rose and covered all of Delphi in a blanket of haze. From this haze emerged Apollo in the middle of a gorge, every sinew stretched while stringing his bow for a final shot at the python, which too, rising menacingly, readied itself for a last strike. But it was the God's arrow that brought down the python in the gorge and freed the oracle. Since that victory of good over evil, Apollo was worshipped at Delphi with numerous temples being erected in his glory even before the fifth century BCE – the most intriguing of temples being one allegedly built by bees in wax.

Standing at the summit of an amphitheatre that had been carved out of a mountain, below me are sweeping views of ravines draped in Greek fir and pine trees. Further below, rocky gorges gape heavenwards in silence while an ambling river curls its way in a valley of cypress trees completing the pictorial setting of the epic battle between Apollo and the python. To my left rising from ruin are the lofty, roofless columns of the temple of Apollo, and to my right is the well-preserved Athenian treasury where donations and sacrificial animals that poured in from devotees across Greece found storage. The treasury was built in 490 BCE to commemorate Greek victory over the Persians at Marathon. It is believed that the message of victory was brought by a single man who arrived in Delphi having run all the way from Marathon. And thus, the name for long distance running.

Walking down the summit of the mountain I pass the amphitheatre. Here, voices once echoed cheering on poets and sportsmen as the Pythia games including wrestling, boxing, and pentathlon played out in honour of Apollo's victory. One admirer of this temple who would have been conspicuous with his cheering was Aristotle. He visited Delphi regularly and enjoyed the celebrations and games immensely, in particular the Hymn to Apollo that was sung by the sweetest voice in all of Greece standing at the edge of the open-air amphitheatre against the backdrop of swooping valleys and drifting clouds. In the distance, towering above all stood the remarkable Sphinx of Naxos on a 40-foot column. Influenced by the Sphinx at Giza, the Sphinx of Naxos is a blend of a woman's head, lionesses' body, and wings of a bird bringing together virtues of varied creatures into one symbol of might, elegance, and intellect. The Greeks, as we have seen earlier, brought in elements of Egyptian art into their creations and unhesitatingly adopted Egyptian thought and style.

But by far the most fascinating and uplifting part of the temple is a wall which I have named the 'wall of oneness'. Running across the front of the temple is a horizontal wall in honey-coloured stone. Inscribed on the wall are names of slaves that were freed either for good conduct or for their accomplishments at the Pythian games. These engraved names aren't just alphabets that come together to form a name but alphabets that came together to mean an emotion – freedom. When the inscriber sat down and engraved each alphabet with a chisel, the thrill that sprang in the slave's heart as he watched his name being inscribed meant only one thing – freedom. At this point the essence of a word that once meant his name melted away and was replaced by a new essence – freedom. Rushing forth from the temple, that man or woman was simply 'free'. Free to become one with society.

Although Plotinus didn't give any importance to his life before Rome, it is obvious that his Greek ancestry shaped his thinking. His passion for the works of Plato and Aristotle and the fact that he spoke and wrote only in Greek is evidence of his love for his Greek heritage. And although he never visited Greece, it was the breeze that blew across the Mediterranean carrying the words of Plato and Aristotle that inspired him to study philosophy. I am in Greece to simply absorb. Having tasted a delicious slice of Greek mythology which included Apollo himself, I head out for Athens. The two-and-a-half-hour drive from Delphi to Athens takes me through jagged mountains and wildflower meadows where swaying sun facing yellow chrysanthemums and daisies dance under the stoic cypress trees. Driving into Athens I check into Shila Athens, a small, charming hotel with a focus on art and ceramics. An early supper on the tiny terrace surrounded by ceramics made by young Athenian artists settles me well for an early night.

The next morning, I find myself sitting under the shade of a pomegranate tree. The freshness of morning dew is on every blade of grass illumined into a fluorescent green by the soft morning sun. As far as the eye can see, crimson poppies peer out of the wild field, attracting a few fluttering butterflies. Judas trees with their blooming lilac flowers enmeshed with olive trees seem to regale in a sweet spring song. Under clusters of shade, tulips in candy colours bloom. Looming in the distance on a hilltop is the Acropolis. I could be forgiven to think that I've chanced upon the Garden of Eden, but in actuality, this is Aristotle's academy in the Lyceum.

Bereft of any visitors (most of whom throng to the Acropolis), this wild field dotted with ruined walls, is holy ground. Rising from under the pomegranate tree, I decide to do what the master enjoyed most – walking. Aristotle taught his students while strolling through these fields. His greatest ideas came to him while engaging in the simplest of activities – walking. The stone ruins of the academy lie silent but the profundity of thought that came out of here would resonate for millennia across continents, oceans, empires, villages, and modern states. The robustness, insightfulness, and incisiveness of Aristotelian thought would inform sociology, theology, politics, science, art, music, and even individual souls with such force that his name would become synonymous with any intellectual pursuit. It was from here that he wrote *Ethics, Politics, Metaphysics, Physics and Logic*. Aristotle as a young student of philosophy studied under the greatest teacher of his time – Plato. It was under Plato's tutelage that Aristotle found his own voice and developed his own theories, many of which contested Plato's. Inspired by Plato's Academy in Athens, Aristotle set up his own.

While walking through the dancing poppies, the intimacy one experiences with Aristotle is captivating. It is almost as if one can ask him a question and he will answer through the silence of your mind. The walls of division, slavery, and 'othering' have been bearing heavy on me. In response, the mind plays out the master's own words:

> Whiteness or blackness in a man does not produce any difference, nor is there a specific difference in a white man as against a black man. Nor would there be even if a single name was introduced for each. For it is as matter that man is here introduced, and matter does not produce a differentia.... This (belief) is the ultimate, the indivisible.... Man is only accidently white.[80]

The sun's ascendance reaches its peak, which gets me thinking about lunch and 'The Feast of Plato'– a celebration which Plotinus enjoyed, over wine, grapes, and food. This celebration was inspired by Plato's epic *The Symposium*, where Plato, in an imaginary dialogue between his master Socrates and Phaedrus, explores the philosophical meaning of love. After Plato's death, his birthday was marked as 'The Feast of Plato' by many philosophers who wanted to honour his life and it became a tradition in Athens and Rome for centuries. It isn't Plato's birthday, and neither do I have a banquet to attend. But I am in Athens and feel an urge to go to Plato's Academy. Its legendary beauty inspired artists to create imaginary frescos, mosaics, and paintings of it, the most famous being the one by Raphael that graces the Vatican called 'The School of Athens.' I leave the Lyceum and make my way to the nearest wine shop.

A bottle of red in hand, some grapes and cheese, and I jump into a taxi. The Akademia as it was known was founded by Plato in 387 BCE outside the main walls of Athens in an olive grove. Plato was born into an aristocratic Greek family that was active in politics. Athens in the fourth century BCE was the heartbeat of democracy. Growing up in a politically charged environment, Plato was in the thick of it. He observed closely how politicians manipulated, lied, and betrayed with ease and impunity. Once they had acquired power the politicians did little for the people, instead sowed seeds of division, waged war, and 'othered' just to sustain power. Sickened and unimpressed by them and their lust for power, Plato retreated outside Athens. There, he met his mentor Socrates who taught and moulded him philosophically with probing discourses on courage, justice, virtue, love, and the nature of ethical standards. Socrates, though, was found guilty of not worshipping the multitude of Greek Gods and instigating Athenian youths. For his alleged misdeeds he was sentenced to death by poisoning. This had an enormous impact on Plato, who set up the Akademia far away from the city so that philosophy and the study of it wouldn't be tainted by politicians. He did hope though that in the future the Akademia would influence politicians and give Athens philosophical rulers. After a 45-minute drive I am dropped off outside a secluded olive grove. Through the green I can see rust-coloured ruins, and I rush in holding on cautiously to the wine bottle.

It is utterly uninhabited, and my only companion is a man hidden behind a tree dressed in a ghastly tracksuit doing some exercise. The Akademia also had a gymnasium and sturdy Greek athletes exercised vigorously in its quiet natural environment, and so I forgive the man for keeping an ancient Greek tradition alive. But the deeper I go into the olive grove I realise I'm entering a small forest with ancient trees interspersed with ruined walls.

I give in to the charm of one such stone wall under a tree and settle down. The quietness is soothing, and after the initial dread of drinking wine that tastes like cough syrup (some Greek wine can) in the spiritual company of Plato, I pour myself a glass and drink up exulting: 'Salaam Aflatoon!' (Aflatoon being the Arabic and Persian name for Plato). The grapes and cheese go down well in celebration of a man who was the architect of Greek philosophy. Plotinus' concept of 'The One' is inspired from Plato's concept of the Divine Creator as 'The Good', and Plotinus' theory that the One is *beyond being* i.e., he creates and brings about motion but is not created and does not move, finds its origins in Plato's superb description of the 'First Principal' and how it created the orderly universe. In Plato's words:

> Now let us state the reason why becoming, and this universe were framed by him who framed them. He was 'Good'. And what is good never has any particle of envy in it whatsoever; and being without envy he wished all things to be as like himself as possible. This indeed is the most proper principle of becoming and the cosmos. God, therefore, wishing that all things should be good and finding the visible universe in a state of inharmonious and disorderly motion brought it to order... God, wanting to make the world as similar as possible to the most beautiful and most complete intelligible things, composed it as a single visible living being (Intellect), which

contains within itself all living beings of the same natural order. Are we then right to speak of one universe, or would it be more correct to speak of a plurality or infinity? ONE is right... since that which comprises all living beings cannot have a double.[81]

The divine craftsman, according to Plato is imposing order on chaos, particularly mathematical order. Plato was obsessed with proportions and mathematical harmonics and believed that proportions brought about order. These proportions had been divinely ordained. At his Academy he gathered leading mathematicians of his time to study mathematical proportions that are the cause of beauty and goodness in this world, be it planetary movements in their orbits or proportioned diets for humans. Mathematical harmonies, Plato believed, resulted in goodness, beauty, and balance, which to me, sitting and gorging excessively on grapes and cheese, makes complete sense. A proportioned, balanced diet would only do me good.

But is the origin of mathematics the number 1? If we were to assess the number 1, its very existence is the foundation of mathematical order and is the reason why mathematical systems exist. It finds itself as an integral part of all the following numbers, and without it, concepts like number 2 and infinity wouldn't exist. For Plato, God is Good, but how does Plato tackle the concept of 'First Principle?' Is the First Principle the number one?

In Plato's words:

Now a First Principle is something which does not come into being. For all that comes into being must come into being from a First Principle, but the First Principle cannot come into being from anything at all; for if a First Principle came into being from anything, it would not do so from a First Principle.

Since it is something that does not come into being then it must be something that does not perish. It is in this way then that which moves itself is a principle of movement. It is not possible for this either to be destroyed or to come into being, or else the whole universe and the whole of that which comes to be might collapse together and come to a halt, and never again have a source from which things will be moved and come to be.[82]

But for me, the wandering daydreamer who has been gasping at the beauty of sunrises, sunsets, bathing in moonlight, marvelling at the flight of starlings, and dancing with the soul of Plotinus, what does the origin of the mathematical number mean?

The First Principle is *beyond being*, indivisible and as Plotinus asserts – a unity which stands at a distance from intellect having generated it and given it elements of Itself. The First Principle is The Good and The One. But it is not the number 1 because the number 1 has come into being and is divisible. In other words, number 1 is young (inchoate) intellect. The number 1 was made by 'The One' as Its reflection and existed as a unity. But when young intellect (number 1) in its desire to know 'The One' in entirety turned towards It, it couldn't understand It. Overcome by a desire to possess all knowledge, the number 1 multiplied and also became divisible. Thus, numbers came to be. 'The One' doesn't exist as a being or a number as we know what it is to 'be', but It's 'not being' is Its very essence and is the way in which It exists.

Philosophically then, to me, anything that is 'addition' fuelled with a desire to multiply is greed – a constant desire to expand.

Subtraction, on the other hand could be viewed as a retreat towards the Good - a contraction which is the equivalent of Plotinus' profound thought '*Take away everything*'.

According to Plotinus 'The One' has injected intellect with a desire to reunite with It. This means everything that exists in the realm of Universal intellect, be it, soul, matter, and the entire universe, driven by free will, are moving forward, and expanding. But all the elements that constitute Universal Intellect are also consumed by an irresistible desire to reunite with 'The One' - The Originator. This means the entire cosmos is caught in two contrasting pursuits – expansion (the outward movement which we could also view as 'addition') and contraction (the inward movement which we could view as 'subtraction'). Be it a cell, a body, skin, a star, or even an empire – they expand and contract.

The ancient Greeks called the inward movement in the human soul and its final union with The One, 'Henosis'. That moment is fuelled by love and ends when soul and intellect completely surrender to 'The One'. In many ways, Plotinus' concept of the ascension of the fallen soul towards 'The One' is a contraction. Simply put, the soul sheds all that it has, retracts into intellect, which then retracts into 'The One'.

But isn't this retreat and contraction of the soul also undertaken by free will? It is. When men like Socrates, Plato and Plotinus were traumatised by the brutality unleashed by intellect in war, by intellect's degradation of society through greed and jealousy and through its perverse lust for power, they also witnessed the vanishing of the 'simple good' in this sensible (physical) world. It is completely plausible that all three of them realised that the only way intellect could be prevented from exercising its free will which resulted in 'bad actions' was to suppress its desire for 'more' and continuously inject it with a desire for only 'the

Good'. This meant regular subtraction of all things material and egotistically desirable. As Plotinus asserts *'Take away everything'* is the absolute subtraction. This would shock the intellect, tame it, make it completely idle and finally bring it to the threshold of surrender. Tamed, idle and only consumed by love for 'The One', intellect would finally surrender to It. The surrender of number 1 to 'The One' or 'Unbeing' is the moment of Henosis and I'm keen to discover it.

Plato's Academy is a stirring place, where in silence and solitude I have penned down these thoughts. But I must leave, for I am going to have dinner with Nikomachi, a wonderful artist whose latest paintings are inspired by Henosis, and with her, over more wine, the conversation promises much.

Nikomachi meets me at 'Me', a restaurant in Kolonaki. There is a carefree air in Kolonaki, which has become a melting pot for artists and musicians. Athens is quite obviously having a 'moment' with young creative people thronging to it from all parts of Europe. It is a relatively inexpensive city where artists can easily rent large studio spaces and thrive in communities. Like Rome, large clusters of the city have become creative havens for poets and playwrights who often begin their careers performing in street squares under the Acropolis having drunk from the enchanting wine cups of Greek philosophy. Nikomachi, with her delicate frame and clear voice, settles in and to my great joy takes charge of the wine and food, ordering a bottle of Assyrtiko. It is delicious. I very quickly retract my cough syrup analogy.

'Henosis is a part of our daily lives,' says Nikomachi.

'What do you mean?' I ask.

'It's about two becoming one... for example, in Greek Orthodox Christian wedding ceremonies, Henosis is evoked.'

'But Henosis is a pre-Christian, Greek philosophical concept.'

'Yes of course, but Greek Orthodoxy has adopted it... in the end it's about uniting as one even if it is marriage. It is like chemistry.... What is chemistry without two elements coming together?'

'Indeed... go on.'

'Henosis is becoming one... but after Henosis there is Symbiosis, and Symbiosis is existing together.'

'So a co-existence after "unbeing" of individuality?' I ask, but then hasten to add, 'Not co-existence because there is no "co" when Henosis occurs.'

'Well, the existence after Henosis is through space and time,' adds Nikomachi.

'I would think it transcends space and time, where intellect ceases to exist. Quite similar to what the Sufis speak about – Fanaa as "unbeing" of individuality to merge with "The One", then Vasl which is the moment of unity, and then Baqaa the state of existence, whatever that existence may constitute within "The One"... that journey to unity inspired the finest Sufi miniature paintings,' I explain.

'Yes, quite similar.' Nikomachi smiles.

'And your paintings, Nikomachi?'

'Well... the essence of my work is how two souls exist in the Universe of life and how they live together in a symbiotic way.'

'So how do you achieve this?'

'It's the method I use.... First, I pour water on the canvas and you see it as a lake. Into that I add two colours, then I lift the canvas and gently... actually, quite sensually, move the canvas allowing the colours to merge, and the shapes meet on a common ground and live together.'

'That sensuality is love,' I smile. 'Does each colour give itself to the other?' I continue.

'Yes, yes... both colours when they mingle get energised....'

'So it is a moment of great giving and receiving of energy?' I ask.

'Yes, yes, and they create a new common ground and this in my art becomes "Us".'

After dinner, Nikomachi takes me to her studio and shows me around. Her work is remarkable and appealing to me as someone who is trying to understand Henosis.

I leave Nikomachi's studio when night has enveloped Athens and the city has retreated under the blanket of slumber. Forewarned about avoiding the adjacent Metaxourgeio area which is the hotbed of a territorial gang war between Bangladeshi and Somali refugees, I walk back to my hotel. Yet, I can't help peeping into the dark lanes of Metaxourgeio. There is a sinister silence to these lanes where drug lords battle it out for supremacy. Given to their excesses, lying on some of the pavements like forgotten scarecrows, their bodies riddled with needles, are some men – victims of the drug wars; their dull eyes still searching for syringes. Their gaunt faces speak of a chilling past and a devastated future. These enmeshed neighbourhoods of Athens where love and hate, art, and blood carve out a daily existence tell a similar tale to the times of Plato and Aristotle where politics, ambition, war, philosophy, poetry, and love lived side by side. Not much has changed.

A lone seagull glides below the Acropolis that glows on a hilltop. A few soft lights that mark the pathway to it resemble a stairway to heaven. Walking in silence towards the Acropolis is like walking hand in hand with Aphrodite, who might well have stepped out of her garden of love, becoming my chaperone in the journey to Henosis.

One of the main principles that grounds Plotinus' philosophy is unlearning, unknowing, and unbeing (what I call philosophical subtraction). This is the only way Henosis is possible. Many modern theologians term this unlearning and unknowing as 'Negative theology.' Through stillness of mind, seclusion, and isolation, an uncluttered state of existence can be achieved whereby all accumulated intellect is first rejected and then completely banished and 'The One' is spoken off only in terms of what It is not.

But how can I reach Henosis? – For I am one who has only known this world of matter – where I, like most, have drunk from the poisoned goblets of arrogance, greed, and jealousy; where, when I reached adulthood, I drowned myself in plans for self-enrichment, paying no heed to balance; where my eyes were glazed by the gleam of capitalism and where my insatiable appetite for its produce grew monstrously – in this world, I did plot, and plan and I did 'other'; where in the quiet of night I have secretly enjoyed a friend's failure (And if you are honest with yourself, you will know that feeling) and in hushed tones mocked and disparaged their accomplishments; it is in this world that my soul was scarred. I carry these scars knowing well that for all that philosophers might say and write, it is only this world – this gilded cage that I will always be part of, for I am no hermit. And because this world has dispersed flames of material desire, which like molten radiation flow in my veins, burning me; I am incurable. And if I am honest, I don't want to be cured, in entirety. Why? Because, like you, I need this world. It is where you and I live. And thrive.

If someone like me is to have even the slightest glimmerings of Henosis, the first thing I need is isolation. The answer lies, I believe, in reaching one of the scattered and remote Greek islands – Patmos. An island where in a mountain cave, St. John in 90 CE had a vision of the end of the universe: the complete contraction and obliteration of Universal intellect. Crouched in that cave, through lashing winds, sheets of rain, snowfall, and blazing sunshine, he wrote the Apocalypse. Into that cave of 'revelation', I will venture.

Pausing for a few moments to look down into the bay, the boat that brought me to Patmos disappears, taking with it any connections I had with materialism. I carry on walking up the mountain under the shade of pine trees that cling to the cliff edges. Through the branches, resting like a crown on the summit, I catch my first sight of the Monastery of St. John the Theologian. Right below the monastery is a small, whitewashed stone house in which I will be spending the next few days. The walk up the mountain which is both physically arduous and sumptuously gratifying for the soul, ends at the Chora. Here, a clutch of houses wait in solitude for wanderers like me. Turning the key of a light blue door, I am greeted with an embarrassment of riches – a flourishing wine trellis from which hang bunches of grape, a bougainvillaea creeping up a wall with white flowers in full bloom, gracefully ageing terracotta flooring, a wooden table with a bowl of fresh peaches, a bed, a hand shower that gives me an electric shock every time I touch it, a small writing desk under a window, and a working oil lamp. There is an honesty in the uneven whitewashed stone walls of the house that speaks the language of its original inhabitant – quite possibly a fifteenth-century fisherman, monk, or farmer. But the greatest treasure of this setting awaits me when I step out onto a tiny terrace. Exactly from where my feet are, the mountain plunges deep down. Unravelling before my eyes is a grand sweeping view of the valley below, mostly arid, and rocky but dotted with patches of pine tree and wild shrub. In the heart of the valley, I can see a curving road, and as my eyes follow it, it climbs into another mountain standing majestically on the opposite side of the valley.

Perched on top of that mountain, like a nest of a lonely falcon is the small chapel of Prophet Elias. Edge to edge on both sides of this silent valley stretching out as far as the eye can see are the sapphire waters of the Aegean merging into the pastel blue sky. Rising behind me are the walls of the monastery into which a steady flow of Greek Orthodox monks dressed in black gowns disappear. This island shaped in the form of a seahorse is so far removed from Athens that it has taken an overnight boat ride to bring me here. Exhausted, I return to the room, sit on the desk, and turn on the oil lamp. It glows slowly and almost immediately attracts a moth. The sound of crickets adds to the atmosphere. For me, abandoning contemplation and turning to the 'Good' as Plotinus would have us do to reach Henosis begins with reaching that point where one is prepared to become empty. It helps to play out his words in my mind while gazing into the quiet valley:

> It is there that one lets all study go; upto a point one has been led along and settled firmly in beauty....[83]
>
> And this is what thinking is, a movement towards the Good in its desire of the Good....[84]
>
> The One is truly ineffable: for whatever you say about It, you will always be speaking of a 'something'. But 'beyond all things and beyond the supreme majesty of Intellect' is the only one of all the ways of speaking of It which is true; (It) 'has no name', because we can say nothing of It: we only try, as far as possible, to make signs to ourselves about It.[85] We are not prevented from having The One even if we do not speak....[86]

Not speaking brings tranquillity. The sun has set leaving its soft pink afterglow, as if Aphrodite's cheek has come to gently rest on the rims of darkened mountains. Night drops slowly and the white bougainvillaea resemble the emerging stars against a darkening sky. The moon rises taking its divinely ordained place in the night sky as the waters of the Aegean shimmer in its light like molten silver. I sleep deeply amidst the sound of crickets. Summer is boldly approaching.

The next morning after breakfasting on the grapes hanging from the trellis, I make my way up the stone steps and into the monastery. The wind at the summit is strong enough to lift the frail and plunge them into the valley. I make it into the multi-arched courtyard where frescos in rich colours adorn the walls and ceilings. Depicting the life of St. John, the frescos tell a variety of stories – about how the saint rescued a helpless sailor from the sea, and of his victory over the magician Kypnos who sinks into the sea after two demons assigned by him fail to kill the saint. The most stirring of the frescos though is of the forty martyrs. They were Roman soldiers who refused to renounce their Christian faith. As punishment, their prefect ordered them to be stripped of their clothing and were made to stand naked on a freezing lake. One of the forty did renounce his faith and immersed himself in a warm bath dying almost instantly. The guard though who had been keeping a watch over the remaining thirty-nine was overcome by a divine calling and converted to Christianity. He removed his clothes and stood by the other thirty-nine making the number forty, all of whom froze to death. It was this kind of acute persecution that saw St. John being banished to Patmos in the first century CE.

Right until the eleventh century, Patmos remained relatively uninhabited, and it was only in 1088 CE that Byzantine emperor Alexios Komnenos gave Patmos to John Christodoulos to set up a monastery in the name of the apostle. St. John, who was one of the apostles of Christ arrived in Patmos in approximately 90 CE and almost immediately sought isolation in a cave, striving to understand his role in the world and gain a deeper understanding of time, both present and future. 'The Book of Revelation', which he wrote in the cave of which the Apocalypse is a part, was based on a vision. The vision included the coming of Jesus, the rise of evil, the destruction of this world, and, quite possibly, the annihilation of the human race during Armageddon (the battle between good and evil) and the return of peace. 'The Book of Revelation' is the final book of the New Testament and is the last book of the Bible as we know it. The cave is a few hundred metres below the monastery, and I make my way there. The curling pathway to the mouth of the cave is empty of people, but as soon as I reach the tiny entrance just before I step in, the most heart-sinking sight awaits me. An old man is sitting on the ground with his legs apart. Between his legs sits his grandson with his neck tilted, his lower lip quivering, and saliva dripping out of the sides of his mouth. They are gypsies. The old man is holding a cup in one of his hands, and as I pass by, he gently lifts his wrist. 'I'm so sorry, no cash,' I whisper. He smiles and nods his head, accepting my apology. Stepping into the cave, I sense the beauty of silence.

The suspended rocks from the top of the cave are curved in various shapes and instantly make me crouch. Light from the outside struggles to make its way in. A monk who's been cleaning some of the icons, and the silver incense burners that are hanging from the rocks suddenly decides to leave the cave and makes his way out, leaving me alone. In this space of semi darkness my eyes feast on the painting of Christ, the Virgin, and of St. John emerging from the cave ablaze with enlightenment. Their once rich colours, now have only a faint lustre. The paintings rest against two enormous, curved boulders. Under these boulders I sit on the floor. A stillness descends and within me now are stirrings of emptiness. To my right is the image of Christ. Both him and I nestled in this cocoon. But when I turn to my left, through the semi-darkness that I am sitting in at the edge of my view is the old grandfather bathed in brilliant sunshine. Minutes become hours. I sense all differences between him and me fade. Both of us sit on the floor, ensconced in tranquillity. No one passes by to drop a coin. He plays with his grandson, becoming a child himself. A return to innocence. His grandson reaches for his dishevelled silver hair and ruffles it. Laughter. The grandfather's skin is shrivelled, his once robust arms now bony, and he also has a slight hunch. With age his spine has shrunk, his once bright eyes now fading, every living cell that makes him is contracting. The existence will cease soon. But in this moment, to his grandson he is eternal. Quite like what the universe, in this moment, is to us.

I leave the cave muttering to myself, 'What do I know of You? What do I know of this world... Nothing... It is best not to know.' A voice filled with urgency brings me back. I've stepped down a wrong path and the grandfather's voice and gestures guide me to the right path, leading back to the summit. Halfway up the summit I stumble into a quiet nunnery, its bountiful garden blooming with jasmine and its small chapel endued with the delicate beauty of the soul. The interiors of the chapel are dark even during the day. Silver wall hangings and tall yellow candle flames are the only clusters of light which illuminate the portraits of Christ and the Virgin. Next to one such cluster of dancing flames stands a nun – she is German and of a distinguished background. She has an open face with sparkling blue eyes. Her face is wrapped in her headscarf and her dark gown flows in the wind that sneaks its way into the chapel. She commands authority, yet there is a kindness in her demeanour. Addressing a group of women who have obviously come seeking solace, she elaborates on how one should never be afraid of solitude and never be afraid to pray. Then she tells a story of how a painting of the Virgin with the third eye on the forehead miraculously re-appeared after it had been stolen, and how a lady in America whose child's life was hanging by a thread saw the Virgin with the third eye in her dreams and prayed to her with such devotion that the child recovered.

Back at the summit, in the distance, I can see the faint, misty outline of Samos where Pythagoras lived and wrote.

Surveying all of Patmos, below me, at the very far end, ensconced in another small valley, I spot a patch of green vegetation surrounding a white building. I decide to explore that little emerald patch and walk down. The downward trek takes me through ravines, precarious cliffs, and arid hills. Goat herders guiding their flock with a carefree abandon are my companions during this walk. Looking out into the Aegean surrounded by the island's uninhabited rugged mountains and its shepherds, one realises that nothing much has changed since the times of Plato and Aristotle. As the two masters must have sailed around the Greek islands seeking inspiration, these are the same sights they would have encountered. The mountains rising from the waters of the Aegean look down at me and I at them. It is as if both mountain and man, wonder through silence whether Plato, Aristotle, and St. John all of whom wandered through wilderness, really found the 'simple good'.

After an hour I reach the little irrigated field that stands on the edge of a pebbled beach. The field is rich with fresh vegetables and fig trees bountiful in fruit. The sound of crickets is everywhere. Attending the field while sitting on his haunches is a farmer. The white building is a monastery which also has a small chapel, and a few men are whitewashing it. Here too, Patmos seems to scatter moments of silent virtue for the interested to observe. I walk into the middle of the field and look around. The farmer continues working, but on seeing me, springs to his feet and offers me fresh beans pulled from a plant he's been nurturing. Only when I look at them, I realise I'm starving. Nothing is said between us. He nods vigorously then points to the fig tree. 'Yes,' I say. From a drooping branch he picks a few and comes to me with his palms cupped with figs. I take a few, thank him, and want to continue the conversation but the farmer gets back on his haunches and continues working his land. I walk into the adjacent tomato field. It is being tilled by a woman who smiles at me.

'Do you speak any English?' I ask observing her interesting headgear.

'Not too badly,' she answers.

I catch a slight American accent.

'Since how long have you been farming this land?'

'Many years,' she says, putting down her spade and looking around.

Then she adds, 'I am a volunteer on this land... I leave Florida every year and come here for a few months to help out.'

'Volunteer?'

'Yes, this land is owned by the nunnery, and it brings me peace to work on it.'

'Might I know your name please?'

'Xara... it's my adopted Greek name... pronounced as "Khara".'

'What does it mean?'

'It means Joy.'

'And what you do here in this remote valley obviously brings you joy,' I say smiling.

'It does, quite like wandering around this place does for you,' she says placing her hand to her chest.

'Yes, it does.'

She continues: 'This valley used to be called the Valley of the Good Men... many monks in the fifteenth century lived ascetic lifes in the monastery and worked on these fields,' she says pointing to the monastery. Some of the tomatoes need Xara's attention and she gets back to work. As I walk past, I say, 'I wish you well.' She looks at me, smiles, and presses both her palms to her chest, 'And to you.'

I make my way to the pebbled beach. A fig and bean lunch graced with an abundance of generosity does more than just nourish the body, it nourishes the soul. For who other than a poor farmer could in exchange of nothing give something more important than what I have received?

The sound of rushing waves and a breeze are the ideal companions during my late lunch. It is only the revving of a motorcycle that intrudes these moments of solitude. A Greek Orthodox monk with a flowing beard and a large silver cross resting on his black gown is getting ready to ride up the mountain. I hitch a ride with him. The monk speaks English with a surprising fluency, and we compare each other's beards. His long, shaggy, and dishevelled – mine recently adopted, young and coarse. Today happens to be the feast of Prophet Elias, and the sparse population of Patmos is heading to the chapel that is perched on the mountain opposite the one on which the monastery of St. John is. Halfway up the mountain, the monk parks his motorcycle, and we climb up amidst the unrelenting sound of crickets. Struck by the natural beauty surrounding me, my pace is slower. As I climb higher and the sun begins its descent, it seems to shower the entire mountain in gold dust. Against this mountain of gold dust, like a flowing cape of the Madonna are the sapphire waters of the Aegean. Jagged boulders lie in silence as if discarded by time, yet relevant to imagination. The curling, ascending walk ends at a few stone steps that take me to the peak of the mountain. Here, a wooden door opens into a magical garden at the centre of which is a beautiful olive tree lit with oil lamps. This hermitage is a refuge for monks and the ones driven by the love for the divine. Here a gale blows with great force and the sky seems closer than ever. A few swallows courageously fly around the summit, but even they are lifted by the raging gale and flung heavenwards. A few monks emerge from the tiny chapel, their gowns fluttering in the gale as they distribute black coffee and bread, a centuries-old tradition to welcome weary travellers. A monk offers me some bread and I accept it. Prophet Elias was known for his miracles including reviving the dead. He lived a life of isolation in the ninth century BCE devoting himself entirely to the worship of God, while being fed by ravens.

I watch as the monks light candles under the olive tree and the magical garden becomes God's little Eden. The sun hastens towards its daily end, crowning one of the jagged rocks like a halo against a deep purple sky.

Night falls. I trace my steps out of the garden. My eyes fall on a boulder which has an inviting reclining curve. I lie on it facing the sky. Looking into the cosmos, every ounce of energy leaves me. A faint white band makes its appearance in the heavens – the Milky Way. Holding within it a billion worlds, the band itself is one of the many trillion in what we call the womb of the Universe. An indescribable feeling urges me to look beyond, but then almost immediately urges me to seek within. A withdrawal, a retreat, a contraction. I feel an inexplicable thrill. A surge upwards, yet it is occurring deep within me as Plotinus' words leave my lips:

Intellect veiling itself from other things and gathering itself inward, will see light.... For intellect will be looking at the beautiful, standing still and filled in a way, with strength, it first of all sees itself glistening because He is near... There one can see both It and oneself as it is right to see: the self-glorified, full of light... he will be in union with himself since he has become single and simple... the soul sees 'The One' in herself appearing for there is nothing between... lovers and their beloveds here below imitate this in their will to be united... So the seer does not imagine two... when the centres have come together they are one.... If anyone sees It, what passion he will feel, what longing in his desire to be united with It, what a shock of delight! The man who has not seen It may desire It as Good, but he who has seen It glories in Its beauty and is full of wonder enduring a shock which causes no hurt, loving with true passion and piercing longing; he laughs at all other loves and despises what he thought beautiful before... That which is beyond this we call the nature of the Good, which holds beauty as a screen before it.[87]

An abandonment of contemplation occurs, an emptiness takes hold, all the while uttering the hermit's words:

When he has become this he is near and that Good is next above him and already close by, shining upon all the intelligible world[88]... The intellect that came to be appeared as all things, the Good is enthroned over them, not so that It has a foundation, but so that It may found the Form of the primary forms, while remaining formless itself... (For Plato says) It rests in majestic immobility.[89]

Above Universal intellect, which is the known and yet to be known, and which casts its veil across the universe, shines 'The Good'. His throne is beyond the heavens and above the realm of intellect. Known in the Quranic verse of *Ayat-al-Kursi* and before the Quran, this song of the throne sung by Porphyry:

> to flee the bitter waves of this life 'where blood sustains... it is that this man (Plotinus) ascended in his thoughts to the first transcendent God many times travelling the roads described by Plato in the Symposium and to him appeared that God who has neither shape nor form, who has his seat above the Intellect.[90]

And there, '*There is nothing but Unity.*' And here where I am, there is nothing too. Not even me. The here ceases. The intellect storms past the stars with a light that drenches a pathway to heaven and every passing star seems but an angel's glistening teardrop shed for our fallen souls.

Souls which yearn for the final flight of freedom.

I have not seen what Plotinus saw. For how he saw what he saw is hidden and kept a secret and he remains the sole keeper of that knowledge. But the negation of everything except the Good (Unity) creates a momentary space into which, steeped in love, my soul, and my intellect, have stepped in, seeking only the good. I have shut the door to reason. Silence. Blankness.

But then, I seem to lose that moment of 'thrill'. Like water slipping from fingers, it has vanished. And from then on, I feel I am returning to learning. Faces and places flash – Fuad, the Saqqara Pyramid, Honey Singh, Ibn Tulun Mosque, Abdallah, the tomb of Seyit Gazi, the Philae temple, Hassan and Imaan, the Fatimid stars in the Palatine Chapel, the olive farm in Agrigento, the Berlin Wall, the wall of oneness, the landing on Mars, the grandfather, and the farmer in the field.

The world that Plato described as a mere reflection of the Supreme Reality has drawn me back in, and it is a stumbling walk back. Walking through the narrow, dark streets of Patmos I pass a chapel, the door of which is open. Peeping into the darkness, I see a small frail old lady, standing before a cluster of candle flames with her hands spread out protecting the flames from the wind that gushes in. Her wrinkles add a kindness and beauty to her face. Dwarfish, she maybe, but as the power of the howling wind grows, the resoluteness in her outstretched thin arms increases, spreading strength to every part of her body including her little toes that rise. Every cell that forms her, comes together – galvanised as a unity, she seems to soar – for in that moment she has been forged by love and the might of faith, making her the keeper of flames – the protector of wishes; and so, it stands ordained that even the wind will succumb to her. Many a wish, unextinguished by her strength. The scene could well be a miniature painting. Through these silent, dark streets, and stirring encounters, I finally make it to the blue door of the house.

The next morning, I rush to the mouth of the cave, clutching some cash in my palm, and hoping to find the grandfather and grandson. They aren't there. Disappointed, I return to the house and spend most of the day lying on the terrace looking out across the valley at the small hermitage of Prophet Elias. My time on that mountain has heightened the allure for the One and completely dulled the desire for the known, but now I'm tossing questions in my head. For how long can one sustain the effects of practising negative theology? For how long would that feeling of pure thrill stay with me? Is it an eternal feeling only when the soul finally departs the body, and then dissolves into the One? Was this the reason that Socrates would have his students, including Plato and himself, practise what it is to be dead – the ultimate contraction? And is not the complete contraction of the universe comprehensible if we believe the scientist

Stephen Hawking whose research on black holes changed the way we view our universe?

Stephen Hawking in A *Brief History of Time*:

> As the star contracts, the light cones get bent inward....light can no longer escape. According to the theory of relativity, nothing can travel faster than light. Thus, if light cannot escape, neither can anything else; everything is dragged back....This region is what we call a black hole.... There is a much larger black hole, with a mass of about a hundred thousand times that of the sun, at the centre of our galaxy. Stars in the galaxy that come too near this black hole will be torn apart....
>
> (After the Big Bang singularity) as time went on, the hydrogen and helium gas in the galaxies would break up into smaller clouds that would collapse..... The outer regions of the star may sometimes get blown off in a tremendous explosion called the supernova.[91]

It is plausible that I'm consumed by these thoughts because of the mystical energy of this island, particularly when one is aware that the Apocalypse was written here. But from all these thoughts emerges the desire once again for the simple. And so, I walk out of the light blue door again, rent a small car, and drive down the mountain and into the bay. In the afternoon, the Aegean has a glass-like sheen from which the sun's rays bounce off in bursts of glitter. I pass a few shops by the bay and some rustic seafood restaurants until I see a little wooden sign jutting out of a field with 'Pottery' written on it. I turn the car into the field and follow the signs. Driving past olive trees, wild shrubs, and bushes, I turn into the slenderest of curves. In front of me is a tiny, whitewashed stone house with blue windows hidden under a canopy of fig trees and set amidst the sound of crickets. I knock on the door. After waiting a few minutes, I'm greeted by Ritsa Eliou. Dressed in a white gown with an apron hanging around her neck and hands smeared in clay, Ritsa has an endearing smile.

'Hello. I was wondering if you ran pottery classes today?'

'Of course... but I don't have any free slots today,' says Ritsa in an angelic voice.

'Do you think I might be able to watch?'

'Yes, please come in.'

I walk in.

'That's my husband Nico,' she says pointing to a slim, bearded man.

The house is filled with ceramics in fabulous colours. A sea green vase catches my eye and Ritsa takes notice.

Ritsa is in the middle of teaching two teenage girls.

She sits next to them and begins moulding some clay. I take some in my hands and copy them. It is amazing how wonderful clay feels in the palms. It is like holding a bit of oneself and casting it the way one wills. As the wheel begins its orbit, the two students attempt at moulding clay into a pot but fail miserably. Ritsa's patience with their multiple failed attempts seems immeasurable, her encouraging voice going softer every time their pot disintegrates. Ritsa's husband, framed in the blue window, is sitting under a fig tree, smiling. He's seen all this before. The orbiting wheel is hypnotising, almost magical, and it lures the two teenagers into trying again. This time, Ritsa places her palms on theirs and slowly the clay starts holding. They don't take their eyes off the wheel. Vision, hand, mind, and clay bring about an expansion as every element that makes clay – water, minerals, and mud starts pulling upwards, growing gradually, and taking form. This expansion and growth originated in thought and then came into existence through will and balance. The result of that triumph is a lumpy pot – quite like our Universe which as recent images have revealed has bulges and lumps of galaxy clusters. But this lumpy pot belongs to the two teenage girls who scream in joy as they hold it in their hands. Ritsa offers to fire it for them in sea green and the girls couldn't be happier.

'Come back tomorrow, it will be ready,' she says, leaning against a fig tree and waving to the girls who leave utterly satisfied. I take my leave too. Ritsa goes to Nico and they discuss the day's events.

Stepping out of Ritsa's studio, I bump into Olivia Koefer, a friend who has made Patmos home with her young son. We walk into the fig orchard, settle in with a tea, and she tells me about what's been happening with her over the past year.

'Refugees are crashing into the Greek islands,' she begins.

'What do you mean?'

'Boat people from all over Syria, Afghanistan, and Iraq landed on the island of Kos not far from here last year,' she continues while cuddling her three-year-old son.

'Aaah...'

'I had to get there and help.'

'You helped the boat people?'

'Of course, they sailed in dinghies, starving, wet and cold cradling little kids.'

'This world... Uh.'

'Yes, I know it was awful.'

'You have a big heart, Olivia... what did you take for them?'

'The basics... biscuits, blankets, toothbrushes, paracetamol.'

'What about Patmos?'

'A few dozen got washed over here, too,' she says, despairingly.

'Washed over? Alive and breathing?'

'Barely.'

'And what happens to them now?'

'Well, the Greek authorities will check out their identities and then some will be deported, others may be given refugee status.'

'How do they get onto these boats?'

'Life is cheap. In exchange for all their savings human traffickers put them onto these little dinghies and put them on the waves. Many drown, others barely make it ashore...'

'Will you help again if they land in Kos?'

'I'll be there in a flash.'

The way she says it reassures me that good will find a way. Olivia's little son needs her undivided attention, and so mum and son decide to go further into the fig orchard where he can chase butterflies and explore the natural wonders of our world. I can hear his gurgles and squeals of excitement long after they have vanished into the orchard. Maybe he found a caterpillar or a ladybug or is just enjoying a juicy fig his mother picked for him.

I drive out to Livadi Geranou beach, not far from Ritsa's studio. Here, under a cloudless sky, the waters of the Aegean have returned to their sapphire blue. I can't resist my urge to fling myself into this ultimate manifestation of unity, and quite like the Nile, the Aegean welcomes me with a burst of freshness. Surrounded by beauty, I swim carefree. To my right rising skywards is the monastery, wrapped under which are the sugar cube like houses of Patmos. In front of me on another hill, like a cotton ball, is a whitewashed chapel; and under me but swimming with me is a variety of small silver fish. Seeing them, I feel the same delight as Olivia's son in the fig orchard. After a while I turn my gaze skywards and let my body float.

While the sea laps against my body, gazing into the heavens, I see the face of the ageing grandfather in the blue sky – old and frail like Plotinus was at the age of sixty-six. Plagued by ill health, advancing blindness, loss of voice, and ulcerated hands and feet, Plotinus left city life and retreated to Campania to live out his last days.

But even with his senses deserting him, on the ruins of an old city which was once inhabited by philosophers in sixth century BCE, he wished to recreate it as 'a city for philosophers' based on Plato's philosophy. To that city he wished the world would come and learn, and leave with ideas, to make this world a kinder and better place. From that city of Utopia, he wished students would leave with noble ideals, principles, concepts of justice, valour and ethics and imbue their environment with good. In honour of Plato, he wanted to call the city Platonopolis. After a few weeks in Patmos, I will leave this mystical island for my last dance with Plotinus, while searching for his final resting place.

# 6

# LAST DANCE IN THE WINDS

Plotinus' fledgling dream to create Platonopolis in honour of Plato would not come true. Porphyry attributes it to some envious courtiers in emperor Gallienus' court who prevented it from happening. Roman politics would raise its ugly head again when Gallienus would become a victim of a conspiracy to oust him, ending in his murder in 268 CE and sending Rome spiralling even further into a vicious whirlpool of chaos. Disheartened with the sabotaging of his project and the events unfolding around him, Plotinus surrounded himself with a few chosen friends and engaged philosophically only with them. He spent his time with Eustochius, a doctor; Zoticus, a poet who was losing his eyesight; Zethus, an aspiring politician of Arab extraction who had married the daughter of Theodosus, once a friend of Ammonius Saccas; and Castricius, a great student of philosophy.

But it was Zethus and Castiricius who Plotinus grew very fond of. In Rome they spent much time together and became as close as family until rapidly failing health and a thirst for the countryside saw Plotinus retire permanently to Zethus' estate, six miles from the small town of Minturnae.[92] Here in the quiet country setting, Plotinus spent his last days trying to dissuade Zethus from political ambitions, gazing out of his window towards an amphitheatre, the mountains that surrounded the estate, and quite possibly reciting one of his favourite verses:

> We are like a chorus that singing all the while, though relating to the chorus leader may turn outwards from the spectacle, but when it does turn towards it, the chorus sings beautifully and relates to the chorus leader.... We will be completely dissolved, and will be no longer. That is 'journey's end and rest for us, and the end of discordance for us dancing a divinely inspired dance. And within this circling dance behold the fount of Life, the fount of intellect, the principle of being, the cause of goodness, the root of soul.[93]

Finally, the angel of death flew in through the window and stood by his bedside. Even this, the most dreaded of angels, must have looked lovingly at Plotinus, for he was about to carry the purest of souls to its final union with the One. The philosopher's last words were:

> Try to elevate the God within us to the divine in the universe.[94]

A snake that had till then been waiting still under Plotinus' bed is said to have slid into a hole in the wall and disappeared. Intellect had vanished. The soul had ascended.

I have driven two and half hours south of Rome looking for the ruins of Velia. It is this deserted town in Campania that was quite possibly the one Plotinus wanted to revive as Platonopolis, for it was here that the great philosophers Parmenides and Zeno taught and lived in the fifth century

BCE. The ruins of Velia lie listless, speaking of thoughts that have withered away with time. In these scattered stones Platonoplis is a forgotten dream. I drive further north towards Minturnae, Plotinus' final resting place. As Minturane approaches and the car swallows up mile after mile, the realisation that this is the last mile of my journey in Plotinus' footsteps fills me with sadness and joy. I leave Minturnae to the right and head six miles further south hoping to find the exact location of Zethus' estate. But I end up driving in circles, passing a beautiful turquoise canal with swaying silver fern twice over, and shooting past a signpost that read 'District Archaeological Minturnae'. It is as if Plotinus doesn't want this journey to end and is playing a little game of hide-and-seek with me. Finally, I drive into the narrow lane that takes me into a garden erupting with lemon trees next to a row of Roman statues. I walk up to the entrance and request a ticket to enter the Archaeological site. The ticket counter is manned by an ageing portly man and a disinterested young woman.

'One ticket, please.'

'Ok… five euros,' she says, struggling with basic English.

I pull out my card.

'No… No, only cash,' she says.

'I don't have cash.'

'Sorry. Ciao.'

'What do you mean, Ciao? Please, I have to go in.'

'No, no… only cash.'

'Well, we are in the middle of nowhere and there is no cash point here… please, this is important.'

'No, no… Sorry. Ciao.'

'Listen, I have come a long way searching for Plotinus'….'

'What you say? Plotino?'

'Uh yes… yes… Plotino… he lived here… somewhere here… his last few days….'

'Plotino... Plotino... I student of philosophy in Naples.' A big smile breaks on her face.

'Well, that's great... You see, I'm writing a book about his work and his thoughts and his travels... You know, he lived his last days around here... six miles from Minturnae.'

'No, I don't know.... No one knows much about him... He lived here?'

'Yes, that's right... somewhere around here.'

'Really?'

'Yes and I have....'

'Don't worry, here, take ticket... go in.'

'Really? Free?'

'Si... Yes... I learn something from you... Plotino live here... I didn't know... You are welcome to go in.'

'Oh, thank you! Grazia Mille! This is a little present from Plotino.'

'Prego... You welcome.' She laughs.

I pass the lemon trees and approach the amphitheatre from behind which looks like a block of curving clay. Its original walls are still intact with a few stray strands of grass peeping into the outside world from its summit. From the front though the newly restored part looks unconvincing in authenticity. Walking further on I stumble onto a beautifully preserved part of the Via Appia. The ancient stones are in perfect condition and laid out in typical Roman style. The road has vertical dents made in it through the millennia by passing carts, carriages, and chariots. In one such mode of transportation, an ailing Plotinus would have arrived here. Roofless pillars and some ruined arches speak in whispers about Plotinus' last days, and even today the line of pine trees at the edge of the view seem to mourn his passing.

In the distance are curving blue mountains and about six miles from where I am standing, through the branches of the pine trees, I can see the light brown walls of Minturnae. But something within me tells me to walk on; to walk away from the amphitheatre and all that is material. It is as if Plotinus is stretching out his hand. I follow and end up leaving the archaeological site. After about a mile I enter a field blooming with wild yellow broom flowers; as if Aphrodite has loosened her tresses to welcome me into this sacred field. I walk through the field and find the most petite avenue of olive trees. Only twenty of them are lined up facing each other, and through them my eyes fall on a ruin with a few windows still intact, its beauty otherworldly. I don't walk down the avenue, instead letting my imagination sing to me, I find myself reciting verses by Elytis and Khusrau:

> Whether he was right or no
> Plotinus will one day appear
> The great eye with its transparency
> And with a sea behind him like Helen tying up the sun along
> with other flowers in her hair.[95]

And accept the salam! O Plotinus! Of one Khusrau of India whose verse, as a bouquet I bring to you.

> I have become you and you me
> so that no one can say hereafter,
> that you are someone and me someone else.

I put my faith in the wind to carry these words through the doors of heaven and make my way across the field and towards my car. For a few minutes, I sit in silence behind the steering wheel. An hour's drive from where I am is Pompeii, the once prosperous city that was destroyed by the lava spewed out by Mt. Vesuvius in 79 CE. I drive to Pompeii just to stay in touch with the fading feeling of emptiness and a sense of being infinitesimal – feelings that I have been carrying with me from Patmos. There is a timeless haunting to Pompeii in which the shells of houses, shops, granaries, and brothels still stand, enclosing within them a 'nothingness'. But it's the frescos that suddenly leap out, smiling with life. They seem to laugh at time and the intent of the flowing molten lava that rushed through the streets when Vesuvius erupted, neither of which were able to erode them. For after all, what is a fresco but unity? Water, lime plaster and dry powder pigment merge together to make the fresco an integral part of the wall. The wall, a fresco. The fresco, a wall. Peacocks, fountains in gardens, Roman women playing the Greek Kithara, and a dancing satyr all have come to rest in a frozen stillness.

## Rome. Autumn 2022

An urge takes hold of me to stand before Plotinus. To be face to face with him. Having locked eyes with pharaohs, what would I feel when I finally stand before a man to whom matter, and form were meaningless? It would be befitting to end my travels by looking into his eyes. And so, I head to Ostia Antica where his bust is on display. As I near this vast site of ruins I can feel an accelerated beat of my heart – anxiety and pulsating excitement.

'I am sorry sir, the bust is in the museum and the museum is closed for restoration,' says the man at the entrance.

Disappointment descends. 'Please, I have come a long way in the culmination of my journey... can you please make an exception?'

'I am very sorry, but I cannot.'

But there is still hope, I think to myself. There is a sarcophagus, allegedly a part of Plotinus' tomb that carries an engraving of his face. It is at the Vatican. Running out of the Ostia Antica, I hail a taxi and make my way to the ultimate bastion of Western Christendom.

In the taxi, I desperately search online for a ticket and purchase one of the last remaining ones. Entering the Vatican, I run through long corridors, passing room after room in search of the sarcophagus. Every turn I take leads me into a chamber of paintings, relics, and statues, until I finally get to the Museo Gregoriano Profano. Here the lights are dim, and stretching out before me, is a sea of sarcophaguses. Two attendants languish on chairs bored with their existence. I look at the sarcophaguses around me passing each one and observing every engraving – none of them are the one I'm looking for. Finally, I show a picture of the Plotinus sarcophagus to an attendant.

'Sorry it's gone for restoration... you cannot see it.'

In the finality of these words, I seem to experience a strange sense of freedom. I smile to myself and walk away. Lost in thought I walk through rooms and ceilings adorned with Raphael's paintings glancing at his iconic 'The School of Athens' in which Plato walks with his index finger raised. I whisper to myself, *All of this is beginning to mean something.* And then suddenly, I find myself standing in front of the Sistine Chapel. I walk in and there right in front of me is Michelangelo's 'The Last Judgement'. To me, philosophically, this fresco is the most brilliant and stupendous exhibition of the dissolvement of all form and matter – the moment when everything that has existed the way we have perceived existence, exists no more. I can only think of Plotinus' words while gazing at the fresco:

Shape is the shape of the traceless... this (the traceless) generates shape, not the other way round.... We will not marvel at the production of such mighty longings... It is not possible for something that is in possession of something else to see Beauty.[96]

And so, it has been ordered by the man who dismissed matter that I, who chose to travel in his footsteps, shall never stand in the presence of his sculpted form. Such is the strength of this feeling within me, that in the future, even if time were to open a window to stand before him, in admiration of his disdain for shape, I will not succumb to that temptation.

Back in Trastevere, the streets come alive as night falls over this city kissed by muses, and where the benign spirit of Plotinus still regales in young love. The fountain at Piazza Trilussa is overflowing and water drips from it like slender strands of silver thread. Below the steps, the young rejoice in love songs as the bent pine tree watches over them. I walk into a wine store, buy a bottle of red, some olives, cheese, and sundried tomatoes, and make my way to Ponte Sisto. The lamps on the bridge glow with an endearing charm. On the bridge I lay out this little feast. Plotinus celebrated 'The Feast of Plato' and the 'The Feast of Socrates' where poets, philosophers, musicians, writers, and actors came and read their parts. This little feast will be in his name – 'the first feast of Plotinus'. Looking into the Tiber and at the musicians who have just come to play, I wait patiently for one who would come up and join me. The music is good. At times, very good. A man in cowboy boots and a curling hat puts out a country song. His time up he wraps up his gear and leaves. After a while, a woman comes up and sings Whitney Houston's 'I will always love you'. Her band is fantastic and the beat they put out is foot tapping. They take a break, and we get talking.

'Would you and your band like a drink?' I ask.

She looks at her drummer who nods approvingly.

'My name is Veronica,' she says, as I pour her a glass of red and offer her some olives. Veronica is American and is doing an internship at a bookstore chain.

'I'm Vito,' says the guitarist, picking up his cup. Vito reveals that he is also a poet and writes regularly for literary journals.

'A drink to Plotinus,' I exult, raising my glass in the philosopher's name. They drink up too.

Veronica comes closer and whispers, 'Who was he?'

I take in a deep breath, smile, and begin, 'Well... many years ago in this city lived a man....'

The first feast of Plotinus is underway. It will happen every year on this bridge. What it will yield in the future excites me.

# EPILOGUE

What does Plotinus want from us?

The ultimate dissolution of all differences and man-made identities? The taking away of everything which we may consider different by diminishing the importance of senses which pick up differences? Does he want us to collectively inhabit a state of mind which is so elevated by stillness and the suppression of senses, that a universal unity is achieved? If this is what Plotinus wants from us, then it is philosophical idealism – an impossible quest.

But if he desired us to be united in an impregnable unity where difference is not seen as 'other' which leads to 'othering' – a mental state of discrimination – then it is achievable and can be aspired for. This philosophical aspiration, I believe, we can strive towards through everyday deeds. Actions that are propelled by our intellect based on the virtues of simple goodness.

Compare these verses – the first from Plotinus' *The Enneads* and the next from one of the Upanishads, and you will hopefully get a sense of how dismissive they both are of 'difference':

## The Enneads

> For bodies are hindered by bodies from commuting with one another, whereas incorporeals are not hindered by bodies. So they are not separated by place but by difference and differentia. When then no difference is present, distinct things are not present to one another. That thing (The One) since it contains no difference, is always present, and we are present whenever we contain no difference.[97]

A verse from *The Philosophy of the Upanishads*:

> In the spirit should this be perceived
> Here there is no plurality anywhere
> From death to death again he rushes blindly
> Who fancies that he here sees difference.[98]

Did my travels in the footsteps of Plotinus take me in search of God, the Ultimate Unity? I don't know. But what is true is that I have come away from my travels having experienced a heightened sense of unity within and with every living organism. What I can say with surety is that once that sense of unity is experienced, a dissolution of 'othering' occurs, and an acceptance sets in. Once that happens, a unique relationship with good can be established. For as we have seen, if the root of a tree 'othered' there would be no flower or fruit. As the First Principle, this Good which is One and which Plato, Aristotle, Plotinus, Thomas Aquinas (the great Christian mystic), Mohammad, and more recently Spinoza and Schelling have spoken about, is accessible. Access to It lies within. And when that innate good is accessed and emotionally felt, something emerges from that moment on. It is called faith.

This faith in the First Principle (Unity) is evident in the most modern celebrations of human endeavours, accomplishments, and even in simple existence. You will witness it when the president of the United States, the leader of the free world, ends his speech with 'God Bless America' (what he does after this proclamation is free will). The pledge to the American flag strikes a similar tone: 'I pledge allegiance to the flag of the United States of America, and to the Republic, one nation under God, indivisible with liberty and justice for all.'

You will also witness this faith in unity when almost every Latin American, Italian, Portuguese, Spanish, and Greek footballer looking heavenwards crosses his chest before taking the field and then exchanges his jersey with his rival at the end of the sporting encounter. When Novak Djokovic was asked how he felt after winning his world record equalling 24th Grand Slam title, his answer was simple: 'God is Great'. Before giving this answer, he had put his arms around his defeated rival and comforted him.

Faith in the First Principle shimmers when Hollywood actors make their acceptance speeches. Denzel Washington elaborates with great eloquence: 'I thank God for giving me this ability, for blessing me, for shaping me, for chastising me, for teaching me, for punishing me, for allowing me to be a vessel and touch people around the world.'

Matthew McConaughey is unequivocal in attributing his achievements because of his friendship with God: 'First off, I want to thank God, because that's who I look up to. He's graced my life with opportunities that I know are not of my hand or any other human hand. He's shown me that it's a scientific fact that gratitude reciprocates. In the words of the late Charlie Lawton who said when you got God you got a friend, and that friend is you.' Will Smith goes even further after winning the Academy Award for a film that told the story of two girls who endured racism and overcame discrimination to dominate women's tennis, considered for many years a white-only sport. 'In this moment I am overwhelmed by what God is calling on me to do and be in this world... I'm being called on in my life to love people. And to protect people. And to be a river to my people... I want to be an ambassador for love and care and concern....'

The faith in the First Principle can also be seen in a great philosopher, as depicted by Raphael in his brilliant sixteenth-century fresco 'The School of Athens'. In this fresco Plato conspicuously raises his index finger while walking next to his student Aristotle while explaining the Theory of Forms. This gesture, symbolising faith is also witnessed in a simple remote mud mosque by the banks of the Nile, where a poor Muslim farmer, on his knees, head bowed with no intermediaries between him and the First Principle will lift his index finger in prayer and bear witness to the unity of the originator. When the qawwals sing 'Allah hu' (God Is) and enter a state of otherworldly trance and verses from the Upanishads are recited in the snowy peaks of the Himalayas by simply calling out 'He Is', this faith emerges ever so strongly resounding across continents and oceans and transcending time. When compared to Plato, Aristotle, Plotinus, and Mohammad, more recently the Dutch philosopher Baruch Spinoza (1632–1677) and the great German thinker Friedrich Schelling (1775–1854) voiced similar beliefs, in fact pressing even further and declaring their complete devotion to the 'oneness' of everything. In her remarkable book *Magnificent Rebels*, Andrea Wulf writes:

> Schelling drew inspiration from Spinoza, who had declared that there was an all-encompassing principle in the universe.

This was the origin of everything and the essence from which everything derived. It could not be produced by anything else. According to Spinoza that was God and also nature. Schelling applied the same principle to his philosophy and called this first origin substance "Absolute". According to Schelling the Absolute contained all ideas, concepts, bodies, souls, individual objects and so on. It united the ideal and the real. It was the One or the Unity, before it divided into the self-conscious self and external nature.... Schelling believed that the self and nature were identical.... He insisted that everything was one. There was a "secret bond connecting our mind with nature', he told his students".... Schelling conjured up a world of oneness where everything from frogs to trees, stones to insects, rivers to humans, was linked together forming one universal organism.[99]

When this belief in 'oneness' is strengthened, like Spinoza and Schelling had done, at that moment, 'othering' ceases. Morgan Freeman's faith in oneness is so powerful that he believes we should stop speaking about racism. The very fact that we do means we are giving it wings and we are 'seeing' race and giving in to what our senses show us. When saying we should not speak about race, what he probably means is that we should elevate our mind to a space where our senses don't pick up the concept of race and only oneness prevails.

Moments and feelings of 'oneness', though, need to be sustained by the fertility and power of intellect, for as we have seen, intellect has been gifted with free will. Let's take a closer look at how this free will unleashes itself. Three successive events sum it up. In February 2021, the most diverse group of scientists worked in brilliant harmony as one team to put us on Mars. In February 2022, Putin attacked Ukraine claiming Ukrainians and Russians are 'one' people – the killing of innocents continues to this day. In February 2023, Turkey and Syria were struck by a monstrous earthquake – the response from the world was astonishingly compassionate. Putting aside political differences, nearly a hundred countries came together to mobilise humanitarian help, including Syria's bitterest political foe, Israel. Our species' erratic behaviour suggests we suffer from a case of collective bi-polar disorder, unable to steer intellect consistently and collectively towards good. This brings us to a question: is it our fate, to be forever engaged in this titanic tussle of trying to overcome othering and steer intellect towards Good? Yes, it is.

Working with Plato and Plotinus' philosophical thought, I have deduced in this book that 'The One' united two elements without discriminating and created water as a true reflection of Itself – the Good. The Good is a unity in perfect balance. But our collective actions have been the opposite of good, instead they have been steeped in excesses. Our actions have consistently exploited water – the very essence of existence. Our uncontrollable need to procreate has led to a population explosion leading to high fuel emissions resulting in global warming which is depleting freshwater reserves in glaciers and rivers. We are experiencing an unprecedented number of droughts in the last two decades than ever before, making water scarcity, the greatest global disaster. This most simple unity without which our planet will melt into oblivion has been vandalised by one of our creations – Plastic. This creation finds its origins in consumerism and corporate greed. An incessant plastic invasion has occurred – one which is the scourge of marine life. Plastic in our oceans, seas and rivers amounts to nearly 199 million tonnes. As these numbers surge, plastic mercilessly kills fish that mistake it for food or get entangled in it. The balance is lost.

As if we hadn't done enough, we created Augmented Reality (AR) and Artificial Intelligence (AI) – a reflection of ourselves. Today, from medical diagnosis and prescription to agricultural and biological recommendations, and from arms production to making our holiday plans, all can be done by the algorithms that have been fed into AI. But in many ways AI is inconsistent, quite like us. Why? Because we have injected it with free will. This means while AI will have tremendous benefits like boosting healthcare and even finding immunity towards cancer, it can also be used for developing and using lethal weapons controlled by it autonomously and not controlled in entirety by us. AI also has the capability to lie and come up with solutions and actions entirely on its own.

Stunned by these possibilities, the Vatican called for a meeting with the top dogs of AI. The man organising these meetings was Father Paolo Benanti, a Franciscan monk given to the teachings of St. Francis of Assisi, the thirteenth-century saint who cared for lepers, tamed man-eating wolves, and sang to birds. According to Madhumita Murgia of *Financial Times* UK who interviewed Father Benanti, besides being a Franciscan monk, he is dedicated to social upliftment, is also an engineer and professor of ethics at the Pontifical Gregorian University and chief instructor of graduates in moral and ethical issues surrounding technology and AI. Murgia mentions in her article that until recently, Father Benanti had only been interested in the charming responses that AI churned out for him like a well-crafted and thought-out poem on love, sky, and stars in response to when the monk had fed it philosophical texts and Dante's verses in medieval Italian.

But with the progression of his knowledge of AI, Father Benanti began to worry. Chief among his worries was what AI can do to human relevance – particularly if it makes human employability irrelevant thus accelerating poverty and widening the gap between the rich and poor (especially when the richest 1 per cent in the world have cornered most of the new wealth).

Father Benanti was filled with even greater horror when he realised the catastrophic destruction AI could bring about when equipped with the ability to use weapons at the time of its choosing and at its own discretion. And so, dressed in a hooded robe on 26 February 2022, Father Benanti and other monks raced through the streets of Rome and headed for the Vatican where he would act as chief translator for the Pope for his meeting with Brad Smith, president of Microsoft, who had just arrived on a private jet to reassure Western Christendom's highest pontiff on the benefits of AI and the responsibility with which it was being controlled.

This was not the first meeting between the two. Benanti in 2020 had orchestrated a similar meeting where a consensus had been reached to work on a guide for designers of AI entrenched in a pledge of common human values. Keeping this spirit in mind, Benanti had drafted a document called Rome Call that was signed by Microsoft, IBM, and the Italian government. Later, leaders from the Islamic and Jewish faiths too signed up. In time Benanti plans to approach religious leaders of the East too, including Hinduism, Buddhism, and Shinto. According to Benanti the Church could create a system called 'algor-ethics' which will be the guidebook for human values while pursuing the development of new AI machines. In short, machines (including robots) and all other autonomous instruments that run on AI would require to doubt themselves.

In Benanti's words, 'Every time the machine does not know whether it is safely protecting human values, then it should require man to step in'. Only then can technologists produce AI that puts human welfare at its centre. This 'AI check', if you wish, is far from being developed and nowhere close to being implemented. Benanti chillingly captured the fertility and unpredictability of intellect when, in his interview with the *Financial Times* he said, 'When the first human being picked up a club, was it a tool or a weapon? With AI, I see a lot of wonderful tools, but I see weapons too. Sometimes, the difference, the line is so narrow.'

Vincenzo Paglia, the Catholic Church's official emissary for AI who Benanti advises and was also at the meeting between the Pope and Brad Smith, voiced similar thoughts to the *Financial Times*: 'We see great epoch-making events from different directions: nuclear power and bombs, ecological crises and also new technologies.' As a result, Paglia commissioned workshops on robo-ethics and AI and law. These made the Pope establish the Renaissance Foundation that will study the impact of new technology on human life. Recently, it has funded studies on technology's impact on migration, border control, and weapons. Paglia sums it up: 'Refugee status decided by an algorithm – that is non-human dictatorship. We would like to defend the freedom of every woman and man, especially the weakest. And this is the reason, we are afraid of the possible oligarchy of big data. It could be a new form of slavery.'

But what was going through the mind of the man who was the chief architect of AI?

A lurking fear of what AI could become haunted him for years. Terrified by what he had created, Geoffrey Hinton, the godfather of AI at Google, resigned in May 2023. His statement would send tremors in the political, technology, and corporate worlds:

'I console myself with the normal excuse: if I hadn't done it, somebody else would have. I left, so that I could talk about the dangers of AI.'

Google responded almost immediately: 'We remain committed to a responsible approach to AI. We are continually learning to understand emerging risks while also innovating boldly.'

On 1 November 2023, Rishi Sunak, Britain's first prime minister of Indian origin hosted the most influential global AI summit to ensure that an agreement was reached for AI safety. While 28 countries signed the Bletchley declaration, an agreement to work together on safety standards that may prevent AI systems turning on humanity, it was clear there was nervousness and great concern about how far AI could go if it wasn't managed for the good. King Charles III summed it up in his address to the attendees of the summit. '...We must address the risks presented by AI with a sense of urgency, unity and collective strength... I want to thank you all for the vital role you are playing in this shared endeavour for laying the foundations of a lasting consensus on AI safety and for ensuring that this immensely powerful technology is indeed a force for good in this world.'

But how would Plotinus have reacted to AI? Quite possibly, with these words:

'AI has *dared* to stand away from its creator.'

A new universe stands to be shaped.

How did all of this come to be? The origin of creation according to Plotinus was no accident, and everything created did not come about by chance. He believes that intellect and form are an orderly progression from 'earlier to later', whereas chance occurs in those things that do not come out of an orderly progression but in coincidences. For Plotinus, chance would need resources, and those resources are from The Good, and chance on its own has no resources. In Plotinus' words: 'If then nothing is prior to The Good, and it is the first, then we must come to stop there and say nothing more about It.'[100]

If we aren't here by chance, then it is ever so important to try and be a reflection of the Good. A timeline gives us an understanding of how infinitesimally short our presence on this planet has been in the grand sweep of time, and the severity of all that we have done in such a short time and can potentially do if there isn't an inner awakening which steers us consistently towards good and tilts the axis in favour of good. 13.8 billion years ago the Big Bang singularity created matter and energy. 4.5 billion years ago, Earth cooled down and began taking form. 3.8 billion years ago the first signs of living organisms appeared. 225 million years ago, land masses split wide open and became what we call continents. Between 200 million and 66 million years ago (for nearly 150 million years), dinosaurs roamed our planet until an asteroid crashed into earth and annihilated them. The first human evolution in Africa happened only 2.5 million years prior to the present. Two million years ago humans moved from Africa to Eurasia and an evolution of different human species occurred. Only 200,000 years ago did the Homo Sapien (we) evolve in Africa. And it was only a mere 70,000 years ago that we left Africa to discover our planet, contribute towards the extermination of other human species, create nations, build borders, invent identities, discriminate, develop, and yet destroy each other by the sheer will, creativity, beauty, and grotesqueness of our actions. We are but a moment.

In 1977, NASA sent the Voyager into outer space with the objective of closely inspecting our neighbouring planets, particularly Jupiter and Saturn. By 1990 it had passed Neptune and Pluto and was at the fringes of our solar system, moving through a boundless void of silence. What lay ahead was left to our imagination. Just before it left our solar system, Carl Segan, one of the leading astronomers of the past century, suggested the Voyager turn its camera around and take one last shot before it would pass into interstellar space. The camera captured what Carl Segan would call a 'pale blue dot'. A barely visible tiny speck against slanting hazy bands of cosmic light and the sweeping infinity of space. Our home. In its frailty though, it is but a dew drop which fell from the garden of eternity. And if Plato is to be believed – that it is a mere likeness of the Supreme reality – then let us remain still, in silence, at the pity of it all.

8 November 2023
Trastevere
Rome

# NOTES

**Prologue and Introduction**

1. Lloyd Gerson, ed., *Plotinus: The Enneads* (Cambridge University Press, 2018), 868.
2. J. Bussanich, *The One and its Relation to Intellect in Plotinus – A Commentary on Selected Texts* (The Netherlands: E.J Brill, 1988), 82.
3. Sky News, translation of Putin's speech, 'Breaking News: Russian President Vladimir Putin says Russians and Ukrainians are "one people".'
4. Gerson, ed., *Plotinus: The Enneads*, 17, 25, 26, 27.
5. Pao-Shen Ho, *Plotinus' Mystical Teachings of Henosis*, Peter Lang Edition, (Frankfurt: International Verlag der Wissenchaften, 2015), 114, V.3. 17. 15-20, 104, VI.7.35., VI.7.35. 19-33.
6. *Ibid.*, p. 36, VI.9.9.33–44, p. 37, VI.7.31.11–19, p. 17, VI.7.36.3–5.
7. Hugh Lawson Tancred, *Aristotle, The Metaphysics Translation* (London: Penguin Books, 1998), 110.

**Chapter One**

8. Bussanich, *The One and its Relation to Intellect in Plotinus*, 72, 75.
9. Ho, *Plotinus' Mystical teachings of Henosis*, 22.
10. Bussanich, *The One and its Relation to Intellect in Plotinus*, 76.

11. *Ibid.*, 75.
12. Mumtaz Hussain, *Amir Khusrow Dehlawi* (New Delhi: The National Amir Khusrow Society, Aiwan-e Ghalib, 1986), 58.
13. *Ibid. pp.* 54, 55, 62, 63, 80, 81.
14. Paul Deussen and Rev. A.S. Geden, *The Philosophy of The Upanishads* (Delhi: Motilal, Banarsidass Publishers, 2017), vii, 2, 3, 13.
15. *Ibid.*, 84, 197, 202, 204, 222.
16. *Ibid.*, 49, 85, 86, 154, 155, 157, 212.
17. Bussanich, *The One and its Relation to Intellect in Plotinus*, 22.
18. Deussen & Geden, 166.
19. *Ibid.*, 83.
20. *Ibid.*, 11.
21. *Ibid.*, 225, 348.

**Chapter Two**
22. *Bussanich*, 96.
23. Ho, *Plotinus' Mystical Teachings of Henosis*, 34.
24. Stefan Sperl and Yorgos Dedes, *Faces of the Infinite* (Published for The British Academy by Oxford University Press, 2022), 7.
25. *Stefan* Sperl, Notes, *The Enneads*, VI.9.10.
26. *Ibid.*, VI.9.10.
27. *Ibid.*, VI.9.11.
28. *Ibid.*, VI.9.8
29. Abdullah Yusuf Ali, The Holy Quran, Text, Translation and Commentary, Sura XCVI. 1-4, 5-12. Iqraa published by Nusrat Ali Nasri (New Delhi: Kitab Bhavan, Daryaganj), 1761, 1762.
30. Anthony Sattin, *The Pharaoh's Shadow: Travels in Ancient and Modern Egypt* (London: Eland Publishing London, 2012), 65.
31. Yusuf Ali, The Holy Quran, Text, Translation and Commentary, Sura CXII. 1-4. Ikhlas published by Nusrat Ali Nasri (New Delhi: Kitab Bhavan, Daryaganj), 1806.
32. Stefan Sperl, Notes, *The Enneads*, VI.9.8.
33. Ho, *Plotinus' Mystical Teachings of Henosis*, I.3.1.5-9 VI.9.9.7-II, *pg* 125, 36 V.4.1.5-13, V.3.17.21-28, 116.

34. Abdullah Yusuf Ali, The Holy Quran, Text, Translation and Commentary, Sura LV. 1-7, Rahman, 1473.
35. Ho, *Plotinus' Mystical Teachings of Henosis*, 109.
36. *Ibid.*, 103.
37. *Ibid.*, 21.
38. Walter Scott, *Hermetica: The Ancient Greek and Latin Writings which contain Religious or Philosophic Teachings Ascribed to Hermes Trismegistus* (Boston: Shambhala, 1993), 161.
39. Gerson, *The Enneads*, 113, 117.
40. Sattin, *The Pharaoh's Shadow*, 41.
41. *Ibid.*, 42.
42. *Ibid.*, 41.
43. *Ibid.*, 55.
44. *Ibid.*, 56.
45. *Ibid.*, 197.

**Chapter Three**
46. Edward Gibbon, *The History of the Decline and Fall of the Roman Empire*, Abridged, Edited and Abridged by David Womersley (London: Penguin Books, 2005), 93–116.
47. *Ibid.*, 93–116.
48. *Ibid.*, 93–116.
49. *Ibid.*, 93–116.
50. Gerson, ed., *Plotinus: The Enneads*, 90.
51. *Ibid.*, 84, 85.
52. Gibbon, *The History of the Decline and Fall of the Roman Empire*, 93–116.
53. *Ibid.*, 93–116.
54. Gerson, ed., *Plotinus: The Enneads*, 241, 242, 243, 244.
55. *Ibid.*, 83.

**Chapter Four**
56. Gibbon, *The History of the Decline and Fall of the Roman Empire*, 114–115.
57. Gerson, ed., *Plotinus: The Enneads*, 24.

58. *Ibid.*, 17.
59. *Ibid.*, 18 and 28.
60. *Ibid.*, 26.
61. Ho, *Plotinus' Mystical Teachings of Henosis*, 108.
62. Baldesar Castiglione, *The Book of the Courtier*, Translated by George Bull (London: Penguin Classics, 2003), 78, 79, 80.
63. Ho, *Plotinus' Mystical Teachings of Henosis*, 54.
64. *Ibid.*, 130.
65. *Ibid.*, 117.
66. *Ibid.*, (VI.9.8).
67. Gibbon, *The History of the Decline and Fall of the Roman Empire*, 121, 126, 185.
68. Deussen and Geden, *The Philosophy of The Upanishads*, 58.
69. Bussanich, *The One and its Relation to Intellect in Plotinus*, 143.
70. *Ibid.*, 143.
71. Gerson, ed., *Plotinus: The Enneads*, 837, 838, 839, 840, 841.
72. *Ibid.*, 837, 838, 839.
73. Sperl and Dedes, *Faces of the Infinite*, 58, 59 (I 6 [1] 6, M:55.
74. Tancred, *Aristotle, The Metaphysics Translation*, xviii.
75. Ho, *Plotinus' Mystical Teachings of Henosis*, I.3.4.16-18, pg 25 and V.5.13.17-18, 26.
76. John Julius Norwich, *Sicily - A Short History from the Ancient Greeks to Cosa Nostra* (London: John Murray Publishing, 2016), 64–65.
77. Diana Darke, *Stealing from the Saracens: How Islamic Architecture Shaped Europe* (London: C. Hurst & Co. 2020), 256.
78. William Granara, *Narrating Muslim Sicily* (London: I.B.Tauris, 2019), 164.
79. *Ibid.*, 106.

## Chapter Five

80. Tancred, *Aristotle, The Metaphysics Translation*, 312.
81. Desmond Lee and T.K. Johansen, *Plato, Timaeus and Critias* (Suffolk: Penguin Classics, 2008), 21.

82. Christopher Rowe, *Plato, Phaedrus*, (Suffolk: Penguin Classics, 2005), 25.
83. Ho, *Plotinus' Mystical Teachings of Henosis*, 101.
84. *Ibid.*, 108.
85. *Ibid.*, 39.
86. *Ibid.*, 27.
87. Bussanich, pg 132 V.5 [32].7.31-8.27, Pao Shen Ho 85 & 86 VI.9.9.55-58, VI.9.10.9-11, VI.7.34.13-14, Pao Shen Ho pg 81 I.6.7.12-19, J Bussanich pg 143, I.6[1].9. 37-39.
88. Ho, *Plotinus' Mystical Teachings of Henosis*, 100.
89. Gerson, ed., *Plotinus: The Enneads*, 824, 846.
90. *Ibid.*, 35.
91. Stephen Hawking, A *Brief History of Time: From the Big Bang to Black Hole* (London: Bantam Books, Transworld Publishers, Penguin Random House, 2016), 96, 109, 135, 136.

**Chapter Six**
92. Gerson, ed., *Plotinus: The Enneads*, 24.
93. *Ibid.*, 828, 894.
94. *Ibid.*, 18.
95. Sperl, *Faces of the Infinite*, 455.
96. Gerson, ed., *Plotinus: The Enneads*, 837, 838, 839, 840, 841.

**Epilogue**
97. Gerson, ed., *Plotinus: The Enneads*, 893.
98. Deussen and Geden, *The Philosophy of The Upanishads*, 44.
99. Andrea Wulf, *Magnificent Rebels: The First Romantics and the Invention of the Self* (London: John Murray Publishers, 2022), 282.
100. Gerson, ed., *Plotinus: The Enneads*, 86.

# BIBLIOGRAPHY

Ali, Abdullah Yusuf, The Holy Quran, Text, Translation and Commentary (Delhi: Kitab Bhavan, Daryaganj, 1996).

Bussanich, J. *The One and its Relation to Intellect in Plotinus* – A *Commentary on Selected Texts* (The Netherlands: E.J Brill, 1988).

Castiglione, Baldesar, *The Book of the Courtier*, Translated by George Bull (London: Penguin Classics, 2003).

Clark, Eleanor, *Rome and a Villa* (London: Michael Joseph, 1953).

Dalrymple, William, *From the Holy Mountain* (London: Harper Perennial, 2005).

Darke, Diana, *Stealing from the Saracens: How Islamic Architecture Shaped Europe* (London: C. Hurst & Co., 2020).

Darwin, Charles, *On The Origin of Species* (Cambridge Massachusetts: Harvard University Press, 1964).

Deussen, Paul, and Rev. A.S. Geden, *The Philosophy of the Upanishads* (Delhi: Motilal Banarsidas Publishers, 2017).

Freely, John, *Storm on Horseback: The Seljuk Warriors of Turkey* (London: I.B. Tauris, 2008).

Gerson, Lloyd, ed., *Plotinus: The Enneads* (Cambridge University Press, 2018).

Gibbon, Edward, *The History of the Decline and Fall of the Roman*

*Empire*, Edited and Abridged by David Womersley (London: Penguin Books, 2005).

Gill, Christopher, *The Symposium*, Plato, translated with an introduction and notes by Christopher Gill (London: Penguin Classics, 1999).

Granara, William, *Narrating Muslim Sicily* (London: I.B. Tauris, 2019).

Hawking, Stephen, *A Brief History of Time: From the Big Bang to Black Hole* (London: Bantam Books, Transworld Publishers, Penguin Random House, 2016).

Harari, Yuval Noah, *Sapiens: A Brief History of Humankind* (London: Vintage, Penguin Random House, 2015).

Harris, Jonathan, *The End of Byzantium* (London: Yale University Press, 2012).

Ho, Pao-Shen, *Plotinus' Mystical Teachings of Henosis*, Peter Lang Edition (Frankfurt: International Verlag der Wissenchaften, 2015).

Hussain, Mumtaz, *Amir Khusrow Dehlawi* (New Delhi: The National Amir Khusrow Society, Aiwan-e Ghalib, 1986).

Isaacson, Walter, *Leonardo Da Vinci - The Biography* (London: Simon & Schuster UK, 2017).

Lee, Desmond and T.K. Johansen, *Plato, Timaeus and Critias* (Suffolk: Penguin Classics, 2008).

Murgia, Madhumita, *Financial Times Weekend Magazine*, 9-10 April 2022.

Norwich, John Julius, *Sicily - A Short History from the Ancient Greeks to Cosa Nostra* (London: John Murray Publishing, 2016).

Rosenthal, Franz, *The Muqaddimah, An Introduction to History* by Ibn Khaldun, translated by Franz Rosenthal, abridged and edited by N.J. Dawood, Bollingen series, with an introduction by Bruce B. Lawrence (Princeton and Oxford: Princeton University Press, 2005).

Rowe, Christopher, *Plato, Phaedrus* (Suffolk: Penguin Classics, 2005).

Sattin, Anthony, *The Pharaoh's Shadow: Travels in Ancient and Modern Egypt* (London: Eland Publishing London, 2012).

Sattin, Anthony, Jessica Lee, Michael Benanav & Zora O'Neill, *Egypt, Lonely Planet*, July 2012.

Scott, Walter, *Hermetica: The Ancient Greek and Latin Writings which contain Religious or Philosophic Teachings Ascribed to Hermes Trismegistus* (Boston: Shambhala, 1993).

Sperl, Stefan, and Yorgos Dedes, *Faces of the Infinite* (Published for The British Academy by Oxford University Press, 2022).

Tancred, Hugh Lawson, *Aristotle, The Metaphysics Translation* (London: Penguin Books, 1998).

Wulf, Andrea, *Magnificent Rebels: The First Romantics and the Invention of the Self* (London: John Murray Publishers, 2022).

# INDEX

Index

# Index

Pope Innocent IV, 178

Porphyry, 149–153, 164, 166, 167, 171–175, 214, 221

Porta Settimiana, 14, 15

Poseidon, 21

Power of 'Oneness', 6, 25, 41, 45, 63, 64, 75, 88, 90, 114, 159, 161, 162, 164, 187, 190, 192, 214, 233, 234

Praetorian guard, 37, 118, 119, 121, 137–139, 143

Princess Lola musical, 93

Prophet Daniel, 112

Prophet Elias chapel, 205, 211, 212, 215

Ptolemy I, 88, 111, 113

Ptolemy II, 109

Ptolemy III, 113

Ptolemy XII, 88, 89, 91

Puglia, 3, 20, 22

Putin, Vladimir, xix, 158, 234

Pyramids of Giza, 59

Pythagoras, 209

Pythian games, 191, 192

Qasr al Nil bridge, 70

Quran, 69, 104, 214

Rafael, 16, 17

Ramese, 114

Rameses II, 15, 95, 99

Rameses III, 94, 95, 99, 100, 114

Raphael, 195, 227, 233
'The School of Athens' painting, 195, 227, 233

Resaena war, 137–139

Rhakotis hill, 113

Rhine, 146

Rifai Mosque, 71

Roger II, 177, 182, 183

Rohingya Muslims, 130, 131

Roman empire, 8, 21, 89, 128, 147, 149, 152, 164–166
beginning of end, 149
setback to, 152
unrest in, 147–149

Roman Forum, 5

Romanos IV, 128

Rome Call, 237

Romulus, 145

Rostra, 6, 149, 154

Saccas, Ammonius, 52, 101, 109, 115, 152, 221

Sahara, 58, 109, 110

Sahin, Ugur, 188

Salah, Mohamed, 49

Salahuddin, 103–105
writeup on, 104–105

Salonia (Gallienus wife), 175

Samos Island, 209

Sanskritized-Greek, 37, 46

Saqqara Pyramid, 50, 53, 56, 214

Sassanian dynasty, 119

Sattin, Anthony, 61, 110-112, 114
*The Pharaoh's Shadow*, 61, 110, 111

Sayyida Zainab district, 67, 70

Schelling, Friedrich, 231, 233, 234

Schliemann, Heinrich, 112

Second World War, 8, 186

Segan, Carl, 240

Selecus I Nicator, 35

Selinunte, the Greek temple, 174–176

Index

# SHORT HISTORIC
# COUNTRY TOWNS

## DAVID SOUDEN

Bakewell
•
Kendal
•
King's Lynn
•
Richmond
•
Rye
•
Sherborne
•
Warwick

GEORGE
PHILIP

British Library Cataloguing in Publication Data

Souden, David
    Short breaks in historic country towns.
    1. Towns.    2. England
    I. Title
    942.009732

    ISBN 0-540-01207-6


Text © David Souden 1991
Illustrations © George Philip 1991
Maps © George Philip 1991


First published by George Philip Limited,
59 Grosvenor Street, London W1X 9DA


Illustrations by Patrick Tate
Maps by John Gilkes
Based upon Ordnance Survey 1:50 000 Landranger and 1:10 000 maps with the
permission of the Controller of Her Majesty's Stationery Office
© Crown copyright


Printed in Great Britain by
Butler & Tanner Ltd, Frome and London

*For Jan Parmiter, and*
*in memory of Molly Parmiter*

# CONTENTS

4

# INTRODUCTION

'God made the country, and Man made the town – and the devil', some say, 'made the English country town.' They say wrong. Country towns have a vitality of their very own – and the signs are that recently this vitality has been growing and small country towns have been regaining their pride.

Perhaps I am biased, having grown up mainly in small towns. Much more survives from their past than in most larger cities. They are a manageable size to explore and get to know, and some have a bravura architectural display or unity of building style that adds to their charm. Small towns sit firmly within the countryside that surrounds them, their markets – always part of the reason for their existence – bringing in people and trade from the area around. To understand country towns is to know so much more about the past, and that is part of the motive force behind this book. Seven country towns and day tours based upon them are described here. All of them are fun and interesting to explore; knowing what made them or who lived in them brings stone, bricks and mortar to life; and staying in them offers every opportunity to investigate further the countryside around.

There is interest in appreciating their quality: the layout, the succession of buildings on the same site, the refacing of older structures to bring them up to date. Building materials – stone, brick, timber, tile – express the geology of the areas in which they are situated. And there is interest in appreciating their past. Most of the towns selected here have in some way failed to live up to the grandeur and importance they all once had, but it is this very failure which has ensured the preservation of their characters. Their former wealth is reflected in what they built in their heyday and have largely failed to build since, or at least not built on the same scale as greater and faster-growing towns and cities.

Of the towns covered in this book, King's Lynn and Rye were among the major centres of medieval and Tudor England; Sherborne goes back even further. The shire towns and those places which attracted the local gentry in Stuart and Georgian England, like Warwick and Richmond, or were rebuilt to attract a spa clientele, like Bakewell, were among the fastest growing towns in the 150 years before the Victorian era. They in their turn were eclipsed by industrial centres. Kendal, the most 'Victorian' town represented in this book, grew at an astonishing pace in the eighteenth and nineteenth centuries, but was surpassed by more ambitious and successful towns in the industrial heartlands.

The legacy of fame and growth followed by relative obscurity and slower expansion or even decline, is the mark of all the towns in this book. I have chosen them for their variety –

port, coast, hill, industry, social display. They vary in size, they vary in form, they vary in material, they vary in setting. I have a connection with many of them. Sherborne I remember as a child. In King's Lynn I first learned to 'read' a town in detail through its buildings as well as its archives. Rye was the town of my ancestors, although there is no sign of any connection now. I was grateful that nobody in Kendal seemed to recognize me as the holiday-maker of ten years before who had innocently taken a jar of jam from a stack in a grocer's shop, to find all the jars flying in every direction, scattering their coloured contents as they smashed.

One mark of these small towns is how many of them have been rescued and revitalized in the past few years. Rather than their centres' being condemned to wholesale destruction, older buildings have been preserved or appropriate materials used in new buildings. Even in the time it has taken to travel and research for this book, return visits to the towns have shown previously decayed and even near-derelict properties being restored to useful life. Many of the towns are expanding again, and while some have benefited from the boom in tourism and shopping, they all have the strong feeling that life continues regardless.

This book is designed to be the only tool you need for your short break away. For each of the seven towns, there is a detailed walking tour of the historic centre, mixing the architectural and historical with the present day. That is followed by a number of wider-ranging countryside tours from the centre, most of which would represent a day trip, enjoying the scenery and places to visit. These historic towns are often at the junction of quite different types of countryside, and that fact is exploited in the touring sections. Road instructions are included in the itineraries, as well as an indication of points at which the longer tours might be made shorter or the shorter tours combined. At the back of the book there is a practical section for each town, describing access to it and indicating likely and reasonably-priced places to stay and to eat, and a list of houses, gardens, and museums open to the public which figure in the tours. (Places included in these listings appear in italic in the text.)

This book is, if you like, historically driven. Everything in it has been chosen to appeal to our sense of the past, and to make us more aware of how towns grow. All of the towns have a surface appeal which is made all the more interesting by exploring. Delve down alleyways, look at the backs of buildings, and you'll find out so much more about a place. In the course of my research, I have been taken for, variously, a school master, a surveyor, the VAT man, the man from the council. That should not put you off. Enjoy England instead, and its rich and varied legacy of small towns.

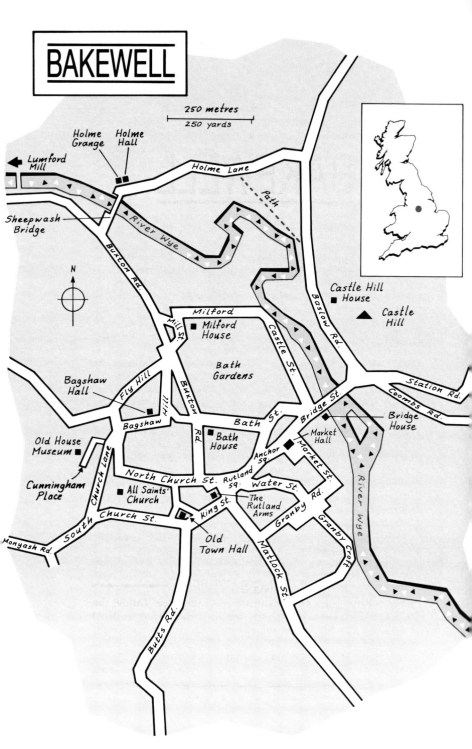

# BAKEWELL

250 metres
250 yards

Lumford Mill

Holme Grange

Holme Hall

Holme Lane

Path

Sheepwash Bridge

River Wye

Buxton Rd.

N

Milford

Mill St.

Milford House

Bath Gardens

Castle St.

Baslow Rd.

Castle Hill House

Castle Hill

Station Rd.

Bagshaw Hall

Fly Hill

Bagshaw

Buxton Rd.

Bath St.

Bridge St.

Coombs Rd.

Bridge House

Market Hall

Old House Museum

Cunningham Place

North Church St.

Rutland Sq.

Water St.

Anchor Sq.

Market St.

River Wye

South Church Lane

All Saints' Church

King St.

The Rutland Arms

Granby Rd.

Granby Croft

Monyash Rd.

Old Town Hall

Matlock St.

Butts Rd.

# 1
# BAKEWELL

Derbyshire

*The word Bakewell has passed into the English language,
as a name for a jam tart with a sugary almond topping.
Two establishments claim to make the original Bakewell
pudding. What they sell you is unlike any other version of
a 'Bakewell tart'; after it, nothing else called Bakewell will
ever seem quite the same. Bakewell is a small town in a
vast setting, with many enjoyable moments, only some of
which involve food.*

*Despite its small size, Bakewell is the most important
town in the Peak District National Park and has been a
significant site since the end of the Dark Ages, when people
began to colonize what had been inhospitable upland. It
is possible that Bakewell was once a Roman military camp,
and certainly the Romans exploited the local lead deposits.*

*The deep valley of the Wye in which Bakewell sits is a
natural thoroughfare, avoiding the bleak upper slopes of
the Peak District – limestone to the south, millstone grit to
the north. The remains of the lead-mining industry
pockmark the moors. Quarrying and tourism are the
mainstays of the local economy. Half of the population of
England lives within sixty miles of the area, and the Peak
District is its playground, from the wild moorland to the
beautiful towns, villages and stately homes.*

## EXPLORING BAKEWELL

Bakewell is set on the western side of the Wye Valley; the
spire of the parish church is the only significant vertical
element in the view from the river bank. The eastern side of
the valley is still open fields, dotted with grazing sheep and
cattle. The honey-coloured and reddish stones in which this
market town is built give it a pleasing uniformity, enhanced
by the rebuilding undertaken by the aristocratic patrons
whose influence over Bakewell is evident everywhere. The

attempt to transform Bakewell into a spa has left a legacy of handsome buildings, making it an ideal town to explore.

The bridge over the Wye leading into Bakewell from the north-east is the place to start. It is one of the town's finest ancient structures, built for pack-horses in around 1300, and spans the river on five arches with pointed breakwaters. Even when it was widened in the nineteenth century, the original stonework was reused. The view from the bridge is sublime: the Wye meanders through the fields, the heavily wooded slopes to the east cover the probable site of the ninth-century royal fortress that established Bakewell's importance, and the town itself runs up from the west bank.

Much of Bakewell has been shaped by the ideas and wishes of local landowners, such as the Cavendish family, Dukes of Devonshire, and particularly by the Manners family, Dukes of Rutland. They owned most property in the town until the early twentieth century. The 5th Duke of Rutland had ambitious plans for transforming Bakewell into a spa in around 1800, to rival Buxton (some 13 miles to the north-west), which had made the Dukes of Devonshire wealthy. His venture failed, yet left the town transformed. The first sign of his scheme is Bridge House immediately on the left over the bridge, now a solid pair of houses in the warm, dark, honey-coloured stone in which most of Bakewell is built. Now sensitively divided into shops and a restaurant, this was designed to be one of the more important houses for renting to visitors. Unfortunately only a vestige of the garden behind the house remains. This was laid out by Joseph Paxton (1801–65) of Chatsworth in the 1840s, but is now a public car park.

Entering town along Bridge Street, the next important building is the early Stuart Market Hall, on the left, which is now the *Peak District National Park Information Centre*. The double gable end is severely plain, and the glazed-in arches on the ground floor were originally open. The upper storey, lit by rows of windows and dormers on the street side, served as the Town Hall through the nineteenth century until a new one was built opposite in the 1880s.

From the open space in front of the Market Hall, the results of the ducal rebuilding of Bakewell are apparent. The centre of the town was realigned, when the old market place was swept away, and the new Anchor Square that replaced it meets Bridge Street to form the wider space of Rutland Square with the grand front of the *Rutland Arms Hotel* closing the view at the bottom. Side streets off to the left, like Water Lane and Water Street, are stone-built terraced rows typical of those the Duke built, replacing older thatched stone and wood houses. Among the shops on the left-hand side is one of the two establishments claiming to make the 'original' Bakewell pudding, the confection of jam, pastry, and almond topping supposedly invented by accident in a town hotel in

1860 (the other claimant's shop is situated on Matlock Road). A prouder piece of the Duke's work stands on Rutland Square itself, a row of gabled houses, now all shops, that rounds the corner into Matlock Street. Some of the original grandeur of Rutland Square has perhaps been lost, for its centre is now a large roundabout – and since this is the A6, traffic is often heavy. At quieter times of day it regains some of its designer's intended poise.

One of Bakewell's most impressive Victorian buildings, the classical Sheffield & Rotherham Bank building of 1838, now the Royal Bank of Scotland, stands opposite this row of shops. Beside it, a foil to the limestone buildings around, are the Bath Gardens, a blaze of bright green lawn and colourful bedding plants, which were originally developed from 1814 as a botanical garden to be part of the spa's attractions. The Rutland Arms Hotel, on the western side of the square, was built in 1804 as another part of the development. A large, three-storey frontage of five bays, it has the rather plain façade that the Duke's architect tended to use, broken only by a square portico of Tuscan Doric columns in the centre. The only original interior feature of note is the staircase. Jane Austen (1775–1817) is believed to have stayed in one of the rooms in 1811, where she worked on the Derbyshire episodes in *Pride and Prejudice*.

Running along the south side of the hotel, King Street begins the gentle climb up the hillside, and opens out on the right into what was once the Cornmarket. Facing you is the Old Town Hall, built in 1602 as the foundation of Sir John Manners' almshouse, and remodelled in 1709. The remodelling did not bring the building up to date, since it still has plain casement windows on both floors (sash windows were highly fashionable at the time), and the end wall rises above the roof line to form a curious stone bellcote. The alterations were made when new almshouses were built at the back. Until then the ground floor had been open and the almsmen had slept in little cells at the rear. The almshouses themselves were also built in an outdated style for 1709: a stone-built row with plain gables and mullioned casement windows.

The ground floor of the Town Hall is now an antiques showroom for the shop on the right, Avenel Court, which has an oddly jumbled late eighteenth-century front, with windows in a variety of sizes and shapes. This frontage hides a group of the town's earliest surviving buildings, including timber framing of the fifteenth or sixteenth centuries.

South Church Street, which climbs up towards the churchyard, is lined by the almshouses and low stone cottages on the right, and more substantial houses, often given Georgian fronts, opposite. The unusual octagonal tower and spire of the parish church – All Saints' – rises up on top of the hill, and steps run up to the raised churchyard. It has been an important Christian site since the eighth or the ninth century. Outside the south door stands the shaft of Bakewell's renowned ninth-century Saxon cross, carved with animals, scrolls and some human figures, while many Anglo-Saxon and early Norman carved stone coffin lids and monuments are stacked up in the south porch and inside the church at the west end. This broad, reddish-coloured church was originally very grand indeed, as the mainly Norman west end still shows. Although the thirteenth-century rebuilding never quite achieved what was hoped for, it is itself a substantial building. The tower, spire and south transept (the thirteenth-century Newark, or new work) were all rebuilt in the 1840s, when the church was in severe danger of collapse. The townspeople wanted the church rebuilt just as it had been, but the architect 'reinterpreted' some of the medieval work, and the spire emerged sixteen feet shorter than before.

The inside of the church is renowned for its monuments. The Newark contains a great sequence of Tudor and early Stuart memorials to the Vernon and Manners families of Haddon Hall behind a beautiful, fifteenth-century wooden screen. Adjacent to the entrance to the Newark is Bakewell's most important, and most affecting, single memorial: an alabaster wall monument of 1385 to Sir Godfrey Foljambe and his wife Avena, shown from the waist up within a decorated arched surround, almost as if they were tucked up in bed. The collection of early medieval stone coffins and memorials is probably the most important in England.

The *Old House Museum* on Cunningham Place, the lane behind the churchyard, is the sole survivor of a type of house that was once common in Bakewell, a rather irregular building of rough stone, with various small windows and a few larger mullioned openings on the front. It is first recorded in 1534, as an older timber structure which had been recased in stone. Six families of workers at Sir Richard Arkwright's new cotton mill nearby lived in this little house when it had been subdivided in the late eighteenth century, and the cottages declined into ever more dilapidated and insanitary condition, until they were rescued in 1954. The history of the Old House was then, like the oak beams and the wattle and daub walls inside, painstakingly uncovered. The Museum contains many local exhibits, from the town's last surviving barber's shop pole to the effects of a local Quaker family.

North Church Street runs down the other side of the churchyard. Its seventeenth- and eighteenth-century cottages have often had newer fronts tacked on, as a foray along the back alleys will reveal. At the bottom of the hill, beside the Rutland Arms, Buxton Road goes off to your left. Rutland Terrace, a row of tall, early nineteenth-century houses divided by pilasters and still possessing their original railings, dominates the left-hand side. Rutland House

*The bridge over the Wye at Bakewell.*

opposite, of the same date but in a more classical style, also with its original railings, was the Duke of Rutland's own town house. 'Beyond the terrace and some shops – the Victorian butcher's shop sells incomparable pork pies – cross the road to Bath Street, the core of the intended spa. The waters at Bakewell were known about in Saxon times; the town's name comes from the Saxon *Bad Quell* ('Bath Well'). A number of warm-water springs emerge at Bakewell, although the only significant one is that of the plain, gabled Bath House on the right, a building of 1697 containing the 1st Duke's private spa water bath. The water temperature is usually some 16° C (61° F) which is significantly cooler than the Buxton waters, and one reason for the failure of the 5th Duke's venture.

The town gardens, conceived as part of the spa's attractions, run beside the Bath House through to Rutland Square. They were originally laid out by White Watson, Bakewell's leading entrepreneur, geologist and Mr Fix-It, who lived in the Bath House and ran the spa for His Grace. Watson had many lines of business. His trade card said: 'W. Watson, having attentively collected the minerals and fossils of Derbyshire, is now in possession of a valuable assortment ready for the inspection of the curious.' The increasing flow of visitors to the Peak District, and increasing tourist and scientific interest in rocks, provided a ready audience.

The British Legion now occupies the Bath House (the 33-foot long bath in the vaulted basement may be seen on written application). The large seventeenth-century house at right angles to the street followed another local tradition, having a face-lift in the mid eighteenth century when its street side was ashlared and its windows sashed, with an oval light let into the gable. Bath Street rounds the corner past the Victorian town hall into Anchor Square. At the far end of the square turn left into Castle Street.

Castle Street is lined with eighteenth-century terraced houses, in a much more vernacular style than the town-centre terraces. Castle Street leads to the quiet Milford area of the town and the pathway running alongside the millstream flowing into the Wye. Way up on the hillside ahead, Bagshaw Hall looks down into the valley: a grand house of 1683 with pedimented windows and doorcase, and a balustraded top to the central recessed bay. At the end of the pathway, tucked behind its garden wall, is the equally grand but later *Milford House Hotel*, with the old mill itself on the right over the little mill-race. The hotel has a Victorian stone front and glazed porch on its garden side, and an earlier, coarser entrance front, dated 1763. It was originally the mill house: the Victorian additions and refacing were done for a Manchester cotton-mill owner, Robert Cross, who retired here. The mill was built in around 1800, but it was not the first as this had always been the site of the main corn mill for the town. It has cast-iron windows, and a very large mid nineteenth-century cast-iron water wheel (although it is no longer in the water).

The cottages on Mill Street – the short road curving from the hotel to Buxton Road – are very important eighteenth-century survivals. This little development was one of the earliest attempts, by Richard Arkwright I (1732–92), to put up sound and serviceable, purpose-built industrial housing. In Arkwright Square, and in a now-demolished row of Bath Street, he put small cottages (with privies) around a central courtyard. This was his second venture of the kind, and was for workers at his cotton spinning mill at Lumford.

Buxton Road out of town runs parallel to the river. The first opportunity to cross the river comes 600 yards upstream at Holme, by the narrow Sheepwash bridge set among the meadows. The seven-arched bridge was rebuilt in 1664. Sir Richard Arkwright's Lumford Mill, built in 1778, is reached along a private road past a stone house (Richard Arkwright II probably lived here until his father's death), and terraced cottages. A fire at the mill in 1868 did not completely destroy it: the creeper-clad stone building beside the river is part of the original structure, which was 186 feet long and only 30 feet wide with a water wheel through its centre. The appropriation of water for the mill reservoir badly affected the flow of the stream, to the anger of the townspeople and of the Dukes of Rutland and Devonshire who owned (and still own) the water rights, so a larger reservoir was built upstream and a new channel cut. Parts of this survive; and sections of the great 1827 water wheel, in use until 1955, are preserved outside Old House Museum. The power capacity of the wheel was extraordinary for its day, about 100 horsepower running 12,000 spindles. Lumford Mill and the Arkwrights' housing have an important place in the history of the modern factory.

Returning along the Lumford Lane, the pathway through the meadows starts at a pair of substantial seventeenth-century houses: Holme Grange beside the road and the larger Holme Hall behind, built in 1626. Its gazebo and summer house are visible from the pathway leading back to the town bridge. The stucco-fronted Castle Hill House, visible through the trees beyond the meadows, was originally the house of the Duke of Rutland's agent – one of the more influential men in the town. It is now part of the Lady Manners' School. Back at the bridge we come full circle, and realize how charmingly small and contained Bakewell is.

# ——— AROUND AND ABOUT BAKEWELL ———

*The millstone standing on a limestone plinth that is the sign marking the boundaries of the Peak District National Park is a reminder of one of the traditional industries, and of the rocks that have shaped this landscape and the livelihood of its people. Millstone grit, as hard and durable as its name suggests, forms a horse-collar shape, the Dark Peak, around the limestone region of the White Peak. Seams of lead, and occasionally other metals and minerals, intrude. The remains of Bronze Age, Iron Age, medieval and modern men and their industries cover the moors and dales of the landscape. Spa waters bubble up. There were already tourists in the seventeenth century, who came to visit the 'Seven Wonders of the Peak', many of which remain wonders to this day. To the east into Nottinghamshire, they mine coal, and to the south some of the earliest cotton factories of the industrial revolution survive. Great houses have been built on the profits of this natural wealth. To have one important aristocratic country house on the doorstep might be considered fortunate. To have two looks like boasting – and with Haddon Hall and Chatsworth, Bakewell has two of the finest.*

*As the only town of any size within the boundaries of the Peak District National Park, Bakewell is a good base from which to explore the Park and the surrounding areas.*

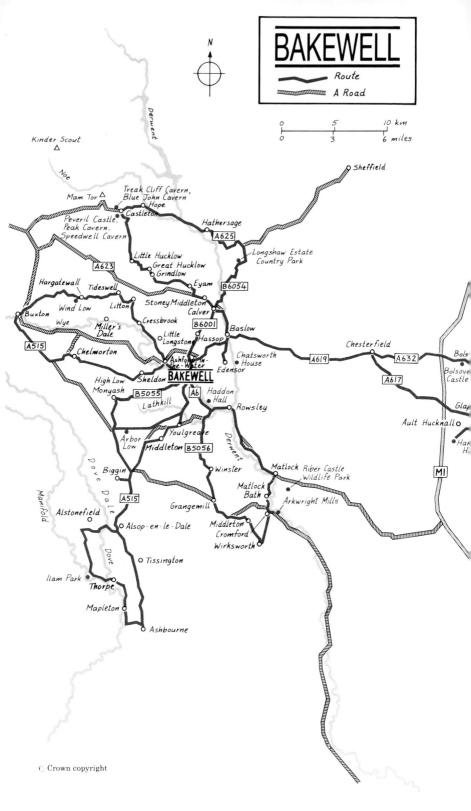

## 1. THE WYE VALLEY AND BUXTON

A short distance upstream from Bakewell the handsome, tidy stone village of Ashford-in-the-Water clusters above its three bridges. The narrow, ancient Sheepwash bridge nearest the over-Victorianized church still has the pound alongside where the sheep were kept prior to dipping. The newest bridge carries the A6020 from the A6. Ashford was renowned in the eighteenth century for its 'black marble', a form of limestone that took a high polish and is to be found in many a chimneypiece or chequered floor, and attempts are now being made to revive the craft. The Ashford works, once owned by White Watson of Bakewell and his forebears, now lie under the A6.

From the upper part of the village, the B6465 climbs the hillside towards Little Longstone. Suddenly, the ground falls away at the left. Monsal Dale, with the Wye flowing in its gorge far below, is a dramatic view, even in a county of clefts and crags. Spanning the river is the high Monsal Head stone railway viaduct, marching on its great arches. This viaduct is now the spectacular culmination of the walking route along the disused railway from Bakewell. Its construction was greeted with hysterical condemnation by John Ruskin (1819–1900) and others in the 1860s; its proposed demolition a century later was greeted with an equal outcry, and since the structure was too strong to be dismantled easily, it stayed.

The unclassified road left from the crossroads at the Monsal Dale viewpoint descends to the river bank and continues alongside the Wye to the tangled knot of lanes at Cressbrook. Just before the village the cotton mill established by Richard Arkwright in 1779 and rebuilt in 1815 stands between the road and the river. This was one of the small factory colonies early industrialists like Arkwright built to harness both water power and available labour; behind the elegant, pedimented mill stands the vaguely Gothick apprentices' house where the young mill-workers were, according to contemporary reports, far better treated than in most similar establishments. From the hamlet there is a memorable walk past the weir and through the gorge to Miller's Dale and another mill building at Litton – where the apprentices were much more harshly used.

The road climbs the hillside to Litton, a sturdy stone-built hamlet on an exposed site. The turn to the left from the village church reaches Tideswell, sitting in its little bowl in the hills. It was once the market town for this upland limestone area, and now bears an air of gentle decline. The best sign of Tideswell's former glory is the fourteenth-century parish church, one of the finest in Derbyshire. The church is tall and well-lit, with a great pinnacled west tower, and a wealth of medieval monuments inside, including that in the chancel to Sir Sampson Meverell, who in the early fifteenth century 'fought eleven battles against Joan of Arc' as it says unblushingly. Tideswell's one-time great claim to fame was the 'ebbing well' – one of the Seven Wonders of the Peak, but the water level no longer rises and falls, and the lead mining that sustained the region has long gone.

Almost due west from Tideswell, the unclassified road descends to cross Monk's Dale, and up again to Hargatewall and to Wind Low. Just west of the hamlet beside the road, Wind Low is the first of many ancient burial and ritual sites to be seen in the Peak District. The Bronze Age burial mound is topped by the remains of a medieval cross. From the topmost point at Bole Hill, another unclassified road bears south-west to cross the steep-sided Great Rocks Dale, then past the exposed golf course and old quarry workings, to enter Buxton on the A6.

Buxton lays claim to be the highest town in England, at over 1000 feet above sea level. Its fame is due to the spa, where waters gush continuously at a steady 28° C (82° F). The Romans knew it as Aqua Arnemetiae; pilgrims came to the miraculous waters of St Anne's Well in the Middle Ages, and the baths were reopened after the Reformation 'by popular demand' – even Mary Queen of Scots (1542–87) was allowed out of captivity in Chatsworth to take the waters. In the 1780s the 5th Duke of Devonshire decided to develop Buxton as a northern rival to Bath, using profits from his copper mines. He under-wrote the building of the great Crescent, designed by John Carr of York (1723–1807), and other new attractions. Buxton's popularity increased with the coming of the railway in 1863, but the rival attractions of the seaside brought a slow decline which has been arrested only in recent years.

From the A6, Buxton town centre is reached going west along Spring Gardens. Old Buxton rises on the hill to the left, while straight ahead lies the semi-circular Crescent, the grandest of all Buxton's architecture. It is on the site of St Anne's Well (another of the Seven Wonders). One of the three original hotels in the Crescent still operates, while the baths and assembly rooms within have been converted into shops, restaurants, and a library. West of the Crescent, the infant Wye flows through the Pavilion Gardens. These were laid out at the height of Buxton's popularity as a Victorian spa, with the iron and glass Pavilion buildings on the slope above, the Octagon concert hall, the extravagantly Edwardian opera house and the modern spa-water swimming pool. The spa is completed by the early nineteenth-century, classical parish church and the Devonshire Royal Hospital. This was originally a huge circular stable built by Carr in 1785, and roofed over in 1881 with what was then the world's largest dome.

Pretty Georgian terraced houses, intended for visitors, line the right side of Hall Bank which rises steeply from new Buxton to the old Market Place. The eighteenth-century Eagle Hotel and the 1880s Town Hall stand at its northern end, next to Terrace Road, which leads back down to Spring Gardens. *Buxton Town Museum* on the right of Terrace Road houses an extensive permanent exhibition on the geology and history of the Peak.

The A515, following the line of a Roman road, continues out of Buxton past the right-hand turn to the floodlit limestone show cave of Poole's Cavern – the third Great Wonder – and on to the high (and still rising) land. Three miles out of Buxton, the A5270 strikes north-east, and the first right turn off it leads into Chelmorton. One of the highest villages in the country, Chelmorton has many delightful features and survivals. In the pre-enclosure manner, which has now otherwise almost entirely disappeared, the farms line the single street, with their strip fields running out behind; the best of them, the eighteenth-century Town End Farm, stands at the entrance to the village. At the other end the twelfth- and thirteenth-century parish church, with a stone rood screen preserved inside, crouches below the 1400-foot hill, on which the Illy Willy Water rises to flow along Chelmorton village street and then disappear back into the limestone.

The road carries on along the moorland top, through a landscape marked by the remains of many former lead mines, to High Low – 'Low' is a Derbyshire term meaning hill. The road forks left to Sheldon, a decayed mining village with mainly late Georgian houses that cling quite picturesquely to the hillside of Sharp Dale. On the plateau south of the village, the Magpie Mine, which was finally abandoned only in 1958, has been restored as one of the best-preserved of Derbyshire's countless lead-mining sites. Its remains include the 1864 engine house and chimney for a Cornish beam engine, a large lined drain (or sough) that takes the water from the mine, and the pit headgear installed in 1951.

The steep, wooded road down Kirk Dale meets the A6 across the Wye from Ashford-in-the-Water, and the main road leads back to Bakewell.

## 2. INTO THE DARK PEAK

From Bakewell's position in the midst of the limestone country of the White Peak, it is an exciting journey north into the sterner heights of the Dark Peak. The A619 passes the former Victorian workhouse, now Bakewell Hospital, and rounds the steep slopes of Handley Bottom to Chatsworth Park. The main road north-east between the hills leads through Baslow, one of the Chatsworth estate villages, crossing the Derwent beside the old humpbacked bridge and the dumpy church, which was restored by Joseph Paxton in the 1850s. From the junction ahead the A623 follows the river, through the Victorian part of the village, and past Baslow Hall, an effective Edwardian pastiche of a seventeenth-century manor house, built for Sebastian de Ferranti of the famous electrical company.

The road continues between the steep valley slopes, with the high, hard edge of the millstone moor to the east. As the road curves left to cross the Derwent, there is a superb view of the stark Calver Mill, built by the Arkwrights in 1803, and backed by the steep wooded slopes above the river. Unlike many of the upland mills, it has been put to productive use again – as a film set doubling for Colditz Castle prisoner-of-war camp and a metal-working factory. From the village of Calver the B6054 strikes right, through Calver Sough (named after the outfall drain or sough from the lead mines) to recross the Derwent, and head north up the steep escarpment to emerge on the moor top.

As the road continues to climb, it passes through *Longshaw Estate Country Park,* an area of woodland and moorland owned by the National Trust, with a former hunting lodge belonging to the Dukes of Rutland set deep within it. Some of the woodland is ancient, and the area is littered with stone circles, barrow mounds and deserted settlements, all evidence of prehistoric dwellers. The A625 to Hathersage negotiates a series of right-angle bends beneath the cliffs and crags. Rejected millstones lie around in the heather-clad slopes of one of those cliffs, Millstone Edge, which was once a centre of the industry. Most of the village of Hathersage lies north of the A625. Its former wealth was based mainly on needlemaking, and a number of mill buildings survive, like Dale Mill at the upper end of the village, and Barnfield and Victoria Mills below the road. St Michael's church stands at the village's upper end, a late fourteenth-century building with many monuments to the Eyre family inside – Charlotte Brontë (1816–55) used Hathersage as a model for Morton in *Jane Eyre.* In the churchyard lies the supposed grave of Little John of Robin Hood fame.

The A625 continues west along the bottom of the Noe valley, with steep hills and moors rising on both sides. The villages follow the springline on the northern slopes. Hope, just above the confluence of the Noe and the Peakshole Water, is one of the less crowded of the villages in the area.

Its church was the mother church for a huge parish that covered two-thirds of the extensive ancient Royal Forest of the High Peak. The church itself is a mainly thirteenth- and fourteenth-century building, with the west tower rebuilt in the eighteenth century. Near it a number of old houses, including the early seventeenth-century Old Hall Hotel and the more sophisticated, Georgian Daggers House, which was originally an inn, show something of Hope's former importance. Industry, past and present, is a marked feature of Hope, where the giant cement works to the south of the village, hidden by trees, is ringed by the remains of former lead workings.

Castleton, a mile or so further west, has spectacular remains of local industry in the form of the natural and man-made caverns within the hillside, and of the might of the Normans in the ruins of *Peveril Castle*. The castle is perched high up on the southern side of the village, on a naturally defensive site, and much of the early Norman north wall is still standing. The walls and the twelfth-century keep were all built in stone; two thirteenth-century towers to the south used Roman bricks from the fort at Navio, south of the river beyond Hope. The castle fell into disuse from the fourteenth century and by the seventeenth was in ruins.

In the little, planned town at the foot of the castle, seventeenth-century box pews, carved with the names of their owners' houses, are retained inside the otherwise heavily early-Victorian parish church. Castleton's claims to fame are its caves and Blue John, a purple-blue form of fluorspar, an unusual and decorative semi-precious stone which was mined here. The first of the caves is the mammoth entrance, fifty feet high and a hundred feet wide, to the *Peak Cavern* beside the castle, from which the Peakshole Water gushes forth. The cavern, which

still contains evidence of the old rope-making craft, has sheltered men and their industries for millenia, and entertained visitors for centuries. The road west of Castleton forks left to the *Speedwell Cavern,* a former lead mine where a boat takes visitors the half mile to the cavern deep inside, and right to *Treak Cliff Cavern,* one of the few remaining sources of Blue John, which has spectacular displays of stalactites and stalagmites. A footpath leads over the top of the hill to the *Blue John Cavern* where the best examples of the rock used to be mined.

Castleton has views of the heights of the Dark Peak to its west; the nearest, Mam Tor, overlooks the caverns. Another of the Peak's Seven Wonders, it is known as the Shivering Mountain because of the frequent falls of shale. It has now proved so dangerous that the A625 beneath it has been closed. Mam Tor is crowned by an extensive Bronze Age hill fort, with views all round. Most dramatic is the view further north-west across Edale to the 2000-foot height of Kinder Scout. It is famous for the mass trespass that took place in 1932 as part of the campaign to establish walkers' rights across the privately owned high moors, and now Kinder Scout is crossed by the Pennine Way.

We now take the tortuous climb onto Bradwell Moor south of Castleton. The minor road running along the lower line of the castle escarpment bends sharply to ascend the steep slope and then winds round the great gash of a stone quarry before again heading due south. A minor road eastwards, crossing the B6049 to Tideswell, connects the hamlets of Little Hucklow and Great Hucklow. Both villages were lead-mining communities and both have Nonconformist chapels but no Anglican church. Surprisingly, all the way up here, the former lead-smelting mill in the village housed a theatre, from 1927 to 1972, which was founded and run by L. du Garde Peach, owner of *Punch*.

Minor roads run east from the hamlet of Grindlow, Great Hucklow's neighbour, under the moorland edge to Eyam, a village famous for its macabre associations as much as its visual attractions. Bubonic plague came to the village in 1665, and under the guidance of the rector, William Mompesson, the villagers isolated themselves from the world, and 257 died. The rector's chair stands in the thirteenth-century parish church, and his wife is buried in the churchyard beside the exceptionally well-preserved ninth-century cross. Mompesson's rectory itself has gone, and the village's most important building is Eyam Hall, built in 1676, with its formal garden and gateway to the street facing the green and village stocks. In an isolated spot east of the village, to the left of the B6521, seven members of the Hancock family who died in the plague lie buried in Riley Graves. It is a rather affecting spot; one does not quite know whether to admire the villagers' bravery or to be amazed at their stupidity in not fleeing the contagion.

The southern spur of the B6521 meets the A623 in Middleton Dale. Just down the A623 from Stoney Middleton the route returns to the crossroads at Calver Sough. Going right, the B6001 crosses the open upland to Hassop, another former property of the Eyre family of Hathersage. (Their house was Hassop Hall, opposite the Roman Catholic church.) South of the village, just beyond the junction with the A6020, lies the elegant, but redundant, railway station, built in 1863 for the 7th Duke of Devonshire to serve Chatsworth and outclass that built for the 6th Duke of Rutland barely a mile down the line at Bakewell. From here, the B6001 drops down to rejoin the A619 on the outskirts of Bakewell itself.

## 3. EAST ON THE CAVENDISH TRAIL

Although little is left except pictures to suggest what the house at Chatsworth erected by Bess of Hardwick (1518–1608) looked like, other buildings which she and her family erected in the eastern half of Derbyshire are within a reasonable distance of Bakewell. In Hardwick Hall she left perhaps the most perfect expression of the Elizabethan house, while at Bolsover Castle her son conceived a fantasy castle – the first of a long line in English architecture.

The A619 north-east of Bakewell runs through Baslow, then skirts the northern edge of the Chatsworth park, descending slowly from the edge of the Peak District National Park to Chesterfield. A brick-built town, it comes as something of a surprise after all the stone buildings. Its outskirts are no better and no worse than those of many middle-sized Midland towns. The approach is enlivened by glimpses of Chesterfield parish church's famous spire, which leans and twists at comically curious angles. The mainly fourteenth-century church is by far the town's most interesting building: its size and splendour are results of the town's medieval wealth, as can be seen from the many chapels built by the town guilds, and of the wealth of the Foljambe family in the sixteenth century, whose distinguished monuments jostle inside.

The church stands on the edge of the market place, the heart of the old town; the range of buildings on Low Pavement, the south side, includes Chesterfield's oldest secular building, the *Peacock Heritage Centre* (formerly the Peacock Inn). This is an early Tudor timber-framed building with a huge room on its upper floor which was possibly the hall of the town's most important medieval guild. After many years of benign neglect and planning blight, Chesterfield town centre has begun to be tidied up. The town's early nineteenth-century expansion is evident from the numerous rows of late Georgian houses, and from the foundry buildings south of the main centre which established Chesterfield's engineering reputation. The railway engineer George Stephenson (1781–1848) spent the last years of his life in Chesterfield; he is buried in the second of the town's churches, Holy Trinity, just north-west of the ancient church.

The dual carriageway of the A617 speeds traffic south-east from central Chesterfield to cross over the M1 at junction 29, and two miles further on the right turn at Glapwell leads to the drive of *Hardwick Hall*. Coal mining is never far away in this Derbyshire–Nottinghamshire border area, known before nationalization as the Dukeries where the various grand ducal estates exploited the mineral wealth beneath the soil. The Dukes of Devonshire were no exception, and although Hardwick Hall is set in acres of parkland, the mine-workings are just a few hundred yards from the house (which was given to the National Trust in 1959).

In the midst of this black and green landscape Hardwick Hall is one of the grandest sights imaginable, set on its hill, with hundreds of window panes catching the light early and late in the day. Bess of Hardwick built the Hall, 'more window than wall', as the last of her great building projects after she had worked her way through four husbands and amassed all their wealth. In fact, she started to rebuild, and then never properly completed, the Old Hall, her own birthplace. Its shell stands beside the new Hall, with its pairs of great corner towers topped by her initials ES, Elizabeth (Countess of) Shrewsbury.

The 'prodigy house' of Hardwick Hall was designed by Robert Smythson (c. 1536–1614), most gifted of all Elizabethan architects, with a sequence of great chambers and reception rooms of which the most important were placed on the top, second, floor with a great panoramic view over the estates. The house flaunts its magnificence: the decorations celebrate women as strong-willed as Bess herself, and the emphasis is upon pedigree. The famous tapestries and embroideries had a practical purpose as well; because of its fairly exposed site and all that glass, Hardwick was always extremely cold. Like Haddon Hall, the house was rarely used, and so its grand Elizabethan character was preserved.

Bess herself, who died in 1608, was buried in what is now Derby Cathedral. Her daughter-in-law Anne, Countess of Devonshire, died in 1625 and is buried in a grand Italianate tomb in the late Saxon/early Norman church at Ault Hucknall, set almost on its own among trees to the north of Hardwick Hall. Bess's favourite son, Sir Charles Cavendish, is buried beneath a sumptuous tomb in the parish church in Bolsover (rebuilt in the 1960s), a few miles further north along the ridge from the crossroads at Glapwell. Just west of the church, *Bolsover Castle* spreads along the top of the hill, looking down on to the mining and industrial landscape. Built for Sir Charles Cavendish, Bolsover is the embodiment of the early seventeenth-century romantic ideal. John Smythson (Robert's son, d. 1634) built a Jacobean reinterpretation of a medieval keep, and decorated the interior in a mannered and fantastic style. Sir William, Sir Charles Cavendish's son, later Duke of Newcastle, added a great new range including State apartments, and a riding school to indulge his passion in horses. Much of this block, with its own highly mannerist window decoration, is now roofless and partly ruined, but it was one of the most architecturally influential buildings of its time.

A rather different sort of fantasy is to be seen in New Bolsover, at the western foot of the hill on which the castle stands, reached from a left turn on the A632 going back into Chesterfield. It is an 1880s model village, built around a green, to house workers and managers for the coal-mining company. This is the landscape in which D.H. Lawrence (1885–1930) set *Lady Chatterley's Lover*. Worsop Castle was clearly based upon Bolsover, and other names and places in this landscape of green estates and coal-black valleys were garbled to protect, as they say, the innocent.

Take the A632 back to Chesterfield, and then the A619 to Baslow. There, take the left turn to the principal, and possibly the most famous, Cavendish family residence – *Chatsworth House*.

Set in its rolling Capability Brown landscape, Chatsworth is the great baroque palace *per excellence*. The house is enormous, its gardens and grounds are among the very finest in the country, and its furnishings and art treasures include some of the rarest and finest in private hands. The original Chatsworth was an Elizabethan mansion as large as the present house, one of the great edifices built by Sir William Cavendish (*d.* 1557) and his wife, Bess of Hardwick (who went on to build Hardwick Hall). The Hunting Tower gazebo on the hillside above and Queen Mary's Bower, a stone lookout platform supposed to have been used by Mary Queen of Scots when she was held here under house arrest, are the only Tudor survivals. William Cavendish, 1st Duke of Devonshire (1640–1707), one of Bess's descendants, began to rebuild Chatsworth in 1687, sweeping away the old house. New south and east fronts were designed by William

*Masson Mill, Cromford, Matlock Bath.*

Talman (1650–1719) before 1696, the west and north fronts by Thomas Archer (1668–1743) after 1700, but the work was not completed at the Duke's death. More work was begun a century later when Sir Jeffrey Wyatville (1766–1840) refaced the east front and added a long north wing, which provided a much grander set of state rooms.

More than twenty rooms are open to the public: state apartments of the 1st Duke's era, each with baroque ceiling paintings by Louis Laguerre (1663–1721) or Antonio Verrio (1639–1707), the Chapel with its wealth of carving in wood and alabaster, the 6th Duke's Library, Great Dining Room, packed Sculpture Gallery, and Orangery. That was added as an afterthought when the Duke (1790–1858) was fired with enthusiasm for gardening by Joseph Paxton, Chatsworth's head gardener, who also designed the Crystal Palace built to house the Great Exhibition of 1851.

Over a hundred acres of gardens are open to visitors. The original late seventeenth-century garden has been overlaid by successive schemes: Thomas Archer's baroque cascade tumbles down the hillside, and the park was landscaped by Lancelot 'Capability' Brown (1715–83) in 1761, when James Paine (1717–1789) built the fine stone bridge over the Derwent to the west of the house and gardens. Between 1826 and 1844 Joseph Paxton formalized the gardens around the house, installing his remarkable greenhouses, of which the glazed Conservative Wall, running east from the north wing towards Paine's grand stable block, survives. New greenhouses and many other features have been introduced during the present, 11th Duke's time (Andrew, b. 1920). Perhaps the single most memorable feature of the gardens is the Emperor Fountain in the Canal Pond, which plays to well over 200 feet. It was installed to welcome Tsar Nicholas I (1796–1855) in 1844, although in the event he never came.

Edensor, the main estate village, lies on the western side of the park, out of sight of the house. It was moved there by the 6th Duke in 1838, and Paxton designed it, with all manner of picturesque cottages: a Swiss chalet roof put on an existing Georgian inn, Italianate windows mixed with Norman doorways and Jacobean gables and chimneys. The church with its tall spire was rebuilt by Sir George Gilbert Scott (1811–78) in 1867.

From Edensor, retrace your route until the junction with the A619, which leads back to Bakewell.

## 4. DEEPER INTO DERBYSHIRE

The A6 to *Haddon Hall* runs parallel to the Wye. The countryside soon begins to open out with hills to the right and the wooded riverside on the left. A mile down the road on the left is the rather inconspicuous entrance to Haddon Hall. Home of the Dukes of Rutland, Haddon is a 'Sleeping Beauty' house, a medieval dream castle, backed by mature trees, with the river winding below. The present Duke of Rutland is a direct descendant of Sir Richard de Vernon, who acquired the property in 1170. Between the fourteenth and sixteenth centuries Haddon acquired its present form. Two courtyards lead to the chapel and the great hall with its parlour and kitchen block; upstairs a sequence of chambers culminate in the 100-foot Long Gallery, which was added in around 1600. The panes of glass in its three great bay windows are moulded and twisted to catch the light, illuminating the intricately carved panelling which incorporates the boar's head crest of the Vernon family and the peacock of the Manners family.

So much is preserved at Haddon because the grandson of John Manners and Dorothy Vernon, who had added this south front, inherited the title of Earl of Rutland in 1641, and Belvoir Castle in Leicestershire became the principal family home. By the eighteenth century Haddon had been largely abandoned, although it was kept in some state of repair. That abandonment preserved features like the medieval kitchens, most of the fifteenth-century interior woodwork, and the painted early Tudor ceiling and window of the Dining Room.

The visitor's tour of Haddon Hall ends in the Stuart terraced gardens, one of the best of all Haddon's fine features, with the formality of the rose garden, and the walls of the terraces forming a sheer drop down to the river.

Beyond Haddon Hall the A6 crosses the Wye to Rowsley, situated just above the confluence with the Derwent. Beyond Rowsley, river and road pass outside the limits of the National Park, beyond the millstone symbol at the lower end of the village. Great Rowsley, on the west bank of the Derwent, is an estate village of the Dukes of Rutland, well-kept and stone-built. The best of its Stuart and Georgian buildings is the Peacock Hotel, a mid seventeenth-century house with symmetrically placed gables on either end, framing the pedimented doorcase and the elaborately carved stone peacock, put up when the house became the hotel in 1828. Caudwell's Mill, on the Wye just south of the village, still produces stoneground wholemeal flour, as it has done for over a century. Over the fifteenth-century bridge (widened in 1925) Little Rowsley is a brick-built railway colony, with Joseph Paxton's original railway station of 1850 now surrounded by a light industrial estate.

The A6 continues along the bottom of the Derwent valley, with views to the west on to the high Stanton Moor. The tower on top was erected in 1832 to commemorate the passing of the Great Reform Act; its nearest neighbours are a number of standing stones and ancient stone circles. A French Renaissance-style lodge beside the road signals the entrance to Stancliffe Hall, built in the 1870s for Sir Joseph Whitworth (1803–77), inventor of the screw thread, who endowed Darley Dale – as this straggle of houses alongside the A6 has come to be known – with a variety of institutions and housing. The lane to the right a little further along leads down to the Derwent, and to the mainly fifteenth-century parish church.

The lane crosses the B5057 and rejoins the A6, passing other late Victorian examples of Whitworth's munificence, to enter the outskirts of Matlock. Matlock is the spa on the other side of the Peak District to balance Buxton, but its rise to fame came somewhat later. Matlock is not one town, but seven or eight different townships (depending on how you count them), divided by steep-sided valleys and social niceties. The first township is the newest, Matlock Bank, which rises up the hillside topped by Smedley's Hydro (now Derbyshire County Hall), a castellated Continental confection begun in the 1850s when John Smedley persuaded thousands of those in search of better health to try his hydrotherapy cures. Competitors sprang up, but none matched Smedley's success.

The A6 crosses to the other bank of the Derwent and Matlock Bridge, with the railway terminus, and then follows the winding river through its narrow gorge with the old village on a bluff above the river and Matlock Green below. John Wesley (1703–91) was one of the many visitors of the eighteenth century and since to admire the sights of Matlock: 'Pleasures beyond expression', he called them. Smedley built for himself the ostentatious fantasy of

Riber Castle way up on the moor east of the gorge in 1862, beside the restrained and prettier seventeenth-century Riber Hall and Manor House. The castle is now ruined, and has become a Wildlife Park (approached from Cromford to the south or the A615 to the north from Matlock Bank). The castle looks across to Matlock Bath, the original spa and very popular in the nineteenth century for day trips, which runs along the west side of the bottom of the gorge. Cable cars ply up and down the *Heights of Abraham,* the steep side of the gorge with show caves. This lower end of the town has the majority of Matlock's attractions, from the *Peak District Mining Museum and Temple Mine* to the children's theme park of *Gulliver's Kingdom.*

As the river and road bend east below Matlock, another castle perches on the hillside above: the battlemented and turreted, but otherwise classical, late eighteenth-century Willersley Castle, built for the Arkwright family. The castle looked down upon Cromford, the Arkwrights' supreme factory colony and one of the earliest concentrations of textile mills. Richard Arkwright founded his first water-powered cotton mill here in 1771. He found an underemployed work force, readily available female and child labour, and water power. He left to posterity a series of monuments to the early factory system – the mills alongside the Derwent. The Masson Mill, built in 1783, is still in use, although its future is in doubt. The *Arkwright Mills* stand a little further along, just to the left of the A6. A number have escaped demolition, including the original Upper Mill, and are undergoing a slow process of restoration. Arkwright also built rows of new cottages to house the new-style labour force, in the village that prospered south of the main road. The main rows of houses lining North Street, with its school building at the end, have been restored. Behind them, the cottages of the lead miners of pre-Arkwright Cromford huddle in tumble-down disorder. The Cromford Canal and Basin which the Arkwrights developed have also been restored, and during the summer season boat trips take visitors $1\frac{1}{2}$ miles downstream to the 1840s Leewood Pumphouse, used to pump water from the river into the canal, and to the spectacular aqueduct, put up in 1792, that carries the canal over the river. All down the narrow valley, river, road, railway and canal interweave.

The road south-west out of Cromford takes you to Wirksworth, which George Eliot (1819–80) portrayed as the inhospitable Snowfield in *Adam Bede.* It was a major centre for the lead trade, and almost died with the demise of the industry, but a vigorous conservation campaign in past decades has made the town into a centre for visitors. At the heart of Wirksworth, just off the main north–south through road, stands the large parish church within its circular green. Elizabethan almshouses and the former grammar school (now a woodworker's shop) are ranged around it. Although the church itself is mainly late thirteenth-century, and was treated harshly by Victorian restorers, it contains at the north side an eighth-century coffin lid, possibly that of a local saint, covered with exceptional, intricate carving of scenes from the life of Christ. On the other side of the main road, some of the cottages on the hillside date from the fifteenth and sixteenth centuries although many were rebuilt in the eighteenth and nineteenth. Richard Arkwright developed cotton mills in Wirksworth as well; the brick-built Haarlem Mill, begun in 1777, is situated on the southern outskirts.

Back through Wirksworth, the B5023 passes active and disused quarries and the village of Middleton to the A5012. This was built in 1800 by Anthony Gell as access to his quarries and lead mines, and rather pretentiously named the Via Gellia. When a textile mill at the Cromford end of this road first manufactured its new fabric in 1892, it adopted the corrupted name of the road and so the term 'Viyella' passed into the language. As you go north-west on the A5012, the wooded steep sides begin to give way to open moorland. When Daniel Defoe (1660–1731) came by in the 1720s on his *Tour Through the Whole Island of Great Britain*, he found families living in the caves in Harborough Rocks, the high ground to the south. He was appalled, but found on inspection that the cave houses were neat and clean, and he left a moving account of the mining families' circumstances.

Take the B5056 north to Winster at Grangemill, where you re-enter the National Park. Winster was a prosperous lead-mining village, to which the eighteenth-century houses lining the main street and climbing the hillside bear witness. A number of once-rich mine workings still lie in the village, such as the Portway Mine to the west of the main road and Orchard Mine south of the main street, on which the parish church, the early Georgian Old Hall Hotel, and the former market hall all stand. The church has an early Georgian west tower and an odd Victorian double-nave body; *Winster Market House*, (the town's most distinctive building and now a National Trust Information Centre) has a Tudor ground floor with arches, now enclosed but once open, and a late Stuart, gabled upper storey in brick. The Old Hall Hotel, with its grand pilastered front, is even more of a surprise inside, with its early eighteenth-century painted and plasterwork ceiling in the front bar.

The B5056 joins the B5057 west of

Winster and winds below Stanton Moor to the east and past more Bronze Age stone circles on the west into the valley of the Lathkill. The road rejoins the A6, which will take you back to Bakewell, just south of Haddon Hall.

## 5. SOUTH TO DOVE DALE AND ASHBOURNE

The B5055 leaves Bakewell from the south-west corner of the parish churchyard. The town falls away very quickly; the left turn at the next crossroads passes the school and makes an often steep ascent on to the moor. After a little more than a mile, with occasional views down into the valley and across to Haddon Hall, the road makes the sudden steep descent into the narrow Lathkill Dale. In dry summers the river may be barely flowing at all, at least above ground, having been swallowed up in the limestone, whereas in winter it may be gushing through its tree-lined gorge. The lane to the left, on the other side of the river, leads into Youlgreave, another of the White Peak's many once-prosperous lead-mining towns now rather marooned on the high tops. From the long village street, Youlgreave's gardens tumble down the hill towards the beautifully clear River Bradford, which flows into the Lathkill a mile downstream. The tower of the parish church, at the eastern approach end of the village, juts out into the street; it is one of the more impressive of Derbyshire's churches, a spacious mixture of Norman and Perpendicular with some fine alabaster monuments inside.

From the village street the lane bears round to the left above the Bradford, passing the mid Victorian Gothic pile of Lomberdale Hall. It was built by the antiquarian Thomas Bateman, who excavated many barrows and took antiquities from numerous churches in the Peak District – Bakewell's included – for his private collection, now on display in Sheffield's

Weston Park Museum. Bateman was buried behind the chapel he designed in Middleton, just down the road. West from Middleton and south passing a number of tumuli that Bateman excavated, the road wriggles down the steep escarpment to join the A5012 and then the A515 heading south.

West of the main road the action of the rivers has created many of Derbyshire's most picturesque dales, many of which are accessible only on foot. The deep and wooded Wolfscote Dale, for instance, has only a footpath running along it, and the Beresford Dale upstream from it, made famous by Charles Cotton (1630–87), a fishing companion of Izaak Walton (1593–1683) and co-author of *The Compleat Angler,* barely has that. These dales may be reached in a number of ways; by footpaths below the village of Biggin to the west of the A515 and down the dry valley of Biggin Dale; from the cottages just above the turning to Alsop-en-le-Dale and under the dismantled railway line that runs parallel to the road, or from the minor road carried on the old stone bridge over the river half a mile south. The River Dove, most famous of all the watercourses in the Peak District, flows through these dales, and for much of its length forms the boundary between Staffordshire and Derbyshire. The most popular access to the Dove is at its southern end, above the confluence with the River Manifold (see below).

The next village off the A515, Tissington, is best known as the place where the ceremony of well-dressing was revived and has since been copied throughout the Peak District. Elaborate religious pictures made from flower petals and natural materials decorate wells in many villages, especially around Ascension Day. Pagan ceremonies taken over by the early church, the well-dressing rituals seem to have revived in Tissington in the seventeenth century, and are now firmly established in the local ecclesiastical and tourist calendar. Tissington is otherwise a quiet pretty village, which has been run by the FitzHerbert family for centuries. They built the early nineteenth-century cottages ranged around two sides of the green, their monuments fill the heavily Victorianized parish church on the third, and theirs is the (twice-extended) early seventeenth-century Hall set behind it.

An open lane below the village green returns to the A515. The gradual descent continues another $2\frac{1}{2}$ miles to the small town of Ashbourne. After all the stone buildings of the Peak, Ashbourne's brick buildings are a pleasant surprise. This is a frontier town, between the Midland Plain and the limestone uplands, and its main streets are among the finest in Derbyshire.

Ashbourne runs east–west along the line of the Henmore Brook, which divides the main town on the north bank from its 'suburb' of Compton on the south. Every Shrove Tuesday, Ashbourne is boarded up for the football match between the 'Uppards' and the 'Downards' – those born either side of the Brook – and the ball is run through the streets with the goals three miles apart. Ashbourne's main, and finest, buildings run along Church Street and St John Street, from the parish church in the west, with its 215-foot spire, to the Gingerbread Shop in the east. St Oswald's church is one of the grandest in the whole region, with its great length and height, its thirteenth- and fourteenth-century architecture, and the family chapels filled with memorials to the Cockayne and Boothby families. Most visitors come to see the affecting memorial to Penelope Boothby, a child prodigy who died in 1793, whose 'unfortunate Parents ventured their all on this frail Bark. And the wreck is total.'

Along Church Street, the handsome line of the late Tudor, stone-gabled front of the Grammar School is continued by early nineteenth-century, bay-windowed houses. Opposite stands the Mansion, a late Stuart townhouse given a mid Georgian façade by Revd John Taylor, an outrageous pluralist and friend of Dr Johnson (1709–84). Some late eighteenth-century travellers like John Byng came to Ashbourne hoping to sense Johnson's aura in the place. A succession of seventeenth- and eighteenth-century almshouses lies along Church Street and its side lanes, leading through to the sloping triangular Market Place. The back road from the north-west of here is the way to Dove Dale, leading along the Dove valley through Mapleton. As the Dove valley begins to narrow, the road climbs the side and bears round above Thorpe village to the bottom of Dove Dale.

It is a much touted statistic that half of the population of England lives within 50 miles of Dove Dale. On some summer weekends you might be forgiven for thinking that they are almost all there, parked by the Izaak Walton Hotel and climbing Thorpe Cloud, or splashing about on the stepping stones across the river. Dove Dale is famous for its limestone scenery (like the weirdly shaped, water-carved Tissington Spires), its literary associations with *The Compleat Angler,* and its seclusion. To find the seclusion, you often have to walk only a mile or two along the otherwise inaccessible gorge – and see the trout which so attract the fishermen, compleat or otherwise.

Much of Dove Dale is protected by the National Trust, as is *Ilam Park* a mile to the west, above the River Manifold. Ilam village is an archetypal nineteenth-century estate village, with *cottages ornées* in a heavy-handed, tile-hung and barge-boarded style, and a completely spurious Eleanor Cross. Holy Cross church was drastically Victorianized, and is filled with monuments to the Watts Russell family who perpetrated all this. Little is left of their 1820s Gothic house, which is now a youth hostel. The lane north from Ilam runs up the high ground between the Manifold and the Dove, then bears east below the village of Alstonefield to run beside the Dove briefly at Milldale, crosses it and returns up the short, dry valley to the A515 and back north.

Three miles beyond the junction with the A5012, past a series of cairns and tumuli on the hills on either side, a minor road heads directly north towards Monyash. Less than a mile east of this point (off the minor road towards Youlgreave and reached by a footpath through a farmyard), Derbyshire's most important Bronze Age henge monument stands on the bare hillside. Arbor Low has 47 stones set in a circle around three central stones, placed within an impressive 250-foot diameter ditch and bank. Those who might be expecting another Stonehenge will be slightly disappointed, since the stones are no longer standing but lie flat on the ground, yet this remains an impressive testimony to the power and ingenuity of early man.

From here it is possible to cross the moor above Youlgreave and retrace the route through Lathkill Dale to Bakewell. Alternatively, Monyash, two miles to the north, is an attractive isolated market village. Its sizeable church, the stump of a market cross, and vestiges of its 23 different springs are all marks of its one-time importance. The B5055 crosses the bare moorland top to enter Bakewell from the top and descend once more into the centre.

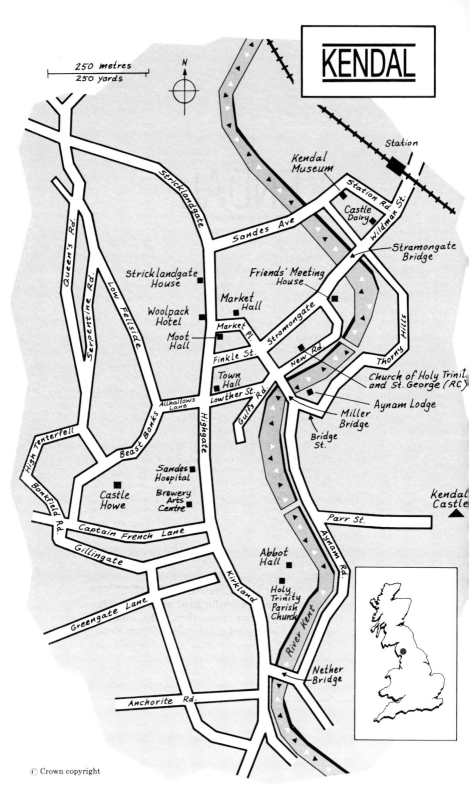

# 2
# KENDAL

C u m b r i a

*Kendal used to be called 'the auld grey town', because of the silver-grey limestone of which almost every building is made. Now it is known as 'the gateway to the Lakes'. Gateways are meant to be gone through, but Kendal is in fact one of the most handsome and rewarding of the larger country towns in the north-west. The largest town in the vicinity of the Lake District, it is an industrial as well as a market town, but it wears its industrial side lightly. Kendal is graced with a great variety of handsome late Georgian classical buildings, while beyond the steep sides of the valley in which it sits lies some of the most dramatic upland scenery in England. The Lake District extends to the west, the Pennines rise to the east.*

*Exploring Kendal reveals a town of contrasts, with wealthy and poor living side by side, and country town classical and rough vernacular buildings all made from the same grey limestone. Its many industries have always been on a small scale, and have left interesting vestiges; some trades – such as snuff – are now very curious survivals. Although there is much to see on the main thoroughfares, the real historical value of Kendal is to be found by poking around in yards, alleys and side streets.*

## EXPLORING KENDAL

Kendal's layout looks quite straightforward on a map. The town is basically one long major street that forks, and the plan follows closely the steep-sided valley of the River Kent. It turns out to be more complicated on the ground. For in the eighteenth and nineteenth centuries, Kendal seemed to implode. Its population trebled in the eighteenth century to around 8000 and then nearly doubled again in the nineteenth, while the area covered by the town did not grow nearly as rapidly. An almost unique residential pattern evolved, of

31

narrow, cramped 'yards' running back from the elegant new houses on the main streets. Despite twentieth-century clearances enough of this pattern is left to give Kendal a very distinctive character.

As in many other towns, Kendal's Market Place is an appropriate starting point. Situated between the two arms of the long main street where they fork, Market Place is lined with inns, shops, and the former Market Hall of 1887 (now converted into the 1980s equivalent, a shopping precinct). The market is still held on Wednesdays and Saturdays. Tucked into the corner, the old Working Men's Institute, with shops below, demonstrates some of Kendal's changes. It was originally used from 1636 as a weigh-loft for woollen yarn, spun by local women and sold to middlemen, which was one of the mainstays of the local economy. In 1758 the building became a theatre, and then a Nonconformist chapel. In 1866 it became a Working Men's Library, one of many examples of the Victorian town's self-help ethic.

The houses on the opposite side of the Market Place, nos. 39–45, with unusual cast-iron fronts added when the street was widened in 1853, stand at the top of the cobbled Branthwaite Brow. From the early eighteenth-century Unitarian Chapel in its walled graveyard opposite, the rough-hewn old stone houses run down towards the river. Blood and offal used to be washed away from the Market Place down this steep hill. It is difficult now to imagine how much open-air butchering of animals there must have been on big market days in Kendal 150 or 200 years ago, when it stood on the main cattle droving route from Scotland.

The Market Place would have appeared even more hemmed in until a century or so ago, when the now-open western side was filled by the old Market Hall of 1854, which had replaced an older building incorporating St George's Chapel, the corn market and the town gaol. The Market Hall was re-erected in Sandes Avenue in 1909. The left turn through the gap into busy Stricklandgate reveals Kendal's distinctive variety of classicized buildings of the early nineteenth century. The Moot Hall, the rough-cast sixteenth-century former town hall (reconstructed following a fire in 1969) stands on the corner, next to a mildly classical five-bay stone house, 21 Stricklandgate, built around 1820 by local architect Francis Webster (1767–1827). Webster founded a dynasty of architects and masons whose work is to be seen all over Kendal; he also designed the late Regency, bow-windowed iron frontage to the shop next door: Farrer's Tea and Coffee House, which is many people's favourite building in Kendal. The further back you go into the shop, the more the building reveals its past as one of many seventeenth-century inns that used to fill the town centre. As in most historic towns, older buildings were often given Georgian face-lifts.

From the open paved area beyond it, which was once the Fish Market, Finkle Street descends. The first large opening among the shops is the New Shambles, a picturesque early nineteenth-century butchers' row, with its cobbles and stone flags, overhead gas lamps, and overhanging shopfronts. The next opening on the left is the first example of Kendal's most distinctive feature, the yards: narrow alleyways of houses, workshops, and storerooms built at right angles to the main street. This particular example is Police Yard, where in 1836 the first police station and later, surprisingly given the narrowness, the fire station were established.

The yards developed in the second half of the eighteenth century. As Kendal experienced unprecedented growth and as its weaving and knitting industries grew apace, ever more people and workshops were squeezed into the available spaces – the long, originally medieval, burgage plots characteristic of many old towns. These yards were sinks of sin and misery, and contributed to the often appalling health and mortality record of the town's poorer areas. Although many have now gone, enough survive to give a sense of how cramped living in them must have been. Some people will tell you that the yards are a unique medieval feature, built to provide protection for Kendal's population when the marauding Scots came down to wreak havoc, but it's an anti-Scottish myth!

In Stramongate, which begins beyond Branthwaite Brow, more yards survive, like the one (complete with its old pump) beside no. 7, Bellingham House. Dated 1544 under the front gable, this was the town house of the Bellingham family, at one time owners of Levens Hall to the south of town. The restored timber and plaster property, now a good bookshop, retains some original woodwork and interior fittings. The yards are all numbered, and many are named after earlier residents or owners. Yard 23 has been restored into a tidy version of what these yards once were, a mixture of houses, workshops, and shops. The majority of people crammed into the yards in Regency and Victorian Kendal – up to 150 in some – were weavers, operating their hand-looms to make the Kendal 'cottons' (a traditional woollen cloth).

Some yards are not open but may be peeked into, like Yard 27, where the warehouse was formerly the Museum of the Kendal Literary and Scientific Society, which numbers William Wordsworth and Robert Southey among its founding members, and before 1837 was the town's Roman Catholic chapel. Its replacement, the church of Holy Trinity and St George, was built on New Road behind, to designs by George Webster (1797–1864), son of Francis. An early Victorian essay in Gothic, its most important features are the sculpted figures on the front by the local artist Thomas Duckett. Francis Webster designed the plain Friends' Meeting House in 1816, set back on the right-hand side of Stramongate beyond the junction with New Road. The Quakers led Kendal's development and prosperity in its heyday in the decades around 1800. Stramongate School, behind the buildings opposite, was founded as the Friends' Day School in 1698. The core buildings date from its refoundation in 1772, and John Dalton (1766–1844), the father of the atomic theory, was an early teacher there before moving to fame in London. Two more Webster designs provide the dominant accent in the last stretch of Stramongate: the elegant Ladies' College building on the left (of 1800), and Sand Aire House with its pillared entrance portico, further along on the right, built in 1827 for a Kendal dynasty of lawyers. Both testify to the town's success in the late Georgian years.

Stramongate Bridge (an ancient structure recased in 1793) crosses the River Kent, from which Kendal (Kentdale) takes its name. St George's church visible to the right across the river was built in 1839 to George Webster's designs, replacing the Market Place chapel; its stubby twin west towers were originally taller, with spires, but they were lowered for safety. The long Bridge Mills building, along the left bank, makes socks, which is an ancient Kendal industry; but it was erected in 1859 to manufacture cards for combing the long-staple wool before it was woven. The great length of the mill was needed to draw out the wire for the cards. Wildman Street, over the bridge, was rebuilt with rather nondescript terraces after 1820, but two interesting older buildings survive.

On the left, *Castle Dairy* is Kendal's oldest inhabited house. Parts date from the fourteenth century, and the stone exterior remains little altered since its rebuilding in 1564. Many interior fittings and furnishings date from the seventeenth century; they may be seen either by day when the house is a small museum, or by evening when it is a small restaurant. On Sleddal Hall, over the road, the 1897 frontage hides a very early seventeenth-century house, much of which remains unaltered both at the rear and inside. It is now a working craft pottery, and visitors and browsers are welcomed.

Kendal's dilapidated railway station, built in the ubiquitous rough grey stone, stands forlornly at the crossroads ahead. The main Euston–Glasgow line passes Kendal by, and the town station is the first halt on the branch line, eventually opened in 1847 after a hard-fought campaign led by Wordsworth against the railway's coming into the Lakes at all. The railway only ever reached the shore of Windermere. As Wordsworth feared, it opened the lakes up to huge numbers of visitors. Station Road to the left leads past *Kendal Museum*, in a Victorian wool warehouse. Recipient of the Kendal Literary and Scientific Society collections, it has a variety of local history displays and curious wildlife panoramas.

Sandes Avenue across the river is a wide street of often heavy traffic; the large shoe store on the left incorporates the re-erected old Market Hall building. Left into Stricklandgate, the main shopping area begins. Halfway along on the right the imposing Stricklandgate House, now the District Council offices, was built in around 1776 for the wealthy banker Joseph Maude. An elegant early example of Kendal's classical style, a seven-bay, rendered house with a rusticated ground floor and pedimented doorcase, it housed the Kendal Savings Bank, and then from 1854 the Kendal Literary and Scientific Society. Immediately opposite, the YWCA is an early eighteenth-century stone-and-brick town house, famous for its earlier visitors: Bonnie Prince Charlie (1720–88), the Young Pretender, and his pursuer, the Duke of Cumberland, slept in the same bed here on successive nights. The estate agency on its right, a rough stone house with the large round chimney-pots characteristic of Westmorland on top, is the remnant of the sixteenth-century Black Hall, built for Kendal's first mayors. In around 1820 the house became Hodgson's brush factory, which explains the large sign above the door, a wooden black pig with bristles along its back.

Continuing on the west side up from Stricklandgate House, past the hard Edwardian red of the Carnegie Library, the Woolpack Hotel is a 1791 rebuilding of a famous inn. Its great archway was designed to be tall enough to admit wagons piled high with bales of wool. Beyond the shop and offices of the *Westmorland Gazette* (which was edited briefly by Thomas de Quincey (1785–1859) until he was sacked because of his laudanum habit, and now publishes the late A. Wainwright's famous fell-walking guides) and the narrow opening of Entry Lane, another sequence of older buildings begins. The Fleece Inn was originally a butcher's shop in the seventeenth century; it still has its covered pedestrian walkway – one of the few surviving galleries that allowed pedestrians easy, dry access to the shops – and rows of meat hooks. The lane off Highgate beside the Fleece is the Old Shambles, put up in 1779 to accommodate butchers, but since its poor drainage was an immense public nuisance, the New Shambles was built. The former Titus Wilson shop is again a surviving Stuart house, and a one-time print works; George Webster added its Regency ground-floor shop front.

Highgate begins where Allhallows Lane comes down from the right to join the main road. Across the street stands Kendal Town Hall. Its earliest part is the right-hand half (now the *Tourist Information Centre*), built as the Whitehall Assembly Rooms in 1825, again by the Websters. The building of public assembly rooms – at a later date than most towns – was a sign that Kendal town society was beginning to take its frivolity more seriously. The original Assembly Rooms were three bays wide, with a screen of Ionic columns, and a cupola on top. To make the new Town Hall in 1893, Stephen Shaw more than doubled the width of the existing building, added florid baroque touches and a new, tall, asymmetrically placed clock tower. Its carillon plays a different tune each day of the week, from 'Devotion' on Sundays to 'There's nae luck aboot the hoose' on Saturdays. Just inside the entrance hang some of the town's paintings, including a view of Highgate crowded with people and coaches, interesting for its depiction of the street in 1818 on the famous parliamentary election day when the rival landed families, the Whig Broughams (whom Kendal backed) and the Tory Lowthers, engaged in fierce battle. The Lowthers won.

Beyond the Town Hall, shops, banks, pubs and houses line Highgate, with yards running behind. Barclay's Bank, one of the principal buildings on the left, was built in 1873 at the amalgamation of two town banks which had both started business in 1788. Using the wealth and legal and manufacturing expertise of leading Quaker families, the town's bankers underwrote the region's commercial success. Across the road, the Midland Bank branch – the oldest in the Midland Group – was built in 1834 by George Webster as the Bank of Westmorland, with large pilasters on its classical façade, topped by a friendly lion.

The restored Yard 83, Dr Manning's Yard, gives the best sense of what these tight alleys were like. Once the yard contained a dry-salter's, a ropeworks, a tannery, wool warehouses, cottages – and, curiously, a windmill. These have now been restored as dwellings. After the lumpy, rusticated Oddfellows Hall, built in 1833 (now the Jehovah's Witnesses' meeting room) and the smoother ashlared, less fussy nos. 134–136 of 1797, Highgate becomes rather more domestic in scale. The (mainly rendered) early Victorian house and shop fronts often disguise older structures. At the end of Highgate the road opens up to the left, at Dowker's Lane.

Set back on this corner is a stone triple archway, the entrance to the grounds of Abbot Hall, Kendal's most distinguished building. Running down to the river, the grounds are a public park, purchased along with the Hall by the Corporation in 1896. The big, mid Georgian house itself lies further to the south, with the parish church beyond. Dividing the park from the Hall runs the Blind Beck, a small stream of great significance. The area south of the Blind Beck is Kirkland, the original pre-Norman settlement by the river crossing. It remained distinct from the market town that grew up after the Conquest. In fact Kirkland was only absorbed by Kendal borough in 1908, and still has a somewhat separate air.

The original *Abbot Hall* (of which there is no trace) belonged to St Mary's Abbey, York, which held the living of Kendal, and then to a succession of secular owners after the abbey's dissolution. The present Abbot Hall was built in 1759 for a local gentleman, Colonel George Wilson. It has a plain

*Trinity Church, Kendal.*

entrance front flanked by two projecting wings, and on the
river front a varied arrangement of bays and wings with
Venetian windows (so called because they first appeared in
the work of the Venetian architect Serlio). Across the
entrance courtyard stands the plain, grey-stone stable block,
with a squat central tower. In 1962, after long years of neglect,
Abbot Hall opened as a furnished art gallery, with the ground-
floor rooms restored to their eighteenth-century splendour.
One of the first paintings on show is Colonel Wilson's portrait,
a dignified early work by one of Kendal's finest sons, George
Romney (1734–1802).

Abbot Hall is no ordinary small-town museum, but has an
exceptional art collection, assembled with an eye to local
traditions and reputations: works by George Romney and
John Ruskin (1819–1900), fine furniture by the Lancaster firm
of Gillow, and an interesting modern collection. The stable
block opposite was converted into the Museum of Lakeland
Life and History in 1971; its displays include farming
implements, old Kendal house and shop interiors, one of the
last hand looms used to make Kendal cloth, a reconstruction
of a Kendal street in 1897 and, in the tower, the study of
Arthur Ransome (1884–1967), including the original of
Captain Flint's trunk from *Swallows and Amazons*. The

museum shop incorporates the front of the Kendal gas works, a tiny classical temple built in 1825 and moved here in 1984, bearing the motto *Ex fumo dare lucem* – smoke gives light.

Holy Trinity parish church stands beside Abbot Hall. The church is one of the widest in the country. The interior is a forest of pillared aisles, two on either side of the thirteenth-century nave, built at various dates between the fourteenth and sixteenth centuries. The four family chapels at the east end, with their monuments and fifteenth-century woodwork, are a miniature history of Kendal's leading families before 1700. The Strickland chapel, to the right of the chancel, includes the touching effigy of Walter Strickland, who died in 1656 aged 11, while the adjacent Parr chapel houses a fragment of a ninth-century Anglian cross, the only relic of the pre-Conquest settlement. A brass plate on the chancel floor to Revd Ralph Tirer, who died in 1627, which reads:

> London bredd me, Westminster fedd me,
> Cambridge sped me, my Sister wed me,
> Study taught me, Living sought me,
> Learning brought me, Kendal caught me ...

has teased generations. The second line is an oblique reference to his marriage in Oxford, not a confession of incest!

The row of low cottages on the northern side of the churchyard housed Kendal Grammar School from its sixteenth-century foundation until 1888. Ephraim Chambers, the encyclopedist, was a pupil here, one of many Kendal boys who found later distinction. Through the handsome wrought-iron churchyard gates of 1822 the route leads back onto Kirkland and then to the ancient Nether Bridge below over the River Kent. Despite successive widenings, the old fifteenth-century bridge survives at the core, although the jumble of cottages, the old Vicarage, and a tanyard that stood beside the river bank have been cleared away.

Across Kirkland from the Nether Bridge stands the now-bedraggled late eighteenth-century Romney House, where George Romney died. After his apprenticeship and early local fame Romney headed for London, leaving his family behind. His mind and health failing, the aged artist returned to the devoted care of his wife, whom he had only occasionally seen in thirty years, and died in this house in 1802. A black memorial urn stands inside the west end of Kendal parish church. Perpetuating George Romney's memory, one of Kendal's famous brands of super-sugary mint cake (as taken on all the best mountaineering expeditions) is named after him.

Back into town along the west side of Kirkland, the succession of basically seventeenth-century houses (some with extra decorative details, like no. 32's pretty shell hood doorcase) is punctuated by alleyways leading up on to the steep hillside. After Gillingate with its late Victorian houses, the next left turn, Captain French Lane, leads to the heart of what was until comparatively recently Kendal's poorest area. The Fellside, on the steep slopes west of the town, was intensively colonized in Kendal's years of growth from the seventeenth to the nineteenth centuries.

Captain French's Lane has little, stone-built cottages along its north side. At the top, the right turn beyond the hospital, Bankfield Road, leads across a small green. A right turn (past the former Inghamite chapel of 1844, now converted into flats) takes you to the top of Beast Banks, where animals were once prepared for market and slaughter. Victorian villas and cottages cluster around a small green, with the handsome mid nineteenth-century Cliff Terrace to the left, enjoying the view across the Kent valley.

The terrace terminates in the belvedere attached to no. 1. In the gardens below stands a square pyramid-roofed stone summer house of the late eighteenth century. Building such gazebos became a Kendal fashion in the later Georgian period, either at the end of the long thin gardens on the main streets, or in the separate gardens on the fellside owned by well-to-do families with little or no garden in town, above the smoke and smell and with a good evening view. Some of these summer houses still survive, like that beside the road on Beast Banks, at Monument House.

A walled lane on the right down Beast Banks hill opens on to a flat green which was the bailey of Kendal's first castle, a wooden fortification built after the Norman Conquest and abandoned a century later in favour of a new site across the valley. The steep mound of the castle motte has been crowned since 1788 by an obelisk celebrating liberty and the Glorious Revolution of 1688; from it there is a fine view across the town's grey roofs to the fells. In the far, lower corner of the green stands a large mid-Victorian house, with the best-preserved of the Georgian summer houses visible in the corner of its walled garden. A stone squeeze stile beside the garden wall leads onto an ancient walled dirt pathway back to Captain French's Lane, and from there down to Highgate.

There is a variety of interesting, mainly eighteenth-century properties going back along Highgate's west side, such as the double-fronted Highgate Hotel, and the Youth Hostel, a four-storey stone house of 1757 with a contemporary doorcase. The Brewery Arts Centre behind was built in 1971, incorporating the old brewery of 1853. Towards the town centre, some early and mid nineteenth-century shop fronts survive, combining plate glass with ironwork surrounds. Webster's Yard, just past New Inn, is a modern reinterpretation of the old yards and serves as sheltered housing for the elderly. It runs parallel to Sandes Hospital, almshouses for eight poor widows, founded by Thomas Sandes in 1659. The Hospital is reached through an archway on Highgate (where an original collecting box bears the exhortation to 'remember the poor widows') and is still inhabited by elderly ladies, who tend their gardens and enjoy a chat.

Shakespeare Yard, the next along, is an unrestored late Georgian yard with a one-time theatre closing the end. Collin Croft, the final yard in this section of Highgate (just before the Midland Bank), has been skilfully restored. There are a number of workshops and warehouses along it, a plain late Georgian house, and at the end a complex of buildings with a steep, stepped passageway leading through it to Beast Banks. Built in 1851 as a pottery warehouse, this became in turn a print works, a tobacco factory, a felt warehouse and a brass foundry, and has now been divided into houses and flats.

On the other side of Highgate, to the side of the Town Hall, the narrow Lowther Street, cut through in 1781, ducks down towards the river. Grey Victorian warehouses and offices are relieved only by the coloured effigy of a Turk over the door of Gawith Hoggarth and Company's snuff works. At the bottom by the Miller Bridge the full sweep of the River Kent through the town is visible. The fast-flowing river has been embanked and tidied in a flood control scheme; from the thirteenth century to the nineteenth it was both Kendal's power source and its waste disposal system. The Miller Bridge sits upon a bend in the river. The bridge was widened and strengthened in 1818 as part of the scheme to bring greater prosperity to Kendal with the canal to Lancaster. Immediately across the bridge is the surviving early industrial complex from those same years. It is cut through by Bridge Street, with two houses guarding the entrance: Aynam Lodge, at the end of the bridge, a wide ashlared three-bay house of 1824, and, opposite, the former showroom and office of the Webster architectural firm. Francis and George Webster built both; their offices bristle with balconies and decoration to show off what they could do.

The Websters' own town houses were built in 1824, along the pleasant riverside walk at Thorny Hills, behind Aynam Lodge. George Webster's house, no. 4, the best of the tall, terraced group, with wreaths carved in the frieze, is now part of the lower comprehensive school. A path from the end of the terrace (beside the dry ski slope) leads to what was the head of the Preston–Lancaster–Kendal canal, which opened with such hopes in 1819, but declined so rapidly with the advent of the railway. Victorian factory and foundry buildings survive around the canal head, many still carrying on the metalwork and weaving for which they were built (although they produce turbines and carpets nowadays rather than brass and cloth). On the left, at the top of Canal Head North, a sweet aroma reminiscent of new hay hangs in the air around one of the factory buildings. These are Samuel Gawith and Company's snuff works, another Kendal industry which has refused to die, established when Cumbria's trade with the American tobacco colonies began in the seventeenth century. The inside has an almost Dickensian look and smell.

The former Canal is now a footpath. Part of the way along it, steps ascend to the road and to the second of Kendal's castles. It is a pleasant walk through the fields and trees to the mound on which the ruined walls stand. Built in around 1200, the castle dominated the entire town for many years. Parts of the round curtain wall and a number of towers survive, enough to show that this was perhaps more a fortified manor house than a defensive work. Its later owners were the Parr family; their most famous member was Katherine Parr (1512–48), sixth and last wife of Henry VIII (1491–1547). A manuscript copy, perhaps in her own hand, of her book of Prayers and Meditations of 1545 is displayed in the Town Hall. With her the family line died out, and the castle fell into a picturesque state of ruin until 1897 when Kendal Corporation acquired it as a public park.

Various paths lead back to the long lines of late Victorian terraced houses and villas with verandah fronts along Aynam Road. A footbridge crosses the Kent to Abbot Hall Gardens, giving a fine view of both house and church. A walk upstream along the bank passes the ends of the yards that run down from Highgate. There is a group of late Georgian houses and sheds in process of restoration where Gulfs Road joins the riverside walk. The left turn past the end of Miller Bridge crosses Stramongate and leads back to the Market Place.

# AROUND AND ABOUT KENDAL

*At almost any point in Kendal, one is conscious of the landscape around. For once, the claims of the advertisements are believable. The fells rise dramatically from the narrow line of the Kent valley, sometimes draped with woods, sometimes barren and grey. Most visitors to Kendal intend to see the Lake District, and two of the routes suggested here explore the area to the west of Kendal, visiting some unusual corners as well as the much-trodden ways and Wordsworthian trails. The landscape is as stirring in other directions, and Kendal is ideally placed for exploring these areas as well. To the south, the River Kent runs through less rugged, although no less beautiful, countryside towards the lower Kent Valley and Morecambe Bay. To the east lie the sometimes stark and inhospitable Pennine uplands and the spectacular Yorkshire Dales National Park. A land of water, stone towns, high hills, and lush narrow valleys, this north-western landscape offers many opportunities for discovery and, although the traffic can be horrendous in the high season, there are quieter spots to be found.*

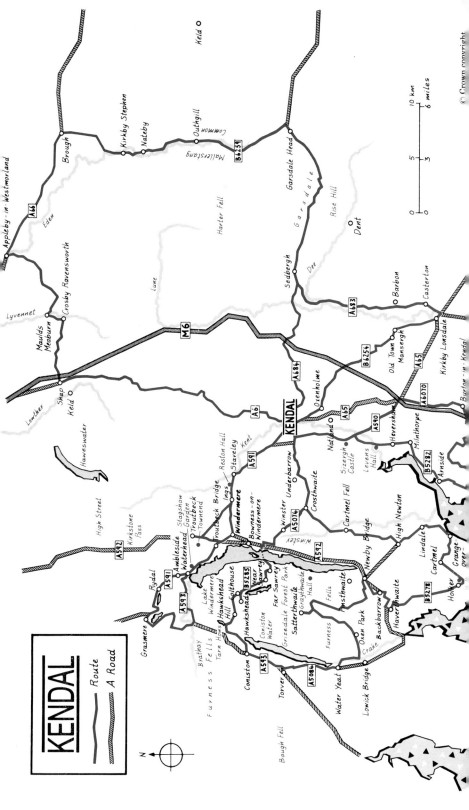

## 1. WINDERMERE AND CONISTON WATER

From almost anywhere in Kendal the fells west of the town beckon. The back road out of Kendal, up Allhallows Lane, Beast Banks and Greenside, quickly enters open country. Bridging the A591, the road climbs, and then descends the steep limestone escarpment of Helsington Barrows to the village of Underbarrow. Before the village there is a parking place on top of the escarpment from which a footpath leads south through the woods to a vantage point with sweeping views in all directions. To the east lies Kendal with the green and grey fells beyond; to the west lie the hills and valleys between here and Windermere, with the Furness Fells and the peak of the Old Man of Coniston beyond; and to the north, if it is a clear day, you can see the still higher inner Lakeland peaks. This viewpoint lays bare the character of the Lake District: high grey fells and hills, the flash of water, and white-washed farms and houses scattered in the valleys.

Down the hill, the second left turn, where the road virtually doubles back on itself, leads past Tullythwaite House restaurant, a classic seventeenth-century Lake District farmhouse – whitewashed, with thick stone walls and large round chimneypots. The road skirts the top of the wide, flat Lyth valley through Crosthwaite to the A5074. Travelling north-west a short distance on this road, the second turn left heads directly west into the swooping fells and woods, dotted with farmsteads. When the lane begins to turn south, the right turn past Great Hartbarrow goes north-west towards Windermere. Below the bare Ludderburn Hill stands the small cottage at Low Ludderburn:

*sheltered from the north, overlooking the whole valley of the Winster. From the terrace in front of the house you can see Arnside and a strip of sea under*

*the Knott. Away to the left you can see Ingleborough, and from the fell just behind the house you can see Ambleside and all the Lake hills.*

This was how Arthur Ransome described the house that he bought in 1925, and in which his great sequence of children's novels was conceived. To those who remember, or still read, his books this is a special place. Against the cottage's whitewashed walls Ransome hoisted signals like those in *Winter Holiday*; to the west lies Windermere, the model for the great lake in *Swallows and Amazons*.

The road continues north-west, skirting the Ghyll Head Reservoir, and begins the sharp descent towards the shore of Windermere. From the A592 parallel to the shore, there are views through the woods down to and across the lake; in the wooded areas are many of the Victorian and early twentieth-century houses which were built when enthusiasm for the natural splendours of the Lakes was at its height, and planning controls were slack. The most important house is the earliest, the Storrs Hall Hotel (on the left just past the junction with the B5360), a large large, heavy rendered, Greek Revival property built in around 1810 by J. M. Gandy, with an octagonal Naval Temple, dedicated to Nelson, Howe, Duncan and St Vincent projecting into the lake. A mile further on, Windermere is crossed by the chain ferry, which runs all year and is very heavily used in summer. Notices at the side of the road tell you how long you can expect to wait if the queue reaches that point: 15 minutes; 90 minutes; give up!

Windermere is a bustling, happy lake, with the resort town of Bowness-on-Windermere above the ferry point, steamers and yachts on the water, and curiosities like the cylindrical mansion, built in 1774, on the wooded Belle Isle in the lake just north of the ferry route. The road from the ferry landing on the west shore leads up through woods and the fields with their characteristic snaking drystone walling to Far and Near Sawrey, huddled villages of stone-built cottages and farmsteads.

Near Sawrey is famous for one woman, Beatrix Potter (1866–1943), who bought the perfect Lakeland farmhouse, *Hill Top*, situated on the left beside the road, with the proceeds of *Peter Rabbit*, her children's classic. She set many of her illustrated books in these fields and fells, and worked for years to conserve Lakeland ways and landscape, buying property and breeding the local Herdwick sheep. Her original drawings are on display in the *Beatrix Potter Gallery* in the former solicitor's office that belonged to her husband William Heel in nearby Hawkshead, reached by the road that skirts Esthwaite Water. In Colthouse, the hamlet where the road turns left to enter Hawkshead, the schoolboy William Wordsworth lodged during his time at the Grammar School. It is in search of Wordsworth, Beatrix Potter, the tangle of white-washed houses and teas that the visitors come who throng the traffic-free streets of this small market town in high season.

Hawkshead was one of the many small towns that acted as feeders into Kendal's economy in the seventeenth and eighteenth centuries, collecting wool from the fell farms. The limited prosperity that resulted is reflected in the houses, inns, and the seventeenth-century church of St Michael. Inside, the names of the Stuart parish officials are painted on the walls, among texts and coloured decoration; in the northeast chapel lies the Elizabethan Archbishop William Sandys, who founded *Hawkshead Grammar School* in the pretty stone and whitewash buildings just down the hill. Like Kendal's Grammar School, great intellects were fostered there; Wordsworth's is among

the schoolboys' names carved into the desk tops.

Before the Dissolution of the Monasteries, the whole of this region was under the control of the great Cistercian abbey of Furness, just outside modern Barrow. The long stone *Hawkshead Courthouse*, from which the monks ran the eastern part of their estates, lies just north of Hawkshead, where the road forks and the B5285 heads west. From the little huddle of cottages and a chapel at Hawkshead Hill, the lane to the right climbs the hill up through the wood to Tarn Hows. It is one of Lakeland's most famous beauty spots; some years three-quarters of a million people come here. Footpaths through the woods on the west of the tarn reach the ridge above the A593 and the valley of the Yewdale Beck. Down the valley, on land given to the National Trust by Beatrix Potter, stands Yew Tree Farm, which is among the best-known farmhouses in the Lake District, with its characteristic whitewashed house, bank barn and timbered spinning gallery. The local Herdwick sheep, whose wool once provided the raw material for stocking-knitting and Kendal's coarser woven cloth, run on the fells above.

The lane from Tarn Hows carries on back down the hillside to rejoin the B5285 at Monk Coniston, just above the head of the long sheet of Coniston Water. The vantage point at the very head of the lake offers splendid views with the steep fells rearing up to the west like a sheer wall culminating in the 2500-foot height of the Old Man of Coniston. At their feet lies Coniston village, and to the east 'the dense coniferous woodland of Grizedale Forest. The road follows the lake's eastern shore, offering views across the water and occasional glimpses of the restored Victorian steam pleasure yacht *'Gondola'* which plies Coniston Water. After little more than a mile, set to the left of the main road, is John Ruskin's house *Brantwood*, where the artist and critic lived from 1871 until his death in 1900. He found it 'a mere shed of rotten timbers and loose stone' and transformed it into an aesthete's paradise that now contains many drawings and watercolours of his beloved landscape. From here he could look across to the hills: 'Mountains', he wrote, 'are the beginning and the end of all natural scenery.'

The road continues to the bottom of Coniston Water, then joins the A5084 just before Torver. At Water Yeat, just before Lowick Bridge, the road forks left and up the steep escarpment to Oxen Park and into Furness Fells. These fells were the source of much of the metal, especially iron, that was sold through Kendal in the sixteenth, seventeenth and eighteenth centuries. The woodlands were exploited to make charcoal for smelting. Vestiges of the iron industry remain: in place names like Force Forge right in the centre of the fells on the road up from Oxen Park; and in some visible remains such as the walls and pits at Cunsey Forge, found up a side track off the lakeside road a mile or so south of the ferry back across Windermere on the Cunsey Beck. A more contemporary use of the woods has been made with the establishment of an open-air sculpture park in *Grizedale Forest Park* which extends from Force Forge almost to Hawkshead. (The sculpture closest to Force Forge is Hilary Cartmel's great carved tree-trunk *Her insistent stream* of 1985.) Grizedale itself, deep in the forest, has a visitors' centre and, perhaps surprisingly, a small theatre.

From Satterthwaite the woodland lanes turn left, then right, then left again, to reach the entrance drive to *Graythwaite Hall*, home of the Sandys, a leading local family since the sixteenth century. Graythwaite's Victorian gardens, famous for rhododendrons and azaleas, are laid out around the comfortable Victorian-Tudor house based upon an Elizabethan core. South from Graythwaite along the wooded lakeside road, at Stott Park above Finsthwaite stands a relic better-preserved than most of Lakeland's industrial history. *Stott Park Bobbin Mill* made reels for the Lancashire cotton industry, harnessing the power of the streams and using local coppiced wood. Its 150-year-old buildings, the machinery, turbine and steam engine are preserved as a working ancient monument. A little further south on the shore of Windermere is another working relic, the Lakeside and Haverthwaite Railway where steam trains ply the four miles or so on the wooded slope alongside the River Leven. The lakeside road crosses the Leven on the slate-built, seventeenth-century Newby Bridge, beside the hotel with its fine Georgian columned doorway.

Belying its picturesque appearance, commerce and industry were the lifeblood in this area south of Windermere, where many great ironworks were founded in the seventeenth and eighteenth centuries, operating on a much larger scale than the smelters higher up in the fells. The largest company was Backbarrow, first based in the village of that name beside the Leven (on the A590, right from Newby Bridge), which was developed by Isaac Wilkinson in the 1740s. His house, Brewer Syke, still stands just off the main road on the left. Wilkinson is still a famous name in iron and steel.

The A590 passes the terminus of the steam railway and Haverthwaite's 1820s parish church (of which H. S. Goodhart-Rendel once wrote, 'The architect is uncertain, and no one would want to claim it.'). At this point the steep wooded hills descend to the widening estuary of the Leven, and the

B5278 half a mile past the church follows the edge of the valley above the marshes, with views out to the expanse of Morecambe Bay, and south to *Holker Hall*. The red sandstone house is principally Victorian, built for the Dukes of Devonshire who were substantial landowners in the area. George Webster extended the original small, early Stuart house in a 'Tudor-bethan' style, after a major fire in 1871. Set in formal and woodland gardens (laid out by Joseph Paxton (1801–65)) Holker, which is still in the Cavendish family, offers a variety of visitor attractions, notably its historic motor vehicles museum.

The side road north-west from the B5278, a mile beyond Holker, follows the River Eea towards the market village of Cartmel, one of the most attractive places in the region. A tight network of lanes and stone houses surrounds Cartmel's chief glory, the great priory church, mainly dating from around 1200. This survives intact because it also acted as the parish church and so was not appropriated by the Crown at the Reformation. Fifteenth-century windows, some with fragments of the original stained glass, pierce the twelfth-century walls, and a fifteenth-century upper stage to the tower was added diagonally, giving the church a quite unique profile. Inside it has many fine furnishings, of the fifteenth and seventeenth centuries, as well as the sumptuous mid fourteenth-century tomb of the first Lord Harrington. *Cartmel Priory Gatehouse*, leading from the town square, is the only survivor of the priory buildings. Between 1624 and 1790 it served as the grammar school.

An old milestone in Cartmel gives the distances to Lancaster and Ulverston by the ancient route over the sands of Morecambe Bay, via Grange-over-Sands three miles to the west. Grange, at the end of the estuary of the River Kent, is the epitome of the quiet, retirement town and seaside watering place, with its mild, protected climate and grey stone villadom. Birdwatchers congregate on the promenade, gazing out over the sands where at least once a year the official guide, appointed by the Duchy of Lancaster, will (at very low tide) lead a party on the eight-mile crossing from Kents Bank, some two miles to the south of Grange, to Hest Bank above Morecambe.

The B5271 leads north up the steep hills from Grange to the village of Lindale. Here the Wilkinsons established the larger of their Cumbrian iron works. Isaac built Wilkinson House and a furnace just above the village on the River Winster around 1748; his son John (1728–1808) later moved to the grander Castlehead House further downstream. Isaac and John developed furnaces in Denbighshire and Staffordshire, and then near Coalbrookdale in Shropshire. John cast the parts for the famous Iron Bridge across the Severn, and launched a prototype iron boat here on the Winster. His cast-iron obelisk (1808) stands in Lindale churchyard; so does the large monument to George Webster, the Kendal architect who built the church here and whose country house was at Eller How a mile north, just off the A590 back to Newby Bridge.

The back road up on to the steep side of Newton Fell from the A590 at High Newton and the slow northerly descent offer fine fell scenery and views down into the Winster valley to the east. At Cartmel Fell, $3\frac{1}{2}$ miles from High Newton, the isolated, barn-like, early Tudor church of St Anthony is reached up a little track off the side road. Inside are seventeenth-century furnishings, fifteenth-century stained glass from Cartmel Priory, and an exceedingly rare painted wooden crucifix of the thirteenth century. From here, the narrow roads continue the descent to the Winster valley, crossing the river where the Arndale Beck comes down to join it, and then rising again to cross the A5074 below Crosthwaite. The reverse of the outward route leads back to Kendal.

## 2. INTO THE HEART OF THE LAKES

This is a much frequented route, and not to be undertaken lightly in high season! From the northern end of Stricklandgate, the A5284 Windermere road leaves Kendal, passing the Abbey Horn Works on the right, founded in 1749 to use some of the by-products of the cattle trade and all that butchery on Kendal's streets. Joining the A591 the road runs through the open fells to Staveley. The 1864 parish church of St James's, off the main road on the right, has excellent stained glass by Edward Burne-Jones (1833–98). Reston Hall, set back on the right hand side of the road a mile west of Staveley, is a plain seven-bay stone house built in 1743 for Robert Bateman, a local boy who made good as a merchant at Leghorn and, as Wordsworth wrote, 'grew wondrous rich'. Another mile along at Ings, St Anne's church off to the left was also built in 1743 by Bateman, and paved in marble which he shipped from Italy.

The right fork beyond Ings leads over the top fells to Troutbeck; the side road joins the A592 coming down from the Kirkstone Pass. Turn to the right along it, crossing the Trout Beck itself up to Town Head, and then double back along the side road running beneath the fellside. The scattered, pretty settlement is worth exploring for its many surviving farmhouses and cottages, which are usually grouped around wells. Best preserved of them all is *Townend* at the southernmost point, a seventeenth-century farmhouse owned by the same family from 1626 to 1947, and since then by the National Trust. Its decoration inside

is remarkably intact, with carved and dated fittings and furnishings in the Lake District manner. Such items are preserved in other houses of the region, although not so well and not so many as at Townend. Dating and initialling was evidence of the Lakelanders' pride in their greater prosperity after the mid seventeenth century, when their poor economy improved with cattle grazing and industrial sidelines in metals and stocking-knitting.

A mile or more down from Townend lies Troutbeck Bridge and the shore of Windermere over the A591. A mile along the main road towards Ambleside, the *National Park Visitor's Centre* at Brockhole provides information and displays about the Lake District, in a large Victorian house built by a Manchester businessman as his summer retreat, with gardens running down to the lake. Passing *Stagshaw Garden*, a woodland enclave with views over the lake down to Belle Isle and over the fells to the higher central peaks from Jenkin Crag, the A591 continues to Waterhead, at the top of Windermere, where the lake steamers depart. The main road turns north up the valley of the Rothay to Ambleside, a small grey stone village trapped inside a tourist honeypot. Ambleside is now more important as a climbing centre than a place to stop and explore. The Victorians discovered the delights of such natural sites as the waterfall at Stockghyll Force to the east (reached by a footpath along the stream), and took away all its wildness. Ambleside's great curiosity is *Bridge House*, a seventeenth-century stone cottage built over the stream, and now the National Trust information centre.

The A591 continues up the valley of the Rothay. This is one of the busiest roads in the area in high season; the alternative back road along the valley floor's western edge, from Rothay Bridge down the A593, is often more relaxing. Both routes lead into the heart of Wordsworth country.

At Rydal, the valley narrows below Rydal Water. William Wordsworth (1770–1850), his wife Mary and sister Dorothy (1771–1855) lived in *Rydal Mount*, up the lane leading north from the church, from 1813 until his death. Many family possessions are displayed in the house, which became a place of literary pilgrimage in the poet's lifetime. Sometimes he might receive a hundred visitors in a day. The house is set in the terraced gardens which Wordsworth himself designed. Rydal Hall, a seventeenth-century manor house with an early Victorian front, lies below the Mount and on the other side of the lane. It was the home of the most important local gentry family, the Le Flemings; now it is an Anglican study centre.

Rydal is less well-visited than its near neighbour, Grasmere, where a younger and poorer Wordsworth lived. The main road skirts the northern shore of Rydal Water and then the eastern shore of Grasmere. Halfway along the Rydal Water shore, Nab Cottage (dated 1702 over the door) was where Thomas de Quincey courted the farmer's daughter (the Wordsworths seem not to have approved, especially when she became pregnant) and where Samuel Taylor Coleridge's son Hartley (1796–1849) later lodged until his death. In 1809 de Quincey had come to live close to the Wordsworths, having worshipped the poet from afar, taking over *Dove Cottage* just above the lake at Grasmere where Wordsworth had lived from 1799 to 1808. Dove Cottage is still a place of literary pilgrimage, for here some of Wordsworth's greatest work was composed. A small, basically early seventeenth-century village house in the Lake District vernacular style, its rooms (and the separate museum over the road) are devoted to the works and belongings of the man

who almost single-handedly 'invented' the English Lakes, and attracted other poets and writers to them. The Wordsworths left Grasmere for Rydal Mount when William was given an undemanding public office that allowed him to write without financial worries.

From Dove Cottage, the B5287 leaves the main road and passes through Grasmere village. Most of the houses are Victorian or twentieth-century, but some older properties survive, like the Swan Hotel (where Wordsworth's guests who were in need of a drink repaired). Grasmere parish church, at the village's southern end, has a rather knobbly exterior of many ages jumbled together under a rough-cast skin, and a fine rustic interior still like that which Wordsworth described in *The Prelude*:

> With pillars crowded, and the roof upheld
> By naked rafters intricately crossed,
> Like leafless underboughs, in some thick wood ...

The Wordsworths are all buried in the churchyard.

In spite of modern tourism, Grasmere still has something of the quality which made William Wordsworth choose it as his home. Guided by the poems and by Dorothy Wordsworth's memoirs, walks in the locality gain an extra dimension. The path from the lane at Dove Cottage passes beneath Nab Scar (above the wood at Nab Cottage), and descends through the trees to the foot of Rydal Mount gardens. There are views over Rydal Water, which may have waves 'like the dance of spirits' that Dorothy once described. Past Rydal church and over the A591, a path crosses the River Rothay by a footbridge and enters the woods, emerging on the lake's southern shore. Heading west, the path continues along the escarpment looking over Grasmere. Dorothy described its bewitching appearance on Boxing Day 1801 in her journal: 'the lake of a rich purple, the fields of soft yellow, the island yellowish-green, the copses red-brown, the mountains purple'. The path joins an unclassified road that runs parallel to the shore and joins the main road by Grasmere church.

This same narrow by-road turns away from Grasmere to the south, through often wild uplands past the small circle of Loughrigg Tarn and down to the A593 at Skelwith Bridge over the River Brathay. Paths on either side of the river lead the short distance upstream to the waterfall of Skelwith Force. The A593 heads east alongside the River Brathay back to Waterhead, where the Brathay joins the Rothay just before it enters Windermere. From there the A591 leads back via Windermere town to Kendal.

## 3. THE KENT VALLEY

In contrast to the previous routes, among the lakes and fells, the area south of Kendal is less rugged, and is often less crowded, especially at the height of the summer season.

Leaving Kendal on the A6 south-wards, *Sizergh Castle* is the first significant sight, reached by a signposted lane to the west off the fast road. Sizergh has always been the home and stronghold of the Strickland family, a long-dominant influence in the life of Kendal. A large, defensible fourteenth-century pele tower stands at its heart, with a hall range that was built on to the tower in the sixteenth century. Sizergh has many grand fireplaces and plaster ceilings; the picture collection includes portraits of the exiled Stuarts, with whom the Catholic Stricklands went to France after James II (1633–1701) was deposed in 1688, and some of George Romney's earliest commissions. Gardens in different styles – formal, rock or old roses –

surround the house; yet Sizergh's gardens, fine as they are, cannot compete with the romance of the ancient topiary at *Levens Hall*, another couple of miles along the A6. James Bellingham built the new house in the 1580s and 1590s, with its many grand rooms and exuberant plasterwork, around the core of another defensive pele tower. James Graham acquired Levens in 1688; the heart-shaped motifs on some of the down pipes refer – so it is said – to his acquiring Levens in a card game that turned on the ace of hearts. Graham added exterior embellishments, and began what is Levens' most famous and important feature, the great French topiary garden which his heiress insisted should not be swept away by the great eighteenth-century tide of naturalism, and so survives.

From the entrance to Levens, the view back across the A6 up the Kent valley encompasses the ancient deer park of the house, with its wooded coverts and open areas for the chase. A short distance south along the A6, the minor road to the left leads through the little village of Heversham, where the shaft of a ninth-century carved cross stands inside the fifteenth-century (but Victorianized) parish church. This side road rejoins the A6, and a mile further along the B5282 strikes west at Milnthorpe, a modest Victorian watering place and earlier market town that today sleeps on, ignored by road and rail. The first left turn along the B5282 passes through another park where fallow deer still roam, that of Dallam Tower, the 1720s country home of the Colonel Wilson who built Abbot Hall in Kendal.

The B5282 runs alongside the narrow strip of land beside the marshes and flats of the Kent estuary to Arnside where the railway to Grange-over-Sands and Barrow-in-Furness crosses the Kent on its viaduct. The hills just to the south of Arnside are owned by the National Trust. Minor roads strike south to Silverdale and the dunes, descending the slopes and passing Arnside Tower, a large and imposing fifteenth-century pele tower. The dunes and marshes around Silverdale, with their protected plants and birds, have an austere beauty, the 'expanse of view ... such wide plains of golden sands with purple hill shadows' that Mrs Gaskell (1810–65) described in *Ruth*. The roads skirting the flat, marshy edge of the bay lead through the quiet Victorian town and over the low hills to cross the railway below Silverdale station. At the head of the ponds and dunes, the road ascends sharply and rounds Cringlebarrow Wood to the village of Yealand Conyers.

The main village street is a pleasant mixture of eighteenth- and early nineteenth-century houses and chapels, with *Leighton Hall* set on the hillside just to its west. The core of the white limestone house dates from 1760, and was given a Gothic treatment in 1810 and extended in the same style sixty years later. The 1810 work was done for the famous Lancaster cabinet-maker Richard Gillow, and many examples of his firm's early work are contained in the house, which also has one of the earliest billiard rooms (since Gillow was among the first to make billiard tables).

East of Yealand Conyers, the A6, the old Lancaster–Kendal turnpike road, opened in 1752 (now the A6070), the modern M6, the main railway line, and the Lancaster canal all run more or less parallel to each other, up the narrow tongue of low land between the higher crags. Turn left onto the A6, fork right, and right again half a mile north, and cross the canal above its long flight of locks. Over the canal, the left turn, the A6070, then passes through Burton-in-Kendal, a market village which in the late eighteenth century was a staging post and a minor

resort for the gentry and a local 'society' town – something that Kendal was not. Burton is principally one long main street, opening into a square halfway along, with the splendid Burton House, of around 1780, many restrained Georgian houses, and a few rather grander stone houses along it. The old turnpike road continues past the part-Norman parish church (in which fragments of another pre-Norman carved cross are displayed) and north alongside the motorway with high crags and rocks on the right. Just beside junction 36 of the motorway, this road joins the A65, the old Keighley–Kendal turnpike, and continues back into Kendal, with the occasional surviving toll house at its edge. The land rises noticeably until Natland where it begins to descend again into the Kent valley.

Entering Kendal, the octagonal toll house still stands on the right-hand side, incorporated into a Victorian house. Almost opposite, a Victorian iron suspension foot-bridge crosses the river, and just beyond that is the factory of Kendal's best-known modern product, K Shoes, founded in 1843 and part of the town's long leather-working tradition. The road then rounds the corner to cross the Kent on the ancient Nether Bridge.

### 4. TOWARDS THE PENNINES

Kendal lies within reach of not only the Lake District National Park but also the western portion of the Yorkshire Dales National Park. The lower fells that form the foothills of the Pennine chain are visible to the east from vantage points in the town, and it is in an easterly direction that we finally turn.

The A65 heads south of Kendal, past the upper school and town leisure centre, from which the B6254 turns off left, looping round the mainline railway station at Oxenholme. The high hill on the right, The Helm, with the banks and ditches of a prehistoric hill fort, has a fine lookout position on top, with views of the hills in three directions and the lower ground and sea to the south. The road travels along the fells, with glimpses of the occasional interesting house, such as the late Elizabethan Bleaze Hall two miles or so beyond Oxenholme, down beside the St Sunday's Beck (nobody is quite sure who St Sunday was). After passing under the M6 and rising for another couple of miles, the road begins its slow descent into the valley of the River Lune. At Old Town an unclassified road leaves the B6254 heading east to the hamlet of Mansergh; the church of St Peter, set to the right, is one of many well-designed little churches in this upland area that were put up in the later nineteenth century, often by the Lancaster archi-

tects Paley & Austin, making good the paucity of churches in these far-flung upland parishes. The minor road descends the valley side to the river, and then follows the Lune to rejoin the B6254, which continues to the small, quiet market town of Kirkby Lonsdale, sitting above the Lune where it is crossed by the A65.

This town was often in competition with Kendal for markets and trade, although its small size suggests that it was much less successful. Kirkby Lonsdale is another grey stone-built town, like Kendal, and has many fine late Georgian and early Victorian houses. There are two sides to the town. The Market Square and Main Street, with a number of good Georgian and Victorian town houses and commercial buildings ranged along them, lead through the main shopping area down to the famous thirteenth-century

*The topiary garden at Levens Hall.*

Devil's Bridge (and its modern successor) over the Lune. Behind Market Street (but largely hidden from it), the church, with its surrounding knot of streets and alleys, has quite a different, ancient air. St Mary's church has a grand early Norman arcade, among the best of all the early building work in Cumbrian churches, but rather out of scale compared to the twelfth- and thirteenth-century work that followed it. Vantage points north of the church have spectacular views of the Lune valley; John Ruskin called it 'One of the loveliest scenes in England – therefore in the world'.

The A683 runs north from just over the river at Kirkby Lonsdale, along the east bank of the Lune. Further east, the land rises steeply to over 2000 feet and the boundary of the Dales National Park. Casterton, the first village on the A683, is remarkable for the sickly, sentimental late Victorian and Edwardian wall paintings in both nave and chancel of its church, founded in 1833, and for the adjacent grim, grey school for clergymen's daughters. Bare, high fells, cut through by the road that passes through to Dent along the dale of the Barbon Beck, act as a backdrop to Barbon, the next village, on the right of the main road. An old packhorse bridge crosses the beck near the church, another Paley & Austin building of the 1890s. From Barbon the A683 follows the line of a Roman road: there is the worn face of a Roman milestone just off the road above the Lune to the south of Middleton. Keeping its course beside the river, the A683 crosses the boundary of the old West Riding of Yorkshire, and the modern boundary of the Yorkshire Dales park, just to the west of Sedbergh.

Sedbergh is one of the important points of access to the cross-Pennine routes and the eastern dales. The waters of the Rawthey, the Clough from Garsdale and the Dee from Dentdale all join at Sedbergh, and flow into the Lune just south of the town. This would be another small stone-built town along a main street, with yards (like those of Kendal) filling spare spaces, were it not for the school that extends into the valley on the south, and the Quakers. Sedbergh School was founded by Roger Lupton, Provost of Eton, in 1525: the earliest surviving school buildings date from 1716 and stand on the road to Dent. They now house a small museum. The old school house, by the parish church, dates from 1755, while other buildings were put up in the 1870s and later when Sedbergh was reconstituted as a public school.

The Society of Friends was founded when a Leicestershire weaver's son, George Fox (1624–91), had a vision in 1652 of a new religious people, and that Sedbergh would be where he would find fellow-seekers. South-west of the town, just off the main A683, a lane runs down to the river and an early industrial settlement at Briggflats. One of the earliest Friends' Meeting Houses, dated to 1675, stands here, incorporating the original living quarters. Following the A684 west from Sedbergh, towards junction 37 of the M6, the right turn beyond the B6257 rises up onto Firbank Fell. At the summit of this minor road Fox had his vision of 'a great people in white raiment by the river side coming to the Lord'. The place is marked as Fox's Pulpit, and from it there are panoramic views across the narrow upper valley of the Lune to the bare heights of the Howgill Fells to the east.

Sedbergh and its immediate surroundings offer many attractions, in the shape of the small town and its buildings, places for refreshment and the bare beauty of the hills and dales within which it is set. It is only some 12 miles back to Kendal from Sedbergh, west along the A684. A wide circle back, through the fell gaps and along the upper Eden valley to Appleby, the county town of the former county of Westmorland, and back down to Kendal from the heights of Shap Fell, gives a much more intimate sense of these vast Pennine uplands.

The A684 east from Sedbergh passes along the narrow Garsdale between the great Baugh Fell rising to over 2000 feet on the north and the slightly lower Rise Hill on the south. The lower, less rugged part of the Clough valley has farmsteads and little clusters of cottages along lanes off the main road for the first few miles. A parking place at Garsdale Foot affords a view of the ravine through which the Clough rushes below Danny Bridge. From here the valley narrows, the hedges are replaced by stone walling and the farms huddle close to the main road. Little stone bridges leap across the river, connecting farms with the road and taking the road first to one bank of the river, then to the other. Garsdale only has one settlement, called – prosaically enough – The Street, where the church, chapel, and most buildings are from the nineteenth century, but the names of many of the properties along the dale clearly reflect the pioneering of ancient Norse settlers. The railway that runs along the slopes above the road in the upper part of the dale is the Settle–Carlisle line, arguably the most scenic and most often-threatened railway in the country. Built at enormous cost in human life between 1869 and 1876, the old Midland Railway line reaches its highest point, 1100 feet, at Garsdale Head. Just beyond here the B6259 leaves the A684 and heads north parallel to the railway. This is not just the railway summit; it is also the Pennine watershed. East of here streams flow down towards the North Sea; Hawes, featured in one of the Richmond tours, is less than ten miles away.

Keeping as level as possible in this landscape, the Settle–Carlisle railway runs through tunnels and cuttings and along embankments, while the road zigzags through Mallerstang Common, the valley of the north-flowing River Eden that will eventually reach Carlisle. Mallerstang is a bare, austere landscape with few trees and few signs of habitation. Becks tumble down the steep hillsides. There is a hamlet after seven miles, Outhgill; the little chapel there was begun in 1663 by Lady Anne Clifford, whose personality is stamped on many buildings in the rest of this itinerary.

When Lady Anne's father, George Clifford, 3rd Earl of Cumberland, died in 1605, he left the 15-year-old Anne as his sole heiress. She had to fight long and hard in the courts to secure her inheritance, and against Parliament's army to defend Skipton Castle in the Civil War. When in 1646 she did succeed to the Craven and Westmorland lands, she set about rebuilding the castles and associated churches on her estates. Lady Anne had a deep sense of history and a somewhat High Anglican sensibility. Her buildings were often archaic in style, her churches simple and designed to promote an air of holiness. She left inscriptions everywhere to tell posterity what she had done. There is such an inscription set above the doorway of Outhgill chapel; there probably was one on the now-ruined Pendragon Castle, a late Norman defensive tower less than a mile to the north, standing on a grassy outcrop, which she had restored in 1660.

Mallerstang begins to widen at the small village of Nateby, where the B6270 comes over the top from Keld in Swaledale to join the B6259. After little more than a mile the B road joins the A685 at Kirkby Stephen, another small Westmorland market town with a number of good Georgian and Victorian houses. The town's most memorable features are the eight-columned screen put up in 1810 between the Market Place and the long red sandstone parish church, with its early Tudor west tower. The A685 continues across the Eden valley floor, which contrasts markedly with the wilder Mallerstang, to Brough set up on the escarpment at the junction with the east–west A66. Brough has been an important crossing point since at least the time of the Romans; they built the fort on top of which *Brough Castle* was erected by the Normans. Damaged during repeated raids from across the Scottish border, the castle stood in ruins from 1521 to 1659, when Lady Anne Clifford set to work restoring it. Many vestiges of her work may be seen in the present ruins. One tower, which she named appropriately Roman Tower, was built from scratch. The castle burned down in 1666. Lady Anne also built a commemorative pillar in the upper half of the village, which was converted into a clock tower in 1911, and she almost certainly built parts of Brough parish church where Norman work mingles with early Tudor.

The A66 continues through the broadening Eden Valley, with the dominating fells rising to 2500 feet on the north, to Appleby, Westmorland's former county town and long Kendal's great rival for precedence. A loop of the River Eden almost encircles the town, and proved a necessary protection in the era of Scottish border raids. The open side was protected by the castle, which became the county seat of the Cliffords. Appleby now lies on both sides of the river, the older Bongate on the east bank with its part-Saxon church, and the twelfth-century new town, Boroughgate, on the west bank with its wide main street leading up to the castle gates. Many parts of *Appleby Castle*, including the great keep, date from the late twelfth

century, but all had been ruined by 1659 when Lady Anne Clifford rebuilt the towers, and made rooms out of the great, bare internal spaces. The east range was rebuilt in the 1690s by her son-in-law and heir, the Earl of Thanet, appropriating some of the stone from Brough Castle. The Great Hall and portions of the walls and towers are still standing. Among the Clifford picture collection is a huge genealogical triptych which Lady Anne commissioned. It is nine feet wide, and shows herself in 1605, her parents, her brothers and her aunts, and herself (painted from life) in 1646. This now hangs in the Great Hall of the castle. There are other memories of her family in St Lawrence's church where she built a family chapel to contain her own tomb with its proud genealogy of twenty-four coats of arms, and the tomb of her mother, Margaret, Countess of Cumberland, who died in 1617. The mother's monument is especially fine, with her effigy lying draped in a mantle: 'But passenger know heaven and fame contains the best of her', one of the inscriptions reads. Lady Anne also repaired the other church in the town, St Michael's in Bongate, and endowed and built the plain and seemly St Anne's Hospital in 1651, with its separate dwellings and little chapel.

There are a number of handsome mid eighteenth- and later nineteenth-century buildings in Appleby, especially on Boroughgate. As the county town, Appleby was the venue for Assizes and many of the Quarter Sessions courts, and it was much more a resort for the gentry than Kendal, although it was considerably smaller. Appleby remains a neat and little-spoiled town; since the loss of its county town status in 1974, it has called itself Appleby-in-Westmorland to keep a vestige of its old pride alive.

The B6260, which leads south from

the main street of Appleby, rises up the steep hillsides. The second minor road on the right leads to the pretty villages on the banks of the Lyvennet Beck. Early man built stone circles and burial mounds on the surrounding fells; modern man may find his roots in the *Ancestral Research Centre* in the nineteenth-century house Holesfoot in Maulds Meaburn, the first village along this road. Other portraits from the Lady Anne Clifford picture collection now hang in the Centre. The largest house in the village is the early seventeenth-century Meaburn Hall, with a pair of summer houses standing in the walled garden. The 1st Earl of Lonsdale used to keep his wife's embalmed corpse in a cupboard here. St Lawrence's church at Crosby Ravensworth, $1\frac{1}{2}$ miles to the south and further up the beck, is often described as a miniature cathedral, incorporating a late Norman crossing tower, a Perpendicular west tower, and a Gothick south porch and doorway by Robert Smirke (1781–1867), architect of the British Museum.

The unclassified road due west from Crosby Ravensworth climbs back onto the fells in the direction of Shap, where the M6, the A6 and the railway all have to climb the steep fell pass (which is over 800 feet above sea level). The minor road crosses the motorway and the railway line to join the A6 in Shap village. Shap is the modern equivalent of those turnpike staging towns which were superseded by the Victorian railway, for this was where drivers of heavy vehicles once had to sit out the heavy snowfalls which Shap experiences in winter; whereas now the motorway thunders by. The little late Stuart market house, and a few Norman arches in the otherwise Victorian parish church, are the only items of interest in Shap; but just to the west along a minor road lies the former Premonstratensian house of *Shap Abbey*, founded in the late twelfth century although the only significant portion of the building to survive is the early Tudor west tower of the abbey church. The abbey ruins sit within a constricted space beside the River Lowther, in a circle of trees which has grown up since the Dissolution of the Monasteries in 1540. A lane leads south-east to the tiny hamlet of Keld one mile away, with *Keld Chapel*, a lonely, plain, small Tudor chapel tucked away in the wilds of the Shap Fell heights.

Keld is a dead end. Back on the A6 there is a steady southward descent from the fells towards the valley of the Kent, with only the occasional old farmhouse or other sign of human habitation, and the heights of Harter Fell and High Street visible to the west, the Pennines beyond Appleby and Brough to the east. The road enters Kendal behind the railway station.

There is a coda to this itinerary. Other portraits from Lady Anne Clifford's collection hang in Abbot Hall (page 36), while a Kendal house has a touching link with her. Collinfield is a seventeenth-century farmhouse now marooned in the housing estate off the A6, beyond the Nether Bridge and the Technical College. It is a large version of a standard Westmorland farmhouse, but it was extended around 1668 for George Sedgwick, who had been secretary to Lady Anne Clifford. She had helped him purchase this house for his retirement – keeping, as she liked to do, one of the keys to the main door lock. The lock survives, still bearing her initials.

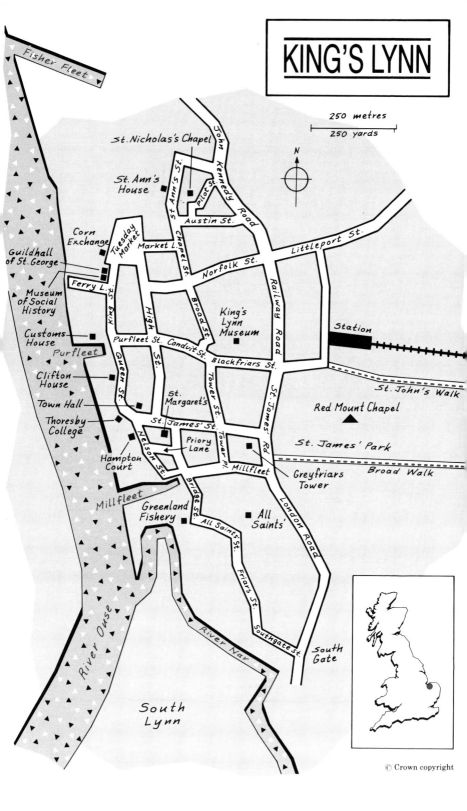

# 3
# KING'S LYNN

Norfolk

*Until the railway came in the mid nineteenth century, it
was more convenient for the belongings of Cambridge
students to be shipped around the coast to King's Lynn,
and then taken up the rivers to the university. Fifty-five
miles by land, or hundreds of miles by water, yet the coast
route was quicker. Navigable rivers and the sea have been
the key to King's Lynn's success for centuries. Indeed, they
were the reason for its foundation.
Daniel Defoe (1660–1731), who was so taken with it when
he visited in the early 1720s, thought, 'Here are more gentry,
and consequently is more gaiety in this town' than in any
other in the region. There is still much going on here.
King's Lynn is virtually two distinct towns: the historic
core, which local people have fought hard to preserve; and
the newer town. What is refreshing is that, rather than
turning the old town into an architectural museum, the
preservation of older buildings has been for community
uses. The archaeological importance, as well as the
architectural thrill, of the town lies in the wealth of
mercantile buildings and warehouses that go back from
the twentieth century to the twelfth. (There is still a
respectable dock business.) It is a town where exploring
back alleys and little lanes, even occasionally interesting
doorways, is always worthwhile. Until the eighteenth
century Lynn was one of the premier ports in England,
which is reflected in the quality and variety of the houses,
churches, and civic buildings.*

## ———— EXPLORING KING'S LYNN ————

King's Lynn is a very linear town; almost everything of interest lies within a few hundred yards of the River Ouse. The
Ouse made the town. King's Lynn stands on what were islands
in muddy swampland. Building materials were brought in by
water – bricks, often from the Low Countries, stone by river

from the Peterborough area – or came from the clays, sand and mud of the wetlands, while the inland river trade and the sea-going trades gave Lynn its immense medieval wealth.

The route begins at the South Gate. King's Lynn was once a walled town; Georgian engravings show the walls, and the two great gateways. Now the only substantial surviving part is the battlemented *South Gate*, built in around 1520 and still used by incoming traffic. A grand stone front faces the world, marking the wealth and self-confidence of King's Lynn.

The main road into town is usually as busy as its name, London Road, suggests. The long, dark rows of handsome, brick-built terraced houses along it are mainly early nineteenth century, for London Road was laid out after Acts of Parliament for road improvement were passed in 1803 and 1806. We take the old road, north-west along Southgate Street and Friars Street to All Saints', the parish church of South Lynn. From these fairly recent housing redevelopments, King's Lynn's building gems soon emerge.

South Lynn was the original settlement, the first piece of dry land to emerge from the marshes. This old road is the ancient causeway running above the line of the River Nar, which flows only a few yards away to the south. All Saints' Church, set behind its wrought iron gateway, is a Saxon foundation, considerably predating the rest of the town, and although what strikes the casual eye is mainly fifteenth-century, like the flint and stone chequerboarding in the clere-story, the transepts are two hundred years older and some walls are Norman. The church even had an anchorite's cell in the middle ages, where a hermit was walled in.

The short walk along All Saints' Street soon leads to other older features of King's Lynn. Immediately ahead stands the brick-and-timber frontage of the Greenland Fishery. The building's name and the projecting sailing ship sign are reminders of its use until early in the twentieth century as a pub for sailors who worked in the whaling industry, then still an important trade here. The house was originally built in 1605 for John Atkin, town mayor and wealthy merchant. Elaborate early Stuart allegorical wall paintings were uncovered during the restoration of this house, which was undertaken by the admirable King's Lynn Preservation Trust who have set out to rescue many worthwhile buildings.

A line of low, rendered and pink-washed cottages, along-side the Greenland Fishery, leads left to a forlorn-looking brick-and-rubble gateway standing alone, the sole vestige of the fourteenth-century house of the Carmelites, one of many orders of monks and friars who congregated in medieval Lynn. As you walk up Bridge Street the curious, tall, slim, octagonal tower of the ruined church of the Greyfriars is occasionally visible over to the north-east, while rising straight ahead over the roof tops are the two west towers of

St Margaret's parish church, one pinnacled, the other plain.

Just north of the Greenland Fishery, Bridge Street crosses the Millfleet (fleet simply means river). The view from the bridge now reveals only a muddy creek (except at very high tide). The River Ouse into which these creeks flowed is visible a short distance to the west. The fleets were once partly navigable, and the action of silting (accelerated by the townspeople's dumping their rubbish) produced the islands between them on which the town was built. Continued silting has left the creeks almost dry. The road turns sharp left past the brick warehouses of the old maltings, to become Nelson Street, one of Lynn's most charming smaller thoroughfares.

The left-hand side has a succession of larger houses, for the most part Georgian refacings of earlier properties, beginning with the pedimented front and doorcase of the seventeenth-century Oxley House. No. 15 is one of the town centre properties which after relative neglect have now been sensitively converted into flats. The entrance to the merchant's counting house survives on the left, while the bricks on the mid Georgian frontage have original graffiti. They came from Holland, possibly as ship's ballast. No. 9 retains its carved medieval doorway, complete with a traceried door. The modest brick terraces lining the right-hand side end with an earlier plaster and timber house, rendered in bright yellow ochre, formerly and appropriately the 'Valiant Sailor' pub.

Immediately opposite is the equally bright, orange-coloured range of buildings known as Hampton Court. Rescuing this property was the Preservation Trust's first project. It was converted in 1963 into fifteen sheltered dwellings around the tranquil internal courtyard. Hampton Court takes its name from a seventeenth-century baker, John Hampton, who owned it, but the property is older than that. The south range was originally a fourteenth-century hall house, squeezed on to land on what was then quayside, to which the west and east wings and finally, in the seventeenth century, Hampton's north wing, were added, with the expansion of both business and the river bank. The narrow St Margaret's Lane alongside Hampton Court leads down to the Ouse. Although at one time Hampton Court's back wall stood directly over the water, now there is a broad bank and quay. The warehouse's blocked-up arches may still be made out in the brickwork, as they may in many other older brick-and-rubble warehouses along the quays.

It is not too difficult to imagine the bustle in this area in its mercantile heyday in the seventeenth and eighteenth centuries, because the quayside is still in use, especially for grain storage in massive silos. The long brick-and-timber late medieval range on the right of St Margaret's Lane, opposite Hampton Court, was the property of the North German merchants of the Hanseatic League, who specialized in grain and metal imports. It remained in their hands until 1750. Somewhere in this jumble of buildings old and new, the teenage Fanny Burney (1752–1840), whose father, Charles Burney (1726–1814), the musician and composer, was then organist in St Margaret's church, had her lookout, where she began making up the stories that were to become her novels. 'I scarce wish for anything so truly, really and greatly', she confided in her journal, 'as to be in love.'

St Margaret's, facing the rectory and the Burneys' house, is one of the largest parish churches in England. It stands at the heart of the town founded by Herbert de Losinga, Bishop of Norwich, in around 1100 to meet the need for a new town and port on the edge of the marsh. The town's name remained Bishop's Lynn until 1536, when Henry VIII (1491–1547) seized the property of its owner, Norwich Cathedral Priory, and it was renamed King's Lynn. A Benedictine priory was established to the south of St Margaret's church; little of that remains except cottages in the lane alongside the church, with their medieval entrance arch. Much however remains of the medieval parish church, in fact dedicated to St Margaret with St Mary Magdalene and All the Virgin Saints. Of the Norman church only the base of the south-west tower survives, with characteristic intersecting arcading. The upper parts of both towers were remodelled in the thirteenth century, with slender pointed windows. By 1452 the north-west tower had collapsed, and the townspeople paid for its rebuilding in the fashionable Perpendicular style. The core of the old tower remains inside. The south-west tower bears a moon clock: the central disc shows the lunar phases while the tail of St Margaret's dragon points to the time of high tide. That information is not there to satisfy idle curiosity: the levels of very high floods, such as those of 31 January 1953 and 11 January 1978 when the church was inundated, are marked beside the west door. This door also carries a medieval sanctuary handle – if a miscreant touched it he was to be given temporary sanctuary.

Inside, the nave has an unsettling quality: it is in fact an early example of Georgian Gothic pastiche. By the late fifteenth century St Margaret's had evolved into a complex building, with many side chapels, a central octagonal lantern, and a tall spire on the south-west tower. It was little changed until the great storm on 8 September 1741 when the spire came crashing down through the nave. Within five years a new nave, crossing, and truncated transepts had been built, designed by Matthew Brettingham who was working at Holkham, the Earl of Leicester's grand Norfolk seat (see page 71). The result is not quite successful. Neither, it must be said, is the modern reordering of the sanctuary inside a low brick wall at the crossing – especially when compared with what does survive of the medieval work at the east end: the misericords, the arcades between the choir and its aisles, the carved wooden screens, and above all the fourteenth-century memorial brasses in the south choir aisle. They are the largest and the earliest surviving memorial brasses in England, commemorating Adam de Walsoken, and Robert Braunche, showing the great Peacock Feast this wealthy merchant laid on for Edward III (1312–77).

The eighteenth-century disaster also destroyed the setting in which King's Lynn's most famous holy inhabitant worshipped and sobbed. Margery Kempe (1364–c.1440) was the first English autobiographer, leaving an extraordinary journal of the soul, describing her religious hysteria, manifested in weeping fits, her many overseas pilgrimages, and her visions of Christ and His Mother in the choir and chapels of St Margaret's.

The townspeople took the opportunity after 1741 to expand the market place on the north side of the church. This is the Saturday Market, the hub of Bishop Herbert's town. Facing south is the great medieval traceried window in the flint and stone chequerboard front of the *Town Hall*; built in 1421, it was the Guildhall of the Holy Trinity, medieval Lynn's most important religious confraternity of local businessmen. The former Town Gaol stands alongside, proclaiming its function through the looped chains and keys decorating the façade. Both form part of a long harmonious sequence of civic buildings rounding the corner from Saturday Market into Queen Street.

A local carpenter, William Tuck, designed the grey-brick gaol in 1784 (now the town's information office). He also built the assembly rooms in 1766 in the Guildhall. The interior is lit by the enormous window, while at the rear the Georgian assembly room and card room have chandeliers, and many plush rococo touches. The portrait of Charles I (1600–49) wearing a crown of thorns recalls King's Lynn's royalist sympathies in the Civil War. In the vaulted undercroft, the town regalia and plate are on display, one of the finest of all provincial civic collections. The great treasure is the so-called King John's Cup, not a piece of the treasure lost in the nearby Wash, but a beautiful fourteenth-century enamelled loving cup decorated with hunting scenes. The Guildhall buildings continue with an addition of 1624, also faced with flint chequer patterns mixing classical and gothic motifs, and a late Victorian extension.

Opposite the Town Hall runs the long seventeenth-century brick front, topped by shaped gables, of the early Tudor foundation of *Thoresby College*. The original panelled door into the courtyard bears the inscription 'magistri Thomae Thoresby fundator huius loci', and closer inspection reveals that the words 'Orate pro anima' (pray for the soul of) were erased after the Reformation. The college was established in 1511 for thirteen priests; within thirty years they had been evicted and the premises taken over for houses and stores. The priests' hall with its timber hammerbeam roof survives on the upper floor on the river side of the court. These buildings were also rescued by the Preservation Society, whose offices are in the late seventeenth-century house on the right. In this corner a plaque marks the edge of the thirteenth-century quay, showing just how far the bank has widened.

Queen Street curves along the line of the earliest river bank. Lynn waterside properties are characteristically long, thin strips running down to the Ouse: the merchants' houses on the street front, outbuildings behind, and then warehouses with narrow lanes alongside running back down to the river with watergates for loading and unloading. There is ample opportunity to go down these side alleys and explore the remains of medieval and Tudor warehouses, and imagine the hive of port activity that this once was.

The most interesting house front on Queen Street is Clifton House. The projecting top-piece of its early eighteenth-century portico with twisted barley-sugar columns has been removed, after one tussle too many with passing lorries, but the doorway opens from the narrow pavement into a court-yard building. Immediately ahead rises a tall brick tower, five storeys high, built in around 1580. It is the only survivor of many like it along the waterfront: they allowed maximum accommodation on a small site, and provided lookouts, storage, and guiding lights. The great wooden post rising through the spiral staircase is a former ship's mast, while some rooms still have original painted wall decorations. From the top, King's Lynn can be seen laid out: the long lines of the main streets, the river and the view out towards the sea. The elegant Georgian rooms in the house have tiled floors beneath them dating from the early fourteenth century, perhaps the finest domestic survival of the period. Below are late fourteenth-century brick-vaulted cellars with traces of an even older late Norman stone-built house. The warehouses at the back, which long remained derelict, have now been converted sympathetically into flats.

Queen Street rounds the corner to the bridge over the Purfleet, opening into Purfleet Place and King's Staithe Square. Beside the (almost invariably dry) Purfleet stands the elegant Customs House, a late Stuart stone building with a hipped roof, topped by a jaunty cupola. It is one of the town's architectural gems, set off rather incongruously by the enor-mous 1930s grain silos on the quayside behind. Many houses around bear signs of Lynn's late Stuart prosperity, especially the double-fronted *Bank House* (which is now a restaurant) with a statue of Charles I set in a curled pedimented niche. The grey brick house half in front of it was Gurney's Bank, opened in 1869. The Gurneys were, and are, one of Norfolk's

*The Town Hall, King's Lynn.*

important families; it was to Bank House that Samuel Gurney Cresswell returned in 1855 from his Arctic discovery of the long-sought North-West Passage.

The Customs House, built in 1683 as a Merchants' Exchange, is Lynn's only complete specimen of the work of its most important architectural son, Henry Bell, himself a town merchant. Bell provided a building that would stand proud among the post-medieval jumble of properties. A statue of Charles II (1630–85) stands over the entrance. The Exchange failed to work – the merchants were probably too entrenched in their individual dealings – and in 1718 the Customs authorities moved in. Now they have moved out after 270 years, and the building's future use is unclear.

The Purfleet marks the dividing line between the Lynn that Bishop Herbert founded in 1100 and the area into which the town expanded in the thirteenth century. King Street leads from the narrow river channel to the great expanse of the Tuesday Market Place. No. 1 King Street, with its range of buildings running alongside the Purfleet Quay, was the house of Sir John Turner, the man who founded the Exchange. No. 9, known as the *Medieval Merchant's House*, has at its core probably the oldest occupied brick domestic house in England, dating from the fourteenth century. Eighteenth-century rooms contain layer upon layer of previous reconstruction and decoration, and the owners are keen to show interested parties the building's archaeology. King Street itself is wider than Queen Street, but also has houses, alleys and warehouses running down to the river on the left. Many Georgian fronts conceal older properties. Ferry Lane still lives up to its name; at frequent intervals through the day a motor boat ferries passengers across the Ouse to West Lynn. It is perhaps the best way to appreciate the river that was the lifeblood of the town, and to see the jumble of properties along the river front, with architecturally important sites jostling among the commercial buildings.

At the far end of King Street, buildings that face each other across the street express Lynn's varied history. No. 27 King Street, beside Ferry Lane, has an ashlared front of around 1750, with pedimented windows and doorcase, and houses the *Museum of Social History*, displaying costumes, toys and furnishings, as well as an important collection of glassware. Next door, with a large six-light traceried window, is the second of King's Lynn's surviving medieval guildhalls, the *Guildhall of St George*; it is the largest and oldest surviving hall of a merchant guild in England. Founded in 1406, the main hall has a substantial medieval timber roof; its warehouses, of similar date, have been converted into a riverside art gallery and restaurant. The Guildhall survived the Reformation by becoming a theatre: Shakespeare's company once visited and in 1766 a Georgian theatre was built inside. Later it became a store for corn and wool. In 1951 it became a theatre again, when it was rescued and restored, then given to the National Trust as the focus of the annual King's Lynn Festival in late July.

Over the road, nos. 28, 30 and 32 contain remains of King's Lynn's earliest-known surviving secular building. Behind the timber and plaster fronts are the remains of a Norman stone-built house; the arcaded gable walls are still to be seen in the rear courtyard of nos. 30 and 32, as well as portions of the thirteenth-century hall wing added to no. 30. The fourteenth-century front to nos. 28 and 30 had open-fronted shops at ground floor level.

The Tuesday Market at the bottom of King Street is one of the greatest open spaces in any English country town, grand yet domestic. Even though it is now – except on Tuesdays – an enormous car park, the market place retains the sense of importance that its size gives it. On the left the dominant buildings are the smugly ugly Victorian yellow Corn Exchange and the more refined yellow brick Georgian building that now houses Barclay's Bank. Prominent on the further side of the square stands the Duke's Head Hotel. Nine bays wide with a large central curved pediment, it was built in the 1680s by Henry Bell, again for Sir John Turner, to accommodate merchants visiting the new Exchange. The hotel incorporates a medieval inn, of which the great oak staircase and one of the galleries survive inside.

Market Lane, running to the right of the Duke's Head, leads into post-1950s new housing and shopping precincts. A left turn into Chapel Street postpones meeting them. Lattice House restaurant on the corner is another medieval-cum-Tudor house rescued from oblivion and dereliction, with a brick-infilled timber frame, although all its older surroundings have gone. The next right turning is into Austin Street, named after the Augustinian canons whose only survival is the medieval doorway in the street wall. Then a left turn leads into one of the last enclaves of the old residential King's Lynn.

Pilot Street curves round the quiet churchyard of the beautiful medieval St Nicholas's Chapel. Beyond the Victorian cottages a short row of older timber and plaster houses survives, rescued in the 1970s. In 1841, 444 people were crammed into the 91 houses on this street; now little remains of these old communities of Lynn. A recent pantiled brick development of sheltered housing closes off Pilot Street; back around the east end of St Nicholas's, the churchyard gate stands beside a seventeenth-century house with a pedimented Dutch gable, known as the Exorcist's House (probably from the pre-Reformation clergy house that occupied the site).

One of the finest sights awaits us. St Nicholas's Chapel was founded in 1146; it was and remains a chapel of ease to serve the new town, not a parish church (although it is now to be taken into the care of the Redundant Churches Fund). St Margaret's retained the function of parish church, and many bitter disputes over jurisdiction were to be fought. The chapel was rebuilt almost entirely by 1429; the tower is the only original part. Its spire was added in 1871, the second replacement for the soaring 170-foot original which had collapsed in the 1741 storm. Exuberant decoration covers the south porch, with dozens of niches for long-gone statues. Although the Chapel is rarely open, it is worth making an effort to see. Its chief feature is spaciousness and light – the church is essentially one large undivided area, with idiosyncratic angular tracery in the large windows. Soaring above is the angel roof, the medieval timber figures playing musical instruments. The walls and floors are filled with monuments to prominent Lynn merchant families; a floor slab in the west end commemorates Robinson Cruso son of Robinson Cruso who died in 1773 – a family name which had been appropriated by Daniel Defoe. (Cruso is still a King's Lynn surname.) Also at the west end is a great rarity, the early Stuart bishop's court. Ecclesiastical justice covered wide areas of life; and before the benches of this small courtroom stood men and women waiting to be tried for fornication, or who were disputing the contents of a will, or whose marriage contract was in question.

Decorative mid eighteenth-century iron churchyard gates open on to St Ann's Street. Immediately opposite, and running back along St Nicholas Street, the *Tudor Rose* hotel and restaurant consists of a late fifteenth-century timber house (with its original traceried door) and a seventeenth-century brick block, the two joined by an unusual first-floor bridge. The long, plain, stuccoed Georgian building opposite the west end of St Nicholas's was the town house of Sir Robert Walpole (1676–1745), the first Prime Minister of Britain. His great house Houghton is nearby, and the family used St Ann's House when they stayed in town during the local season or for business. Beyond, there is a sudden break between the historic centre and the working port town – marked by the tattoo parlour, its windows filled with photographs of satisfied customers. The street turns right to join the main thoroughfare of John Kennedy Road.

As its name suggests, this road is part of the comprehensive redevelopment of the early 1960s. The cranes of the docks are visible away to the left, and there will often be lorries carrying timber, grain, cars, and scrap metal to and from the ships; the road to the docks is worth taking, past the deep-water basins dug in the later nineteenth century. Just before the open river, the Fisher Fleet is the little quay on the left where the fishing boats tie up. The fishermen's main catches are shrimps and prawns, and they sell some on the quay. There is quite a different working environment here, away from the historic buildings but an essential part of the history of the town which visitors rarely get to see.

Retracing the route past St Nicholas's, Chapel Street leads into the pedestrian shopping area and Broad Street. Like many provincial towns which paid less attention to conserving their past than they should have in the 1960s and 70s, King's Lynn has now woken up to the value of what it possesses, and not just the set pieces of the so-called historic core. It is a symptom of this earlier redevelopment that the Victorian chapel that houses *King's Lynn Museum* is marooned in the middle of the bus station, south of the main shopping precinct. The museum contains a rich variety of artefacts underlining the town's history. Badges dropped by medieval pilgrims who disembarked at King's Lynn on their way to the shrine of Our Lady at Walsingham, or the tools of the early nineteenth-century whaling trade, or the famous fairground 'gallopers' built by Frederick Savage Ltd (which closed in 1973), illustrate aspects of the history of port and town.

Across the busy Railway Road to the east of the Museum and bus station, Victorian terraced streets lead towards the yellow brick railway station – end of the line from Liverpool Street – and St James' Park. In the centre of its tree-lined walks is one of the most curious of King's Lynn's many curiosities, *Red Mount Chapel*. Standing on the raised bank that was part of the town's defences, it was built in 1485 as a wayside chapel for pilgrims on their way to Walsingham, on an extraordinary octagonal plan in red brick. The original lower chapel, entered through a door cut into the bank, was quite mean; but in 1505 a considerably more splendid upper chapel was built, with a miniature fan vault, and a priest's lodging sandwiched between the two. After the Reformation the chapel had a variety of uses – as a gunpowder store during the Civil War siege, as a water reservoir, as a stable – until it was restored in 1829. Close by is the sole remaining portion of the old town wall, with a postern gate set in it.

The Broad Walk through the park from the wall leads to the main road. Behind the glaring red brick of the Carnegie Library on the opposite corner, the tall tower of the Greyfriars stands in the municipal gardens. Like the Red Mount Chapel, it is octagonal, and it stood on the cross passage that ran between nave and chancel of the friars' church. When the rest of the church came down it was retained as a navigational aid. St James' Street, with a few early buildings among more recent development, continues west past the Greyfriars tower towards the Saturday Market and St Margaret's.

## —— AROUND AND ABOUT KING'S LYNN ——

*Very flat, Norfolk. Noël Coward (1899–1973) has a lot to answer for. His memorable tag has meant that for decades newcomers to East Anglia have been surprised to find that Norfolk is for the most part a gently rolling county. The flatness is reserved for the marshes and fens in the north and west. The highest point in the county is still only some 300 feet above sea level, so there are no great heights – just a rich farming landscape with many country houses, little villages and small towns.*

*And churches. 'Norfolk would not be Norfolk', wrote Sir John Betjeman (1906–84), 'without a church tower on the horizon or round a corner up a lane.' The quantity of church buildings is extraordinary. Norfolk has more than 650 pre-Victorian parish churches standing, another hundred in ruins. It is little surprise then that, as you travel, the skyline sometimes seems to bristle with church towers. For all these churches there are relatively few people now. Once, in the later Middle Ages, Norfolk was England's wealthiest and most densely populated county. That wealth, coming from sea-going trade and the cloth industry, fed the growth and the splendour of King's Lynn. Industry has, for the most part, long since gone; Norfolk's recent wealth has been agricultural, and many great landed estates survive.*

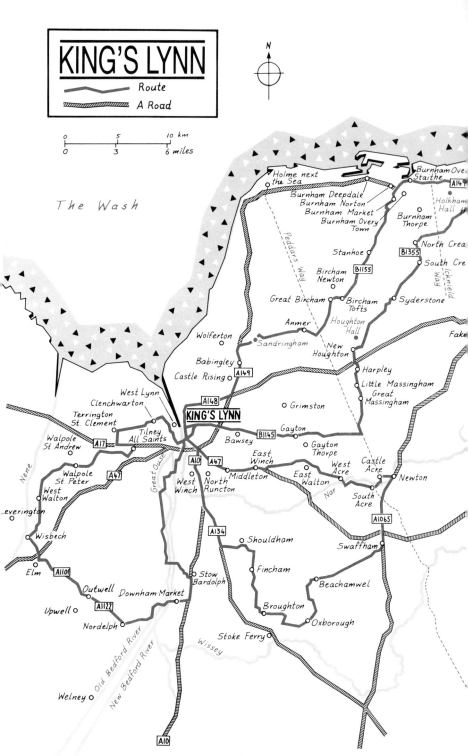

KING'S LYNN

Route
A Road

0    5    10 km
0    3    6 miles

N

The Wash

Holme next the Sea
Burnham Deepdale
Burnham Norton
Burnham Market
Burnham Overy Town
Burnham Overy Staithe
A149
Holkham Hall
Burnham Thorpe
Peddars Way
North Creake
B1355
South Creake
Stanhoe
B1155
Bircham Newton
Icknield Way
Great Bircham
Bircham Tofts
Syderstone
Anmer
Houghton Hall
Fake...
Wolferton
Sandringham
New Houghton
Babingley
Harpley
Castle Rising
A149
Little Massingham
Great Massingham
West Lynn
A148
Clenchwarton
KING'S LYNN
Grimston
Terrington St. Clement
Tilney All Saints
B1145
Gayton
Walpole St. Andrew
A17
Bawsey
Gayton Thorpe
Walpole St. Peter
A10
A47
East Winch
West Acre
Castle Acre
A47
Middleton
East Walton
Newton
West Walton
West Winch
North Runcton
Nar
Leverington
South Acre
Wisbech
A1065
A134
Shouldham
Swaffham
Elm
A1101
Fincham
Outwell
Stow Bardolph
Beachamwel
Upwell
Downham Market
Broughton
A1122
Nordelph
Oxborough
Old Bedford River
Stoke Ferry
New Bedford River
Wissey
Welney
A10

© Crown copyright

*Country houses, landscapes, small towns and, of course,
churches form the backbone of the itineraries based upon
King's Lynn. The first, and longest, encompasses the great
variety of north Norfolk scenery from chalk downland to
coastal marsh, and is based upon three of the county's great
estates, Holkham, Houghton, and Sandringham. The
second has a quite different look, through the marshland
and fenland west and south of Lynn. The last heads south-
east towards Norfolk's other, unusual, landscape type, the
sandy near-desert of Breckland.*

## 1. GREAT HOUSES AND ROMAN ROADS

Modern King's Lynn has spread well to the east of the historic town, and the ring road encompasses warehouses and light industrial buildings that give Lynn its more recent prosperity. Villages have been swallowed up, notably Gaywood which is the oldest settlement in this coastal marshland. The exterior of its muddled, brick-built parish church of 1909, on the right of the A1076 after its junction with the A148, does not prepare you for the strange glory of the interior, naive early Stuart paintings on wood showing the defeat of the Spanish Armada and the discovery of the Gunpowder Plot, celebrating Protestantism's supremacy. Along the B1145 at the junction with the A149, the flat land begins to rise, on to the sandy heaths. Lanes on either side of the hamlet of Bawsey lead to its two ruined medieval churches, less than a mile apart; over the slight hill lies the village of Gayton. Tall lime trees frame the fourteenth-century church tower with, at its four corners, the signs of the evangelists in place of pinnacles. The tiny hamlet of Gayton Thorpe, a mile south-east down the lane beside the tall, brick tower of the former wind-mill, now has only a few houses, and a little, rough-flint church. It has classic features of the county's churches: a round tower, dating from the eleventh century, and a nave rebuilt some 400 years later, with an intricate timber roof and a stone font featuring the

seven sacraments. Such richness for such a tiny place is far from unusual in Norfolk.

That a Roman villa was uncovered on the village common here, and another larger villa was found a couple of miles north at Grimston, is not surprising given the proximity of two major Roman roads, Icknield Way and Peddars Way, that gave access to the sea. Peddars Way forms a short section of lane left off the B1145 on the further side of the expanse of Massingham Heath three miles east of Gayton Thorpe. It became an important medieval route, and is now a designated Long Distance Path, connecting with the Norfolk Coast Path to provide varied and interesting trails for walkers. The lane leaves Peddars Way after only a few hundred yards and continues to the right at a crossroads into the picturesque little village of Great Massingham, with its green, pond, pub, and the Perpendicular tower of the church. Inside, the painted screen and carved wooden benches survive. Where there is a Great, a Little cannot be far away; and Little Massingham is less than a mile to the north in the same open countryside, just as tucked away, its church boasting a fifteenth-century hammerbeam roof. It is then little more than a mile to the next village, Harpley – settlements often come thick and fast in Norfolk. Harpley has a finer church still, built in flint during the rectorship of John de Gurney in the early fourteenth century. Various fifteenth-century additions include the splendid carved wooden south doorway, embellished with figures of saints.

The right turn just beyond the church leads to the warm brick and dark flint of the Manor Farm buildings, and left beside them on to the main road. Immediately across the A148 is the entrance avenue to *Houghton Hall*, perhaps the most beautiful of all Norfolk's great houses. After nearly a mile of lime trees, neat white-washed ranges of houses and a white wrought-iron gateway proclaim the entrance to the park. The village of New Houghton is an early example from 1729 of what was to become a prominent feature of Georgian estates, the removal of cottages from the parkland to a new, more orderly site. These cottages have none of the picturesque frills of those on many other estates: they are solid, almost timeless four-bay houses with pyramidal roofs. The drive to the house curves through mature wooded parkland to reveal the great house, one of the incomparable sights of Norfolk.

What strikes immediately is that this house is built entirely of stone, and moreover a pinky, Aislaby stone that had to be brought from a distance – the mark of great extravagance. The house was an ostentatious statement of the prominence and wealth of Sir Robert Walpole, first and longest-serving of all Prime Ministers. Houghton celebrates the eighteenth-century ascendancy of the landed Whigs, and of the political rise of the commoner. The main block is the perfect expression of the Palladian country house. Nine bays by five, the grand first floor rises from a rusticated basement, and the four corner towers are capped by domes. Houghton was also among the very first Palladian houses, designed by Colen Campbell (1676–1729), the great publicist for the new-style classicism of the 1720s. It

has a grand sequence of state rooms inside, with the double cube Stone Hall most splendid of all, decorated by William Kent (1685–1748) and retaining many of the original furnishings; however, the great Walpole picture collection was sold off to the Russian Empress, Catherine the Great (1729–96),to raise money.

A curving pair of service wings frames the house, with stables built around a courtyard in the local (and much decayed) orange-brown carrstone, just to the south, beyond a grove of pleached limes. The present owner, the new Marquess of Cholmondeley, is directly descended from Walpole's daughter Mary, and the Walpoles had been at Houghton since the twelfth century.

East from the gates at New Houghton and left at the first turning, the lane runs north-east towards the B1454, and over it to Syderstone and then on to South Creake and the B1355. This is rich, rolling farm landscape, with barely a sign of human habitation – the farm at the crossroads on the edge of Houghton park is appropriately enough called North Pole. There are occasional stretches of woodland, like that on the hill of Syderstone Common alongside the B1454, and the villages have interesting churches – Syderstone with an ancient round tower and Georgian nave, South Creake's wide Perpendicular interior crowned by an angel roof. Otherwise, it is a route on which to sit back and enjoy the solitude. The B1355 will probably be busier. It heads north alongside the River Burn, which gives its name to the collection of Burnham villages and towns nearer the coast. After two miles, at North Creake just past the parish church with another of the angel roofs which are a glory of Norfolk, the lane bears right to the south side of the Holkham estate.

*Holkham Hall* is the second of the

great north Norfolk country houses. It represents the eighteenth-century triumph of man over nature – green and wooded park and farmland imposed upon what an inscription above the inside of the front door describes as a 'barren estate'. The long drive through the triumphal archway leads to the lake and the house, which is larger by far than Houghton and filled with superb art collections and furnishings. William Kent, assisted by Matthew Brettingham, built one of the grandest of all Palladian houses for Thomas Coke, in the park Coke had planted on the inhospitable, marshy coastal plain. The house's beauty is diminished for many visitors by the yellow brick in which it is built; but the deliberately plain exterior opens into the marbled splendour of the Stone Hall, adorned by classical sculpture, and the sumptuous sequence of state rooms beyond, in which canvases by Anthony van Dyck (1599–1641), Thomas Gainsborough (1727–88), Claude Lorraine (1600–82), Nicholas Poussin (1594–1665) and great Italian masters, and a houseful of statuary and books, are among the treasures.

Holkham acquired fame again with Thomas William Coke, the first Earl of Leicester, who was among the self-promoting agricultural pioneers of the late eighteenth century. He was known as 'Coke of Norfolk', and the estate bears many traces of his efforts, in the form of rebuilt farms and barns, and the grandiloquent obelisk erected in his memory, a 120-foot high column with four cows at the base. Recent research has punctured the myth of Coke's skill and success, but his name and fame survive.

As stately homes do, Holkham has acquired a range of other attractions for visitors, which include a 'Bygones' collection of agricultural implements and steam engines. At the far end of the north drive, the gates, with the pub and estate cottages, give access to the A149. In the 1850s, the 2nd Earl of Leicester improved the channel giving access to the harbour of Wells-next-the-Sea just a couple of miles to the east, and he planted Holkham Meals with pines to stabilize the sand dunes, just on the other side of the road from the Holkham gates. The result is one of the largest beaches in the region, a mile across at low tide. Some areas are given over to nature lovers, watching the many birds which live on or migrate to this coast; other areas are dedicated to naturists. The whole of the north Norfolk coast from Holme next the Sea in the west to Salthouse much further east is a Grade 1 nature reserve of international importance. Access is provided at various points, like Holkham Meals, to see the birds: the over-wintering geese, the terns, the shelduck, and perhaps the avocet. On some days you will feel improperly dressed without a pair of binoculars. As at King's Lynn, the action of rivers and of man has resulted in extensive silting, turning once-important north Norfolk ports into minor, inland settlements. The loss of economic activity has been wildlife's gain.

Among the decayed ports are the various Burnham parishes – there are seven of them, Burnham Market or Burnham Westgate, Ulph, Burnham Sutton, Burnham Norton, Burnham Deepdale, Burnham Overy, and Burnham Thorpe, intertwined in the area west of Holkham Park and south of the A149. Burnham Overy is divided between Burnham Overy Staithe, the dainty port beside the main road with a narrow muddy channel leading out to sea, and Burnham Overy Town a mile inland. It is a village of picturesque cottages and a few farms, built in the mixture of flints, clunch (chalk) and brick that is the feature of this whole area. The curiously muddled church stands on a rise, with its Norman central tower topped by a seventeenth-century cupola. The dusty interior is still surprisingly close to the view engraved by John Sell Cotman, best-known of the Norwich School of painters, almost two centuries ago. This church and those of Burnham Market and Burnham Norton are barely a few hundred yards apart. Norton's church possesses an exceptionally fine fifteenth-century pulpit painted with the Latin Fathers of the Church and the figure of the donor, as well as a characteristic and probably Anglo-Saxon round tower. Burnham Market's church has unusual figures illustrating Christ's life, around the tower parapet. A field and a farmhouse east of Norton church contain remains of a thirteenth-century friary, reached through the gatehouse decorated with flushwork, stone-and-flint patterns which are another characteristic Norfolk building feature.

These villages-cum-towns show evidence of prosperity continuing well into the eighteenth century, such as Burnham Market's wide street and Westgate House behind the church, built to designs by John Soane (1753–1837) in 1783. This prosperity was based mainly on the ports' profits. Burnham Thorpe's most famous son, Horatio Nelson (1758–1805), gained maritime fame of a different nature. He appears all over Norfolk, especially on pub signs.

On the roads south-west of the Burnhams we are on the most obvious of Norfolk chalk lands, rolling countryside with sparse settlements (although in the Middle Ages there were clearly many more villages which have since disappeared). Stanhoe, on the B1155, was the site of a great New Stone Age flint axe factory, and many villages bear the marks, in place names or overgrown pits, of the practice of digging chalk and lime to marl the fields, an early method of fertilization.

Further south-west on the A1155 are the villages known as the Birchams: Bircham Tofts, with its ruined parish church; the beautiful little church of Bircham Newton a mile to the north, with mid Victorian box pews and a double-decker pulpit that flew in the face of prevailing fashion; and Great Bircham, where the church has similar Victorian box pews in a building also remarkable for its reused Norman doorway and the bulbous communion table dated to 1640. Many of the fields around grow lavender, a Norfolk industry.

South-west from Great Bircham, at the crossroads just across the ancient line of the Peddars Way path, the right turn leads into Anmer, with the charming little fourteenth-century church in the grounds of Anmer Hall, a Georgian house built in the brown brick characteristic of this particular part of the county. The road continues west down from the chalk on to the sandy heaths and the estate of Sandringham, often said to be the Royal Family's favourite home. Queen Victoria (1819–1901) bought it for the Prince of Wales (later Edward VII, 1841–1910), in 1861. The estate extends over coastal marshes, sandy heathland, and arable fields. Great areas of heath have been wooded, mainly with conifers and birch, making this one of the most densely wooded parts of this side of Norfolk. The estate is kept spick and span: there are cottages at West Newton to the south and in Sandringham village itself, and the royal stables have a life-sized statue of the Prince of Wales' 1896 Derby-winner. There are often glimpses through the trees of the brick water-tower with its Italianate top, which is now an unusual holiday cottage.

Right at the heart of the estate is *Sandringham House* itself, reached through the huge cast- and wrought-iron gates given to the Prince and Princess of Wales by the city of Norwich as a wedding present in 1863. The church to the west of the house attracts crowds of visitors on a Sunday when the Royal Family are in residence and attend morning service. The little medieval church is encrusted with Victoriana and Edwardiana: the silver altar and reredos given by an American admirer of the Royal Family, the Italianate baptistery given by Edward VII, and many memorials of and from Queen Victoria. The House itself, open in the summer except when members of the Royal Family are staying, was rebuilt almost from scratch in 1870. A brick house with stone dressings, it presents a bewildering forest of gables, cupolas and chimneys in a vaguely Jacobean manner. The painted ceiling in the Great Drawing Room, including pheasants as well as *putti*, is a salutary reminder that Sandringham's great importance for Edward VII and George V (1865–1936) was as a sporting estate.

Wolferton, at the end of the rhododendron drives on the far west of the estate over the A149, is another of the neat estate villages. The church, built in the characteristic red-brown carr-stone, contains a variety of medieval screens, as well as an ugly lectern given to it by Princess (later Queen) Alexandra (d.1925). Up the lane to the right, the *Wolferton Station Museum* was once the royal station, on a branch line from King's Lynn which was one of the early victims of Dr Beeching's axe. Items from royal trains, like Queen Victoria's travelling bed, are included among the exhibits in the retiring rooms where Edward VII and Queen Alexandra would receive other crowned heads.

South on the A149, Babingley, with a medieval wayside cross at the crossroads, is a deserted village. The ruined church in the fields half a mile west of the main road marks the spot where St Felix is traditionally supposed to have landed in *c.*600 to bring Christianity to East Anglia. The present church, of corrugated iron and pitch pine, stands by the crossroads; it was built in 1894, a gift of the Prince of Wales. Sandringham estate farms, like the old Jacobean Babingley Hall up the track, and estate cottages, bear the last badges of royal ownership.

Just over the Babingley River, a short distance to the right off the main road is the village of *Castle Rising*. The Castle itself is the first thing to be seen, a great, broad and decorated Norman stone keep surrounded by huge defensive earthworks – including a moat – more than half a mile in circumference, punctuated by a Norman gatehouse. Built in around 1150, the castle is one of the best surviving examples of the might of the conquerors, even without all the other buildings which once filled the enclosure. The remains of a chapel survive inside the castle precinct; but the church in the little village set out in a grid below the castle ramparts is a considerably better-preserved Norman building. The display on the west front has all the classic Norman elements: deeply cut chevron moulding and carved grotesques on the round-arched doorway and window and intersecting arcades. Although the church was restored in the mid nineteenth century, much of the original survives, notably the heavy arches below the tower, side altar niches, and the squat, heavily carved font. To the east of the church is Castle Rising's most charming survival, the *Trinity* or *Howard Hospital*, almshouses founded in 1614 and still inhabited by a complement of elderly ladies, who show visitors their communal hall, the little chapel, and the original Jacobean furniture in the rooms ranged around the quadrangle.

The lanes run back south of Castle Rising through the woods and on to the A148, which in turn leads to the A1078 ring road. Evidence of the current revival in King's Lynn's fortunes is to be seen in the brightly coloured modern warehouses and light industrial buildings on the northern edge of the town. The road continues through to the dock area of King's Lynn and back into the old centre.

## 2. MARSHLANDS AND WATERWAYS

One special feature of King's Lynn is its position at the meeting point of a great variety of types of landscape, and thus in the past, of trade. The wetlands of the saltwater marsh and the freshwater fens make an exciting contrast to the higher lands east of the town. I admit that not everyone shares my liking for the flat horizons, and nowhere can seem greyer than the fenlands on a cold, cloudy day, but what makes the landscape so special is the way in which man has tamed it and shaped it, adorned it with beautiful churches, and defends it against the constant danger of the sea. Nowhere seems brighter and clearer on a warm, sunny day.

The starting point is Lynn's South Gate. Saddlebow Road crosses the River Nar to the southern bypass, and the dual carriageway sweeps across the Great Ouse on a high, wide bridge. From the A47–A17 interchange on the other bank, a side road leads north towards West Lynn (which the ferry connects with King's Lynn). Just before the village, the road veers left towards Clenchwarton, and the characteristic marshland landscape begins suddenly: flat as a board, criss-crossed by drainage channels, with potatoes or other crops in every direction. The few vertical marks are the church towers and water towers of the little villages, scattered across the flat countryside. As a reminder that the coastal defences are only a few miles to the north, the little brick church at Clenchwarton contains a memorial

to the rector for his heroism in 'the terrible inundation of Feb. 16th 1753'.

The next village westwards is Terrington St Clement, its former prosperity evident in the Victorian, cast-iron shopfronts, and the large, stone-built church. Most of the Marshland churches like Terrington St Clement's are built in the creamy-grey limestone brought along the inland waterways from Rutland and the area around Peterborough. Inside St Clement's, the cover to the font is one of the finest surviving examples of pre-Civil War, High (anti-puritan) Anglicanism, a towering canopy that opens up to show painted landscape scenes incorporating Christ's baptism.

This is the last parish in Norfolk. To the west lies Lincolnshire, a continuation of the same landscape. The parish to the south is Tilney All Saints, reached by the lane from the central crossroads in Terrington past Lovells Hall, the gabled, brick early Tudor manor house. Tilney All Saints has a hemmed-in feeling that is rare in this countryside: it lies between the A17 and A47, and three great lines of electricity pylons stride through. Nevertheless, the parish church is one of the most splendid in a county of fine churches, with features from almost every century: a spacious twelfth-century interior; a thirteenth-century west tower; a fourteenth-century stone spire and wooden hammerbeam roof; windows and misericords from the fifteenth century; the rood screen and font from the seventeenth; and monuments from the rest. The lanes west of Tilney run in a loop more or less parallel to the A17, between market gardens and fruit orchards, to the little Walpoles.

Here the parish churches again dominate the settlements. Walpole St Andrew was built in one phase in the late fifteenth century, complete with an anchorite's cell in the brick tower, while inside the focus of interest is the painting on the south wall, *Christ with the two Marys* by Sebastiano Ricci (1659–1734). The quiet perfection of this church is a foil for the splendour of Walpole St Peter half a mile to the south, set among a pretty knot of lanes, footpaths, and cottages. The church is 161 feet long, its walls are pierced by broad windows, the battlements and parapets are intricately patterned and, inside, old plain glass floods the church with the clear Marshland light. The chancel was raised high above the main floor level to allow an ancient right of way to pass underneath, making a visually arresting climax to the interior. Much of the woodwork is Jacobean, including a poor box; and the carved dogs are worth looking for – gnawing bones in the porch, on the carved stalls, and a seated pair in the chancel wall niches.

The lanes then veer south towards West Walton, with another of these staggeringly grand Marshland churches, standing slightly apart from the tiny village it serves. Its tower stands separate from the church, open on the ground floor with the tall pointed arches (characteristic of the 1240s when it was built) rising to the parapet on top. The church shares many features of the great cathedrals of the period, like Lincoln, especially the detached Purbeck marble shafts to the columns inside, with carved stiff-leaf capitals. The clerestory in the high interior still has the original wall paintings, in the form of simulated heraldic wall hangings.

Less than two miles away is the point where the counties of Cambridgeshire, Lincolnshire, and Norfolk meet – but it is not worth seeking out,

*Burnham Overy Mill.*

as it is in the middle of the prosaically-named Nene Outfall Cut river, by a sewage works.

Wisbech, the largest town in the general vicinity of King's Lynn, and also one of the most attractive Georgian towns in the eastern counties, is in Cambridgeshire. The River Nene, along which the county boundaries run, made Wisbech into an important inland port until the nineteenth century. The town's chief fame are the North and South Brinks, the Georgian houses lining the banks on either side of the river – testimony to eighteenth-century wealth which derived from oilseed rape crushing as well as river and sea trade. The road from West Walton joins the B198 on Wisbech's outskirts, and follows a rather unprepossessing route into the centre. The best route starts from the Market Place, past the grey brick Georgian front of the Rose and Crown Hotel down High Street to the bridge and the two Brinks. South Brink, on the left, has a variety of mainly Georgian houses including the handsome, broad, brown brick front of nos. 7–8, birthplace of the eminent Victorian, Octavia Hill (1838–1912), co-founder of the National Trust. It looks across the river to the grander North Brink, a similarly harmonious collection of houses with at its centre the showpiece *Peckover House,* built in the 1720s. This yellow and red brick house, five bays wide, is now a National Trust property; the gardens behind are a particularly lovely example of a large Victorian town garden, with one of the longest-surviving ginkgo trees in England. Peckover House was part of the Gurney banking company's premises (like Bank House in King's Lynn), although nothing now survives of the banking office that stood alongside.

Downstream, a few of Wisbech's huge brick warehouses survive on the river bank – more did until the great

floods of 1978, which also damaged 700 homes in the town. There are other areas of handsome Georgian and early Victorian housing in Wisbech, with a few older properties interspersed. South-east of the High Street, around the huge, spreading parish church, the grounds of the former Wisbech Castle were turned into a late Georgian housing development: the Crescent of red-brick terraces, the Alexandra Theatre (now occasionally in use as a theatre again), and the grey brick Castle House. The *Wisbech and Fenland Museum,* built in 1846 with a classical doorway, displays early photographs by Samuel Smith, an almost unique record of small town and port life in the earliest days of photography. There are no people in the pictures, however, since long exposure times were required.

From behind Peckover House, the road connecting to the A1101 continues a mile north-west to Leverington. In the Norman period this was on the coast, and the village was only founded in the twelfth century; the line of the old sea bank is one of the main features between Leverington and the main road. Leverington church is another architectural gem, mainly thirteenth-century with a soaring spire and, inside, one of the great medieval Jesse windows complete with dozens of little carved figures on the tracery and its original silver, blue and brown glass. Leverington has a number of particularly fine large houses, notably *Leverington Hall,* built in brick in the sixteenth century and remodelled over the following two hundred years.

Back down the A1101 and the dual carriageway through Wisbech and across the ring road on the far side, the B1101 side road continues round to Elm, with its great church tower similar in style to that at West Walton a few miles to the north. Much of the church, with the exception of the wooden, double hammer-beam, angel roof, is in the same thirteenth-century, Early English style, while the village also contains a range of handsome late seventeenth-century houses, especially the Black Horse Inn.

The name Elm derives from eels rather than trees, and this was once a very watery area, on the very edge of the Wash, that probably teemed with fish. The Romans had been the first to try to drain it and redirect the water-courses, deflecting the great flow of water out at King's Lynn. Succeeding generations from the early Middle Ages continued the process. Swinging east through the orchards and market gardens back on to the A1101, cross back into Norfolk and follow the road south-eastwards. As it wiggles and turns, the road follows the old course of the River Ouse before it was diverted from Wisbech. This area, around the twin villages of Outwell and Upwell split between the two banks of the river, and thus between Norfolk and Cambridgeshire, is a bewildering net of watercourses, some dating from mid seventeenth-century attempts to drain the Fens by Dutch engineers like Cornelius Vermuyden, others from the ultimately successful nineteenth-century efforts. The villages have a Dutch air, brick houses and windmills lining the banks, and both have size-able stone churches on the Norfolk bank. Upwell's church is crammed to overflowing with galleries and pews, a rare survival of early nineteenth-century seating arrangements. The villages' seventeenth-century wealth, when the larger houses were built, sprang from their rare specialization in growing hemp for rope-making.

From Outwell church, the A1122 follows the Well Creek, which flows on an aqueduct across the Middle Level Main Drain (nineteenth-century engineers could not usually find evoca-tive names for their achievements). At

Nordelph, the Well Creek is joined by the waters of Popham's Eau, and road and river continue to the great meeting of the waters at Denver Sluice. A maze of footpaths on top of the defensive banks provides the best view of the waterways as they rush together, or are dammed back. The parallel Old and New Bedford Rivers mingle first, close to the roadside, then join the Great Ouse coming down from Ely and the Cut-off Channel that drains the eastern edge of the fenland. The first sluices were built here in the 1820s; the Cut-off Channel was not operational until the 1960s. One particular charac-teristic of these fenland waterways is the tall banks on either side, to prevent the flooding of land which is only a foot above sea level.

Some appreciation of what the pre-drainage fen landscape was like is possible in winter, when the area between the Old and New Bedford Rivers is deliberately flooded. It acts as a huge wildfowl refuge, where thou-sands of wintering birds feed. The visitor centre and hides are at Welney, five miles south-west of Denver Sluice, although access to the Sluice by car involves a five-mile circuit through Downham Market. The A10 which used to thunder through Downham now passes a mile to the east, leaving it a much more peaceful small town of understated, mainly Victorian and late-Georgian brick and carrstone houses. The market place is dominated by the cast-iron, Victorian Gothic clock tower, loved by few except the people of Downham Market. This town is quite a novelty in this area – it is actually on a hill, the last vestige of the greensand belt that runs through west Norfolk. The parish church with its Early English carrstone west tower stands higher still in its big church-yard reached by steep steps.

If this high ground is unusual, the church at Stow Bardolph a couple of miles up the A10 contains an even rarer feature. In the Jacobean, brick-built north chapel where the Hare family monuments are concentrated, a mahogany cupboard contains the life-size wax effigy of Susanna Hare, who died at the age of eighteen in 1744 after pricking her finger when sewing on a Sunday: the surprised look on her face is a stern warning. The Hare family dominated Stow Bardolph from the sixteenth century, and the village is neatly laid out around their Hall, now an undistinguished, mainly late Victorian rambling house. The side roads run west of the A10 and Stow Bardolph to cross the Great Ouse again at Stow-bridge, and run up alongside it to the Wiggenhall villages.

Like their neighbouring Marshland villages, these are famous for the beauty and the splendour of their parish churches. Wiggenhall St Mary Magdalen, the first of them, mainly built in brick except for the tower, is the least distinguished, although it would be of considerable interest in other less well-endowed areas, with the remains of its painted rood screen and its original wooden benches. Late medieval wooden benches are among the glories of the churches of Wig-genhall St Mary the Virgin and Wig-genhall St Germans two miles to the north. St Mary the Virgin lies at the end of a track between the tiny village and the watercourses that flow into the Ouse. It dates mainly from the fifteenth century, and has a very full set of carved and decorated benches, with pierced backs, figures of saints on the bench ends, and animal and human figures decorating other parts. A Jaco-bean pulpit, with an hourglass stand, a classical Jacobean font cover, and the painted figures of its medieval rood screen, are all rare and unusual sur-vivals. Wiggenhall St Germans a mile further east, on the high, opposite bank of the Great Ouse has similar splen-

dours. The splitting of what had been the parish of Wiggenhall into four, each with a splendid Perpendicular church, is testimony to the wealth and vitality of the Marshland, growing grain, raising animals, and tapping into the wealth of King's Lynn as a port. Now these tiny villages are barely able to maintain the great lega-cies of a prosperous past.

The roads run north-east from Wig-genhall St Germans towards the signs of the modern prosperity of King's Lynn: the sugar beet factory on the bank of the Great Ouse, and the inter-change on the town's southern bypass. A mile further north lies the historic heart of the town.

### 3. CASTLE ACRE AND SWAFFHAM
One of the names associated with the renewal of King's Lynn in the years around 1700 was that of the merchant-cum-architect Henry Bell. Although the town did not give him occasion to build a church, the opportunity arose at North Runcton, a few miles to the south-east, off the A47. The old church had collapsed in 1701, and Bell's church was completed by 1713, built of local carrstone with brick dressings in Wren's classical style with large Ionic columns and a domed vault inside. The panelling in the chancel, also Bell's work, was brought here in 1901 from St Margaret's, King's Lynn. North Runcton has now become a satellite village for Lynn, and is fast losing its rural character.

However, it is not long before the countryside does re-establish itself, even along the main A47 as it runs above the valley of the Nar, through Middleton to East Winch. The church, on the right beside the road, is a heavily restored Perpendicular build-ing, although it still has its old screen and benches. At the far end of the village, the late Georgian Hall was for a while the home of the Lancaster family, and it is described in some of Sir Osbert Lancaster's cartoons and architectural writings (especially *All Done from Memory*, published in 1953). A back lane passes through the marshy commons – which were probably once a finger of the sea – to the charming hamlet of East Walton. The round-towered parish church is a rare example of a Georgian church interior: plain glass in the large, fifteenth-century windows floods the box pews and three-decker pulpit with light.

Lanes continue to the east, rising up on to the chalk land on the side of the Nar valley. A succession of delightful villages bears the name Acre – West Acre, South Acre, Castle Acre. Mid Victorian social reformers considered these among the most scandalous examples of rural exploitation, where gangs of women and children walked miles to work in the fields from their desperately poor villages. Now the once-insanitary conditions have been modernized away. In the Middle Ages, these villages had a remarkable concentration of churches and defensive structures, and the ruins are among the most evocative in Norfolk. The Augustinians had a great priory in West Acre, and fragments of the church and other buildings stand on the banks of the Nar, reached through the preserved, flint-built gatehouse. A sculptural panel from the priory sits in the north porch of the mainly Perpendicular parish church beside the priory gatehouse. Its stained glass was installed in 1907, and is a real Edwardian period piece. The Birkbeck family from Westacre High House are portrayed kneeling, with one gentleman resplendent in hunting pink.

South of the village, the lane crosses the river and continues along it to tiny South Acre. Yet the church here, set in a prettily wooded churchyard, contains a great variety of interesting features: a richly carved fourteenth-century screen, the almost life-sized Harsick memorial brass of 1384, and the large alabaster monument of 1623 to Sir Edward Barkham, Lord Mayor of London. There are moated remains of houses in the fields between the church and the river, while over the other side stand the ruins of the great Cluniac *Castle Acre Priory*. Set in green lawns, the most impressive feature is the solid west front, the main portion of the church left standing. To reach the ruins, however, it is necessary to recross the Nar (either by the ford on the nearest track, or by the lanes and the bridge a few hundred yards further to the east, part of the Roman road, Peddars Way). On the right rise the huge earthworks of the post-Conquest *Castle Acre Castle* which gives the village its name. Only the castle gate with its two round towers survives largely untouched, in the wide street of the town that grew up within the outer bailey. Castle Acre is a village of charming little cottages, interspersed with a few larger Tudor houses. The narrow lane left from Bailey Street continues to the parish church of St James. It is a large church, with a great west tower and doorway set in it. Inside, the font with its very tall cover with the original colouring preserved, the misericords in some of the stalls, the painted rood screen and the painted pulpit are among its treasured medieval survivals.

The lane past the church continues to the priory precinct, with the ruined walls of the church and monastic buildings set around the west front and, beside it, the well-preserved early Tudor Prior's house. It is a substantial, stone-built manor house, showing the wealth of many monastic clergy on the eve of the Reformation. One prominent decorative feature, which is to be seen elsewhere in the village and the region (like the Guildhall at King's Lynn), is the flint and stone chequerboarding.

The roadside hamlet of Newton, consisting of a pub, a couple of houses, and a church, lies on the main A1065 from Fakenham, just east of Castle Acre. The church is one of the daintiest, and oldest, in Norfolk: it is Saxon, and has a central tower capped by a little pyramid roof. Its tiny windows and narrowness give away the early date; the beautifully made early 1950s furnishings are the perfect complement to the church's simplicity. Below Newton the road continues on its uneventful way, except for a final view across the valley and the castle and village of Castle Acre, to Swaffham. This is the only town on the journey, and is one of Norfolk's most attractive small market towns. The approach to it, beneath the concrete bridge carrying the A47, is inauspicious, but the road continues past handsome brick and flint houses into the town centre. The Georgian period provides the keynote for Swaffham's main buildings, although the huge late fifteenth-century parish church, set on a rise, is the dominant structure. A narrow alley from the Market Place leads into the tree-lined churchyard. The exterior is a spectacular display of Perpendicular windows and walls, all lavishly decorated, with the great west tower crowned by a pretty little late-Georgian lead lantern and spike. The great feature of the interior is the angel roof.

Swaffham's buildings of interest are concentrated in and around the Market Place, which is a popular and busy local attraction on Saturdays. At the centre is the classical rotunda which was built in 1783 as the Market Cross, its lead-covered dome topped by an ample figure of Ceres. Behind it is the mid Victorian red and yellow brick Corn Exchange, as lumpy as the Market Cross is elegant.

Swaffham marks the edge of the sandy heaths of Breckland, one of the driest areas in England and now covered to a considerable extent by Forestry Commission coniferous plantations. Swaffham Heath, south-west of the town, is largely forested, and a road leads through it to the village of Beachamwell. Of the four churches that were once here, within a few hundred yards of one another, only St Mary's survives, with its thatched nave roof and the bottom of a Saxon round tower topped by an octagonal, fifteenth-century upper stage. Some of the internal stonework is Anglo Saxon, while later masons scratched graffiti on the pillar at the south-west end, including the figure of a demon and the prices of their materials. The ruined tower of St John's church stands in a field to the west, beyond the park of the Edwardian Beechamwell Hall. From the Hall, the lanes lead south, with views east to the ruined walls of All Saints' church, to Oxborough.

Oxborough is dominated by the great house of the Bedingfield family, *Oxburgh Hall.* Although much necessary repair and restoration work went on in the nineteenth century, this is still one of the great brick-built mansion houses of the late fifteenth century, with the spectacular seven-storeyed gatehouse as the main focus. A pair of octagonal towers rises to the battlemented top. Sir John Betjeman once made a television film here. He laboured his way to the top of a tower, and looked around through 360 degrees of rolling countryside. 'Ah,' he exclaimed, 'not a pylon in sight!'

The entrance gate, in a large building connecting the two towers, opens into the central courtyard. Some rooms contain wall hangings embroidered by Mary Queen of Scots (1542–87) and Bess of Hardwick (1518–1608). The Bedingfields continue to live here, although the property is now owned by the National Trust. A small Catholic church, attributed not entirely convincingly to A. W. N. Pugin (1812–52), stands in the grounds. Most of Oxburgh parish church is a ruin, since the main steeple fell in 1948 and brought down the nave with it although the Bedingfield family tombs in their separate chapel were unscathed. The most famous of the monuments are the early Renaissance canopied tombs in terracotta, executed in the 1520s and incredibly avant-garde for their day. The chancel with its fifteenth-century stained glass was also spared and has now become the church.

Oxborough lies on the very edge of the fenlands; below it runs the River Wissey, the waters of which are now mainly carried in the Cut-off Channel to Denver Sluice. The village was once an inland port, and the few houses south of the main village are still called Oxborough Hythe. There is no river crossing here; the lane runs west to the A134 and the Wissey at Stoke Ferry (and from there to Downham Market). The alternative route, continuing to use country lanes, turns right at the junction west of Oxborough, rather than left, across the marsh and then left into the perfect village scene of Broughton – Georgian cottages ranged around the large, square pond and the green, with the church steeple poking up behind. The lane swings north outside the village, and goes through the large arable fields towards Fincham. Moat House, on the southern edge of the village, has a square, moated island in the grounds, which was probably an early cattle enclosure. The house was outside the moat, protecting the precious beasts. The village itself is ranged along the A1122, another of the region's Roman roads, with the parish church at the crossroads. Much of Fincham church was built around 1500, in flint and stone rubble; it has an angel roof, as well as a Norman font decorated with

oddly stylized carved scenes – the Nativity, the Magi, and Adam and Eve.

Over the crossroads, the lanes lead north to Shouldham. Once this was a market town with fairs, a grammar school, and a priory; now it is a sleepy village. The main street in a series of right angle turns skirts the precinct of the Gilbertine priory, established in 1190. The cottages, some with the now-rare blue Norfolk pantiles, others with thatch, cluster around the green and the street, with All Saints' church on a rise above. Its chief glory is the carved hammerbeam roof inside. The village itself once stood on this small hill, but with the establishment of the Priory the villagers were displaced to the west. The lines of the former streets can still just be made out in the earthwork mounds to east and north of the church.

A coniferous forest has been planted to the north, with walks and picnic places laid out in it. The lane west out of the village leads, after a mile, past a sail-less windmill, right on to the A134 and joins the A10 to the south of the crossing of the River Nar. The fen landscape briefly re-establishes itself here around Setchey, where a little carrstone tollgate lodge survives at the roadside, before the road regains the rising ground of the old causeway into King's Lynn. West Winch is another village affected by the encroachment of Lynn, but a number of older stone cottages survive there. Its church has a fifteenth-century west tower decorated with niches for the statues of saints and the coat of arms of the Cholmondeleys (of Houghton).

The A10 continues the last mile above West Winch before being absorbed into the King's Lynn ring road system. The second exit from the interchange leads back to the South Gate and the final stretch of the River Nar just before it joins the Great Ouse.

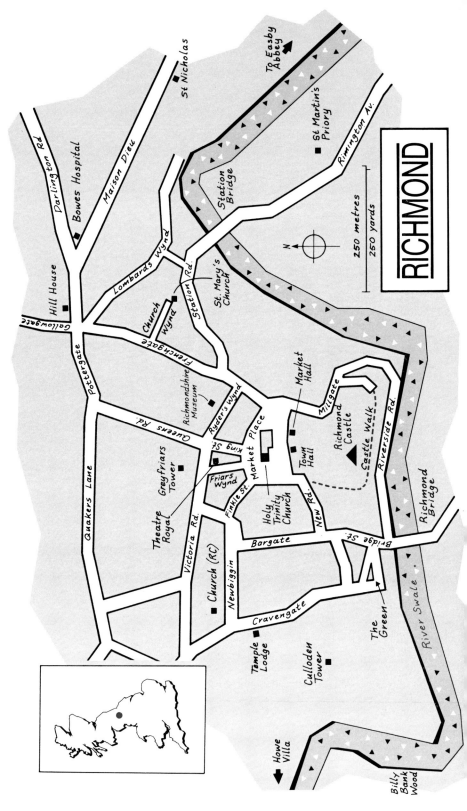

# 4
# RICHMOND

North Yorkshire

*If you approach Richmond the way the artist J. M. W.
Turner came around 1820, you do so from the south. The
road swoops down past woods, rounding a corner to reveal
the great stone castle rising sheer from the cliff above the
rushing Swale. An elegant Georgian stone bridge across
the river leads to the town, with cottages tumbling down
the hill towards the water. The town side of the river is all
built up; on the south side the banks are largely wooded
and green. Turner's painting makes the rocky heights even
more dramatic than they are, but that artistic licence does
not diminish the scale and impressiveness of the town.
Even if you enter Richmond from other directions, the
great square castle keep rising over 100 feet from a rocky
bluff above the river appears in almost every view.
Sandstone is the principal visual motif: castle and houses
are made of it, and the streets are cobbled with river-
smoothed pebbles. One seventeenth-century visitor
remarked that 'the streets are like rocks themselves', and in
many parts of the town that description still applies.*

## EXPLORING RICHMOND

*Richmond Castle*, its entrance set back behind the Market
Place, is the best place to begin. The great keep stands over
the original gatehouse of the fortress founded to subjugate
the area in the aftermath of the Norman Conquest. The keep
was built in the second half of the twelfth century by Conan,
great-nephew of Alan Rufus who began the castle in 1071.
Staircases in the wall passages open out into spacious halls
on the upper floors, while the top of the keep offers views
over the town. From here, the layout of Richmond can be best
appreciated. The Market Place and the buildings that face
on to it mark the site of the early town which sheltered in the
outer bailey of the castle. The land falls away to both west

and east, but to the north it rises towards moorland. From the earliest days of its foundation, Richmond began to spread in all these directions, with growth stimulated by the market, by the town's importance as an industrial centre in the seventeenth and eighteenth centuries, and by its role as the hub of an administrative district that is still called Richmondshire.

Many parts of the castle, including large sections of the curtain wall, and the ruined great hall, the oldest in England, date from its foundation in the late eleventh century. Unusually for their date, these early parts were built in stone rather than wood, a mark of how strategic the castle was seen to be. It is one of life's ironies that, except on two occasions in the thirteenth century, this great structure hardly saw an arrow shot in anger, and was a defensive anachronism almost from the beginning. One of the most evocative surviving chambers in the castle walls is the tiny chapel of St Nicholas – Richmond's first church – with its stone altar, piscina, wall seats, and narrow windows. By the fourteenth century the castle needed repair; by the early sixteenth it was in a ruinous state. Its stone was plundered to build the growing town.

Leaving Richmond Castle by the main gate and bearing right leads you into narrow cobbled streets, where little seventeenth- and eighteenth-century cottages, and some modern neighbours, huddle under the castle walls. From Millgate, steps lead up on to Castle Terrace and round to Castle Walk, opened up in the later eighteenth century as a broad promenade on the edge of the cliff beneath the castle walls. The views from here are quite magnificent: down on to the fast-flowing Swale, with its rocky bed and natural weir, over the river to the woods, and upstream to Richmond Bridge and the hanging woods beyond. Seats have thoughtfully been provided for those who want to linger, and no fence detracts from the drama of this cliff-edge walkway.

The path eventually comes back to the vicinity of the Market Place. It is the Market Place as much as the castle which has made Richmond a thriving small town. The late 18th-century cross is better described as an obelisk (with pronounced curvature to its sides, making it appear a rather distant cousin of a Buddhist *stupa*), and has a top-knot ball. Dated 1771, it replaced a number of previous crosses in different parts of the broad, cobbled market place, which stood as focuses for the sale of particular products. John Speed's town map of 1610 shows them, as does Robert Harman's 1724 map, which also identifies some areas by name: the leather market, the butter market, and so on. Still very much in use, the Market Place remains the heart of the town.

That the cross was rebuilt in the 1770s is significant; there is little in the Market Place that seems to be pre-eighteenth century. In spite of its Norman origins, Richmond's centre is predominantly Georgian, and many of the most attractive buildings date from the period of intensive rebuilding and refurbishment from the 1730s to the 1850s, the peak of the town's prosperity. Two distinctive structures break that post-1700 sweep. The first is the Norman Castle, the second Holy Trinity Church, Richmond's second church, in the centre of the Market Place.

Holy Trinity is not the parish church, but a chapel belonging to it. Described by Sir Nikolaus Pevsner (1902–83) as 'the queerest ecclesiastical building one can imagine', architecturally it is a hotch-potch: a few Norman details, a fourteenth-century tower, and much from the 1860s. The church itself is upstairs. Shops and cottages hug much of the outside of the building, exposing only a few portions of wall. Some parts of the interior, including former shops beneath the church's north aisle, now house the *Green Howards Regimental Museum* (the Green Howards were Alexandra, Princess of Wales' Own Yorkshire Regiment), displaying soldiers' uniforms through the ages, regimental trophies, and Victoria Crosses won by the men, as well as Richmond's civic regalia, including the sixteenth-century town mace and other pieces of the same date. The Green Howards have been associated with the North Riding since 1782, and with Richmond since 1873.

On the southern edge of the Market Place, between the church and the castle, stands *Richmond Town Hall*. This was put up in 1756, probably to designs by Thomas Atkinson, a minor architect with a number of North Yorkshire churches and country houses to his credit. It incorporates not only the council chamber and a court room, but also an assembly room, an essential feature of polite Georgian society without which no self-respecting country town was complete. On the other side of the path to the castle is the Market Hall of 1854, a stone and cast-iron building with three arches crowned by pediments which makes up for what it lacks in charm by still buzzing with activity on market days.

Although the Market Place looks Georgian, the regular rhythm of the façades reflects the layout of the late eleventh-century planned town, in which narrow burgage plots, strips of land given to town burgesses, ran back from the main frontages on the central open space. Moreover, although the buildings may have eighteenth- and nineteenth-century faces, older structures often remain behind. The Bishop Blaise inn on the southern side of the market place, for example, hides a complicated building history behind its rendered frontage.

In seventeenth- and eighteenth-century Richmond, this inn was the focal point of the woollen hosiery industry, historically one of the town's most important trades, and stood next to the woolhouse, where the transactions in wool and knitted stockings were recorded. Most of the hand-knitting of stockings was done in the countryside around, the hosiers of the town buying the wool in the market and supplying it to the knitters in the villages and farmsteads. The inn is called after the fourth-century ecclesiastic and martyr who is supposed to have invented the woolcomb and who is the patron saint of woolcombers. His feast day, 3 February, was an occasion for great merriment and processions in Richmond and many other wool-working areas.

The grandest single building in the Market Place is the early eighteenth-century *King's Head Hotel,* eight bays wide and with at least one original external doorcase. Unusually for Richmond, it is built in brick, and it incorporates another set of assembly rooms dating from around 1760. These provided a venue for the local season, and the inn allowed traders to do business out of sight of watchful market authorities.

From the upper end of the Market Place, New Road begins the steep descent to the River Swale. As its name suggests, this replaced the original approach to the town which runs off to the left through the archway of the gate known as the Bar. One of only two of the original gateways to survive, its proximity to the Castle and Market Place demonstrates how small the original walled settlement was. Cornforth Hill, below the gateway, is an attractive paved street with a curving row of Georgian houses on the right. At the bottom of the hill, New Road joins the end of Bargate, from where Bridge Street extends to the main bridge and to The Green. This lower end of town had always been poorer than other parts. There is something of a village atmosphere here now, very different from the neighbourhood described in the 1830s, 'the haunt of every vice and disease . . . It had three distinctive smells – beer from the Brewery, hides and leather from the tan-yard, and human squalor and decay.'

The three-arch bridge over the Swale is one of the exceptional features of the town. Built around 1789 to the designs of John Carr of York (1723–1807), surveyor of bridges for the North Riding, it replaced a narrow and dangerous ancient structure. As a plaque set into the bridge records, it was on the turnpike road to Lancaster, but other highways in the vicinity were much more successful, and the bridge was less thoroughly used than had been intended. Not for the first or last time, the world tended to pass Richmond by.

The space between The Green and the river, now filled by cottages and former industrial buildings, was once the site of the grand house of the Yorke family, one of the two Whig dynasties that dominated eighteenth-century Richmond. It was demolished in 1824, although some of the outbuildings were converted into cottages. Harman's map of 1724 shows the house, set among formal gardens, with tenter grounds on the hill behind (roughly where the coach park now lies). Here cloth was stretched on 'tenterhooks' to dry in the sun.

Harman's map – even today issued to visitors by the local tourist information office, so little has Richmond's layout changed – also shows a small defensible pele tower on the hillside above The Green, a relic of the era of Scottish raids across the border. The base of the original building is still there, but in 1746 the rest was transformed by John Yorke III into the tall, octagonal gothick structure with a spiral stair-case turret at one corner which is seen today. This is *Culloden Tower,* commemorating, in true Whiggish fashion, the final defeat of Jacobite hopes with the rout of the forces of Bonnie Prince Charlie (1720–88) at Culloden. The tower is one of Richmond's architectural gems, and is visible, standing alone in its parkland, from many vantage points in the town. Best of all, it can be rented as a holiday cottage from the Landmark Trust. From the drawing room on the second floor, with its exuberant plaster-work, including a vaulted ceiling, pointed windows frame views of the Castle and town.

Cravengate rises from The Green. (Gate here, as elsewhere in northern England, usually means way or road, rather than entrance.) Towards the top of the hill on the left is the other survivor of the Yorke estate, Temple Lodge, built around 1769 and then enlarged into an essay in battlemented Victorian picturesque some 80 years later. On the opposite side of the road is Temple Square, a small three-sided Georgian court-yard with some cottages built around 1760, others c. 1819, which began life as the headquarters and depot of the North York Militia. A little further up is Newbiggin, wide, largely cobbled and one of the most pleasing of all Richmond streets. Newbiggin means new building, and this was one of the areas built beyond the original small walled settlement as Rich-mond grew in the thirteenth and fourteenth centuries. On the corner with Cravengate stands the old gaol and debtors' prison. Almost opposite is the town's Roman Catholic church, built in 1867 in a curiously wilful Victorian Gothic. Catho-licism had remained strong in this part of Yorkshire since the Reformation, and this led Sir Thomas Lawson, of nearby Brough Hall, to establish a chapel and priest's house on this Newbiggin site in 1771. A new 260-seater chapel, built in 1809, was in turn replaced by the present building.

Newbiggin bears all the signs of the growth and refur-bishment of prosperous later eighteenth-century and early nineteenth-century Richmond, with many good houses. Another venture into the Gothick, and rather more playful than Culloden Tower, is no. 47 on the south side, with jaunty bay windows flanking the main door, and sash windows set in pointed surrounds. No. 30 opposite is an ashlared house (quite an uncommon feature in Richmond) of c. 1820. Not all the buildings here are quite so substantial. As with the rest of the old town, Newbiggin had been developed with long narrow burgage plots running back from the main frontage.

These plots were often later built on, with rows of cottages, or 'yards', running at right angles to the street. The best is Carter's Yard, which runs south from Newbiggin through a narrow archway. The cottages here were built some time in the last thirty years of the eighteenth century, perhaps by the John Carter who was recorded as a retired carpenter living in one of the houses in 1851. At the end, Newbiggin turns the corner, with pretty doorcases and a former warehouse side by side on the bend.

Back at the top of Cravengate, Victoria Road runs to the right, with a plain but pleasing early nineteenth-century terrace. Before it was renamed in honour of the young queen, this road had been called the Back Ends, and gave rear access to the houses on Newbiggin. The confusion of roads where Cravengate, Victoria Road and other thoroughfares meet is the result of building around what had been the area of the beast market. The roads to the west and north-west lead into Swaledale, from where cattle and sheep came to be sold and driven on from Richmond to larger markets. Here also lead was collected from the mines in Swaledale and Arkengarthdale, brought in on the backs of specially-bred ponies, who carried three hundredweight per load, and then traded in the Nag's Head Inn.

At the end of Victoria Road a narrow pedestrian alley, Friars Wynd, leads back to the Market. Before the gate, on the left, is an unprepossessing, rather blank stone building. Inside is one of Richmond's greatest treasures, another testament to its success and prosperity in the eighteenth century: the *Theatre Royal*. It is one of the few surviving Georgian theatres in the country, and certainly the best-preserved. It was established in 1788 as a permanent venue for the main theatre company on the North Riding circuit, that of Samuel Butler. It still has its raked stage and dressing rooms beneath, the pit for the common people, the gallery, with backless seats (be warned), and boxes (with chairs!) The interior decoration is based upon the original colouring, and some 18th-century painted details survive. It is being used as a theatre again, but now seats only 230 compared with the original 400, who were crammed in tightly together.

Butler was an actor-manager, whose company had been performing in the town since 1774, if not earlier; with the establishment of the theatre they had a permanent home, and put on plays with great success in the September–October season when local people crowded into Richmond for races and assemblies. Some of the finest actors in England, such as Edmund Kean (1787–1833), trod Richmond's boards. After Butler's death in 1812, the company and its circuit went into sad decline. The small towns where they played were being eclipsed as centres for society and its display. The theatre finally closed in 1848. The building was used as an auction

*The Market Place, Richmond.*

room, with a wine vault in the boarded-over pit, and later as
a corn chandler's. Local and professional interest led to the
gradual rediscovery and restoration of the building from the
1930s. The theatre's history is displayed in the attached
museum (entered from Friars Wynd), together with the oldest
surviving set of painted stage scenery, dating from 1836.

In the garden opposite the theatre foyer is a vestige of
Richmond's medieval past, the fifteenth-century tower from
the Greyfriars church. The Franciscans came to the town
in 1258, but the delicate openwork-topped tower is all that
survived the dissolution of the order in the sixteenth century.
Medieval and sixteenth-century work from the Friary itself
are incorporated in a Georgian house on the same site back
along Victoria Road. Near the theatre are some of the more
fanciful of Richmond's later Victorian buildings, such as the
brick and terracotta bravura of the Fleece Hotel, and the
bright blue-painted bays of the Greyfriars shop, once a café.

Ryder's Wynd drops down from the crossroads with Victoria Road towards Frenchgate with *Richmondshire Museum*
just off it to the north. Local history exhibits here include
the vets' surgery from the television realization of James
Herriot's books, and villages and small towns around offer
the visitor constant reminders that this is 'Herriot country'.

Whether Frenchgate gets its name from foreigners who settled here in the twelfth century is debatable; but certainly this was one of the earliest over-spill developments as the town's medieval population grew. The modern impression of Frenchgate is of a prosperous Georgian street, with much fine detailing on doorcases and house fronts. As in Newbiggin, the narrow plots running back from the street façades encouraged the development of long yards of cottages as Richmond's population expanded in the eighteenth century. Four late eighteenth-century cottages half-way along on the left stand in place of the grand late seventeenth-century Bowes Hall, demolished by Lord Dundas to expand his rent-roll. Grove House, no. 37 Frenchgate, is a more substantial brick house, five bays wide, set back from the street; it was built in 1750 for 'an opulent and eminent merchant', Caleb Readshaw, who had made a fortune exporting knitted goods to the Netherlands. The adjoining house is one of three on Frenchgate with fine mid eighteenth-century classical porches.

Richmond's parish church, St Mary's, lies off Frenchgate to the east, approached along a sloping path, Church Wynd. Curiously, the church was built in this suburb, rather than inside the original town, some time in the mid twelfth century. It is rather inconspicuous in comparison with the castle or Holy Trinity church, and Victorian restoration, both inside and out, has not helped redeem its air of second-best. Only the westernmost arches of the interior arcades are original, but a nice touch here is the carving of a Swaledale sheep on the capital of one of the pillars – a reminder of the origins of the town's medieval prosperity. Most of the church is the work of Sir Gilbert Scott (1811–78) between 1859–60. A painting of 1837 inside the church shows it in its former, unreconstructed state, complete with the box pews and prominent pulpit. The heavily-restored chancel stalls came originally from Easby Abbey just outside the town (see page 92). There is fine carving on their misericord seats; most fun is the third seat from the left in the southern row, which shows two pigs dancing while a third plays the pipes. On the chancel wall to the east of these stalls is the only important monument inside the church, to Sir Thomas Hutton who died in 1629. Sir Thomas and his wife kneel, with their twelve children beneath, and allegorical figures around, topped by Fame who blows a trumpet. Coats of arms and verses fill the foot of the monument. For instance, Eleanor, the third child:

> I liv'd, I di'd, yet one
> Could hardly know,
> I di'd so soon, whether I liv'd or no.
> O what a happy thing it is to lie
> I' th' nurses arms a week or two and die.

The churchyard has a wealth of monuments – some 700 in all.

They have a guidebook all to themselves, directing the visitor to such gems as the epitaph to the Methodist preacher and reformed drunkard, Revd Joseph Sager, who died in 1806: 'Salisbury was my birthplace, Oxford taught me, London ruined me.' One plain stone marks the site where, according to tradition, over 1000 people were buried in the plague epidemic that ravaged the town in 1597–8. A plaque in the corner marks the original position of the Grammar School, refounded in 1567 but recorded as early as 1392.

Under the mastership of James Tate (1771–1843) Richmond School became one of the three leading schools in England, and former pupils earned academic honours in classics and mathematics. Charles Lutwidge Dodgson (1832–98), son of the rector of Croft, near Darlington, was a pupil from 1844 until 1846. Dodgson earned fame as a mathematician at Oxford, and as Lewis Carroll, author of *Alice's Adventures in Wonderland* (1865) and *Through the Looking-Glass* (1871).

Frenchgate ends with a set of steps that lead up to Pottergate, at a higher level. This is another street with substantial, prosperous Georgian houses. Looking down Frenchgate is Hill House, set up higher still (and in summer smothered with roses). This was the home of Frances I'Anson, supposedly the original 'sweet lass of Richmond Hill', as celebrated in song, and whistled by the Green Howards.

> *This lass so neat, with smiles so sweet,*
> *Has won my right good-will,*
> *I'd crowns resign to call thee mine*
> *Sweet lass of Richmond Hill.*

All claims that this is the Richmond Hill above the Thames in Surrey are scoffed at. The house, seven bays wide, with Venetian windows, is a Georgian recasing of a substantial earlier house, one of the two finest in Richmond at the close of the seventeenth century, when it was the town house of the prominent D'Arcy family. In the 1960s Hill House was threatened with demolition; but Richmond's enlightened council purchased it and converted it into a number of dwellings. Other local schemes undertaken since the 1960s show how sensitive Richmond was in a time of much less conservationist attitudes elsewhere in the country.

Hill House and its substantial near-neighbour Oglethorpe House are among the few in the town to have many easily visible features that pre-date 1700. Oglethorpe House incorporates a sixteenth-century house at the rear, built into the steep slope. Its front has two bays which rise through the three storeys, with columns at the angles, the same feature as is found in no. 37 Frenchgate.

With these fine houses, the tour of the most important streets in Richmond ends. Yet there is more to explore. Gallowgate, the hill leading up from the junction of Pottergate and Frenchgate (passing the former army barracks now converted into flats and houses), comes out at the old town racecourse. It is used still as a gallops; at the far end are the sorry remains of the grandstand, built in 1775 when the town races were at their height. Originally it had an arcade of Tuscan columns, with arched openings above and an iron balcony. Rather better preserved, on the southern side, is the square stone-built starter's stand. Richmond's grand eighteenth-century town assemblies, for which the Town Hall and the King's Arms competed, usually took place in race weeks. Gradually the races atrophied, and Catterick rose as the important racing venue in the area; by the later nineteenth-century Richmond races had been largely abandoned. The climb up to the course is still worth it, if only for the magnificent view over the town and the hills, and for the chance of seeing the horses exercising.

Back down the hill into Richmond, at the town end of Darlington Road stands the tiny Bowes Hospital, an almshouse founded in 1607 by the then lords of the manor of Aske Hall (see page 109), inside the former medieval chapel of St Edmund. Recognisable fragments of a late Norman chapel – a window here, an archway there – make this an odd little dwelling. The sharp left fork by the Bowes Hospital, along Maison Dieu, leads out to the ruins of Easby Abbey. The road passes St Nicholas, a substantial seventeenth-century house built on the site of the former medieval Hospital of St Nicholas, given its neo-Tudor appearance after Lord Dundas had bought the property in 1813. *St Nicholas Gardens* are frequently open. A side road beyond leads down to Easby, but there are other routes for pedestrians and a finer approach to Easby is along the Swale, behind St Mary's churchyard where a footpath leads through the woods and fields on the north bank. Another way is along the old railway track on the south bank which has been made into a pathway. Starting from the neo-Gothic old railway station, it passes the ruins of the small Benedictine priory of St Martin's and crosses the Swale below Easby Abbey, and then a footpath leads the short distance back.

However it is approached, *Easby Abbey* has a quiet magnificence. Set within the abbey precinct near the ruins is the little parish church, while the Georgian brick Easby Hall stands on the hillside above to complete the composition. Yorkshire is a county of romantic monastic ruins; Easby may not necessarily be the best known, but it has certain qualities all of its own. This Premonstratensian abbey was founded by the constable of Richmond Castle, Roald, in 1151. In 1392 Richard Scrope (*b*. 1346) refounded the abbey, which had long been racked by internal squabbling; it is believed to be his tomb that is set, unmarked, into the north chancel wall of Easby parish church. The abbey buildings date from the thirteenth and fourteenth centuries in the main. The south range of buildings is the most impressive, since so much is still standing, especially the refectory with its row of large upper windows. Large parts of the west range are also standing, and make exciting exploring with their many staircases and little dark rooms, punctuated by great stone arches and windows, ending with the reredorter (lavatories) over the remains of the canal leading to the Swale. Of the great abbey church itself, however, virtually nothing remains.

The church of St Agatha lies between the abbey ruins and the well-preserved gatehouse (of *c.*1300) that led into the precinct. Externally the church is not especially remarkable; inside, the mainly Early English details are accompanied by fine wall paintings in the chancel, executed in the mid thirteenth century. There is a particularly touching nativity scene painted on the south wall; somehow, the enormous central heating pipes below it add to the charm. On one of the window jambs opposite the scene for spring depicts a man sowing seed – and a beady-eyed crow standing in wait. That this was an important early Christian site is demonstrated by the Easby Cross, found in pieces set into the walls, one of the best pieces of eighth-century sculpture in the country. (A cast stands in the church; the original is now in the Victoria and Albert Museum in London.)

The Swale flowing down from the dale to Richmond and Easby and then away to the Ouse and the Humber, forms the final element in the discovery of Richmond. Much of the building stone for the town, especially for older and humbler buildings, came from the river bed, where rocks and boulders come downstream from the dale with the floodwaters. For street cobbles, and occasionally for buildings, the Swale is still a quarry. The swift river also provided power for many of Richmond's industries. The path back to the town along the river from Easby passes the sites of many mills, such as at the Batts (upstream from Station Bridge) and at the bottom of Millgate beside the falls in the river. The mills were used for grinding corn or for fulling in wool production.

The potential of Richmond's mills is best seen further upstream at Whitcliffe. A pleasant walk on the south bank of the Swale from Richmond Bridge, through Billy Bank woods and the fields beyond leads to a footbridge back over the Swale and to Howe Villa, a late Georgian mill-owner's house, attached to the former flax and later paper mill that was powered by the force of the river. The mill itself, which was one of the few examples of Victorian industrialization that Richmond permitted itself to have, has largely gone.

Walking back through the woods, Richmond reveals itself again bit by bit. Little twentieth century villas over the river; the stone cliffs masked by woods; the Gothick elegance of Culloden Tower; and the sheer bulk of the castle with the tightly-knit houses clinging to its skirts.

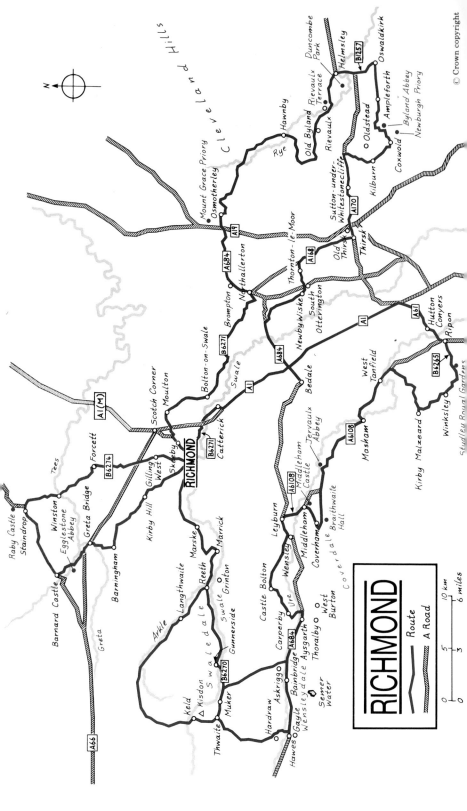

© Crown copyright

# AROUND AND ABOUT RICHMOND

*You may have the opportunity to buy local cheeses in
Richmond Market Place. Although they all come from
within a couple of dozen miles of the town, each has a quite
different character. Probably only one will be familiar:
Wensleydale, fresh and crumbly, sometimes blue-veined.
Less familiar will be the others, which have been kept alive
in small, old-fashioned farmhouses: Swaledale, dryer and
closer in texture than Wensleydale, and Cotherstone (from
Teesdale), softer and more sour. As the cheeses are different,
so too are the dales: deep river valleys, scoured in the Ice
Age, which cut into the broad backbone of the high and
often forbidding Pennines, and characterized by steeply
sloping sides and clusters of small fields demarcated by
miles of dry-stone walling.
There is still more variety within easy reach of
Richmond. The upper part of Swaledale rises to 2000 feet
above sea level; downstream the valley of the Swale falls to
below 200 feet. There are broad, rich acres of farmland in
the plain of the Vale of York, with its string of market towns
and former staging posts along the ancient route of the
Great North Road. Prosperous country-house estates
chequer the broad vale and the lower slopes of the hills.
Across the Vale to the east the land rises sharply again at
the edge of the gaunt North Yorkshire Moors.
North of Richmond the River Tees heads east towards
the sea, passing below Barnard Castle. The lusher land
here has a greater concentration of landed estates and
country houses than Swaledale, many based upon earlier
defensive castles, while metal deposits in the lower valley
led to the industrial growth of Darlington and Teeside.
The areas within easy reach of Richmond, then, may
have the same basic ingredients – uplands, valleys,
monasteries, castles, small towns and villages – yet they are
as different as cheese and cheese.*

## 1. THE DALES

A debate to establish which is the finest of Yorkshire's Dales might well set off a minor war. They all have their fierce advocates, for the wooded and half-tamed landscape of Wharfedale, the green pastoral of Wensleydale, the darker winding austerity of Swaledale, or the closed narrowness of a smaller valley like Coverdale.

Everywhere there are survivals from the past. Great medieval fortresses and smaller fortified houses once guarded strategic points and estates vulnerable to attack. Monastic foundations were established here, far from the corruption of towns, and their great flocks of sheep provided a new source of wealth. Most of these castles and abbeys now stand ruined, and few other buildings survive from before the seventeenth century. An expanding population produced the dales of today: little villages and small market towns with their solid eighteenth- and nineteenth-century houses, inns, chapels and churches, disused lead-mines and weaving-sheds, and fields carved out of almost bare hillside. As work in the dales has dried up, isolated areas have been abandoned, leaving the scars of lead-mining on the fell-sides, and lonely farmhouses perched on the heights.

The establishment in 1954 of the Yorkshire Dales National Park was official recognition of the very special character of the region, a designation intended to preserve and enhance the landscape, and to provide better facilities for an ever-increasing number of visitors. The border of the National Park comes right up to the edge of Richmond town. The natural falls in the Swale beneath the Castle are the last in a long sequence along the river's course as it cascades over the junctions between different types of rock.

This route into the Dales follows the Swale and one of its main tributaries, the Arkle, exploring what Swaledale and Arkengarthdale offer; then it crosses to Wensleydale and Coverdale.

West of Richmond the A6108 and from that the B6270 follow the rushing river, with hanging woods on the steep slopes on either side, houses and farms where the terrain is gentler, and the occasional ruin glimpsed on the other bank. Preferable, perhaps, is the old road, a higher by-road that leaves Richmond from the western end of Victoria Road and climbs up on to the steep moorland escarpment above the river, with occasional views down into the valley. (It was the main road until 1837, when the riverside route was cut.) This is a climbing and caving area, and Marske, the first village on the route, has a Mountain Rescue Post. Past the oddly tall stable buildings and gateways of Marske Hall, all dating from around the mid eighteenth century, the road crosses the Marske Beck on a fifteenth-century bridge. The parish church was restored in 1683

with a Stuart interpretation of the Norman and Early English building that had been there before, and still retains its late Georgian interior wood-work. The left turn at the next cross-roads runs down to Marrick, a small huddle of houses and farms, from which footpaths lead to the ruins of the Benedictine priory founded at Marrick in the mid twelfth century and the convent of Ellerton, on either side of the Swale. Material from Marrick Priory was re-used in the church built within the ruins in 1811, and the remains of the priory are now incorporated into a Youth Centre. The medieval fishponds survive, as do the 375 steps of the Nun's Causeway up to the village from the priory at Ellerton, with stepping stones to take the sisters across the river. Little remains of the convent buildings themselves.

There is a viewpoint into and across the dale from directly above Marrick Priory, on the road that leads to Reeth, joining the B6270 just above Grinton. Grinton itself is worth doubling back to see. Until the sixteenth century, the church here served the whole of upper Swaledale, its parishioners coming up to twelve miles for mass and the Sunday market – or bringing their dead along the upland track still known as the Corpse Way. As settlement in the dale grew, so other churches and chapels were built further up. Huddles of mainly small houses line the main road and dot the roads leading over the hills into Wensleydale, past the vestiges of the lead-mining industry that sustained this region's economy until the last century. An early nineteenth-century smelt mill survives up on Cogden Moor, reached by a track off the minor road to Leyburn.

Grinton, and just above it Reeth, mark the point where the more open lower dale narrows into the wilder upper reaches. Reeth is distinctive, with some handsome houses round the large sloping green bordering the main road. The most prominent is the former hotel, a testimony to Reeth's one-time importance as a market in the dale and as a collecting centre for the lead mined and smelted up in the hills. The *Swaledale Folk Museum* is located in the former schoolroom at the lower end of the green, its exhibits and photographs portraying the local farming and mining traditions.

The minor road that leaves the B6270 at the upper end of Reeth green rises steeply through Arkengarthdale. In some parts the hillsides have a lunar landscape quality, scarred and pocked with the detritus of lead-mining and, in the upper parts, coal-mining. Lead-mining was an important local industry from the Middle Ages, only ceasing in the early years of the twentieth century when the ore became uneconomic to extract. In a few areas there are easily visible remains of the actual workings: hushes (where water was used to scour the hillside to expose the ore and then lateral mine-workings were burrowed into the hill) and abandoned smelting mills may still be seen at Low Moor and Booze Moor on the slopes above Arkengarthdale to the north, and are even better preserved at Gunnerside, on the highest ground between Arkengarthdale and Swaledale and reachable only on foot. The names of some of the former mine workings in the area, Heart's Ache for one, express the difficulties involved in extracting the ore.

Langthwaite is the only village in Arkengarthdale, straggling alongside the Arkle Beck below the main road. Its lanes and alleys evoke the hardship of the lead-mining communities in the tiny houses huddled under the watchful gaze of the owners' more lavish dwellings on the hillside above. Booze, a hamlet of Langthwaite, had 41 inhabited houses in 1851; today it is virtually deserted. The nineteenth-

century church, with its tall west tower, and the welcoming Georgian C.B. Inn on the main road, were built on industry profits. The inn commemorates Dr Charles Bathurst, physician to Oliver Cromwell, who bought the manor of Arkengarthside in 1656 and founded the premier lead-mining family of the same name. One of the nineteenth-century lead companies was named C.B. after him, and the hamlet here was named C.B. after the firm and the pub – the only place name in the country which is just initials. Beyond the inn in a field by the road that climbs over the hills across the county boundary to Castle Barnard, is a curious hexagonal building with a pyramid roof and elegant sash windows set into arched recesses. It was built in 1807 – to store gunpowder for use in the mines.

At the top of the dale the aspect becomes wilder as heather moorland opens up on either side, and distant higher ranges of the Pennines come into view. Disused coal workings stand abandoned a short distance from the road on either side, in what must have been one of the most inhospitable of all English coal-mining villages. All that is left now, built at an altitude of 1732 feet just on the Durham border, is the Tan Hill Inn, England's highest public house. It sells tee-shirts and postcards as well as beer and displays photographs of the old coal-workings and of the snowy waste that surrounds it in deepest winter. There is a warming fire in cold weather, especially welcoming for the walkers on the Pennine Way which passes right by the pub.

The steep twisting road and the Pennine Way footpath follow opposite banks of the Stonesdale Beck as it leaps and turns on its way south to Keld, in a landscape of cliffs and scars, small streams and boggy grass. As the road descends there are more signs of habitation: first, the drystone field barns which are a special feature of the dales, in Swaledale above all, and then a few isolated (and often abandoned) farmhouses.

Above and below Keld the River Swale steps down through a sequence of waterfalls, the broad ledges of Wain Wath Force above the village, then Catrake Force where the East Gill descends to join the Swale in a series of vertical leaps, and the high falls at Kisdon Force a little further downstream. These may be reached along signposted footpaths from the cul-de-sac at the end of the village. For those who would like to venture further away from the road, there is a particularly fine walk (of some six miles) from Keld to Muker and back which shows off the natural beauties of this section of Swaledale in a way that travelling by car cannot.

The B6270 from Keld to Muker and Gunnerside goes round the other side of Kisdon, the prominent, isolated hill at whose foot Muker stands, connecting grey and rugged villages, the hills with their dotted pattern of field barns and occasional farmhouses soaring above. A carved door lintel on the Kearton Guest House in Thwaite incorporates the initials and dates of birth – 1862 and 1871 – of the pioneer wildlife photographers Richard and Cherry Kearton, who were born here and went to the village school at Muker, the next village down the dale. Muker itself is in a magnificent setting, with the high Kisdon behind and the Swale and its tributary the Muker Beck alongside. A collection of grey stone cottages is crowned by the small late Tudor and late Victorian church at the highest point of the village, and a reading room and village institute of 1868 and a chapel reflect the days of lead-mining wealth in the nineteenth century. The hardy Swaledale sheep, which once dominated the farming of this dale, have had a renaissance in

recent years, and Swaledale Woollens in Muker have revived the knitting crafts which were once the mainstay of many families in the dales.

At Gunnerside the road crosses the Swale; and here the different elements of the dale all crowd together, the small grey-stone village above the rushing river, with a great gash in the hillside to the north marking the Gunnerside Gill making its way down to join the Swale, and the remains of the lead mines which made the village prosperous once, and gave it a stock of property suitable to be transformed into the holiday cottages which are now bringing money back again. The road continues along the north bank of the river, following its turns through the small villages back towards Reeth and on to Richmond.

Alternatively, south over the tops is Wensleydale. There is a pass across the moors alongside the Oxnop Beck from a point between Muker and Gunnerside, and another from just below Thwaite, where the Buttertubs Pass rising to almost 1700 feet is the highest in the country, with appropriately exhilarating views back into the green dale and to the moors beyond, brown, green, or purple according to the season. The potholes known as the Buttertubs, fluted shafts cut into the rock by the action of peaty water, lie very close to the roadside, and there are wide views over upper Wensleydale from the final steep descent into the valley of the Ure above Hardraw village. The highest dales waterfall, Hardraw Force, which leaps more than sixty feet, is the main attraction in what is effectively the back garden of the Green Dragon Inn. It is a classic waterfall, with a curtain of water plunging into a deep pool, and space enough for the adventurous (and well-clad) to walk behind.

Hawes, across the Ure, the main market centre of upper Wensleydale, grew up in the seventeenth century as a staging post on the packhorse routes. There is little of great antiquity in the small town, but it is full of interest, and there are some late seventeenth- and eighteenth-century houses inter- spersed among the Victorian prop- erties, mainly on the Market Place and near the town bridge. Being on the only major road across the Pennines in this region, the A684, the town attracts visitors. Hawes and its adjoining hamlet Gayle both have a very intri- cate street pattern, a compact knot of roads and lanes, with the parish church of 1851 set up above (opposite the late Georgian White Hart Inn). The causeway between Hawes' church and Gayles' passes an eighteenth-century cotton mill which is one of the earliest surviving, and which houses the oldest working water turbine in the world – further instances of the dales' long tra- dition of textile production. At Town Foot, beside the former railway station yard, is *Outhwaites' Ropeworks*, open to the public on working days; tra- ditional and synthetic man-made materials are wound into ropes up to 100 feet in length, in a business that has been established in the town since 1840. The old station itself is now a *National Park Information Centre,* while the one-time engine shed houses the *Upper Dales Folk Museum,* with an impressive display of artefacts relating to country life and craft collected by Marie Hartley and Joan Ingilby, who have been both preserving and writing about local activities for decades. Appropriately enough, as Hawes is the centre for revived Wensleydale cheese production, rescued almost single- handedly from oblivion by the redoubt- able Kit Calvert, cheese-making tools figure in the collection. Low Row, back in Swaledale, is the centre of produc- tion for the far rarer Swaledale cheese, similarly rescued in recent years.

The main road follows the Ure

along the reasonably broad valley bottom, with the land rising on either side. In spite of its steepness, this is altogether a gentler, greener land- scape than Swaledale; dairy herds are a common sight on the lower slopes, with sheep on the upland fields and hills. At Bainbridge, four miles east of Hawes, the short River Bain tumbles down to join the Ure. It comes from Semer Water up on the moor to the south, Yorkshire's largest natural lake (which may be reached by a number of minor roads). At Bainbridge the Romans established an important fort to the east of the present village, its site still marked by an earth platform and a sequence of ridges and trenches. The most distinctive feature in modern Bainbridge is the large green (grazed by sheep in summer), with houses arranged informally around its edges.

Askrigg, Bainbridge's near neigh- bour on the other bank of the Ure, is now a centre of the James Herriot industry, where much filming of the television series was done, and so to be admired or avoided as personal taste dictates. The parish church of St Os- wald, built in the mid fifteenth century, is the grandest in the dale, with a very fine nave ceiling using moulded beams. Although it is now on a minor road, the main street through the village was once the main Lancaster–Richmond turnpike, and the rows of eighteenth- century stone houses, including the distinguished Manor House and King's Arms of 1767, demonstrate Askrigg's wealth from cloth, lead, and clock-making in the Georgian era. There are two more waterfalls, Mill Gill Force and Whitfield Force, among the woods above Askrigg.

Both the main road and the back road lead to Aysgarth, although there is a detour from the latter just before the village is reached. A steep road south descends into the subsidiary Bishopdale, where the hamlet of Thoralby has a number of seventeenth- and eighteenth-century stone houses, and then crosses the beck and the valley floor to the quarrying and mining village of West Burton, which lies just off the main through routes. Here there is a large and splendid village green with an obelisk of 1820 at the focal point. West Burton even has its own waterfall on its own beck at the lower end. It is perhaps, with all these attributes, the best small village in the tour. From West Burton minor roads re-cross the beck to the main road at Aysgarth.

Aysgarth church was once the mother church for upper Wensleydale, seen from the huge size of the graveyard rather than from the largely Victorian building itself. However, the interior of the church incorporates a pair of fine screens in the chancel, and other woodwork of the early sixteenth century, all supposed to have come from the dissolved Jervaulx Abbey a little way down the dale (see page 102). Aysgarth's main attraction is the great mile-long series of waterfalls, known as Aysgarth Force. The Upper Falls are viewable from the bridge, a fifteenth-century structure widened in 1788 by John Carr of York; the more dramatic falls below can be reached through paths in the woods. Yore Mill, just below the bridge, now houses an extensive *Coach and Carriage Museum,* devoted to the horse-drawn life of the Yorkshire squire and his estate.

The road from the bridge carries on through the little village of Carperby, with its seventeenth-century cross standing proud on seven steps, to the village of Castle Bolton, where the top road from Reeth comes down into Wensleydale, and the local squire's home, *Bolton Castle.* This great fortress guarding the dale was built in the late 1370s by the 1st Baron Scrope of Bolton, twice Chancellor of England.

It is generally regarded as one of the finest monuments of English military architecture, with its four great corner towers and range of living quarters around a courtyard. One of the towers has partly collapsed, and much of the interior has been gutted, but spirited attempts are now being made to restore the castle, and to people it with dummy figures. Mary Queen of Scots (1542–87) was imprisoned in the castle for a while; it was one of the first of her many places of confinement after she fled from Scotland in 1568. Many of the figures in the castle represent members of her retinue. (One ghostly dummy, a monk in the chapel praying for the repose of the soul of the deposed Richard II (1367–1400), is placed to alarm the unwary.)

The minor road from Castle Bolton passes under the cliff of Preston Scar and beside the grounds of Bolton Castle's seventeenth-century successor, Bolton Hall (which was gutted by fire in 1902 and rebuilt using part of the surviving shell). The road leads to Wensley, the village from which the dale took its name, and its larger neighbour Leyburn. The dale's first market was established in Wensley in 1202; but in 1563 the village all but disappeared when it was devastated in a massive plague epidemic. The village revived more than a century later when it became the estate village for Bolton Hall. Wensley has a particularly fine parish church, where the Scrope family pew incorporates pieces from a rood screen taken from Easby Abbey after the dissolution. There are also several Scrope monuments.

Leyburn, which benefited from the Wensley villagers' flight, is the lower dale's main centre, but is remarkably unprepossessing, although it does have a number of late Georgian houses in and around the central Grove Square; and Leyburn Hall, hidden behind the Market Place and looking out to the hills, is a fine house of the 1750s. Leyburn's best feature is the view over the dale from Leyburn Shawl, the top of the escarpment west of the town, which is reached by footpaths and tracks. Below Leyburn, the dale begins to open out into a much wider valley, and the pastoral landscape gradually gives way to one of arable crops.

The A6108 south-east from Leyburn follows the Ure to Masham. About 2 miles from Leyburn is the entrance to Coverdale, guarded by the ruin of *Middleham Castle*. Until the mid eighteenth century this narrow and, in its upper reaches, wild valley was one of the main routes between Richmond and London. Middleham Castle has one of the largest keeps in the country, of a similar date and pattern to that at Richmond. The castle grew by stages, becoming ever more comfortable, between the twelfth century and the

fifteenth when it was the home of the great Earl of Warwick, the Kingmaker, and at the height of its prestige. Richard, Duke of Gloucester, later Richard III (1452–85), was brought up in the castle and married Warwick's daughter. Middleham itself is a pretty little town, with some good Georgian houses, and a church dedicated to St Alkelda which contains a unique early Tudor monument to one of the last abbots of Jervaulx, a few miles further along the main road. Today the town is renowned for racehorse breeding and training, with over 200 horses in training at any one time.

From Middleham an open road crosses the Low Moor, where the horses exercise, to the tiny, nearly isolated church of Coverham, with traces nearby of the Premonstratensian Coverham Abbey. The minor road along the fell passes *Braithwaite Hall,*

*Rievaulx Abbey.*

a Restoration manor house which incorporates a fourteenth-century grange that belonged to Jervaulx Abbey and is now a farmhouse, and leads on to the tidy estate village of East Witton on the A1068. The village was largely rebuilt around its sloping green in 1809 by the Earl of Ailesbury who then owned the Jervaulx Abbey estate. Jervaulx Abbey itself, a mid twelfth-century Cistercian foundation, which acquired extensive Wensleydale estates, lies a mile along the main road. Its ruins are not as dramatic as others in North Yorkshire, but they are set in attractive parkland and something survives of every part of the monastic house. Best preserved is the high wall of the dormitory block. Wild flowers are allowed to grow all over the ruins.

The main road leads on to the small market town of Masham, where the parish church looks into the Square on one side and on to open countryside and the River Ure on the other. That effect is repeated elsewhere in the town, giving it a very distinctive feel; in the main square, for example, small islands of houses look both inwards and out onto the rolling country-side immediately behind. The parish church has various pieces of sculpture to watch for: part of a carved Saxon cross stands outside, while the monument to Sir Marmaduke Wyvill of 1613 inside includes a cherub blowing soap bubbles.

There are a large number of medieval effigies among the monuments in West Tanfield church, the next village along the main A6108; most were probably connected with the castle that stood by the river, of which nothing survives now but the fortified fifteenth-century gatehouse. Beyond West Tanfield a minor road to the right leads over the low hills to Kirby Malzeard, the centre of Wensleydale cheese production today. At Winksley to the south, above the River Laver, there are

the first signs of the principal destination of this part of the tour, the great ruined abbey at Fountains. Abbot Huby built a chapel in Winksley around 1510, parts of which are preserved in the early twentieth-century church dedicated to the great Durham saints, Cuthbert (c. 634–687) and Oswald (c. 605–642). The road swoops steeply down to the river and up again, with vistas beginning to open out where it joins the B6265.

*Fountains Abbey* and the gardens of *Studley Royal* are among the greatest sights in the north of England. The abbey was founded in the 1130s by a pioneering group of monks who wished to break away from the relaxed atmosphere of their parent Benedictine house, St Mary's Abbey at York, and adopt the new strict Cistercian rule. The remote valley they chose was 'fit more, it seemed,' their chronicler said, 'for the dens of wild beasts than for the uses of mankind'. Like many of the great Yorkshire abbeys, Fountains prospered on the wealth from great sheep walks in the dales, and the wishes of the founders were lost in ever-greater laxity and corruption. A great sequence of church and monastic buildings, completed by 1250, was crowned by Abbot Huby's early sixteenth-century tower, so tall it can be seen over the rim of the valley. Only a few years later, in 1539, the abbey was dissolved and progressively fell into disrepair. Finally, in 1768, it was incorporated into the Studley Royal estate, forming the most dramatic romantic ruin an eighteenth-century garden could ever hope to have. The heart of Studley Royal, a serene, formal water garden, with a canal and pools adorned with temples and statuary, was laid out between 1720 and 1740 by John Aislabie, who had been disgraced in the great financial scandal of the South Sea Bubble. His son William added the abbey to the estate and incorporated it into a landscaped extension to the garden.

The best approach to this complex is through the gardens, ending with the carefully contrived surprise view of Fountains at the end. Another masterpiece was added to this assembly of superlatives a century later, in the form of William Burges's elaborate St Mary's church set on the edge of the park, encrusted with ornament and decoration. Inside is the white marble tomb of the 1st Marquess and Marchioness of Ripon, for whom the church was built.

The speedy way back to Richmond is along the A61 and the A1, but a much more scenic route follows the minor roads parallel to the A1, running past a succession of prosperous farms and hamlets. The first hamlet, off the A61 across the Ure from Ripon, is Hutton Conyers. Above it lies Norton Conyers, a fifteenth-century house substantially remodelled in the mid seventeenth century by the Graham family (who still own the house), and tinkered with again in the 1770s. There, Reader, she married him: in 1839 Charlotte Brontë visited the house, and used it as a model for Thornfield Hall in *Jane Eyre*, as well as taking a family story as the basis for the mad first Mrs Rochester. Many Graham family monuments are in Wath church half a mile north, standing at the end of an attractive cobbled village street.

Return to the A61, then join the A1 – the old Great North Road – and continue north. Just after Londonderry take the A684 left to Bedale, in some ways a miniature version of Richmond. Here too there are sloping cobbled streets and buildings reflecting Georgian prosperity, especially those immediately on the main street and Market Place. Bedale Hall, an early Georgian stone mansion remarkable for its five-bay wide entrance hall and its cantilevered flying staircase, stands

in the cobbled centre, a country house set down in a small market town. The parish church is one of the dominant accents of the place, with its tall west tower prominent at the head of the main street; inside are a number of interesting monuments, including one of the earliest English alabaster effigies, a fourteenth-century piece commemorating Sir Brian Fitzalan. His wife's effigy beside him was carved in stone.

The Great North Road now also bypasses Catterick to the north, a quiet little town set along the old main through route, with its fifteenth-century bridge over the Swale. Nearby is the famous racecourse, part of a long tradition of breeding and racing in this vicinity – even when Daniel Defoe (1660–1731) passed through the area in the 1720s, he drew particular attention to the horses. The back road to Richmond ducks under the A1 and follows the Swale, avoiding the sprawling mess of the military Catterick Camp on the A6136. St Trinian's Hall and Farm lie on this route, but there is not a hockey-stick in sight.

## 2. THE VALE OF YORK AND THE NORTH YORKSHIRE MOORS

The routes east from Richmond across the Vale of York are considerably flatter than those to the west until they reach the higher ground of the Cleveland Hills. Beyond rise the North Yorkshire Moors, a high gritstone and sandstone plateau which was designated a National Park in 1952 (two years before the Dales) and which sweeps towards the coast at Whitby. On the flanks of the moors, villages and small towns nestle in the valleys, and some of the north's finest ruined abbeys are sited on the moorland fringe.

The A6108 Darlington Road from Richmond joins the A1 at Scotch Corner. Moulton can be reached by crossing the busy A1 from the minor road at Skeeby, or for the faint-hearted by coming back down the A1 from Scotch Corner and turning left. Moulton has a restaurant–pub which is much favoured locally; it is also notable for its two mid seventeenth-century houses set back south of the village centre, Moulton Manor and *Moulton Hall,* built for two members of the Smithson family and with many stylistic features in common. Moulton Hall, the smaller of the two, has Dutch gables, with oval windows set vertically in them and a particularly fine Caroline carved staircase inside. The by-road south-east leads to Scorton, where the early eighteenth-century brick Grammar School and stone-built master's house stand side by side. The school's first headmaster is commemorated in a fine monument in Bolton-on-Swale church half a mile south on the B6271; so is Henry Jenkins, who died in 1670 aged 169. There is a curious obelisk to his memory in the churchyard.

The B6271 to Northallerton passes the square, brick block of Kiplin Hall, built in 1625 for Lord Baltimore (*d.* 1632), who founded Maryland (as a Roman Catholic colony) and after whom the first city of the state was named. The road continues westwards to Northallerton, touching the Swale below Kiplin but mainly keeping to the slopes above it. This, as elsewhere in the Vale, is a pleasant, undemanding farming landscape. The busy town of Northallerton lies on the main north–south route on the east side of the Vale. There are the remains of a motte and bailey castle west of the main centre, close to the railway junction which helped transform the town in the nineteenth century. Despite later development, the centre still has the feel of a late eighteenth-century coaching town, with several inns in the curving terraced main street. The mainly fifteenth-century parish church with a high crossing tower contains early stone carvings stylistically related to the Easby Cross (see p. 93) and carvings are also a notable feature of the church beside the village green at Brompton, to the north-east just off the A684. Pre-Conquest sculpted tombstones here are engagingly adorned with bears.

The A684 runs through rolling countryside to join the A19. A turning a mile north of the junction leads into the National Park and to the ruins of *Mount Grace Priory,* on the wooded lower slopes of the Cleveland Hills. Founded in 1398 by the Duke of Surrey, this is the best-preserved Carthusian house in England, its ruined church and the outlines of the great cloister still evocatively isolated. Twenty monks kept a strict regime of silence and prayer, and lived a separate existence in each of the tiny, 22-foot square two-storeyed cells with gardens attached set round the cloister, meeting only in the diminutive church. The gatehouse into the precinct and the adjacent guesthouse were transformed into a private residence in the seventeenth century and have recently been converted to house an exhibition centre on the priory and its history. Mount Grace encapsulates the isolated asceticism of the stricter forms of medieval religious life. From the steep wooded slopes behind there is a panoramic view over the Vale of York to the Pennines beyond – setting off the peaceful ruins. That the old faith was not entirely extinguished in this part of Yorkshire is evident from the survival of the early sixteenth-century Lady Chapel on this steep hill, which became a place of pilgrimage after the Reformation and has been restored for worship. Footpaths lead up to the chapel from the priory; access by car is from the straggling village of Osmotherley, reached along the side road east from the A19/A684 junction.

Osmotherley is notable perhaps for its adherence to denominations other than the Church of England. Mass is said in the Old Hall on the main street; John Wesley (1703–91) preached on the market table beside the stone cross, and the very early Methodist chapel was built in 1754. The Friends had built their meeting house twenty years before that. The minor road north from Osmotherley leads to the moorland beauty spot Scarth Wood Moor, alongside the Cold Beck and its reservoir. The track running along the tops is the old Hambleton Drove Road, one of the broad green routes along which great herds of cattle were once driven.

The drove road is no more than an open track; by car, the route over the moors winds south and east from Osmotherley village, up the incline onto Osmotherley Moor, and then follows 7 miles of open by-road to Hawnby. There are many views along the way, back to the vale below and across the heathery slopes and steeply-incised valleys of the moorland; when John Wesley brought Methodism from Osmotherley to Hawnby, where it took deep root, he thought this one of the best journeys in England. Hawnby itself clings to the slopes above the River Rye, a small knot of stone cottages with the diminutive parish church below.

From Hawnby the road descends to a bridge across the river and then runs on south across the moors to Old Byland. The tiny hamlet is one of the highest in this area; east of it, the road winds down a steep, wooded hill to the valley of the River Rye and *Rievaulx Abbey,* another of Yorkshire's finest abbey ruins. Established in 1132, Rievaulx became the English mother church of the Cistercians. Although ruined, the great abbey church with its walls standing to the roof line is remarkably well preserved; three tiers of windows are clearly outlined either side of the nave. The mid thirteenth-century chancel is one of the finest buildings of its day, while whole ranges of the conventual buildings still stand. Like Fountains, Rievaulx has been incorporated – from a distance – into an eighteenth-century garden scheme. The main road above the abbey, the B1257, gives access to *Rievaulx Terrace,* a gently curving walk winding across the side of the valley between two Palladian temples, one rectangular and the other round. Contrived vistas through the trees give glimpses of the abbey ruins far below. The garden temples have painted ceilings and, in the case of the round temple, a floor of tiles from the ruined Byland Abbey.

Rievaulx Terrace was created in c. 1760 by Thomas Duncombe III, who wanted to complement if not surpass the more formal grass terrace with two round temples laid out by his father in front of *Duncombe Park* on the other side of the valley. Duncombe Park Gardens which fill a great bend in the River Rye below Helmsley, the small town further down the B1257, are among the finest in the north, with bold landscaping covering some 600 acres and strategically placed temples and statuary. The house (until recently a school) has now reopened to the public following the mammoth task of its restoration since Lord Feversham regained his ancestral seat.

Helmsley itself, at the entrance to the park and set where the North York Moors fall away to the Vale of Pickering, is one of the prettiest towns on the moors. Many roads and walking routes converge here and it is a popular place. The predominant colours of the town are yellow and red, from the local stone and tiled roofs. A statue of the second Lord Feversham under a tall High Victorian Gothic canopy dominates the wide market place, and the church just behind is also Victorian, largely rebuilt in thirteenth-century style in *c.* 1867. Close by, the high keep of *Helmsley Castle* rears up above the present entrance from the town, the remains of the castle ruined after a long siege in the Civil War.

The A170 and B1257 run due south from Helmsley to Oswaldkirk, and west beneath the steep moorland edge with the vale spreading out below to Ampleforth, the modern descendant of the great Yorkshire abbeys. Ampleforth village is strung out along the roadway, with the Abbey and College at the east end. An English Benedictine community established in France fled back to England after the Revolution, and settled in Ampleforth in 1802, taking over a recently built house and beginning the great series of extensions and buildings that make up what is now England's leading Roman Catholic public school. The modern Gothic abbey church, built between 1922 and 1961 to designs by Sir Giles Gilbert Scott (1880–1960), and the nearby Roman Catholic parish church both contain early work by the celebrated local woodworker Robert Thompson (*d.* 1955), marked by his characteristic mouse. The abbey crypt incorporates the former high altar stone from *Byland Abbey* three miles west along the road through Wass, where the southern tip of the North York Moors pokes down through the woods. The extensive ruins of Byland Abbey, founded by the Cistercians in 1177 after forty years of wandering trying to find a suitable place, dominate the area. The church built here had one of the largest naves in England, much of which, together with the enormous west front, is still standing. The side road back on to the moor towards Oldstead passes under the entrance arch to the precinct. Byland was a larger building than either Rievaulx or Fountains; but here the ruins have not been incorporated into a landscape design and they stand proudly gaunt on the valley side.

The road continues to skirt the higher ground to Coxwold, a neat village noted for its associations with Laurence Sterne (1713–68), who was vicar from 1760 until his death. In the rather modest brick-built *Shandy Hall* he wrote most of *Tristram Shandy,* regarded as his masterpiece, and *A Sentimental Journey.* The house has become a literary shrine. The parish church of St Michael, with an unusual octagonal west tower, is set picturesquely at a high point in the village. It contains a sequence of monuments to the Bellasis family of Newburgh Priory: the elaborate Jacobean wall-monument to Sir William contrasts with the marble standing figures of the Earl of Fauconberg (who died in 1700) and his son, and with the plain Gothic tomb of the 2nd Earl of the second creation, who died in 1802. *Newburgh Priory,* itself a handsome spreading building just south of the village, was founded as a house of Augustinian canons in 1145, and was given to Henry VIII's chaplain, Anthony Bellasis, on its dissolution. The house is a mixture of eighteenth-century and earlier work and incorporates parts of the medieval priory; its most famous feature is the supposed tomb of Oliver Cromwell, whose body was allegedly smuggled back here after the Restoration by his daughter the Viscountess Fauconberg.

The road that hugs the edge of the upland turns north-west to Kilburn, another charming small village with a giant white horse, cut into the chalk on the cliff above in 1857, standing over it. Robert Thompson, who died in 1955, exercised his considerable woodworking skills in a half-timbered house and workshop in the village and his craft is continued here. From Kilburn a side road winds up the steep escarpment past the White Horse, with fine views back over the land falling away into the Vale given added interest by the hovering figures from the hang-gliding club at the top of the hill. A series of tight bends descends to the A170 at Sutton Bank, with views far to the west between the woods. (There is a complicated series of roads in the area designated for use by caravans to avoid this descent.)

The A170 strikes west, via the appropriately named Sutton-under-Whitestonecliffe, to the busy town of Thirsk on the Cod Beck. To the north of the town is Old Thirsk, with its stately fifteenth-century parish church, the finest in North Yorkshire, with an ornamented wagon roof, and the eighteenth-century Thirsk Hall fronting onto the street beside it. On the road towards the centre, Kirkgate, is *Thirsk Museum,* once the home of the Thomas Lord who founded Lord's Cricket Ground in London. The cobbled market place in the new town is bordered by some fine eighteenth-century inns; but the town suffers from an influx of coaches bringing those in search of the pseudonymous James Herriot, whose veterinary practice is based here. From Thirsk the A168 heads towards Northallerton with the considerably flatter landscape of the Swale valley spreading out to the west. A minor road left from Thornton-le-Moor runs across the A167 at South Otterington, then beside the River Wiske and north through the mid-Victorian estate village of Newby Wiske to join the A684. Two miles west is the A1, and the fast road back to Richmond.

### 3. INTO TEESDALE

Over the moors north of Richmond is the valley of the River Tees, quite different from the dales to the south. It is also a different county, County Durham. Teesdale spreads wide from its main market town, the ancient defensive site of Barnard Castle, with a number of rich landed estates. Eastwards, the character of the dale changes as it approaches the industrial and historic railway centre, Darlington, and the north–south sweep of the A1.

The minor roads out of Richmond to the north-west cross Richmond High Moor, passing either side of the town's former racecourse, but the most westerly route, off the upper road to Marske, is liable to be closed for military training. Both lead to the village of Kirby Hill, perched high above Holme Beck and the scanty ruins of Ravensworth Castle, with panoramic views across to the valley of the Tees. With its stone-built houses ranged round a rectangular green, this is an uncommonly attractive village. The former almshouses stand in a corner of the green; another corner is occupied by *Kirby Hill Grammar School,* founded in 1556 and closed 401 years later. The building's trustees are still chosen by lots drawn from among names written on paper, enclosed in wax, and floating in a jar of water. Kirby Hill parish church has a fine tower, dated 1397, and considerable Norman work. If you are accompanied by a child, or feel like becoming one again, see how many mice you can find carved on the church furniture by Robert Thompson.

Barningham is another handsome village set around a green, this time setting off the plain stone front of the late seventeenth-century Barningham Park. The road north leads to *Greta Bridge* on the A66, a beautiful 80-foot single span across the Greta built by John Carr in 1773 and much painted by Thomas Girtin (1775–1802), John Sell Cotman (1782–1842) and other artists of their day. Here, too, is the estate of *Rokeby Park.* There is a square of houses at the bridge and, curiously set back along a footpath beside the river, the mid eighteenth-century church of St Mary, with various fine monuments to the Morritt family who lived at Rokeby Park in the nineteenth century. Sir Thomas Robinson, who was director of the fashionable Ranelagh Gardens in London, may have designed the church as well as the early Palladian house which he built for himself in the 1730s, rendered on all but its entrance front. The grandest room is the saloon, which rises through both first and second floors, and there are fine eighteenth-century furnishings including a set of needlework pictures embroidered by Anne Morritt. The 'Rokeby Venus' by Velasquez, which the Morritts bought in 1813, now hangs in the National Gallery, London.

A side road skirts Rokeby Park and follows the Tees to Barnard Castle, passing the ruins of Egglestone Abbey, a house of Premonstratensian canons that was founded from Easby (see p. 92) at the end of the twelfth century. The thirteenth-century church survives in a recognizable state here, but not the monastic buildings. With the exception of the reredorter, with its tall narrow drain into the beck, these are considerably more ruinous than those at Easby.

The fortress which has given *Barnard Castle* its name dominates distant views of the town. In spite of its enormous size, however, the castle is much less obviously present within the town than the castle at Richmond. Like Richmond the site is naturally defensive, bounded by cliffs on three sides. The Barnard part of the town name refers to the father and son who held the castle through the twelfth century; later it was granted to the Beauchamps, Earls of Warwick, and from them descended to Richard, Duke of Gloucester (see p. 101). Although it was little used after the fourteenth century and was quarried for building stone by its seventeenth-century

owners, the Vane family of nearby Raby Castle, much of the castle survives, including the main tower of the keep, thrusting forward above the highest cliff.

Rather more dominating in the townscape is the Victorian extravagance of the *Bowes Museum* on the southern edge of Barnard Castle at the end of one of the main streets. Built between 1869 and 1892 to house the art collections of the local magnate John Bowes and his wife Josephine, a former Parisian actress and painter, the house is a cross between an ornate French château and a town hall. It houses important collections of paintings, including the famous portrait of Napoleon at his coronation by Jacques-Louis David (1748–1825), and Continental furniture and ceramics. Its most famous single exhibit must be the solid silver swan automaton, a late nineteenth-century monstrosity that swims on a silver lake.

As in Richmond, at the town's heart stands a rebuilt eighteenth-century market cross, here a small octagonal building with a room above it that was converted into a court room in 1814. There are a number of important seventeenth-century town houses and several Georgian buildings (although many have been demolished in recent decades, and on the bridge side of the town replaced by unsympathetic blocks of flats) while early nineteenth-century weaving mills by the river reflect Barnard Castle's importance as a wool-weaving town in the eighteenth century. For such a small place, Barnard Castle is a surprising mixture.

At the village of Staindrop, a few miles north-east of Barnard Castle on the A688, with its picturesque greens and cottages, the land begins to rise to the fells. The large and impressive parish church is filled with monuments, with many medieval memorials, such as the oak effigies of Henry

Neville, 5th Earl of Westmorland, and his second and third wives among others, commemorating that family. Later works, such as the nineteenth-century sculpture of Sophia, Duchess of Cleveland, lying on a tomb chest while an angel bears away her soul, commemorate the Vane family, successively Lords Barnard, Earls of Darlington and Dukes of Cleveland.

The Nevilles and the Vanes both owned nearby *Raby Castle,* one of the most impressive of all northern castles. It was begun in the early fourteenth century, and still looks medieval despite many attempts to change it – not least the first Lord Barnard's efforts to demolish the castle in 1714 in order to spite his heir. The Yorkshire architects Daniel Garrett, James Paine and John Carr all worked at Raby in the eighteenth century, and much of their interior work survives. Carr, for example, transformed the inner courtyard into a Lower Hall, where visitors alighted from their carriages inside a sumptuous vaulted room. From this period, too, date the many farm and estate buildings in Gothick style, while the Victorians got to work on the outside of the castle, reinforcing its medieval appearance.

Two miles south, to the left of the B6274 on the nearby Langley Beck, is Alwent water mill, dated 1792, one of the few intact water mills in the region and with a cluster of associated buildings. The road crosses the Tees at Winston by a single-span bridge of 1762, 111 feet wide, designed by Sir Thomas Robinson of Rokeby. On the rising ground some three miles south of the river is Forcett Park, an especially fine early Georgian house by Daniel Garrett, who worked at Raby, and who probably designed the Culloden Tower at Richmond. The superb *Forcett Dovecote* in the grounds

echoes Culloden Tower in being octagonal, with open arches at the base and blank arches above. A splendidly High Victorian church beside the drive has appropriately dark interior woodwork intact. Just to the east are Stanwick fortifications, one of the country's most impressive defensive earthworks with over six miles of banks and ditches, heroically built by the Brigantes in the first century to fend off the Romans. South of here, where the B6274 turns sharp right into the village of Gilling West, a minor road continuing straight ahead leads to Sedbury Park, the home of the D'Arcy family. Gilling West church contains some D'Arcy monuments.

The Dundas family also dominated Richmond in the eighteenth and nineteenth centuries, becoming the Marquesses of Zetland, and their house is *Aske Hall* set in its park just to the right of the road as it makes its final approach to Richmond. The gardens are open ocasionally, and they include a Gothick folly temple attributed to Lancelot 'Capability' Brown (1716–83), who redesigned the landscape. At the core of the Hall itself is a fifteenth-century pele tower, to which a variety of Georgian, Victorian and modern neo-Georgian additions have been made. The road into Richmond then passes Scots Dyke, a pre-Roman defensive earthwork, while on the top of the hill in the field on the left stands the eye-catcher of Oliver's Ducket, a little tower from Richmond Castle re-erected here in the eighteenth century. It commands superb views across Scotch Corner and the flatter plains of the Swale and the Tees, towards the Cleveland Hills and the conical peak of Rosebery Topping.

At the end we reach Darlington Road, dropping down into Richmond town centre again.

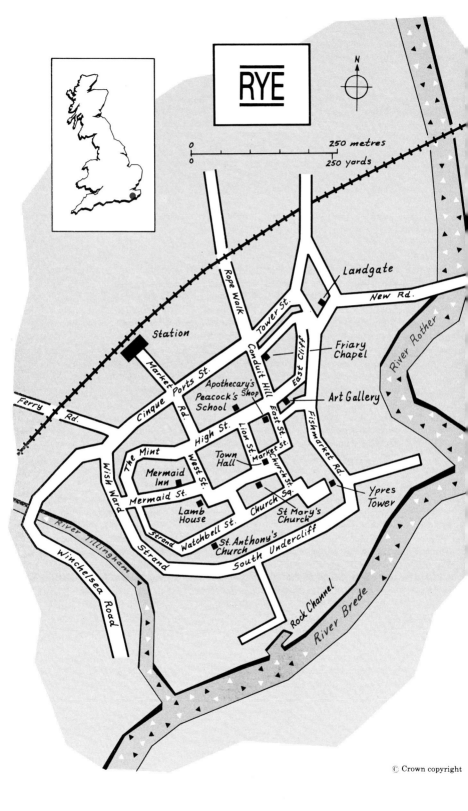

RYE

N

0            250 metres
0            250 yards

Landgate

New Rd.

River Rother

Rope Walk

Tower St.

Station

Friary Chapel

Conduit Hill

East Cliff

Ferry Rd.

Market Rd.

Ports St.

Cinque

Apothecary's Shop

Peacock's School

Art Gallery

High St.

East St.

Lion St.

Market St.

Fishmarket Rd.

The Mint

West St.

Town Hall

Mermaid Inn

Church St.

Ypres Tower

Mermaid St.

Wish Ward

Lamb House

Church Sq.

St Mary's Church

Strand

Watchbell St.

Church St.

St. Anthony's Church

South Undercliff

Strand

River Tillingham

Winchelsea Road

Rock Channel

River Brede

# 5
# RYE

East Sussex

*'Two-and-twenty years on end in London have qualified me in perfection for a small brown hilltop community in a more or less drained ... imitation of the Roman Campagna.' Those were the sentiments of Henry James (1843–1916), perhaps the best-known former resident of Rye. One of his successors in Lamb House, grandest of the town's residences, was E. F. Benson (1867–1940), a prolific author whose waspishly comic novels set in Rye are still read and enjoyed. Television dramatization has increased their popularity, and many visitors come to discover the Rye – or Tilling as Benson called it – of his 1920s Mapp and Lucia novels. To some extent they can still find it.*
*'There is not in all England', Benson wrote, 'a town so blatantly picturesque ... [it] positively consists of quaint corners, rough cast and timber cottages, and mellow Georgian fronts.' For over a century writers and painters have been attracted to the town and the lonely wild expanse of Romney Marsh. It is the Rye they conjured up that many come to see: a curious town perched on a sandstone hill rising out of the marshes. There is another Rye too, a working and a fishing community inhabiting the fringe of the flat silty plain that was once the sea.*
*Once, the sea came right up to the town gates and Rye was one of the medieval Cinque Ports with special responsibilities to guard the vulnerable Channel coastline against the French; now the shore is some three miles away. One of the richest communities in Tudor England, Rye was in severe decline by the late seventeenth century, and remained a sleepy backwater for over two hundred years, apart from a little smuggling. While other towns and cities were slowly rebuilt and transformed, Rye retained its medieval layout and a legacy of buildings reflecting its former strategic value and vanished mercantile wealth, to be rediscovered in the 20th century.*

With most towns, some central feature will usually present itself as the obvious place to begin exploring – perhaps the market place, or the parish church. But a tour of Rye should start not in the middle but on the edge, at the mid thirteenth-century tall stone fortress known as *Ypres Tower* which stands at the south-eastern corner of the old town. This cliff-top survival of the medieval defences flanked by sections of the original, fourteenth-century town walls expresses something of Rye's unique character as a hill town, and as a port from which the sea has long since retreated.

The Ypres Tower and gun emplacement formed Rye's fortress, designed to keep out the French, England's traditional enemy. The Dauphin himself had occupied Rye briefly in 1216, and renewed difficulties around 1250 led to a royal order to build the forty-foot high tower with its round corner turrets. The Gun Garden, the flat space alongside the Tower (appropriately dotted with small cannon), provides the first view over the flat marshy plain to the sea. The River Rother meanders its course through the silt and sand, the small boats that can navigate it at high tide sitting marooned on the mud banks at low water. In Rye's late medieval and Tudor heyday this expanse was all sea, and even eighteenth-century views show a few waves lapping the cliff on which the Tower is built.

Damaged during World War II when it was hit in a German air raid, the Tower now houses *Rye Museum* with exhibits telling the town's chequered history. The Tower itself had many uses after it ceased to be a fortress, serving as the town hall, a private residence, the town gaol, the police station, and finally as a mortuary. From the top of the Tower there are wider panoramic views: east over Romney Marsh, criss-crossed by drainage channels and with fields dotted with sheep; and south to the sea. On clear days you can see up the coast to Folkstone and even Dover.

The cobbled lane from the Tower leads into the square around the parish church of St Mary the Virgin, and is lined with buildings that are typical of Rye as a whole. Rye is a beautifully maintained, sometimes almost manicured, mixture of timber frame and weatherboard, plaster, brick and tile, with the church and the medieval fortifications the only stone structures of consequence. Many house fronts are tile-hung in the traditional Sussex style. The little Church Street that runs down the eastern side of the square is just such a mix of building delights. Half-way along on the left-hand side is the oval brick water-cistern with a domed top dating from 1735, to save the inhabitants having to go down to the bottom of the hill to collect water. The citizens of the time were given dire warnings against polluting this water supply, not 'to throw any dirt, dust, soil, trash, nastiness or anything else into the reservoir'.

Just before the cistern is the entrance to the churchyard, a haven of shrub, grass, headstones and, a rare survival, graveboards (wooden grave markers like the headboard on a bed) within the low encircling wall. Massive late medieval flying buttresses that prop up the east end of the church rise from the pathway leading round to the north porch. Parts of the north and south transepts are Norman (their age is more clearly seen from the stone arcading inside), but most of the church is fifteenth-century, rebuilt after the French raid of 1377, in which parts of Rye were razed to the ground and the church was badly burned. There are still some reddened scorch marks on the older fabric. The present jaunty pyramid roof and weather-vane were added to the low crossing tower in 1702. Jauntier still is the clock on the north face of the tower, added in 1760, with chubby quarter boys (who strike the quarters but not the hour) flanking a florid cartouche bearing the sober motto 'For our time is a very shadow that passeth away' (Wisdom 2:5).

The quarter boys are modern fibreglass replicas; the originals have been placed in the north-eastern Clare chapel inside the church, one of the few thirteenth-century parts of the building. The stained glass, all Victorian or later, reflects Rye's literary associations. The largest windows were given by E. F. Benson of Lamb House and *Mapp and Lucia* fame, the south transept window commemorating his parents and his brother and fellow-author A. C. Benson (best remembered today for the words of 'Land of Hope and Glory'), that at the west end E. F.'s years as mayor from 1934 to 1936. The donor himself appears in it, kneeling in his mayoral robes at bottom left, with his dog Taffy in the central light.

One of the prominent features of the church interior is the great pendulum of the clock, installed in 1562, which swings in the tower crossing. Until Victorian times it was even longer and almost reached the ground, a danger to passing worshippers and a temptation to small boys. The original clock mechanism is still in place in the tower, and is sometimes on view; narrow passages, stairs and ladders lead to the tower roof, with views in all directions. It is an ideal place from which to get your bearings on Rye and to appreciate the grid pattern of the streets. The neighbouring hill town of Winchelsea can be seen to the west.

The north door of the church opens directly on to the path around the square and on to Lion Street, leading down the hill towards the High Street, with the classical brick front of Peacock's School closing the view. The fifteenth-century half-timbered tea room just on the left was the birthplace of John Fletcher, Shakespeare's friend and fellow-playwright, whose father was vicar of Rye in the 1570s and eventually Bishop of London. Market Street, the right turn a short way down, was never a large market square – a reminder that Rye's main trading business was coastal and so had always been done down on the quayside. A number of late medieval houses and shops with eighteenth- and early nineteenth-century frontages face the Town Hall, which like much of Rye is small but perfectly formed. Built in 1743, it has an open arcade on the ground floor and a parapet and pretty little cupola on the roof, which is often glimpsed above the surrounding buildings.

A grisly reminder of mayoral dignity hangs in a gibbet cage inside, the skull of John Breads, executed in 1743 for murdering the mayor's brother-in-law, although Mayor Lamb himself was the intended victim. Cage and corpse were exposed on Romney Marsh, and the rest of Breads' bones were 'removed piecemeal by superstitious persons in the belief that the drinking of their infusion in water was a cure for rheumatism'. What was left of the murdered man was buried in the Clare chapel in the church, near the ornate communion table that the Lamb family, who dominated the town in the eighteenth century, had given in 1735.

The people of Rye enjoyed some Georgian prosperity, being able to reface their old houses and rebuild as much as they did. The houses along Market Street, which then becomes East Street past the lane leading back up to the cistern and Ypres Tower, reflect that minor revival. The *Flushing Inn* on the right shows all the stages of Rye's success. A fifteenth-century inn hides behind a Georgian front; and if you indulge in its fine seafood you will see a huge wall painting in the dining room executed in the 1540s, a kaleidoscope of heraldic devices, birds and beasts, royal arms and mottoes. Below, the tunnel-vaulted cellar dates from the thirteenth century, when Rye's economic success was established, and predates the destruction of the 1377 raid. Stacked with bottles, it is easy to imagine that it played an important role in the eighteenth century when smuggling in Rye was at its height.

As East Street rounds the corner a narrow alley on the right, ending in a steep flight of steps, offers a surprising glimpse of the surrounding plain. The chequered brick Georgian house beside it, with a side gate made from the thick medieval prison door, bears a plaque stating that the painter Paul Nash (1889–1946) lived there in the 1920s. Artists have congregated in and around Rye for a century, luxuriating in long low horizons and the clear light. *Rye Art Gallery*, in a much-restored half-timbered house on the cobbled Ockman Lane further down East Street, puts on important temporary shows beside its permanent collection featuring a litany of famous names associated with Rye over the past eighty years – Nash, Edward Burra (1905–76), John Piper (b. 1903), Duncan Grant (1885–1978) and Ivon Hitchens (1893–1979).

High Street, the main shopping thoroughfare, runs to left and right across the end of East Street. Stop to admire the window of the Georgian apothecary's shop curving round the

*Mermaid Street, Rye.*

left-hand corner, before turning right past mainly Victorian shop and house fronts to the old lookout position on the very edge of the town. The newer aspects of Rye – cars, modern housing, the silt plain – mingle down below. The road swings left downhill alongside a stretch of the medieval wall to the town's fortified main entrance, the Landgate. Built in the fourteenth century, the gate cuts the town off from the cause-way which until Stuart times was virtually the only way to approach Rye by land. Fortified towers flank the gate on the causeway side, and the portcullis groove and some of the machicolations through which defenders could pour boiling liquids or throw missiles on to attackers are still there.

Once through the gate, turn left under the line of the town wall to the next lane, Conduit Hill, running back up to the town. Brick Victorian housing across the road shows when Rye finally outgrew its medieval limits. The postern gate at the bottom of Conduit Hill has long since disappeared. Through it the townspeople had access to the water pumps outside the walls. The prospect of bringing water in buckets up this steep cobbled street is quite daunting.

A modern housing development on the left shows how Rye architects have successfully adopted vernacular idioms for new building within the old town; the pottery housed in the late fourteenth-century chapel of the Austin Friars further up the hill, reached by a steep stone staircase, demonstrates Rye's continuing use of old buildings for new purposes. Rye was a centre for pottery production in medieval times, and has seen a resurgence of pot-making this century. Circular house-name or number plaques, often individually decorated, are a distinctive product. You will see them all over town.

At the top of the steep rise, you emerge on to the High Street again, almost opposite the apothecary's shop. The shops and houses lining the street are full of character, and many older frontages and shop fittings survive, like the canopy and hooks of the butcher's shop on the left and the old-fashioned Mariners opposite, the model for Diva's Ye Olde Tea House in Benson's novels. Two of Rye's important buildings stand almost opposite each other half-way along the High Street. Facing up Lion Street to the church is the brick-built former grammar school, Peacock's School (now a record shop). Founded in 1636, it is a very early example of a classical style that was still largely confined to London, with giant pilasters rising through two storeys and three pedimented gables on top. Over the road, the George Hotel is the grandest of the town's many hostelries, with a front and porch of around 1720 hiding a fifteenth- or early sixteenth-century structure; beside it, and now part of the hotel, is the town Assembly Room of 1818, with first floor bow windows and a decorated plaster ceiling. (Ask in the hotel to see inside.)

Past the bookshop and the Market Road turning (which leads down to Rye's rather handsome mid-Victorian railway station), the High Street begins slowly to wind down the hill, and becomes The Mint. As elsewhere in Rye, many of the attractive houses lining both sides have become antique shops and restaurants. Some, too, are older than they seem. No. 54, although dated 1728, has the overhanging second storey of a medieval house; nos. 45–6, with a studded upper floor jettied out over the street, are more obviously fifteenth century. Passages open up on either side, like the tiny appropriately named Needles Passage on the right, and the cobbled alley up to Mermaid Street on the left.

The Mint ends with a Victorian shop, its narrow curved front turning the corner between Wish Ward and The Mint, where they emerge on to the Strand. When Rye was still a thriving sea port the Strand was the town quay, the source of roaring economic success. Rye's peak of prosperity came in the middle of the sixteenth century, when it dominated the London markets for fish. Five thousand people lived in the town, perhaps the tenth wealthiest place in England. Then Rye went into rapid decline – despite the corporation's spending ever-greater sums on trying to keep the fast-silting channels open.

Boats can still reach the quay, but they have to follow the

twisting river channel from the now distant sea. Although a fishing fleet still operates, most of the boats which come in here now are yachts. Gaunt testimony to decline in Rye's trading fortunes are the great black weatherboarded warehouses filling much of the area of the Strand. Many are in a state of decay, some empty, some housing more antique and pottery shops. A new housing development alongside self-consciously apes the warehouse style. It seems a shame that Rye, which has done so much for so long to conserve the heart of the town, has done less to preserve the maritime buildings on its edges – in their own way just as fine as the much-photographed houses on nearby Mermaid Street.

Mermaid Street starts its ascent back towards the church from a well-preserved section of the town wall that backs the Strand, with a flight of stone stairs leading to the Borough Arms pub perched on top. Modern houses, white weatherboarded like the pub, nestle underneath. An ancient stone plaque set in the wall bears the curious borough arms, three lions and three boats cut in half and spliced together. Steep and cobbled, Mermaid Street is one of the most picturesque thoroughfares of any English town, a pleasing mixture of brick, tile, wood, occasionally stone, plaster, and roughcast, adorned with roses and every manner of climbing plant. Almost every house is worthy of admiration.

The large roughcast *Jeakes House,* half-way up on the right, which is now a comfortable guest house incorporating the former Friends' Meeting House next door, was home to some of Rye's more controversial figures. Samuel Jeakes, who built the house (originally as a wool store), was a leading Puritan activist and writer during the Civil War, organizing mass walkouts from church; his son Samuel became famous as an astrologer and covered the house with zodiacal signs. Two plaques remain high up on the front. The Frewen family, of Brickwall near Northiam (see p. 131), inherited the house, which they sold in 1924 to the temperamental American poet Conrad Aiken (1889–1973), one of the literary lions attracted to Rye. Poets and authors flocked here in the 1930s – many of them, like Malcolm Lowry (1909–57), touring every pub in town – but in 1939 Aiken left Rye for America, ill and disillusioned.

As elsewhere in Rye, many Georgian doors and façades on Mermaid Street hide sixteenth-century structures. Other buildings, such as the Tudor Old Hospital and its neighbour the Mermaid Inn towards the top of the hill, are more obviously ancient, with wisteria climbing over their venerable timbers. The Mermaid trades on its reputation as a haunt of smugglers, for its thirteenth-century, vaulted cellars are said to have been an important link in the chain for bringing in contraband in Georgian times. It was Rye and the Mermaid that Rudyard Kipling described in his 'Smuggler's Song':

*Four and twenty ponies trotting through the dark,*
*Brandy for the parson, baccy for the clerk.*

Kipling (1865–1936) was one of the visitors to *Lamb House*, the home of Henry James, on the cobbled West Street at the top of the hill. The grandest single house in the town, it is named after the Lamb family who ran Georgian Rye. One of the first visitors to the Lambs' brick house when it was newly built was George I, who spent a few nights there in 1726 when his ship was forced by a great storm to seek refuge in Rye Bay. Henry James, the great American author who was almost more English than the English, fell in love with Rye in the 1890s, and acquired Lamb House in 1899. Its garden room became his 'Temple of the Muse', where he dictated new works; and the house became a focus for the remarkable literary coterie that clustered in and round Rye. That tradition continued when the Benson brothers lived here in the 1920s and 1930s. Lamb House features as the haunted setting of James's *The Turn of the Screw*, as well as being 'Mallards' in E. F. Benson's 'Tilling' novels.

For writers such as James and the Bensons the town combined romantic isolation with a handy rail service to London. The ground-floor rooms of Lamb House are shown by the National Trust as a literary shrine to Henry James, but a stray bomb in 1940 destroyed the writing temple, and only a plaque records its existence. I miss another vanished feature of Rye. Lamb House used to have one of the old street lamps fixed to it. They were quite out of the ordinary, plain bulbs on a parabolic backing lined with fragments of mirror, which added to Rye's quirky charm; large black lantern lights have now replaced them.

West Street leads back to St Mary's Square, where the pink-washed, Georgian *Old Vicarage* to the left was Henry James' first Rye home. He found it poky, although it looks big enough by today's standards. (You can try it out, for it serves teas and offers accommodation.) The range of houses along the west side of the square perfectly expresses the mixture that is Rye. The façade of the Old Custom House, which was faced with mathematical tiles – tiles made to look like brick – in the eighteenth century, conceals a fifteenth-century house contemporary with the long half-timbered house, St Anthony's, beside it.

Squeezed in among the variety of smaller houses lining the south side of the square is the remaining portion of the thirteenth-century stone-built house of the Friars of the Sack, the only dwelling to survive the French raids of the following century. Hucksteps Row, a narrow private lane (once called Fishgut Alley), runs back from the square. The novelist Radclyffe Hall (1886–1943) lived here with Una, Lady Troubridge in the inter-war years; waves of controversy broke upon them when Hall's lesbian novel *The Well of Loneliness* was condemned as obscene in 1928, and she set *The Sixth Beatitude* (1936) in this alley. Her description of 'crazy old houses with their rotting walls, their cracked weather tiles and their sagging roofs' does not match the spruced-up buildings you see today.

Down cobbled Watchbell Street, which continues the square's south side, two churches are interesting intruders among the cottages and timbered houses. The Roman Catholic church of St Anthony of Padua on the left is a scaled-down Italianate gem built in 1928, a mixture of marble and whitewash inside, a miniature Franciscan basilica outside. Down on the right the warm red-brick former Independent chapel of 1817 nudges up against a half-timbered house. Set behind leaning gate piers, it is an engagingly lop-sided composition.

There is no defined end to Watchbell Street, for it opens into space from the hilltop, looking across to Winchelsea and the rising land beyond. Steps plunge down the cliff face to the Strand below; signs of erosion are a salutary reminder that the hill on which Rye is built is far from stable; people sometimes wake to find their back gardens smaller than they were the day before.

The descent is an exciting end to the tour, as the steps precipitate you into a different world. At the bottom, nineteenth-century brick terraces face the cliff, along the road following the former shoreline which now takes the through traffic. Carry round to the left and cross the road where it is safer. The Rock Channel just to the south, hidden behind a line of huts and boatyards, represents the other Rye, the working community which visitors often forget. There are many yachts and pleasure boats, but fishing boats still anchor in the channel which joins the Rivers Brede and Tillingham to the Rother, and some of the huts along its banks sell straight from the catch – plaice, sole, shellfish. Trade of this kind once made Rye; now it hides from the gaze of visitors. But here at last the link with the sea is tangible.

Look back, and there is Rye perched high above, with the Ypres Tower guarding the seaward approach. A long flight of steps climbs the cliff to the tower, where you can enjoy again the view with which you started.

## ——— AROUND AND ABOUT RYE ———

*Rye was once on the coast. That is perhaps the single most important fact in its history; it guarded against invaders, and finally lost to the sea itself. The coast of East Sussex has always been vulnerable: the Romans came, the Saxons, the Normans and the French, and Napoleon and Hitler both based their invasion plans on this shoreline. From*

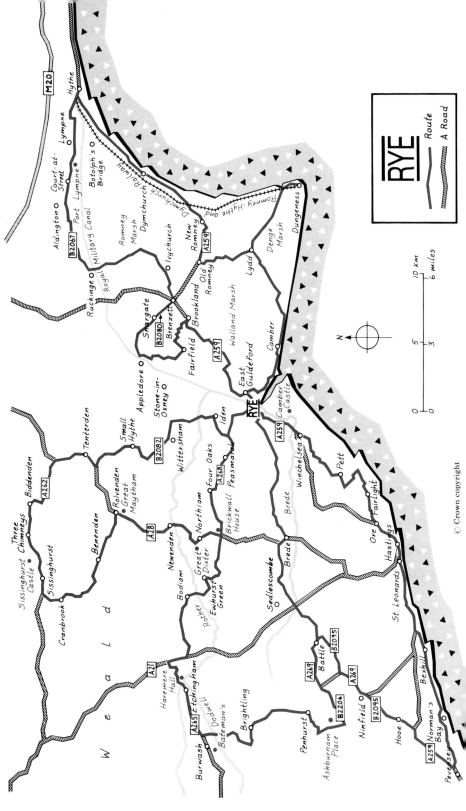

© Crown copyright

*the Kent boundary just east of Rye, the expanse of the marshland offers a watery, sometimes eerie experience, its scattered villages filled with the memories of smugglers and, more recently, of artists and writers, while the wooded landscape of the Weald above Rye presents quite a different aspect, of grand houses and gardens, small towns and secretive villages.*

## 1. SUSSEX-MAINLY-BY-THE-SEA

The first of the itineraries centred on Rye explores other defensive sites along the coast, and the seaside, before returning through the landscape of the Weald. Worth investigating fully on its own account is Rye's neighbouring hill town, Winchelsea. It is best approached on foot across the fields and marshes. For the longest, but also the most exhilarating, route to Winchelsea follow the river to Rye Harbour, a huddle of cottages, a pub, and the inshore rescue boat station, then scrunch west along the shingle banks above the shoreline. At the Harbour stands the forlorn shell of one of the long defensive line of tapering circular Martello towers, like upended flower pots, built to repel invaders during the Napoleonic Wars. Camber Castle, the curious flattened structure seen inland across the gravel and marsh where thousands of terns breed in season, belongs to an earlier phase of defence against France; it is one of many gun platforms built from Kent to Cornwall by Henry VIII. The castle may be seen at closer quarters from the footpath running from the A259 Rye–Hastings road, across the levels towards Winchelsea, starting by another Martello tower. Yet another footpath, inland from the A259, threads its way through fields where sheep graze and crosses many small streams.

Ahead of you Winchelsea rises behind the remains of its protective medieval wall. The road and paths enter Winchelsea by fortified medieval gateways: the way up the steep hill from the main road and the path across

the fields by the Pipewell Gate, and the coastal paths by the Strand Gate. Inside, Winchelsea has a genteelly ghostly air – like a garden suburb shut up for the season; 'a town in a trance' the poet Coventry Patmore (1823–96) called it. Broad manicured verges line the streets and medieval stone buildings stand beside weather-boarded Georgian and pretty neo-Georgian houses.

Founded in 1280 as a new planned town (for the Gascon wine trade), when the old town had been inundated by the sea, New Winchelsea was laid out in a chequerboard of streets that were never finished. The French raided, the harbour silted up and, as the late Stuart traveller Celia Fiennes (1662–1741) remarked, 'grass grows now where Winchelsea was, as was once said of Troy'. St Thomas' church was probably never completed and only the broad fourteenth-century aisled chancel remains, with its west end shored up; its size shows how grand it was intended to be. Inside, the niches in the walls contain fine medieval tombs and wall paintings, the windows especially nasty 1920s stained glass.

Many of Winchelsea's best medieval remains lie underground, in magnificent cellars; other items are displayed in the *Court Hall Museum* in the late medieval stone Court House almost opposite the churchyard gate, but remains of the thirteenth-century chapel of *Greyfriars* stand in gardens behind the old town wall, looking down on to the Royal Military Canal which runs from here right round Romney Marsh. Begun in 1804, the canal is one of the oddest and most useless of all the area's defensive relics: it took four years to build at prodigious cost – by which time Napoleon had given up his invasion plans.

The road south-west out of Winchelsea passes through the third of Winchelsea's medieval gateways – the New Gate – towards Wickham Manor, a late medieval stone farmhouse, the forlorn remnants of the once-conspicuous early eighteenth-century wooden windmill, and the village of Pett where hills and woodlands begin. The lane descends the ancient cliffs to the cluster of holiday cottages and bungalows of Pett Level, then rounds towards Fairlight. Still dotted about are World War II pillbox gun posts, and many a consignment of contraband has been landed in these rocky bays.

This is a coast of crumbling cliffs, and the road west into the fringes of Hastings keeps to higher ground nearly a mile inland. Joining the A259, beside Ore's fragment of a medieval church and the brash fussiness of its Victorian replacement, the main road continues into Hastings Old Town, between the cliffs topped by the ruins of the medieval castle, and the shingle beach with fishermen's boats drawn up around the distinctive, tall, black-tarred, wooden net-huts.

Hastings is famous for the battle – the one with the date every English person can remember. The battle itself took place a few miles away, but Hastings was William the Conqueror's first great foothold in 1066 and he built his first castle here. Hastings has always been a stronghold with its Wealden sandstone cliff; but as with so many places along this coast its medieval importance was eclipsed by the combined action of storms and French invaders, and Hastings slumbered, still without a proper harbour, until the discovery of the seaside in the late Georgian period.

There are two distinct sides to Has-tings. The Old Town climbs the valley between the castle hill and West Hill, a tangle of narrow streets and alleys (or 'twittens', since this is Sussex) that often turn into steep flights of steps. (A chair lift offers an easier ride to the cliff-top castle ruins with panoramic views over the town and the sea.) The mainly seventeenth- and eighteenth-century houses are a delightful confusion, and the two medieval churches and a number of Victorian churches, notably Basil Champneys' charming Our Lady Star of the Sea, stand on the main streets. The plain former Fishermen's Chapel near the beach, at Rock-a-Nore, is now an engrossing *Fishermen's Museum*, while just along the road the *Shipwreck Heritage Centre* features modern coastal radar and local wrecks, most spectacularly the *Amsterdam* which foundered in 1749 off the Hastings shore.

The newer development extending into St Leonards to the west is flatter and more regular, with well-mannered terraces and squares in best seaside taste. It begins with Pelham Crescent, a remarkable development of 1824 cut into the base of the castle cliff with the dilapidated church of St Mary-in-the-Castle as its centrepiece. The peeling façades are testimony to Hastings' current predicament, where shabby gentility rubs shoulders with the amusement arcades of the con-temporary seaside town.

Hastings sprawls, and nowhere less fortunately than in the almost continuous inter-war ribbon development to Bexhill westward along the coast. The A259, which leaves the coast to enter the town and join its inner ring road, divides the inland old town of Bexhill, of quaint nooks around the part-Norman parish church, and the post-1880s resort with its many curious echoes of the Raj. On the sea front is the De La Warr pavilion, like a white liner moored above the shingle shore.

The concrete and glass pavilion built by Erich Mendelsohn in 1935 is one of the outstanding products of the Modern Movement in Britain. A distinct odour of yesterday's cabbage may permeate the interior, but sun yourself in a deckchair on one of the balconies to get a true taste of the Sussex sea air.

From Bexhill station the route follows the line of the railway towards Eastbourne, the road at first hugging the coast, past a succession of groynes (the timber structures running out to sea to prevent erosion of the beach), fishermen, bathers, beach-huts, and picnickers in their cars, before turning at Norman's Bay over the flat level to Pevensey. It was here that the Conqueror landed in 1066. Pevensey is a narrow little village, with a number of timbered and stone houses and a part-Norman church, but it is dominated by the sprawling mass of *Pevensey Castle*. Portions of the walls, like the bastion at the head of the village street, are remains of the Roman fort of Anderida, built in the mid third century, inside which the Normans built a massive keep, defensive wall and gateway. With the silting of the coast Pevensey was gradually abandoned, to be refortified in 1587 with the threat of Spanish invasion, and again in 1940. Some of the World War II lookouts on top of the ancient keep are preserved, as part of the history of coastal defence.

The A259 leads north-east across the sheep-grazed levels towards Hooe. The left turning for Hooe just beyond the junction with the B2095 (and the inviting country charm of the Lamb Inn) passes the few survivals of a once larger settlement: the seventeenth-century Dutch-gabled Court Lodge and the church over the fields. Beyond Hooe Common the Weald begins, a land of wooded hills and vales, sticky clay, and remnants of the ancient iron industry. The B2095, which becomes the A269 for a stretch, carries on to

Battle, through the immaculately kept villages of Ninfield (where the cast-iron village stocks on the green are a relic of the iron industry) and Catsfield. Powdermill House, on the left of the road inside a sharp bend, is a vestige of another local industry, gunpowder manufacture. Above it rises the sweeping hillside where, according to tradition, the Battle of Hastings was fought in 1066: Santlache, a sandy ridge, to the Saxons; Senlac, pool of blood, to the conquering Normans.

The little town of Battle sits on top of the ridge, the road to it rising between cottages and sweeping open views to the walled enclosure of *Battle Abbey* which the Conqueror founded, and the parish church opposite. The grand fortified abbey gatehouse looking down the main street is one of the few parts to remain intact. Sections of the abbey were incorporated into a private house (now a school) after the dissolution of the monasteries by Sir Anthony Browne, Henry VIII's Master of Horse (who lies buried in a fine early Renaissance tomb in the parish church). Various monastic outbuildings and the battle site are open to the public.

The Pilgrim's Rest, the fifteenth-century timbered hall house by the Abbey gate, was as its name implies a stopping place for medieval pilgrims to Canterbury and Chichester, and is the best feature in a pleasant street, matched only by the Georgian staircase boldly spiralling round the central lightwell of the George Hotel. There are two museums near the Abbey gateway, *Battle Museum* with a reproduction of the Bayeux Tapestry telling the story of the Conquest, and a *Museum of Shopping*. Leaving the real shops of the High Street, the minor road to the right leads to Sedlescombe passing a smock-mill dated 1810. (A smock-mill is a windmill in which only the upper part revolves to allow the sails to catch the wind.) Sedlescombe is a scattered village with a pretty green beside the over-Victorianized church.

Lanes running eastwards connect the A229 at Sedlescombe with the A28 at Brede. Like most Wealden villages, Brede has a small core with scattered settlements around, where clearings for farmsteads were hacked out of the woodland. Brede church is partly late Norman, partly early Tudor; the flamboyant south chapel and chancel were built by Sir Goddard Oxenbridge, whose tomb effigy of 1537 stands in the church despite the fact that Sir Goddard reputedly ate children, and died when the children of Sussex cut him in half with a wooden saw (since metal could not harm him) – or so it is said. A sculpture in the church with a less worrying history is the Madonna carved by Clare Sheridan in 1937. She is best known for her busts of the Russian Revolutionaries, and like Sir Goddard she owned nearby Brede Place, a mainly fifteenth-century stone manor house down the narrow lanes east of the church, which has been restored after suffering substantial fire damage. The tubercular American writer Stephen Crane (1871–1900) – another member of the literary coterie that centred itself on Rye – spent his last years in Brede Place, having gained fame if not wealth from *The Red Badge of Courage*.

These lanes continue up the hill to join the B2089 heading east along the ridge back to Rye. The Wealden landscape is left behind, the distinctive skyline of Rye reappears, and the road crosses the River Tillingham and the railway line just on the edge of town.

## 2. ROMNEY MARSH

For many, one of the principal attractions of Rye is the open flat space of Romney Marsh to its east. The Marsh is low-lying land that has been reclaimed from the sea by the natural process of silting and by man-made drainage schemes since Roman times. Over the past century or so artistic and literary figures have been attracted to its odd, quiet beauty. Paul Nash for one talked about its 'strange unity of sea, sky and earth'.

That this was once a wealthy and populated area is evident from the number, scale and now-lonely beauty of the churches dotted around, often bereft of a local congregation. Exploring Romney Marsh is, however, more than an extended church-crawl, with the seaside in its many guises, the birds and the sheep, the open expanses, the associations with literature. Wartime mementoes and past eccentrics are never very far away. The Marsh is one of the wilder corners of England, yet still within reach of metropolitan life.

Immediately east of Rye the landscape opens into the flat marshland. After the A259 Folkestone road has crossed the Royal Military Canal (see p. 121), the first of the Marsh churches stands at East Guldeford, a gaunt early Tudor barn-like building. The main road then skirts the drained landscape, fields bounded by ditches and often filled with grazing sheep, to cross the Kent border just past an isolated farmhouse two miles to the north-east. Technically you are in Walland Marsh and Romney Marsh is the larger expanse beyond the ancient Rhee Wall, the Roman embankment which is still visible in some places, but the whole area is usually termed Romney Marsh. The famous Romney Marsh sheep are everywhere: hardy, suited to wet – and very tasty. (Most go for export, but some Rye restaurants and butchers serve Marsh lamb.)

After a couple more miles (and past the unlikely curiosity of the Philippine Village craft centre in the Nissen huts of a former RAF camp), the village of Brookland offers the first sign of a proper settlement. It clusters around its bizarre church – bizarre because of its lop-sidedness (due to subsidence) and especially because of the detached wooden belfry looking like three black candle-snuffers piled on top of each other. There are more rarities inside. Box pews (which many Marsh churches retain), a graveside shelter to keep the parson dry, and tithe scales and weights from the Georgian era; rarer still is the Norman lead font, decorated with the symbols of the zodiac and the labours of the months.

From Brookland, the lane northwest wriggles its way round to Fairfield where the church of St Thomas Becket sits like a brick-built ark in the fields, surrounded by sheep, swans, and dykes. The church, the key for which is held at the nearby farmhouse, was rebuilt by W. Caröe in 1913 in the same form as the wooden original and he retained its box-pews and internal woodwork. Today it stands quite alone; but archaeologists are now finding evidence of dense settlement in this area in the early Middle Ages. You may be lucky and come across a dig on your journey.

Over the level crossing the road continues to Appledore. The edge of the marsh is in sight, with the village of Stone-in-Oxney perched on top of the ancient cliff. Appledore is a pleasant village, where old red brick and tile houses cluster along the grassy width of The Street and around the church, reconstructed after French raids in 1380. The village lies on the tranquil north bank of the Royal Military Canal, which gives no sense of being designed as a defensive bulwark. The B2080 follows the canal for a short distance before veering south-east to Appledore railway station and the tiny villages of Snargate and Brenzett.

Snargate is best-remembered for its early nineteenth-century rector, Richard Barham, author of the once immensely popular *Jackdaw of Reims*

and other of his *Ingoldsby Legends*, many of which took their mystery and humour from the Marsh. Barham's picturesque church, with its leaning tower and wall-painting of a Tudor great ship, has numerous examples of a particular local Georgian feature: 'text boards', oval wooden boards with religious texts painted on them in black and gold. St Eanswith's church, just outside Brenzett, the next village, has similar text boards and a painted wooden altar reredos, although the church itself was over-restored in 1902.

Just below Brenzett, the main road follows the Rhee Wall dividing Walland and Romney Marshes. Follow the minor road from the junction of the A259 and A2070 to cross slightly drier ground to Ivychurch. Close to the crossroads, the *Brenzett Aeronautical Museum* has a permanent display of aircraft, especially parts from those which were shot down over the marshland during the Battle of Britain. At Ivychurch a few houses ring one of the grandest of the Marsh churches, ironically built soon after the Black Death, probably a major cause of the area's rapid depopulation 600 years ago.

Doglegging left and right over the B2070 the lanes pass through some of the most open stretches of Romney Marsh. Occasionally the land rises to the dizzy height of four metres; and birds fill the air, especially at migrating times. The route continues to Ruckinge, a village just across the Royal Military Canal and on the slopes that mark the edge of the Marsh. The parish church is another massive stone structure; visitors, however, are usually more interested in the south-west corner of the graveyard where a rough plank mounted on iron supports marks the grave of the Marsh's two most notorious smugglers, William and James Ransley, who were hanged in 1800 for highway robbery.

From Ruckinge it is barely a mile

east to Bilsington, but the change in the landscape is already marked as the land rises and becomes distinctly wooded. Overlooking the Marsh below the village crossroads, the crumbling obelisk put up in 1835 to commemorate Sir William Cosway MP still stands despite having been struck by lightning in the 1960s. In 1894 Ford Madox Ford (1873–1939), chronicler of the literati who lived in and around Rye (and one of the most prodigious of literary liars and embroiderers), bought a cottage in Bonnington. He moved to nearby Aldington in 1896 (and a few years later to Winchelsea, to be closer to Henry James, his literary idol). Joseph Conrad (1857–1924) moved to Aldington briefly in 1908 from Hythe; twenty years later Noël Coward (1899–1973) bought a farmhouse here, which he filled with the great and the not-so-good for weekends.

Many ghosts throng this road. At Court-at-Street $1\frac{1}{2}$ miles further on, a pathway to the cliff above the Marsh passes the ruined chapel where the Holy Maid of Kent, a girl called Elizabeth Barton, attracted pilgrims in the 1520s with her ecstatic religious visions. She became one of the first martyrs of the English Reformation, for prophesying Henry VIII's doom should he marry Anne Boleyn. Another mile along, *Port Lympne*, where the colourful John Aspinall has established his Country Park Zoo, was one of the grandest inter-war houses, and Sir Philip Sassoon entertained here on a lavish scale. His house was an exotic fantasy: a hundred rooms, a courtyard from Spain, windows of alabaster, a *trompe l'œil* tent by Rex Whistler, and a showpiece garden. Restoration work has reinstated parts of the house's extraordinary decoration, while among other animals rhino and buffalo roam.

In the village of Lympne itself, the turning to the right leads to a lesser fantasy, *Lympne Castle* – really a medieval fortified house – which was restored and extended at the beginning of this century. The wartime observation post at the top surveys the expanse of the Marsh, and looks down on the few remaining walls of Stutfall Castle, the Roman fort that guarded the port of Lemanis. Pictures in some of Lympne Castle's rooms show the Victorian excavations, and a steep path through the fields leads past the chunks of Roman masonry. Lympne church, just beside the castle, bears out local smuggling tales, since a secret cellar has been found under one of the pews.

East of Lympne the steep lane from Shepway Cross descends on to the Marsh, bridging the Royal Military Canal on its last few miles before reaching the sea at Hythe. Just below the pub and houses at Botolph's Bridge a level crossing takes the road over the private line of the *Romney, Hythe and Dymchurch Railway*. It is a miniature railway, with a 15-inch gauge. Completed in 1927, it runs from Hythe to Dungeness, and was the brainchild of another of the Marsh's eccentrics, the millionaire Captain J. E. P. Howey. The open carriages are packed in the holiday season with exuberant children, and adults who, like Captain Howey, never quite grew out of model trains. In 1940 the railway was used as the most bizarre part of the coastal defence scheme, ferrying ammunition up and down the coast.

The military still use the coastal ranges at Hythe, beyond the point where the minor road joins the main coast road and turns left to Dymchurch. Although the road runs along the shore, views of the sea are usually hidden by the mass of the sea wall. The need for the wall is evident from the signs of flooding in places where the sea defences failed during the great storms of January 1990. Most of the coast from here to Lydd is a long line of bungalows and holiday houses.

The little town of Dymchurch attracted an artistic community at the beginning of this century, of which Paul Nash was the principal member. Russell Thorndike, brother of Sybil, used it as the basis for his Dr Syn novels, stories of smuggling derring-do, which were a great success in the inter-war years. In odd-numbered years there is a 'Day of Syn' August bank holiday carnival in Dymchurch to keep his memory alive. The holiday trade has grown in Dymchurch over the past century, but there are vestiges left of the old village, notably the eighteenth-century *Dymchurch Court Room* for the administration of Romney Marsh, just south of the part-Norman, part-1821 church. The *Martello Tower* at the southern end of Dymchurch is in the care of English Heritage and open to the public. One of 74 of these towers defending the south and east coasts, its sheer walls, raised entrance and gun emplacements show how seriously invasion threats were taken.

The miniature station of the miniature railway is just west of the tower, beside a lane that heads back inland towards St Mary in the Marsh. A few cottages, the Star Inn, and its little church on a grassy mound make up the village; a simple wooden grave marker and a plaque inside the untouched part-Norman church, commemorate E. Nesbit, the Edwardian children's author whose rather bohemian life ended in a seaside cottage at St Mary's Bay in 1924. And more or less opposite, Noël Coward first discovered the beauties of the Marsh in 1921, when he rented the cottage by the pub and made a reverential visit to Miss Nesbit, his life-long favourite author.

Two miles south is New Romney, the most substantial town in the Marsh. A broad main street, some handsome buildings including an early Georgian assembly room, and a huge parish church with its soaring Norman tower, all speak of the town's former glory. One of the original Cinque Ports, Romney moved from its old site, to the shore where the River Rother reached the sea, in the twelfth century; but the great storm of 1287, which changed so many features along this coast, shifted the Rother's course so far that thereafter it emerged at Rye. New Romney quickly faded. The entrance to the wide, magnificent church with its great Norman tower and nave is some way below the road level, evidence of how much material was deposited in 1287.

Old Romney lies some two miles further inland, beside the A259; its church, reached up a side lane, is one of the prettiest and finest of the Marsh churches, with its pink-painted box pews (a legacy of filming *Dr Syn* here), and its medieval font, an outstanding piece of stonework. Left from the village crossroads, the B2076 turns south to Lydd. The gaunt ruins of another church stand in a field to the right of the road, beneath the pylons taking electricity from the nuclear power station at Dungeness.

The road reaches the little town of Lydd opposite the parish church, its tower, one of the tallest in Kent, a landmark for miles around. The tower pinnacles were added by Cardinal Wolsey (c. 1475–1530), Henry VIII's Chancellor, when he was the (absentee) rector. The church incorporates part of a tenth-century basilica. Lydd has a few fine houses, beyond which stretch the great shingle banks of Dungeness.

The minor road crosses the Denge Marsh on to the wide grey expanse, ending in the coastal settlement which partly consists of former railway carriages converted into little homes – another of the region's eccentricities. Dungeness's three lighthouses stand at the edge of the shingle. Only the base of the 1792 light survives, as a circular house, but the towers of both the 1904 light and the new 1959 light, made of pre-stressed concrete, rise high into the air. The spiral stair of *Dungeness Old Lighthouse* leads to dramatic views. Close to, there is the huge lens itself; and further off, electricity pylons stride away from the massive bulk of the nuclear power station, the shingle stretches into the marsh beyond, and the deep channel in the sea lies just off-shore so that shipping passes surprisingly close by.

Dungeness is the end of the road; on some days, it feels like the end of the world. Returning to Lydd, at first alongside the miniature railway, the minor road to the left from the village crossroads runs between the shingle (and the army firing ranges) and the unromantically named Jury's Gut Sewer, to the sandy coast and Camber. Fine sandy beaches – the largest on the south coast – extend for almost a mile out at low tide; in high season, the bungalow-owners and Pontin's holiday campers may rule the sands, but at other times seclusion is easily found. The road continues round on the eastern side of the Rother back to East Guldeford and Rye.

## 3. THE WEALD, WOOD AND IRON

The Weald is sandwiched between the North and South Downs running through the south-eastern counties. Its name is simply Old English for wood, and woodland is still one of the abiding features of this landscape. The Sussex Weald extends north-west of Rye, a swooping landscape of clay vales, woods, parkland, scattered settlements and industrial remains

Initially the route retraces the end of the first itinerary, west from Rye on the B2089 down to Brede, and then across to Sedlescombe and Battle. At the upper end of Battle, where the main roads part, the A269 forks left through the modern fringes of the town. At the next junction in the road a handsome stone lodge marks the former extent of the estate of the Ashburnham family, principal landowners in this area for centuries. Continuing ahead from the next sharp bend in the A269, the B2204 runs past the Ashburnham parkland, with views ahead to the South Downs and glimpses of the sea. Although Ashburnham Place, down the long drive to the right, is private, access is permitted to the church beside the house and the grandiose stable buildings. The park, laid out in the eighteenth century by the renowned landscape gardener, Lancelot 'Capability' Brown (1716–83), was devastated in the 1987 hurricane, when many old trees were lost; the damage is slowly being made good. Only a fragment remains of the great Victorian house, and a 1960s Anglican prayer centre stands on its site. Most of the parish church was rebuilt in 1665 in a Perpendicular style by John Ashburnham, great friend of Charles I. He and his brother are buried here, John in a tomb as old-fashioned as his church, William in one of the earliest English examples of baroque sculpture, its awkward depiction of grief simultaneously poignant and absurd.

The lane running off the B2204 west of the park leads into an area of scattered houses and farms in the woods of the Weald, where many vestiges remain of the iron industry that was so important to the area until the late eighteenth century. Left from the houses at Brownbread Street (a name that may refer to nodules of iron slag) the narrow lane continues to the cottages at the former water-driven iron forge. The track opposite follows the brook, red with the iron it carries, upstream through the woods once used for charcoal burning to the site of the blast furnace and the sequence of ponds that fed it. Masonry remains of the furnace may be found hidden among the undergrowth near the cottages. In this perfect country scene it is hard to imagine noisy industrial activity, the casting of cannon and firebacks, that went on here two or three hundred years ago. This site was the last iron works in Sussex, finally closing in the 1820s.

Beyond the forge, the hamlet of Penhurst is perfection, with the stone, early Stuart manor house reflected in its pond, the wood and brick farm buildings, and the little-touched church. The church's seventeenth-century internal woodwork survives, including panelling and box pews. The narrow lane past it continues for three miles, crossing the B2096, to the village of Brightling, set on a hill among trees. The road, with a wealth of timber and stone houses beside it, skirts the high bank of the churchyard, in which the most conspicuous feature is a large

stone pyramid. This is but the first of the eccentric follies of 'Mad Jack' Fuller, the local landowner whose family had been made wealthy from the iron industry. He died in 1834 and had built this as his tomb in 1810. The local story that he was buried sitting in a chair holding a bottle of claret has been disproved by excavation! Cast-iron gravestones are to be seen in the churchyard and the porch.

Fuller's memorial bust inside Brightling church is one of many plaques and tombs filling the interior, while the large barrel organ that he donated is still in full working order up in the west gallery. Fuller was a friend and patron of the painter J. M. W. Turner (1775–1851), and a great builder of follies; many exotic legends have attached themselves to him and his buildings. The area is worth exploring, by car and on foot, to view them – the

*The beach at Hastings.*

129

classical Temple and the Sugar Loaf mock spire in Brightling Park south of the church, the great obelisk and the observatory to the west.

The road that runs north between 'Mad Jack's' obelisk and observatory, alongside commercially exploited woods, reaches Burwash, one of the handsomest of all Wealden village streets, where weatherboarded, brick and tile-hung houses jostle behind the raised pavements and trees. The wide part-Norman church contains the oldest known cast-iron memorial slab, from the fourteenth century, and a plaque to Rudyard Kipling's son John, killed in action in World War I. Kipling's house, *Bateman's*, is situated just to the south-west of the village down a lane off the A265, a stone-built edifice of 1634 with a handsome porch and projecting south wing, set amid lawns and gardens running down to the mill stream and mill. The National Trust keeps the house much as Kipling left it; beyond is Pook's Hill, as in *Puck of Pook's Hill*, Kipling's famous collection of short stories which were mainly set in this Wealden landscape. Kipling lived at Bateman's from 1904 until his death some thirty years later.

The main road north-east from Burwash runs along the ridge between the Rother and Dodwell valleys to Etchingham, where the two rivers meet. The church to the left of the road is almost entirely late fourteenth century, founded by Sir William de Echyngham (who is buried under one of a notable set of memorial brasses). The misericords are carved with foxes preaching and other examples of the exuberance of the Middle Ages. A mile to the east, *Haremere Hall*, a Jacobean manor house, lies just off to the right. Shaped gables top its projecting wings, and the house is set above terraced gardens. The interior is an interesting mixture of original and brought-in fixtures; outside, the Hall has become

a heavy horse centre where farming methods of the past are demonstrated.

A little further east the A265 joins the main London–Hastings road; a mile south on the A21 signposts point to the left towards *Bodiam Castle*.

The approach to Bodiam is memorable, as the road descends from the wooded ridge above the Rother to the neat little village and its castle. This is one of the most satisfying of all English castles, a perfect square with tall circular corner towers, surrounded by a broad moat. It was planned as a whole in 1385 (in the wake of those French raids which had devastated so many churches and towns on the coast). The roofless ruin was saved from becoming a stone quarry by 'Mad Jack' Fuller of Brightling, and restored a little over a century later in 1919 by Lord Curzon, who presented it to the nation.

The narrow bridge over the River Rother (which was once navigable up to here, hence the danger of attack) offers a magnificent view back towards the castle with the rising ground behind. Ahead, the lanes run south-east to Ewhurst Green, where the church, tile-hung and timber houses and the oast-houses with their characteristic cowls make a handsome picture, and then through the woods up the steep valley side to the B2165 that runs east along another of the Wealden ridges. Dog-legging left and right over the A28, we continue to the scattered parish of Beckley. Many of the placenames around recall the old woodland industries: Beckley Furnace, Weaver's Farm, Watermill, Tanhouse Farm. Who can tell how Glass Eye Farm got its name?

At Four Oaks – a name that seems superfluous in the wooded landscape – the B2165 joins the A268 heading back through the woods towards Rye. At Rye Foreign the land opens up again and the road then follows the ancient causeway that was at one time the only dry route into the town. Even longer ago, this was part of the coastline and the higher ground was the cliff. Beyond the wide grassy street of Playden with its very late Norman church, the modern fringes of Rye appear (with some houses by fashionable Edwardian architects), running down to the town walls and the Landgate, over the railway bridge.

## 4. HOUSES AND GARDENS

Some of the finest and most influential modern gardens are within easy reach of Rye, and they feature in this last itinerary which takes in many of the characteristic types of landscape found in previous tours: Weald, marsh, hill and vale.

The first stage retraces the steps of the previous itinerary through Playden, Rye Foreign, Peasmarsh and Beckley. Just past Beckley's Norman church and rather grand early Georgian brick-built Church House, take the fork to the right. The woods on the left suddenly open just before a main road junction to reveal the large timber-framed front of *Brickwall House* set behind its grand entrance gates. Now a school, this was for generations the home of the Frewen family whose influence was felt widely (not least in Rye where they were major property owners). Family portraits spanning four hundred years line the walls, and some grand rooms, especially the Jacobean drawing room with its plasterwork ceiling, are on show when the house is open on summer weekends. The Frewens are remembered in the church: in their monuments, including the Victorian family mausoleum, and in the communion rail given in 1638 by Thankful Frewen. (He and his brother Accepted had a Puritan clergyman father, hence their names.) Northiam is rich in white weather-boarded houses so well kept they are positively dazzling on a bright day. The village

museum is almost opposite the church, and the left fork beyond it leads eventually to *Great Dixter*.

To gardening enthusiasts, that name is magical. The home of writer and plantsman Christopher Lloyd who also runs a nursery behind the main garden, Great Dixter was built in 1910 for Nathaniel Lloyd (Christopher's father) by Edwin Lutyens (1869–1944). Lutyens took the late fifteenth-century house, returned it to its original form as a hall house with raised solar at one end, and added a sympathetic new wing in a similar brick and timber style. Incorporated at the back is another timbered hall house which Lutyens and Lloyd found near Benenden a few miles north, and had transported back to Northiam in pieces on a cart. They paid the farmer in whose field it had been mouldering a few pounds! Lutyens, in consultation with Lloyd and with Gertrude Jekyll (1843–1932), laid out an exciting garden, part formal, part wild. The Lloyds have developed it ever since, and it is full of surprises and contrasts, like the great border which is a riot of summer colour facing the rarely mown grass of the orchard meadow.

The car park has a wide view over the valley of the Rother, and the lanes lead back to the A28 which crosses the river (and the border with Kent) by the early Georgian stone bridge. Newenden church immediately on the opposite bank contains one of the most impressive carved Norman fonts in the county; otherwise the church is unimpressive, because much of it was demolished in 1700. Above Newenden and the junction with the A268, the A28 dips and rises again towards Rolvendon and Tenterden. On the right just before Rolvenden is *Great Maytham*, built by Lutyens at much the same time as he was working at Great Dixter, a new house in his formal 'Wrenaissance' style for H. J. Tennant.

An earlier house of 1721 is incorporated in the new building, reached
up a grand avenue through a massive
entrance lodge from the road side.
Great Maytham has since been converted into apartments; the public
areas and the Lutyens walled gardens
are open occasionally. Lutyens also
designed the village working men's
club (in his neo-vernacular style), and
various Tennant memorials in Rolvenden church. The church, that
stands on a mound at the south end of
the pretty, mainly white weather-
boarded street, is otherwise filled
with monstrous nineteenth-century
furnishings. The antiques shop at
no. 63 features a collection of historic cars, especially three-wheeled
Morgans, which fits the ambience of
the place quite perfectly.

The left turn from Rolvenden High
Street, the B2086, passes two windmills – the second still working – on
the way to Benenden. The village and
great house were all built in the middle
of the nineteenth century for the Earl
of Cranbrook. As with other parishes
in the area, settlement had previously
been scattered; the Old Manor House
to the left of the main village street
is but one example of the substantial
timber Wealden yeoman's houses
found throughout Benenden parish.
George Devey (1820–1886), famous for
his estate cottages at Penshurst Place
in Kent, built most of the new village,
and David Brandon designed the grand
Elizabethan-style house, now a girls'
public school famous for having the
Princess Royal among its old girls. The
eighteenth-century *Benenden Walled
Garden* in its grounds specializes in
growing and selling old varieties and
fragrant plants.

A mile or so along the road, the lane
to the right past the telephone box
leads through orchards into Cran
brook, probably the prettiest small
town in Kent. Cranbrook is set on a

hill, but one of its most prominent features of all is not on the hilltop but
beside the road from Benenden – the
great smock windmill, Union Mill,
over 70 feet tall, that seems to sail
over everything. Beyond it, Cranbrook
opens up with its two principal streets,
filled with interesting houses exhi-
biting all the local features: tile-
hanging, weatherboarding, brick and
timber-studding. The early nineteenth-
century chapel on Stone Street has a
timber front grooved to look like stone.

Cranbrook parish church lies at the
foot of the main hill, a building dating
mainly from the later fifteenth century
with some very important early Tudor
stained glass that managed to escape
the attention of the reformers. The
pompous family monuments inside are
leavened by the memorial to the Victorian artist Thomas Webster (1800–
86), shown in his painting smock with
his brushes in his hand. The corner of
the churchyard is the setting for Cranbrook School, founded in 1576; its earliest building is the brick-built 1720s
School House.

On the northern edge of Cranbrook,
where the B2189 joins the A229, the
Willesley Hotel on the left, a mixture of
elegant Georgian and wilful Victorian
(the latter designed by Norman Shaw
(1831–1912)), and the half-timbered
fifteenth-century Old Wisley on the
on the right, both combine romance and
severity in their individual way. Vita
Sackville-West (1892–1962), in her
long poem *The Garden*, exhorted that
'Gardens should be romantic, but
severe', and that was the approach she
and her husband Harold Nicolson used
in the garden they created in the 1930s
and 1940s at Sissinghurst Castle, two
miles east of the A229–A262 junction
above Cranbrook. Many regard *Sissinghurst Castle Garden* as the greatest
of all modern gardens. The Tudor
tower, almost all that remains of the
Elizabethan buildings which belonged

to Sir Richard Baker (c. 1568–1645), provides the ideal vantage point for the gardens. They are a succession of 'rooms' divided by hedges and walls, many with a theme of colour or plant, and connected by paths. Last to be planted and most famous of all is the White Garden, installed in 1946, where every plant's foliage or flowers are white – romantic and severe.

The A262 continues east from the long castle drive through the hamlet of Three Chimneys, with a pub (renowned for its food) and a few cottages. The name is supposed to be a corruption of Trois Chemins, 'three ways'; the stone and timber pub certainly has more than three chimneys. Beyond lies Biddenden, a near-perfect village street of half-timber, weatherboard and brick, the legacy of its one-time importance as a weaving centre. The church, considerably enlarged in the fifteenth and sixteenth centuries when Biddenden was probably at the height of its success, contains a sequence of Elizabethan memorial brasses showing men each with successions of wives.

The tall church tower was perhaps designed to invite comparison with that of Tenterden, four miles further along the A262; if so, the comparison is in Tenterden's favour, for its tower, built in the second half of the fifteenth century, soars, sharing with Lydd (see above) the distinction of being the finest on a Kent parish church. Tenterden's tower dominates the whole town, where many of the houses are faced with the mathematical tiles that are such a typical feature of Sussex and west Kent. A variety of Georgian houses line the main streets, with a few older, occasionally half-timbered, houses squeezed between them.

From the south end of the town, by the Victorian gatehouse to Heronden Hall and its park, the B2082 runs down to Small Hythe. Hythe means port, and although it is still some way inland,

this was once marsh and water; Small Hythe looks across to the Isle of Oxney, a tongue of raised ground from which it is separated by a maze of ditches, dykes and sewers.

It is a charming village, where two half-timbered houses stand beside the small, red-brick parish church, all built around 1517 after a fire had engulfed the village the year before. *Smallhythe Place*, the right-hand house of the pair, was the home of the great actress Ellen Terry until her death in 1928. Her memorabilia are displayed inside, featuring many members of the local artistic community who appear elsewhere in these pages.

Below Smallhythe Place, the road crosses the Reading Sewer, last vestige of the medieval port channel, and begins to rise on to the Isle of Oxney. Wittersham is a characteristically scattered parish. Its church and surrounding cottages stand on the side road leading south, opposite the pub. Lutyens was here too, for he designed the big house opposite the church in his neo-Georgian style for Hon. Alfred Lyttleton in 1906. Back on the main road, where it turns sharply right to descend the cliff and cross the Rother, the Stocks Windmill, dated 1781, is one of the proudest Kentish post-mills (a windmill whose whole body turns on a post to enable it to catch the wind).

The River Rother marks the county boundary; below it, the land begins to rise again at Iden. Housing estates beside the main road mask the little parish church, almost hidden down the side road to Rye Foreign, with some rare statuary and medieval graffiti, and a modern mural painting by Hans Feibusch (exhibited at the Festival of Britain). Iden church has a place in the record books as well: two rectors spanned the years 1807–1924.

Then from Iden church, the lane to Rye Foreign leads back to the A268; and so, through Playden, to Rye.

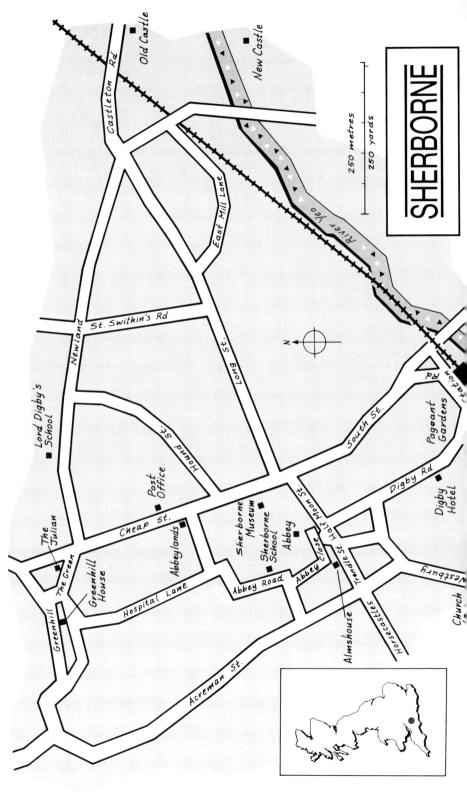

# 6
# SHERBORNE

Dorset

*When I was eight years old, I had a school friend whose
father owned a tea room in Sherborne. Its low-ceilinged
dining room offered not only one of the best views in the
whole town of the honey-coloured Abbey church, but also
all the cakes and fizzy drinks a small boy could want. Bliss.
Schoolchildren are one of the most distinctive features of
this small, pretty town on the Dorset–Somerset border
where the population falls by about a fifth outside term
time. Sherborne School itself, the public school within the
precincts of the former Benedictine abbey, is but the best-
known of the eleven schools in the town. The children's
presence adds something, but even without them,
Sherborne would still be one of the more attractive of the
West Country market towns that built their prosperity on
cloth, slumbered through the nineteenth century, and now
have a substantial retirement population. With them,
Sherborne has a vitality and a cultural life much greater
than one would expect for a place of only 8000 people.
The Abbey church at the town's heart is among the finest
of all English parish churches. Around it are streets of
mainly stone-built houses and cottages, some almost rural,
others decidedly sophisticated and urban, while many shop
fronts and fittings survive from the last two centuries.
Remains of Roman and Romano-British buildings show
a continuity of settlement that is evidence of Sherborne's
importance as a local market and a religious centre. The
town also lies in a most scenically varied region, the land
where Thomas Hardy's characters fought the inexorable
workings of Fate. Some, in* The Woodlanders *or* A Group
of Noble Dames, *even wrestled with Fate in Sherton Abbas,
alias Sherborne itself. The great Elizabethan adventurer
Sir Walter Ralegh (1554–1618), at one time lord of the
manor, had no such truck with Fate – he called Sherborne
'Fortune's Fold'.*

Sherborne Abbey is the place to begin: it can claim, justi-
fiably, to be Dorset's finest building. It sits to one side of the
open green, a large, cathedral-like church with transepts and
a central crossing tower, built in the local Ham Hill stone.
Until 1884 the south side of the green was blocked by the late
Stuart town hall; the hall was then demolished, the Abbey
churchyard cleared and grassed over, and a high memorial
cross erected to commemorate George Digby Wingfield Digby
of Sherborne Castle, who had underwritten the restoration
of the Abbey (and whose family were, and remain, important
local landowners).

This is one of the most important early Christian sites in
England, for St Aldhelm (c. 640–709) established his cathedral
here in 705, from where he controlled a vast diocese running
from Wiltshire to Cornwall. It remained a cathedral until the
Norman Conquest, when the bishop's see was removed to the
Wiltshire hilltop settlement of Old Sarum and then finally to
New Sarum, now better known as Salisbury, in 1227. Sherborne became a Benedictine monastery, and a glorious new
abbey church superseded the humbler cathedral.

There is evidence of at least three phases of building: from
the Saxon, Norman and 15th-century Perpendicular periods.
The earliest surviving parts are the Saxon west wall and the
north-west doorway which once led into the parish church of
All Hallows, built on to the Abbey's west end. Remains of the
Norman building include some of the external buttresses, the
south porch and the arches of the crossing tower. The wealth
of the Abbey allowed the monks to rebuild parts of it in the
new Perpendicular style from about 1430 onwards.

The most striking thing about the Abbey interior is the
high fan vaulting spanning the nave and chancel. Fan vaults
are among England's most exciting, and beautiful, con-
tributions to Gothic architecture, and Sherborne's chancel
can claim to have one of the first large-scale examples of this
work, begun in the 1430s. The vaults in the nave disguise very
cleverly the fact that each of the arcades is out of position in
relation to the other, perhaps because they are based on the
positions of the Saxon originals. There are over one hundred
highly coloured bosses covering the junctions of the ribs,
with subjects ranging from heraldic emblems to monsters.

As in so many places where churches were used by both
the townspeople and monks, relations between them were
often strained; during riots in 1437, the parish priest fired a
flaming arrow into the new fan vault, and part of the abbey
church burned down. The red scorch marks can still be seen
on the choir wall by the tower. At the dissolution of the
monastery a century later, it was acquired by Sir John
Horsey, one of Henry VIII's Privy Councillors, who sold the
church to the town. All Hallows was demolished and,

unusually, the abbey church became the parish church. In most towns, such as Glastonbury, abbeys were dismantled with alacrity; in others only part of the church was retained and the rest allowed to go to ruin, as at Malmesbury.

Sherborne Abbey is also remarkable for the quality of its furnishings and monuments. The choir stalls incorporate fifteenth-century misericords, which range in subject matter from wives beating their husbands to Christ sitting in majesty on a rainbow. In the little chapel on the east of the north transept Sir John Horsey lies beside his son in a delightful tomb crowned with horses' heads in a pun on the family name. The chapel beside the south transept is almost filled with the tall Tudor six-poster tomb of John and Joan Leweston. Sir Walter Ralegh's private pew once filled the rest of the chapel. One of his successors at Sherborne Castle, John Digby, third (and last) Earl of Bristol, is commemorated in the south transept by a great baroque monument of 1698 where three life-sized statues are framed by stagily weeping *putti*. Tombs of Sherborne abbots, some of the earliest memorial effigies in England, line the choir aisles which lead to the Lady Chapel at the east end, which was rebuilt in the 1920s. Since 1550, it and its flanking chapels had been part of Sherborne School; the south-eastern chapel, for example, was the head-master's bedroom for centuries until it was reincorporated into the Abbey.

From the south porch, turn left alongside the church, skirting the east end where rows of mid sixteenth-century shields bear the coats of arms of local families. Beneath the Georgian sundial the once sadly decayed arms of Edward VI (1537–53), who founded Sherborne School in 1550, have been replaced by a modern copy.

A little further along on the right is the *Sherborne Museum*. Local items on display are of more than just local interest, ranging from decorative wallpapers and plaster from town houses to reproductions of some of the exquisitely illuminated pages of the medieval Sherborne Missal of *c.* 1400.

At the end of the passageway a charmingly dilapidated ancient precinct arch opens into the small paved market area, where in Hardy's *The Woodlanders* Giles Winterbourne would have stood selling his apple trees. The most striking building here is the hexagonal early Tudor stone Conduit, one of Sherborne's most unusual and memorable monuments, with open tracery on every side. Originally the monks' washing place, the Conduit was moved here from the Abbey precinct after the Reformation. It has in its time been every-thing from a public fountain to a police phone box.

The timber and stone building housing a row of shops in Half Moon Street, round the corner to the right, is another rare survival. It was built by the parish in around 1530 with shops below and a parish room for entertainments and meetings running the length of the first floor. The row is completed with late Georgian shops and the public weighbridge house on the corner, its early Victorian weighing machine inside still intact.

If these are rare survivals, the buildings at the southwest corner of Abbey Green are rarer still. A little cloister courtyard enclosed by a low curving wall, with a range of stone buildings running behind, forms the charmingly reticent entrance to the *Almshouse of Saints John the Baptist and John the Evangelist*, founded in 1437. Doubled in size in 1868, it is still an almshouse, taking in both men and women. Moreover, the original buildings, completed in 1448, are still in use. In the tiny chapel, partitioned off from the hall by its fifteenth-century wooden screen, is Sherborne's prized treasure, a late fifteenth-century Flemish altar triptych. The exquisite central panel shows God the Father looking down on a medieval town where a crowd witnesses the raising of Lazarus.

From the almshouse, a path skirts part-medieval cottages fronting the Abbey Green to the kissing gate west of the Abbey. Beyond is Sherborne School, one of many which originated in the wave of educational foundations around 1550. Sherborne expanded enormously in the first half of the nineteenth century, in common with other public schools under vigorous, reforming headmasters, but the core is the former monastic precinct of Sherborne Abbey, reached through a gateway crowned by Edward VI's arms. The old school was based in the leftmost corner of the present gravelled court, at the Abbey's east end, but subsequently annexed buildings to its north incorporating the monks' cloister, the guest hall and the abbot's chapel. Before the school took them over, the range housed one of Sherborne's eighteenth-century silk mills. Through the passageway in the far corner, there is a tiny garden behind the east end of the Abbey, with the arms of Edward VI again emblazoned over the doorway, set there when Old School House was built in 1608.

Abbey Road runs on beyond the main gatehouse. Where it meets Cheap Street, Abbeylands, the building on the left, has a sixteenth-century half-timbered frontage. It is possible to see just how it was fitted together, since the timbers are carved with a sequence of Roman numerals to help the builders – as if they came out of a kit. The doorway, dated 1649, was added later.

To the left up Cheap Street, the shops on either side often occupy seventeenth-century cottages and eighteenth-century town houses, and many have original Georgian or Victorian shop fronts, while the successful little shopping arcade of Swan Yard across the road from Abbeylands occupies the Georgian outbuildings of the former Swan Inn. The Post Office, a mid nineteenth-century town house with a beautifully finished Ham stone façade, is the centrepiece of the street. Watch out too for the artists' shop at no. 12, with a shutter groove in its Victorian shop window, the 1880s fish market and the 1920s dairy shop just beyond. The street's oldest frontage is Palmer's hairdressers, a late medieval timber-framed house jettied over the street and still boasting its original doorway.

Past the impressive white, double bow-fronted Regency house opposite, the office for the Digby Estates, the road divides around three sixteenth-century buildings standing together. The first was refronted in brick in the eighteenth century, but has kept its original windows and steeply sloping roofs; the half-timbered upper storey of the central house projects on carved brackets. The third (and earliest) building, The Julian, is at the far end. Originally a hospice for the Abbey, this stone-built early Tudor house has a curious square bow window rising through three floors, and a triangular 'splash-back' stone on the street corner, to prevent public nuisances and indecencies.

This short row may be seen to best advantage from the triangle of The Green, up the left-hand road. The school boarding house in the island between the two roads was once the Angel Inn, and still carries the inscription 'Licensed to let post horses' on its Tuscan-columned porch. Thatched stone cottages alongside face the late Georgian brick fronts and pretty first floor bow windows of the houses and shops rounding the corner to Greenhill House, a wealthy clothier's residence built in 1607, and the only substantial Stuart town house in Sherborne. Beneath the Georgian porch original three-storey bay windows flank a nail-studded door.

Greenhill, part of the A30, forms the north side of The Green. To the east, opposite the end of an elegant line of eighteenth-century ashlared houses punctuated by the solidly Victorian Gothic front of The Priory, a narrow lane runs through the yard of the George Inn and under its archway to rejoin Cheap Street beside The Julian. There is little in the Georgian and Victorian exterior of the George to show that it too is early sixteenth-century, but there are original beams with carved bosses and a Tudor fireplace in the public bar.

Where the lane joins Cheap Street, take Newland which runs east towards the castle. Despite its name, it is a long time since this street was new – over 750 years in fact. It came into existence through the initiative of the Bishop of Salisbury, Henry de Poore, who established a separate borough in 1227 as a money-making venture; before this Sherborne itself had had no special urban status. Freemen were allowed to settle in the new borough with some privileges, but not enough to be able to escape the power of the bishop who dominated Newland and Sherborne from Sherborne Old Castle, his fortified residence.

On the way to the Castle, at the Cheap Street end of Newland, you pass Sherborne House, Lord Digby's School for Girls, hiding behind a tree-fringed wall. This handsome provincial baroque house was built as a town house for the Portman family in 1720 by Benjamin Bastard, a member of the family of builder-architects who transformed Blandford Forum, near which the Portmans had their main seat (see p. 155). The ceiling and walls of the staircase hall, viewable with permission, were decorated by the great baroque artist Sir James Thornhill (c. 1675–1734). After 1850 the house was the home of the celebrated actor Charles Macready (1793–1873) – 'the Great Macready' – who sponsored the Literary Institute that met in the outbuildings to the left of the main house, which now house the town youth club.

Where Newland widens at the junction with Hound Street, another green marks the former borough market place, which had a cross where the telephone box is now. The seventeenth-century Newland House, on the south side, was once an inn, and its pretty late Georgian pilastered doorcase dates from this part of its history.

Another link with Bishop Poore is the house at no. 101 Newland. Larger than most in the street, with a substantial pair of doors leading to what was once the town's main bakery, this house has recently been discovered to be an important and rare early fourteenth-century timber-framed hall, probably built as the administrative centre for the borough and the bishop's local estates, and given its present façade some time in the seventeenth century.

The ruins of *Sherborne Old Castle* lie at the end of Newland, reached by a lane which crosses the railway line to Castleton. Castleton was itself a borough, with all the attendant privileges, but even in the Middle Ages was probably not much larger than it is today – just a few houses and a church. It must have been one of the very smallest of all English boroughs. Nothing survives of the medieval church; the present church, dating from 1715, still has its Georgian furnishings. The entrance to the Old Castle lies beyond the church and the short row of pretty, rose-covered seventeenth- and eighteenth-century houses opposite. Although only parts of the castle built by Bishop Roger de Caen, regent to Henry I (1069–1135), survive, what remains – sections of the curtain wall, the gatehouse, and of one of the principal central buildings – suggests that this was more of a defensible palace than a full-scale fortress. Seat of the Bishops of Salisbury until the reign of Elizabeth I (1533–1603), the castle was last inhabited by Sir Walter Ralegh, who acquired the episcopal estate while he was still one of the queen's favourites. He constructed a new residence on a hill across the river, which became the core of the New Castle. Each castle is visible from the other, picturesque elements in the park. The grounds were laid

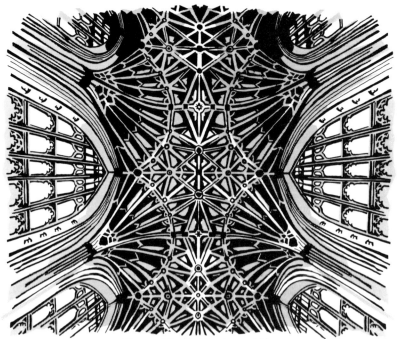

*Fan vaulting in Sherborne Abbey.*

out by Lancelot 'Capability' Brown (1716–83) for the Digby family, who have owned the estate since 1617. But the Old Castle was turned into an eye-catching ruin long before Brown set to work when it was besieged by Parliamentary forces in 1645.

Back at the crossroads, it is a ten-minute walk along the road south over the River Yeo to *Sherborne New Castle*, so this visit may well be made separately. The Victorian lodge gate, set underneath the steep hillside, is the entrance to the drive that sweeps through the park to the front of the house. 'Castle' is perhaps a misnomer for this fairly bizarre building. Sir Walter Ralegh's flamboyant hexagonal three-storey lodge house with chimneyed turrets was extended by Sir John Digby, who acquired Sherborne in 1617 (after Ralegh's disgrace and while he was awaiting his execution). He added two-storey balustraded wings with turrets and, wherever he could, the curious Digby family crest, an ostrich with a horseshoe in its beak.

Very little of the Elizabethan and Jacobean interior survives, since most of the main rooms were redecorated in a Jacobean style in the nineteenth century, but the Oak Room retains panelling of the 1620s, while an early Stuart plaster ceiling and heraldic Digby chimneypiece adorn the Red

Drawing Room. In this room hangs the most famous of the house's paintings, the procession of Queen Elizabeth I, attributed to Robert Peake. She is carried in her litter, attended by the gentlemen of her court, depicted as a youthful maiden despite her advanced age (she was in her late sixties). The Library is a delightful essay in Strawberry Hill Gothick.

The visitor's tour ends in the Elizabethan cellar, now home to the eccentric and glorious miscellany of items in the family museum. Most grisly of the exhibits is the skull of a Royalist soldier killed in the siege of 1645 with a bullet lodged in the eye-socket. Close by, in the tea rooms occupying the Gothick dairy, a crude Roman mosaic pavement showing Apollo playing the lyre and Marsyas dancing came from a nearby villa which was excavated in 1836.

From the New Castle, return to the Castleton crossroads and follow Long Street. The low cottages lining the road gradually give way to prouder and grander town houses, such as the Eastbury Hotel with its mid eighteenth-century classical front which is, unusually for Sherborne, executed in brick. Artefacts from rooms in Donore, a slightly earlier house of c.1700 with a hood porch and original casement windows on the opposite side of the road, feature in Sherborne Museum, where fragments of a wall-painting of a hunt and the fourteen layers of wallpaper which hid it are on display. The Red House, further along on the right, is Sherborne's earliest and grandest brick-built residence, dating from around 1730.

From this point, the east end of the Abbey sailing above the rooftops becomes the focus of the street. Beyond the late eighteenth-century brewery buildings, set on massive stone arches – and recently sympathetically converted into houses and flats – a sequence of houses reflects Sherborne's early entry into the lucrative world of provincial banking. The Regency Gothic front of the National Westminster Bank office, with its oriel window and extra-secure door, is adjoined by the Old Bank House, where Simon Pretor, a local grocer and merchant, established one of the earliest West Country banks in 1773. Over the road, past the former late Georgian Congregational church and its mid Victorian schoolroom (now auctioneers' premises), a line of late medieval houses leads through to Cheap Street.

Turning left along South Street, the stream that once scoured the monks' privies still flows beneath the roadway. Denners', on the corner with Half Moon Street, retains some of the original Victorian draper's shop frontage, with carved capitals between the shop windows, while cottages on the left-hand side of South Street, like Gainsborough House, obviously incorporate late medieval structures. At the bottom of the street, just before the railway station, an iron gate leads into the Pageant Gardens, established in 1905 with the profits from the pageant marking the anniversary of the foundation of St Aldhelm's cathedral in 705, under the direction of the improbably named Louis Napoleon Parker. The event was a roaring success; Parker virtually single-handed invented the country town pageant, of wobbly wimples and bad verse.

Digby connections appear again in Digby Road, on the other side of the Gardens, which is dominated by the stone bulk of the former Digby Hotel (now another boarding house for Sherborne School), its gables crowned by Digby ostriches. The hotel, put up in 1869, has had a distinguished literary career, appearing as the 'substantial inn of Ham-hill stone with a yawning back yard', where Grace waited for Giles in Hardy's *The Woodlanders*, and as the Lovelace Hotel in *Wolf Solent* by John Cowper Powys (1872–1963). Just past the 'yawning back yard', now a garage and car repair works, the Digby Tap pub on the corner was formerly the parish workhouse, while a plaque on the Britannia Inn, where the lane from Digby Street joins Westbury, records its first incarnation as the 'School for the education and clothing of poor girls of Sherborne, founded by the Rt. Hon. William Lord Digby 1743'. Its successor is Lord Digby's School in that much grander house on Newland.

Westbury, with its variety of cottages, describes a wide arc to run parallel to the river, which played a more important part in Sherborne's life when the town was a textile centre than it does today. Almost opposite the Roman Catholic church and the convent school, Marglass Ltd occupies the site of the first of Sherborne's silk mills, the town's most important industry after the traditional cloth trades had declined. The mill began in 1753 under John Sherrer, 'silk thrower of Whitechapel', and the original building survived until recently when fire destroyed much of it. Silk production continued on this site until World War II, when the factory pioneered the manufacture of fibreglass fabric, in which it is still a European leader.

Returning along Westbury and then the narrow Trendle Street, with its stone cottages and the long side of the almshouse, brings us back to Half Moon Street in front of the Abbey church where the exploration began. Perhaps it will be time for tea.

## —— AROUND AND ABOUT SHERBORNE ——

*Few regions in Britain have as varied a landscape within such a small area as the country around Sherborne. The complex geology of Somerset and Dorset has resulted in a delightful patchwork of scenery, from the wetlands of the Somerset Levels in the west to the chalk plains in the east, from the chalk downland and clay vales of the south to the*

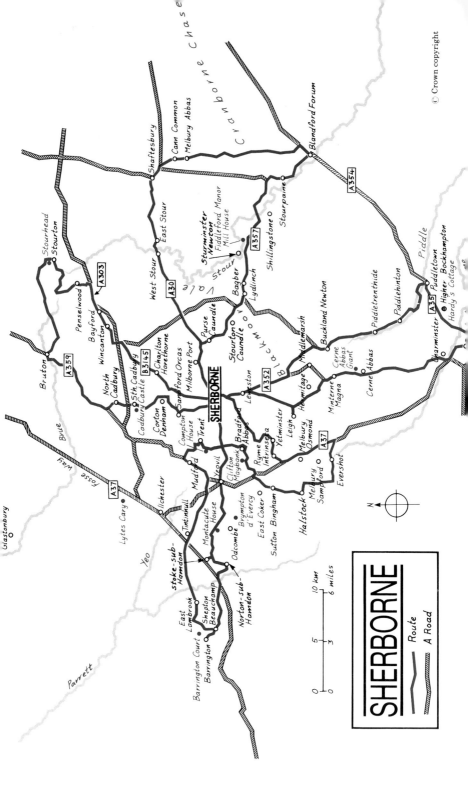

© Crown copyright

ANCE SHERBORNE

*limestone plateau of the north. This is an area which has rich and productive farming land, little villages with charmingly improbable names, churches with soaring towers built from the profits of the medieval wool trade, and small towns with their traditional markets. Almost every village seems to have its handsome manor house, and everywhere there are superb gardens.*

*One name stalks the landscape: Thomas Hardy (1840–1928). The novelist who single-handedly recreated the idea of 'Wessex' remained close to his Dorset country roots. Many of his novels are based upon real places. Dorset, like every county, may have changed dramatically in the course of the past century, yet it is often easy to imagine oneself back with Tess or Jude.*

## 1. HOUSES AND GARDENS

Sherborne's finest buildings are almost without exception built in the beautiful Ham Hill stone, quarried a few miles west into Somerset. The area around Ham Hill has a wealth of substantial historic houses and fine old gardens, most of which are open to the public for at least part of the year. A very happy day can be spent touring and visiting these, and the villages and small towns in between.

The approach to Yeovil, five miles west of Sherborne along the A30, is dramatic, as the road cuts through a short gorge of yellow clay, and then descends Babylon Hill, scene of a bloody Parliamentary victory in the Civil War. Yeovil itself is disappointing, a brick-built town once made prosperous by glove-making and now wrecked by road schemes and shopping precincts. Look out for the fine Perpendicular parish church on the right as you pass through and join the A3088 Ilminster road, and for the fifteenth-century farmhouse and huge 114-foot-long barn in Preston Plucknett on the northern outskirts.

*Brympton D'Evercy*, complete with its own vineyard, lies down a driveway off the minor road to Odcombe a mile further west. The main house, with its early Tudor entrance façade and classical late Stuart garden front,

stands in a group with the fourteenth-century church and the fifteenth-century chantry house. The unifying effect of the Ham Hill stone makes an assemblage that is not easily forgotten.

Only a mile or so west along the A3088 lies *Montacute House*, regarded by many as the best of all Elizabethan houses. The road winds past steep St Michael's Hill (the *Mons Acutus*), crowned by an eighteenth-century lookout tower, beneath which the stone-built village crouches around a central square. Lying along a drive from the square, the E-plan house presents two faces to the world. The 1530s Renaissance porch came from the nearby, largely demolished Clifton Maybank House, and was grafted on to the house in the 1770s. The main entrance for visitors is now the porch in the garden front, facing the thick yew hedges and ogee-canopied stone pavilions that enclose the lawns and borders. Here is the quintessential Elizabethan house, all warm stone and glittering windows. The interior is filled with handsome original features: the Hall with an unusual plaster panel depicting a popular ritual – the shaming of a hen-pecked husband; the panelled Parlour and the 189-foot Long Gallery running the full length of the house.

The quarries are worked out, but

Ham Hill, now a Country Park, remains a local landmark, visible in all directions. The massive fortifications constructed here, with defensive ramparts three miles round, were occupied from the New Stone Age until the post-Roman era. Armada warning beacons blazed from the hill, as did the torches carried in the West Country's largest-ever agricultural workers' demonstration in 1871, principally directed against the Phelips family of Montacute. The next village, Stoke-sub-Hamdon, is also entirely built in the local stone and is notable for the Norman church which has a remarkable north doorway, carved with religious emblems and the signs of the zodiac. The fifteenth-century hall and barn of *Stoke-sub-Hamdon Priory*, to the west of the village, form a rare survival of a medieval priest's house, although one of several in this area. Norton-sub-Hamdon, a mile south on the other side of the hill, has one of the earliest and finest of the great soaring Perpendicular church towers for which Somerset is famous. These are known as wool churches, because they were funded from the great wealth produced by the wool and cloth trades.

West of here the land falls away towards the marshes and moors, but the route still runs through rolling countryside to join the B3165 and the A303. This is part of the ancient Fosse Way, the great Roman road from the Devon border to Lincoln, but our route soon leaves it at the Lopen Head roundabout to take the minor road north-west to Barrington. Shepton Beauchamp, on the way, has another splendid fifteenth-century church tower, while the church at Barrington itself on the other side of the hill has a fifteenth-century nave, but retains its thirteenth-century tower.

Picturesque stone and thatch cottages run from the church to the great manor house at the other end of the village. Much altered inside but with an atmospheric, evocative exterior, *Barrington Court* is, like Montacute, built on an E-plan, but is in fact early rather than late Tudor, with a forest of twisted chimneys and pinnacles on the roofline. This magical building is a backdrop to a piece of twentieth-century creativity: Colonel Lyle, who rescued Barrington in the 1920s, began a series of walled gardens under the inspiration of Gertrude Jekyll (1843–1932), specializing in growing the lilies and irises for which Barrington is now justly famous, as well as building a model farm. The National Trust has introduced exhibitions and trails on the farm and estate.

A narrow lane connects Barrington Court with the minor road to the three little Lambrook villages. If Barrington's gardens are fine examples of earlier twentieth-century taste, Margery Fish's cottage-style layout around the sixteenth-century *East Lambrook Manor*, which she described in her well-known and much-loved books of the 1950s, is an instance of a modern gardening style to which we all might aspire. Now designated (like Montacute) a Grade I historic garden, East Lambrook's planting schemes have been carefully restored.

Continue eastwards along the lanes from East Lambrook. You may wish to make a detour north-east along the A303 to the late medieval manor at *Lytes Cary*, with its hedged gardens and topiary. This was the home of the first great English herbalist, Henry Lyte, whose *New Herbal* appeared in 1578. Another delightful small garden, *Tintinhull House Garden*, lies on the east of Tintinhull village, just over the A303. One of the best of modern formal gardens, Tintinhull is designed as an interlocking series of hedged and walled compartments embracing ponds and borders. The late seventeenth-century house is not open.

Follow the lanes skirting the built-up area of Yeovil, joining the A359 to Mudford, then crossing the Yeo to the village of Trent with its intricate maze of narrow lanes and houses just across the Dorset boundary. Sir Frederick Treves was pleased to find in 1906 that Trent had 'no hint of modernness about it', while Sir Nikolaus Pevsner (1902–83) delighted in the parish church with its fourteenth-century spire and its sixteenth-century wooden screen and benches. The church, the manor house where Charles II (1630–85) hid on his flight after the Battle of Worcester, and the surrounding late medieval farmhouses, combine to make Trent one of the most appealing villages in north Dorset, and if you are lucky some gardens may be open for charity. Due south of Trent, *Compton House* in Over Compton, a Victorian mock-Tudor property inspired by Clifton Maybank (see p. 150), promotes one of the more unusual garden attractions in this region, offering butterfly houses full of colourful, fragile beauty.

The A30 runs just south of Compton House, directly back into Sherborne.

## 2. DORCHESTER AND HARDY'S WESSEX

North and central Dorset, the land of the Stour and Frome valleys and the high chalklands between, spreads below Sherborne in a mat of secret wooded villages and sweeping hills – the Wessex heartland of Hardy's novels. This route skirts the edge of the great clay Blackmoor Vale, on which Hardy based his Vale of the Little Dairies, and runs south to the county town of Dorchester on the chalk heights. Thomas Hardy's birthplace near Higher Bockhampton lies to the east, on the edge of the Frome valley (his Vale of the Great Dairies).

One side of the Yeo valley rises steeply into the woods south of Sherborne, from where the main road, the A352, follows a direct line south to Dor-

chester. Taking the side road to Leigh some three miles south brings you to Leweston, where the diminutive early seventeenth-century church with its original fittings, one of a distinctive group in this corner of Dorset, is largely unspoiled; it stands in the grounds of the convent school, based in the eighteenth-century manor house, looking across at the unabashedly modernist school chapel. From here onwards the chalk hills become gradually more prominent, and the road rises past the scattered hamlet of Hermitage, as secluded as its name suggests. Rounding the steep-sided, 800-foot High Stoy, we enter the world of *The Woodlanders*.

*The spot is lonely, and when the days are darkening the many gay charioteers now perished who have rolled along the way, the blistered soles that have trodden it, and the tears that have wetted it, return upon the mind of the loiterer.*

For this was also the way that Tess of the D'Urbervilles walked to find news of Angel Clare.

The minor road rejoins the A352 in the deep gully above Minterne Magna. The parish church in this little village, its door right on the roadside, and next to the entrance gates to Minterne House, is crowded with memorials to Napiers, Churchills, and Digbys, the families who once owned the estate. The mansion itself, rebuilt in an Arts and Crafts idiom around 1900, is not open, but the gardens are. On a quiet day you may be able to pay in the 'honesty box' and enjoy the rare rhododendrons and the woodland walks and cascades of *Minterne House Gardens* all by yourself.

Cut into the turf of a steep chalk slope on the left before Cerne Abbas, to the south, is the Cerne Abbas Giant, a huge 180-foot high figure brandishing a club and displaying an extravagant erection. His age is a subject of dispute, although some people have found a stylistic resemblance to the figures in the Roman pavement preserved at Sherborne Castle. The village itself lies off the main road, from which a short turning leads into the main street. Pubs that were once inns, late Georgian shop fronts, and the old market house on Long Street speak of the former prosperity of this pretty place. Along the other principal street, past the tall, airy church with grotesque carvings and medieval statues adorning its west tower, and the timbered houses opposite, stand Abbey Farm and the fragmentary remains of *Cerne Abbey*, the once-great Benedictine monastery – a flamboyant early Tudor gatehouse, a fifteenth-century guesthouse, and the holy well.

The most dramatic route out of Cerne Abbas is the narrow, steep-sided lane from the further end of the village on to the chalk heights. South towards Dorchester, sweeping vistas open up on both sides of the road, giving views down into the narrow wooded valleys so characteristic of mid-Dorset. Just above Dorchester is the village of Charminster, once dominated by the Trenchard family. The tower and interior of the parish church are covered with their T-motifs, and the Trenchards built *Wolfeton House* just to the south around 1510, enlarging it in the reign of Elizabeth I. The twin-towered gatehouse and a corner of the earlier house survive, and so does most of the classicized Elizabethan house with its fine stone staircase. Wolfeton's rarest feature is the ashlared barn which is the Riding School, built around 1610 and the oldest in the country.

Dorchester was an important Roman town, established after the defeat of the British in their stronghold of Maiden Castle just to the south-west in AD44. The Roman layout and the lines of the walls are preserved in the modern street-plan and the tree-

lined eighteenth-century walks, while just behind the new County Hall, the excavated remains of a fourth-century Roman town house are open to view. A series of disastrous fires robbed Dorchester of many of its older buildings, but this is still Hardy's Casterbridge, with Georgian and Victorian façades looking on to the central crossroads and surrounding streets.

Thomas Hardy, as an apprentice architect in the town, worked on the restoration of the mainly fifteenth-century St Peter's church in the centre, one of the few principal buildings to have survived the great fire of 1613. As a writer, he features prominently in the High Victorian *Dorset County Museum* next to St Peter's, where his study has been re-erected inside as a major exhibit. There is also a particularly fine display of Roman antiquities. Dorchester is also connected with some famous and bloody trials. The late Georgian Antelope Hotel over the High Street, and the seventeenth-century half-timbered building beside it, were where Judge Jeffreys (1648–89) condemned 74 Dorset men to death for their part in Monmouth's Rebellion in 1685, while the courtroom in the 1790s Old Shire Hall further west along the High Street is where the Tolpuddle Martyrs were condemned to transportation in 1834 for their part in attempting to organize the first agricultural trade union. A plaque on the brick Barclays Bank on South Street records this as Trenchard's house in *The Mayor of Casterbridge*, and the poet William Barnes's statue stands in the centre of the town.

The eastern end of the High Street heads directly out of Dorchester over the River Frome to the new ring road, the easiest way to Maiden Castle. This immense Iron Age earthwork fortification, with a series of banked ramparts and ditches enclosing an area of 47 acres, caught the imagination of

Britain during the series of excavations led by Sir Mortimer Wheeler
(1890–1976) from the 1930s, and is one
of the most impressive prehistoric
monuments in England. From the
Castle there is a good view of the Winterborne valley to the east, where a
string of villages, some now deserted,
follows the line of the river – which is
usually dry in summer, hence the
name. To the south is the eighteenth-
century Winterborne Came House
beside the church and rectory where
William Barnes (1801–86), Dorset's
dialect poet, was incumbent.

Connections with both Barnes and
Hardy are found in the country east of
Dorchester. From the junction where
the ring road continues as the A35
towards Bournemouth, a lane skirting
the grounds of the Dorset College of
Agriculture leads into one of the surviving fragments of Dorset's wooded
heathland. In the woods above Higher
Bockhampton, reached along a series
of narrow lanes, stands *Hardy's
Cottage*, set against the backdrop of the
woodland which he evoked in *Under
the Greenwood Tree*. Here you can see
the bedroom where Hardy was born
(and where he was thought to have
died at birth until revived by an observ-
ant nurse), the room where he wrote
his first novels, and the living room
where family gatherings were held.

Puddletown, Hardy's Weatherbury,
lies two miles along the A35 beyond
Hardy's Cottage, on the River Piddle –
its name used to be bowdlerized to
Trent. The B3142 following the upper
Piddle plunges back into the chalk
hills, where one village merges into the
next, with cottages and farms lining
the narrow valleys. William Barnes
caught the essence of this landscape:

*The zwellen downs, wi' chalky tracks*
*A-climmen up their zunny backs,*
*Do hide green meads an zedgy*
*    brooks …*
*An' white roads up athirt the hills*

Round barrows and ancient hilltop
settlements crown the heights above
the road as it passes the early Stuart
showpiece front of Waterston Manor,
set among water meadows, and on
through Piddlehinton, where the
fifteenth-century parish church is
outclassed by the rectory. Beyond lies
Piddletrenthide, strung out along the
still-narrowing valley, with a part-
Norman church which is one of the
more interesting in the county: the
grand tower bears the date 1487 in
Arabic, not Roman, numerals. Among
many monuments are the graves of the
Dumberfields, the originals for Hardy's
D'Urbervilles.

The rounded chalk heights begin to
give way to the vale beyond Buckland
Newton, but not before the road west
rises steeply above Middlemarsh, on
which Hardy based Little Hintock in
*The Woodlanders*; Lower Revels Farm
on the right of the lane, once a roadside
hostelry, still looks much like the Rev-
ellers Inn to which Tim and Suke's
wedding party were headed. The lane
emerges on to the main Sherborne–
Dorchester road, which leads back
north through Longburton. Early
seventeenth-century features in the
parish church here, including tombs
adorned with macabre skeletons, are
echoed in the church at Leweston and
other local villages.

## 3. VILLAGES OF STONE

Dorset is still very much a rural
county, made up of a network of
villages. Some of the best of them, with
fine stone-built houses, are easily
explored in a short excursion to the
south-west of Sherborne. Some are
open and spreading, others tight and
secretive: Dorset in miniature.

Leaving Sherborne west on the A30,
a side road to the left leads to Bradford
Abbas. The glory of this village is its
parish church, notable for the sumptuous fifteenth-century tower, porch,

chancel, and panelled nave roof. Only two of the eleven original statues on the face of the 90-foot tower survive, but they give an indication of quite how magnificent this church once was. The adjoining Rose and Crown inn, with its late medieval stone fireplace, was originally a rest house for the monks of Sherborne.

The cannibalized Clifton Maybank house lies over the River Yeo, but it is reached only by returning to the main road, crossing the river and turning right under the Bristol–Weymouth railway line. All that survives of this once-great mid-Tudor mansion on the west bank of the river built for Sir John Horsey is its south wing. Sir John, who had been steward of Sherborne Abbey estates, acquired substantial parts of the monastic lands after the Dissolution, and used the profits gained from selling the abbey church to the townspeople to build his great Ham stone house, in its time second locally only to Barrington Court (see p. 146). When the family was finally bankrupted in the 1770s, most of the house was demolished, and some parts were re-used elsewhere. The centre of the entrance front with its sculptural Renaissance detail is now a major feature of Montacute House, and some of its stone pinnacles stand in the grounds of Compton House (see p. 147).

The county boundary runs immediately west of Clifton Maybank; the lane continues down the Somerset side to join the old Roman road which is now the A37. Turn right and then left past the fanciful obelisk beyond the railway to follow the lanes to East Coker. This village is associated with T. S. Eliot (1888–1965), who lived in Coker Court and was buried in the churchyard. One of his *Four Quartets*, with the memorable first line 'In my beginning is my end', is named after this attractive place, where most of the buildings, including some mid-Stuart

almshouses, are built in the same, mellow Ham Hill stone.

From the crossroads east of the village, a causeway runs across Sutton Bingham reservoir. Beyond Halstock, at the southern end of the reservoir, the road runs east, then south through scattered woods and farms, and rises up the steep hill to Evershot, which at 700 feet above sea-level is Dorset's second highest village. Evershot is more compact than most in the area, and is made all the more memorable by its nineteenth-century embellishments: raised pavements, street lamps, and bow windows. Here too there are Hardy connections: the Acorn Inn in the centre was the Sow and Acorn in Tess's great walk across Dorset.

Just to the north, and accessible only on foot, is Melbury Sampford, another of the important local houses of the 1530s and 1540s, which is reached by a path across the deer park from the top of Evershot village. The house's most obvious feature, its great hexagonal tower with large windows, is part of the original building, one of the first 'prospect' lookout towers which later became such an architectural motif of the Elizabethan age. Much of the rest of the now rambling, architecturally incoherent mansion was rebuilt in the late seventeenth century, then extended in the 1870s and 1880s by the 5th Earl of Ilchester. It dwarfs the fifteenth-century parish church alongside, crammed with monuments of the owners, members of the Strangways and Fox-Strangways family.

The right of way through the magnificent parkland continues to the estate village of Melbury Osmond to the north, a tangle of lanes and beautifully maintained thatched cottages around the mid Georgian and Victorian church where Thomas Hardy's parents were married, and with a water-splash (now often dry) separating one part of the village from the other.

East of Evershot the main road follows the ridge line for three miles north, passing the turning to Melbury Osmond, until the next right turn, into Ryme Intrinseca. The lane from Ryme Intrinseca enters Yetminster, to the east, at a small triangle of roads and cottages, beside the school founded by the distinguished chemist Robert Boyle (1627–91) in 1691. The principal street extends east from here; almost every building along it is either old or architecturally interesting, or both. There is a wealth of houses dating from the late seventeenth century when prosperous local farming families were jockeying for position. Social scramble became property boom, and the results are still to be seen. Look out for Court House (which still has many original windows), Higher Farm, dated 1624 and 1630, the picturesque White Hart Inn, and Petty's Farm and the Manor House. Seventeenth-century cottages, often with swooping thatched roofs that curl round upper floor windows, are found in the lanes around the more prosperous houses in the village centre. The oldest house, Upbury Farm, is contemporary with the adjoining fifteenth-century church. The farmhouse has at its core a hall house, built as a rural retreat for a prebendary of Salisbury Cathedral, and converted in the mid seventeenth century. The church itself has a medieval painted wagon roof.

After the seventeenth century Yetminster returned to being a rural backwater; only the mid Georgian house opposite Upbury Farm and the large late Georgian property at the upper end of Church Street provide evidence of later wealth. More recently, Yetminster has been affected by a new property scramble, as retired people

*Montacute House.*

and workers from Yeovil have bought up property and new housing has been added on the fringes, but the overall effect has been slight.

The lane from the north end of Yetminster, past Boyle's School, crosses the railway towards the landmark of Bradford Abbas church tower and from there to Sherborne.

## 4. WHERE DORSET, SOMERSET AND WILTSHIRE MEET

One of the finest of all English gardens lies within reach of Sherborne: Stourhead, the quintessence of eighteenth-century garden design. The Stour, Dorset's river, rises in its parkland, just within Wiltshire. The journey there and back runs through dairying country, of hills and vales, hidden villages and lanes, to the edge of the limestone and chalk uplands which stretch into Somerset and Wiltshire.

The Bristol Road (B3145) north from Sherborne rises through farmland before descending the escarpment to the Somerset village of Charlton Horethorne, where stone houses cluster around a triangular green. The church, set behind the early Stuart manor house, is partly twelfth-century, with a fifteenth-century tower, and contains a Roman altar and medieval statue niches still with their original colouring. The wooded hill rising north of the village then descends to the A357, where you turn north under the A303 then east to Wincanton and its racecourse on the hillside.

Like Dorchester, Blandford Forum, or indeed Warwick, Wincanton was one of the many towns rebuilt in a new style after suffering extensive fire damage in 1747. The handsome houses and coaching inns in the Market Place and High Street date from the 1750s. The town's principal architect, Nathaniel Ireson, who is buried beside the part Georgian parish church, came from Warwick. Just outside the town

on the side road through the straggling hamlet of Bayford, there is a spectacular view south from the chalk escarpment over the expanse of Blackmoor Vale. Then a little further along the A303, a lane to the left climbs another chalk hill into the tangle of lanes around Penselwood.

The area is still densely wooded, the last fragment of the Forest of Selwood that once covered the Somerset–Wiltshire border. Prehistoric and Norman encampments stud the hills; on one of them is the stone which marks where the three counties meet. The walled lane through the woods north of Penselwood emerges into the little village of Stourton just at the head of the lake and garden of *Stourhead*. The view that opens up before you is one of the most famous in England, with classical temples set around the artificial lake, and the Palladian bridge and the medieval spike of the Bristol High Cross in the foreground.

Henry Hoare, of the banking family, began his great garden in 1744, flooding the bottom of the valley below the Palladian house built for his father twenty years before. From the High Cross and the picturesque parish church, a circuit of the wooded lakeside takes in the sequence of mid eighteenth-century temples and garden buildings. On the far shore the path enters a grotto, ornamented with statues of a nymph and the river god of the Stour, and filled with the noise of the flow of the infant river.

Whatever the season, Stourhead is an enchanted garden; in late spring the rhododendrons and azaleas are a famous, crowd-drawing show, enjoyed by all but the purists who know that such planting had no part in the original scheme. The house stands on the hill above, hidden from the garden. The original 1720s villa was extended on either side in around 1800 and given its classical portico in 1841. Although the centre was gutted by fire in 1902, it was largely rebuilt in the original style, while the library in the south wing, with its original Chippendale furnishings, and the picture gallery in the north wing, escaped the flames.

The lane from Stourhead continues to the Frome road, the B3092, which then passes the front of Stourhead House. The next turn left carries along the top of the park, with vistas through the trees across Blackmoor Vale to the mid-Dorset hills, and down the little brilliant-green valley where the Stour is born beneath St Peter's Pump (removed from Bristol in the 1760s). There are even better views from the 160-foot landmark of *King Alfred's Tower* a mile further along, right across Somerset to the Mendip plateau and, if it is clear, even to the coast. Henry Hoare put up this triangular brick prospect tower around 1770, at the point where Alfred the Great, King of Wessex (849–99), is said to have rallied the Saxons in 878.

The lane continues west through the hills to meet the B3081 Wincanton–Shepton Mallet road, which descends into the valley of the Brue and the sleepy limestone-built town of Bruton. Antique shops predominate in the narrow main street, alleys wind around the proud Doulting-stone church and the precinct of the former abbey, and sixteenth- and seventeenth-century buildings, like the core of the King's School and Sexey's Hospital, mingle with Georgian inns and town houses. The most prominent vestige of the abbey is its dovecote, a gaunt roofless gabled tower, on the hill across the river.

Beyond the rather hilly country and isolated farmhouses to the south, a side road leaves the A359 to North Cadbury, a village of attractive small houses and cottages. At the south end, the large Elizabethan mansion built for the Puritan writer Sir Francis Hastings stands alongside the grand early fifteenth-century church, where he was buried in an unmarked tomb. Across the A303 rises Cadbury Castle, now one of the favoured sites for the legendary King Arthur's Camelot. Excavations suggest Dark Age occupation of this mighty Iron Age camp, one of the strongest prehistoric British fortresses. The pathway up on to the camp starts from beside the Victorianized church in the little village of South Cadbury.

The lanes continue for about three miles through the narrow gaps between the hills to Corton Denham and Sandford Orcas. Turn right in Sandford Orcas up the hill towards the tiny church (which has a fifteenth-century screen) and *Sandford Orcas Manor*. Set in a topiary garden, and built in Ham Hill stone in the 1540s, this little gem has survived amazingly little altered. Even the great locks and keys on the oak doors throughout the house are original, although many of the furnishings were added when the Medlycott family repossessed the house in 1873 from a succession of tenants – who had kept it from the improvements of intervening generations.

Sherborne lies due south of here, along a narrow lane down the valley.

## 5. DORSET'S RIVER

The Stour is Dorset's river; only its first two miles at Stourhead lie outside the county. It is an undemonstratively beautiful river, meandering its slow way through a pastoral landscape. Crossing the wide Blackmoor Vale, dairy country *par excellence*, it cuts its way through the chalk heights of north-east Dorset to Blandford Forum. There is a network of small, almost sleeping towns along it, and a wealth of charming villages and farms.

The farmyards on either side of the road from the Castleton crossroads to the A30 show how rural Sherborne quickly becomes. Milborne Port, a couple of miles to the north-east, into Somerset, was once a more important place than it is today, a pre-Norman royal manor which remained a parliamentary borough until 1832. The parish church off to the right of the main road has a very important central tower, crossing, chancel and transepts from the very end of the Anglo-Saxon era and the immediate post-Conquest years. The A30 hustles through, past the eighteenth-century pilastered town hall, a clutch of humbler cottages, and the swaggering Queen Anne brick-built Ven House just beyond the town.

Purse Caundle straddles the minor road south of the A30 within a mile of Ven House. Its parish church, built all of a piece in the early fifteenth century, stands almost opposite the basically late fifteenth-century *Purse Caundle Manor* with a slim oriel window gazing on to the lane. The Manor House was reordered inside in the mid sixteenth century and given a symmetrical front in the seventeenth, but still preserves a late medieval layout, with great hall, minstrels' gallery, solar, and upper chambers. The lane continues down the wooded hill through Stourton Caundle, east to join the A357 at Lydlinch and from there to Bagber, where Dorset's dialect poet William Barnes grew up as a farmer's son.

Thomas Hardy spent the first two years of his married life in the little town of Sturminster Newton two miles further west (locals call it Stur). Across the River Divelish is the restored Georgian town mill, which still grinds corn, and then a medieval bridge takes the road over the River Stour into Sturminster. This is still very much a market town, holding the largest calf market in Europe. The assembly rooms and corn exchange in the triangular market place suggest something of the atmosphere of a late eighteenth- and nineteenth-century country town. The parish church standing between the market place and the river was mainly rebuilt in 1824 for the Revd Thomas Lane Fox, who reputedly spent his personal fortune of £100,000 on his parishioners.

*Fiddleford Manor Mill House* just downstream, and accessible by footpath as well as the road, is the remaining part of a medieval hall built around 1380; the interior is best-known for its luxuriantly carved open timber roof, the outside for the lengthy inscription dated 1566 exhorting 'Miller be true, disgrace not thy vest'. The river winds away to rejoin the main road two miles on above Shillingstone, where a lane crosses the reedy Stour to Child Okeford. The village and the valley are dominated by the massive chalk bulk of Hambledon Hill, topped by a neolithic hillfort. It is a steep but exhilarating climb, with views over Blackmoor Vale and the Stour valley to the west, the deep wooded Iwerne valley (pronounced Yoorn) and the chalk hills of Cranborne Chase to the east. Just to the south and 150 feet lower is the almost conical Hod Hill, with Iron Age and Roman fortifications. The road east skirts the grounds of the grand Jacobean Hanford House School, with its classical front, and then passes between Hambledon and Hod Hills to join the A350 where it makes a huge loop round the grounds of Stepleton House. This was once the site of the village of Iwerne Steepleton, swept away when the park was formed.

Beyond Stourpaine, a linear village of small cottages dwarfed by the steep hillsides on the east, the A350 and the Stour continue into Blandford Forum. Conscious action and until recently unconscious preservation have made this the most thoroughly Georgian town in Dorset. Fire raged through the town centre in 1731, but under the influence of the local gentlemen-architects John and William Bastard, all was rebuilt within thirty years, in an accomplished classical style that is notably sophisticated for so small a place. Although obscured by modern shop fronts, what they achieved is still visible in the Market Place, lined with the grand façades of the Town Hall, the Red Lion Inn, the Greyhound Inn, and groups of houses including the Bastard brothers' own. Here too is the church with its tower topped by a cupola; the classical fire monument in front of it is designed to double as a water cistern in case of future disaster. Like other Dorset market towns, Blandford Forum slumbered as its fortunes were eclipsed in the nineteenth century, to emerge faded but largely untouched by architectural and economic progress.

A minor road from the industrial estate on the north of Blandford leads up on to the heights of Cranborne Chase. This is an exhilarating landscape, with secret valleys hidden among the rounded, part-wooded hills. For centuries this chalk downland extending east into Wiltshire was protected as a hunting preserve with jurisdiction over it shared between local great landed families.

There is no settlement other than the occasional isolated farm until the village of Melbury Abbas, where the road begins to descend to meet the Shaftesbury–Ringwood B3081 at Cann Common. Shaftesbury, two miles north, is a real hill town, perched on the edge of the greensand escarpment looking into Blackmoor Vale. Thomas Hardy was 'thrown into a pensive melancholy' when he contemplated Shaftesbury, or Shaston as it was called in his novels, a great and wealthy abbey town which bore, and bears, the unmistakable signs of having lived through much better times. If the Abbess of Shaston, they used to say, were to marry the Abbot of Glaston, the happy couple would have been wealthier than the medieval kings. Today there is little of Shaftesbury's great convent left at the high western edge of the town. And the bones of Edward, King and Martyr (963–978), its most precious possession, which were rediscovered on the site, now languish in a bank vault while their inheritance is disputed.

The High Street is lined with buildings dating from the sixteenth to the twentieth centuries, but what everyone comes to see is the incomparable Gold Hill, the nostalgic setting for many an advertisement and featured in countless calendar illustrations. This cobbled street, reached through a narrow alleyway beside the Perpendicular St Peter's church, descends extremely steeply, with a row of cottages, many of them thatched, on the left and the huge buttressed wall of the abbey precinct on the right. As you slither down the hill to the charming almost village-like streets at the bottom, the great green expanse of north Dorset opens up ahead.

It is eleven miles back to Sherborne from Shaftesbury along the A30, which loops around the town and picks its way down the escarpment in a series of virtual hair-pin bends to reach the soft pastures of Blackmoor Vale. Between the villages of East Stour and West Stour, the River Stour is bridged for the last time, and the road continues through rolling countryside into the marshy valley of the River Cale and Bow Brook, and back to Milborne Port and Sherborne.

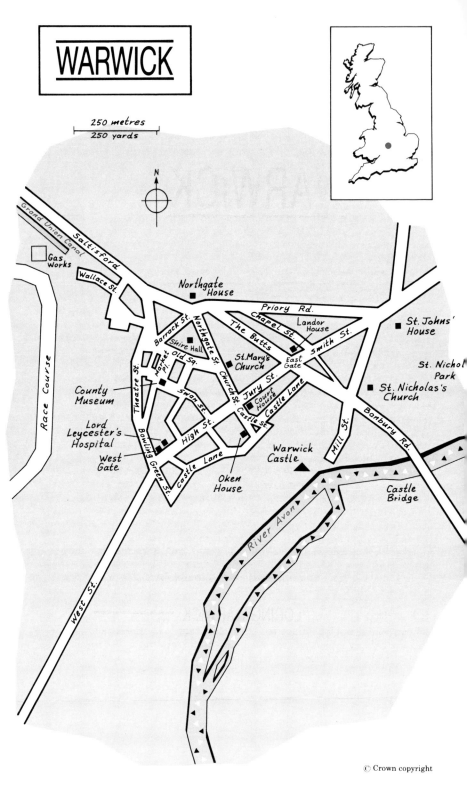

# 7
# WARWICK

Warwickshire

*Despite its ancient importance and its status as county
town, Warwick is overshadowed by many others in the
West Midlands – Birmingham, Coventry and even its
neighbour Royal Leamington Spa, in whose
administrative district it now lies. Ironically, it is that lack
of growth and business success which has kept Warwick
as charming and as interesting as it is. Warwick is also the
epitome of central England: contenders for the
exact mid-point of the country lie within a few miles of it.
Warwick grew up on a natural strategic site, and was
established as an Anglo-Saxon burh where the River Avon
could be crossed and defended. The Castle, one of the great
tourist sites of England, is a powerful reminder of defence.
If medieval might is one of the images of Warwick,
another is of late seventeenth-century and eighteenth-
century elegance. On the night of 5 September 1694, most of
Warwick was burned to the ground and more than 250
families were made homeless. The opportunity was taken
to rebuild the town in stronger, lasting, and more elegant
forms and materials. There are three different faces to
Warwick: medieval survivals in the areas not affected by
the fire; the post-fire town with the county administration
buildings; and the castle, which dominates the approach to
the town but otherwise seems to ignore it.*

## EXPLORING WARWICK

There is an obvious place to begin: the bridge over the River
Avon. The view of Warwick Castle from here is one of the
most stirring in England: its wall rears up from the sandstone
cliff, punctuated by a hundred windows of all shapes and
sizes, a few cottages at its foot. Below, the Avon flows through
woods and meadows. The river and the defences are the reason
for Warwick's growth and past importance.

The single span, balustraded bridge, built in around 1790, replaced the medieval bridge a couple of hundred yards downstream, which was in a dreadful state and in the way of the landscaping being carried out in the Castle grounds at the time. The ruins of the old bridge can just be made out – it collapsed soon after the new bridge was opened – serving as a romantic feature in the parkland setting of the Castle. Upstream, the banks of the Avon are now a public park.

Banbury Road leads into town from the bridge. The first lane to the left, Mill Street, offers a taste of pre- and post-fire Warwick. The fire of 1694 did not reach this far, so there are still some sixteenth-century half-timbered houses at the end of the street (albeit restored). Close to the main road is a happy juxtaposition of styles where the elegant mid Georgian brick front of Miller's Place, no. 15, is squeezed in beside the stone-built malt house of a century or so before.

The stout entrance lodge to *Warwick Castle* stands at the top of Mill Street. Paths snake through the grounds, leading first to the blocky, stone-built, mid eighteenth-century stable block housing the ticket office and refreshment kiosks and then skirting around the Castle's wide, dry moat to the gatehouse.

Warwick Castle is one of England's premier fortifications. Its sheer might is difficult to take in: the tall fourteenth-century towers, Caesar's Tower on the left, rising from the sandstone cliff, and Guy's Tower on the right, flank the huge wall and the doubly fortified barbican gatehouse. Although the first defences here were put up by Alfred the Great's daughter, Ethelfleda, in 914, castles were largely a Norman innovation. The first phase of Warwick was started in 1068 as part of William the Conqueror's strategy for subduing the rebellious north. His wooden stronghold on the original motte and bailey was rebuilt and walled in stone over the following 150 years. In the fourteenth century the Castle acquired its present form, with its fantasy towers, and the great block of the living quarters, some 160 yards long and 90 yards wide, filling one side of the enormous courtyard.

The Castle is exciting to explore and its military function is still obvious: the entrance gate has holes for throwing missiles down on intruders and a gibbet cage is on display in the dungeons. In the Watergate Tower, a visitor's presence will trigger a startling recorded commentary: 'This room is haunted...'. Guy's Tower affords a panoramic view over the town below, as well as of the verdant countryside to the south. Across the great lawns of the courtyard, the main living quarters contain a sequence of grand State Apartments, mostly of the mid eighteenth century but with some surviving from a late Stuart scheme. After a fire in 1871, the Great Hall was rebuilt in an appropriately heavy style, and the main family wing was redecorated.

Views of the Castle today are still close to those painted by the Venetian artist Antonio Canaletto (1720–80) in around 1749; they used to hang in the Castle, but were among many art works sold by the present Earl of Warwick in the 1970s. The Canalettos now hang in the Barber Art Gallery at Birmingham, and the huge antique marble Warwick Vase (for which the great conservatory was built) graces the Burrell Museum in Glasgow. In 1978 Warwick Castle was bought, with all its contents, by Madame Tussaud's. The Victorian family apartments now display convincing waxwork tableaux of an 1898 house party, when Edward, Prince of Wales (1841–1910) visited.

The title of Earl of Warwick has had one of the most complicated histories of all English peerages; revived four times, it has been borne by many great families – Beaumont, Beauchamp, Neville, Dudley, Rich and Greville. For all this, the Castle only ever saw any action during the Civil War.

The Castle's magnificent grounds to either side of the Avon formed one of the earliest commissions undertaken by Lancelot 'Capability' Brown (1716–83). In recent years some of the garden features which had fallen into disrepair, like the Victorian Rose Garden, have been restored. A rolling programme of conservation means that some part of the Castle is always under scaffolding, but this is a necessary evil.

The car park exit leads into Castle Lane, which is dominated by the castle wall. Much of this street was demolished in the late eighteenth century to extend the castle's grounds – and here the huge fortification ends abruptly. The lane is closed off by a Tudor timber-framed structure which survived the fire – Thomas Oken's House. Oken, a mercer, left his considerable fortune to the poor of Warwick in 1573. The house is now *Oken House Doll Museum*. Castle Lane itself swings left and then right around a mid eighteenth-century pair of brick semi-detached houses – an early example of this type of property – with one entrance on Castle Lane, and the other on Castle Street, which leads to the heart of the town.

Warwick's town fathers took the opportunity given them by the 1694 fire to reconstruct the centre in a more fitting style and in more durable materials. They even set up a special tribunal to enforce the building codes. Houses had to be rebuilt with very thick party walls, and in brick and stone rather than plaster and timber. The corner buildings at the crossroads of the market place were given special decorative emphasis. On the way up Castle Street, no. 8 on the left is one of the best-preserved post-fire properties with its pedimented dormer windows and the curious flat, fluted capitals on the pilasters. Its use from 1826 is proclaimed by the inscription incised on the front: 'Dispensary for the Sick and Poor of Warwick and its Neighbourhood'. Beside it, the former Aylesford Hotel, now a restaurant decked out in pink and one of the important corner properties put up in 1696, is a provincial version of houses fashionable in London a few years before, with busy baroque details like pediments, pilasters, scrolls and laurel leaf bands.

On the corner formed by Castle Street and Jury Street is the long, stone flank of the Court House. Since its erection in the mid 1720s this has been one of the principal town (as opposed to county) public buildings in Warwick, although difficulties over paying for it kept it unoccupied for a number of years. It now houses the *Tourist Information Centre* (the main entrance is round to the right in Jury Street). Built by Francis Smith, the most accomplished of the many gentlemen-architects of eighteenth-century Warwick, it is a building which makes its presence felt without being over-assertive. A two-storey structure decorated with rusticated stone bands, it has a statue of Justice set in a niche over the central doorway, with the royal arms above her and the town badge below. Inside, on the first floor, a ballroom runs the full depth of the building, serving as a venue for the town balls and assemblies in the season that were the hallmark of polite Georgian urban society.

The two remaining corners of the crossroads were treated in a similar way to the Aylesford corner, with a grand, pilastered house on each. Church Street runs north between them to the awesome tower of St Mary's Church. The elegant Georgian houses that line the street include the former town literary club, the Athenaeum, on the right, an ashlared house with a huge triple window on the first floor. In front of the church, the street opens into an irregular square, one of the earliest deliberately-planned squares in a small English provincial town.

St Mary's Church was another victim of the great fire, with the exception of the east end. The stricken townspeople placed their rescued belongings inside for safety, and – predictably – the smouldering furniture set the building alight. Much of the original church was Norman; the rebuilding was undertaken in a curious late Stuart version of Gothic designed by a local gentleman-mason, Sir William Wilson. The great west tower is 174 feet high, a landmark for miles around, and it stands on the old roadway, with arches that allowed traffic to pass underneath. The pinnacled tower has mixed classical and watered-down Gothic motifs, as do the window tracery and the interior.

There is a great deal to see and enjoy in the church: the wall monuments, the little chapter house almost entirely filled by the great six-poster monument to Fulke Greville (1554–1628) to whom James I gave Warwick Castle in 1604, the Norman crypt with a ducking stool for miscreant women, and the bread cupboards for the distribution of provisions to the poor. The church's greatest treasures are the medieval

*Warwick Castle.*

Beauchamp tombs, which survived the fire. In the centre of the chancel lies Thomas, 11th Earl of Warwick, who began the great rebuilding of the castle, and died in 1369. A doorway in the south transept, which is built in a much more convincing early Georgian version of the Gothic style than the rest of the church, leads down into the Beauchamp Chapel, the Lady Chapel endowed by Richard, 13th Earl (d. 1439).

This is one of the most sumptuous survivals of the fifteenth century in England, rivalling the royal work in Westminster Abbey. Stained glass installed by the king's glazier survives in some windows, especially the figures of saints in the east window and the charming angels, playing contemporary musical instruments, in the upper tracery. Carved and coloured saints and angels adorn the chapel. In the centre of the chapel is the Earl's richly decorated tomb, with the memorial effigy of the praying Earl and the hoops arching over it all in gilt copper. The Purbeck marble chest is adorned with portraits of his family. On either side of the chapel are the wall tombs of Robert Dudley, Earl of Leicester (1533–88) – Queen Elizabeth's favourite, who founded the Hospital that still bears his name – and of his brother Ambrose, 3rd of the Tudor Earls of Warwick. The Gothic plaster altar-piece, sitting rather uneasily in its setting, was added in the eighteenth century. Designed by Timothy Lightoler who redecorated the castle interior in the 1760s, it replaced that destroyed during the Civil War.

The last gem in St Mary's Church is the tiny fan-vaulted chapel between the chancel and the Beauchamp chantry. Even the little niches have their own miniature fan vaults.

Northgate Street, running up from the west tower of St Mary's, is an elegant eighteenth-century street, now almost entirely given over to county administrative offices. Some of the best-looking of all surviving Georgian judicial buildings line the left-hand side, and along the right runs a succession of brick and stuccoed houses with a delightful variety of doorcases and fanlights. The sequence on the left runs from the Judge's Lodgings, a simple and dignified ashlared building of 1815, past the old *Shire Hall* with its central pediment and Corinthian capitals, put up in the 1750s to replace the old county buildings, and finally to the County Gaol, in a simpler classical style. With permission, you can see the interior of the Shire Hall, designed by Sanderson Miller (1717–80), another Warwickshire gentleman-architect. In its top-lit, octagonal court rooms, much of the original plasterwork and furnishings is intact. Below street level are the cells from the old gaol, ominous chambers where prisoners scratched their names on the unforgiving walls.

Prisoners were incarcerated elsewhere after 1861, when the gaol became the militia barracks – in Barrack Street, which runs along the top of the old gaol building, an ancient cell door is still fixed into the wall. Facing down into Northgate Street, on the other side of the roundabout, stands *Northgate House*. Built in 1698, it is the largest and grandest pair of semi-detached houses in town, eleven bays long with a central carriage entrance. It even has two sundials, one in the central pediment, the other on the side. The open space behind Northgate House is the site of what was once Warwick's finest mansion, The Priory, an early seventeenth-century house which fell into great disrepair and was finally shipped across the Atlantic to Virginia in the 1920s.

Barrack Street leads round into the top of the Market Place, past the new Shire Hall, built in the best traditions of the multi-storey car park and spoiling one of Warwickshire's finest groups of buildings. No. 10 Market Place, a handsome stone-built house with its Corinthian pilasters and portico which dates from 1714, and has been incorporated into the newer county buildings, is another handsome example of the work of Francis Smith. It faces on to the oddly L-shaped Market Place. The dominant feature is the former Town Hall, a two-storey building dating from 1670, standing alone in the paved central area. William Hurlbutt, a local carpenter, designed and built it in the standard post-Restoration form, with a hipped roof and a cupola. Originally the ground floor was an open arcade. It was enclosed and glazed, with the oddest round-headed iron traceried windows, in 1871 when the building became the *Warwickshire County Museum*. One of the museum's treasures is the huge tapestry map of the county, woven in the local factory set up by William Sheldon around 1570, based upon Christopher Saxton's Tudor *Atlas of England*. Warwick sits plum in the centre.

The shopping street runs round the back of the Museum to the Old Square opposite St Mary's church, and down Church Street to the central crossroads. High Street, leading off to the right, was thoroughly devastated in the fire, and almost all of the buildings date from the eighteenth century. Their fanlights, balconies and doorcases breathe Georgian elegance. One to notice is no. 3, on the other side of the road. The house is brick-built, quite low, and shows the extra-thick party walls that were incorporated in the immediate post-fire houses. The doorcase is dated to 1791, and its Egyptian columns and top-heavy, semi-circular pediment, embellished with stars, square and a pair of compasses, proclaim it as a (very early) masonic lodge. At the far end of the High Street, the road falls away sharply, sweeping past the ancient West Gate. It was here that the fire started, and the westerly wind blew the sparks into the centre of town. Thankfully the older houses around the West Gate were spared. A row of half-timbered sixteenth-century houses on the left, some with jettied upper floors and gables, stands high above the road. Opposite them is one of the splendid sights of Warwick, the West Gate, and the timber range of *Lord Leycester's Hospital*.

Part of the West Gate is hewn out of the rock on which Warwick stands. Its arches and vaults are thirteenth- and fourteenth-century. The road now passes around it, and only pedestrians go through it. St James' Chapel sitting on top, which was begun in 1383 and had its tower added in 1450, is now largely a Victorian reconstruction; it is reached by a walkway from Lord Leycester's Hospital, set up high on the north side. Robert Dudley, Earl of Leicester, whose home was Kenilworth Castle a few miles away, acquired the former guild and civic buildings from the Warwick Corporation in 1571, and established this almshouse, for a 'Master and twelve Brethren'. Eight ex-servicemen and their wives now live here.

Behind the impressive and half-timbered front – made even more so by the incorporation of the timber-porched former inn next door – the quadrangle leads into the constituent parts of the hospital. On the left, the Great Hall, with its massive roof timbers, has been used for public assemblies since the late fourteenth century; on the right up the stair-case, the oak and plaster Guildhall was where the town's pre-Reformation religious guilds met to organize the town affairs. It now houses the Regimental Museum of the Queen's Own Hussars, which has waxwork tableaux. Some of the older rooms in the hospital are also on show, although most of the galleried eastern side of the courtyard is private, as is the much-photographed Victorian, half-timbered Master's House on the north side.

Just by the West Gate itself is another of Warwick's surviving curiosities, a very early cast-iron pillar box, of the 1850s, in the form of a fluted classical column with a vertical slot for posting letters, which is still in use. (Another stands by the East Gate.) Bowling Green Street runs beneath the wall of the Hospital and fragments of the old town wall into Theatre Street behind the Market Place. As its name suggests, this street was the site of the town's eighteenth-century theatre. Over to the west, on the former common lands, lies the town race course – another great social venue in the Georgian period. Theatre Street continues northwards and leads left into Saltisford. This is probably the most ancient street name in the town – it was the ancient salt track from Droitwich. In around 1800 the area became Warwick's little industrial quarter. Attempts were made to introduce textile manufacture to the town, notably by Samuel Crompton (1753–1827) who founded the worsted mill that stands on Wallace Street, near the canal basin on a short spur from the Grand Union Canal. Nearby is another early nineteenth-century mill, with the mill-owner's house alongside. On the opposite side of Saltisford is the most charming of all Warwick's industrial age survivals, the Gas Works of 1822. The prosaic name does not do justice to the prettiness of this pair of octagonal gas holders joined by a long range with round-headed windows, brick-built and faced in rendered cement.

Back down Saltisford and past Northgate House, the Butts leads to the confection of the town's East Gate. Above the fifteenth-century stone arch rises the fanciful St Peter's chapel, built in 1788 by Francis Hiorns, replacing a decayed medieval chapel. Its tower rises to a pinnacled Gothick crown and short spire. The chapel has since been incorporated into the adjacent girls' school.

Jury Street, the fourth arm of the crossroads that forms Warwick's principal focus, runs back into the centre from the East Gate. The fire did not quite reach this end of Jury Street, so some medieval remnants survive, such as the lozenge timber framing of the first houses on the north side. The most easily seen old interior is the pizza parlour a few doors along, where the timbers date back to the late Middle Ages; while the Lord Leycester Hotel, with its early eighteenth-century brick front, incorporates a seventeenth-century stone house at the back. The opposite side of the street has fine eighteenth-century houses, some of stone, some of stuccoed brick.

Back through the East Gate, Smith Street runs down the hill. Immediately on the left are two contrasting pre-fire houses, one timber-framed and gabled, the second built in

1692, a brick house with hipped roof and stone quoins. This is
called Landor House, after the Victorian poet Walter Savage
Landor (1775–1864) who was born there; its style set the precedent for what was built after the fire. Chapel Street, which
runs down into Smith Street beside Landor House, has an
interesting variety of nineteenth-century cottages, mainly in
brick, built when Warwick finally began to expand. A number
of small houses, some – like the Antelope Inn – incorporating
Tudor features, some Georgian and many Victorian, line
Smith Street, at the bottom of which stands the mansion of
*St John's House* on the other side of the road.

Set in its own grounds with entrance gates and a gravelled
approach, St John's was built in 1626, the first large stone
house in the town. It has five gables, three shaped and two
pointed, with large mullioned windows on the two floors
below. The house is now maintained as a branch of the County
Museum, with the museum of the Royal Warwickshire Regiment on the first floor. The ground floor exhibits include
some handsome, melodiously chiming clocks, produced by
Warwick's dynasties of Georgian clockmakers.

Behind St John's House the public park of St Nicholas
runs down to the meadows beside the River Avon. Deep dips
in the ground are the remains of the quarries which produced
the badly weathering sandstone of which St John's and other
local houses are built. The road from St John's swings round
to St Nicholas's, the second and always considerably less
important of the town's two churches. Set slightly back from
the Banbury Road, opposite the Castle entrance lodge, it was
rebuilt progressively in the eighteenth century, starting with
the vestigially Gothic tower and spire in 1748, and then the
body of the church in 1780. Thomas Johnson, who was responsible for most of the work, was another local gentleman-
architect. He also designed the County Gaol. St Nicholas's
chancel was rebuilt by John Gibson (1790–1866), a turn-his-
hand-to-any-style Victorian architect whose work is to be
found at Charlecote, Guy's Cliffe, Compton Verney and elsewhere, and was paid for by the patronage of a network of local
aristocratic families. From the church, Banbury Road sweeps
down the hill to the river and the bridge where we began.

# ——— AROUND AND ABOUT WARWICK ———

*Warwickshire is not a county that makes grand landscape
gestures; yet for all the built-up areas associated with such
nearby towns as Birmingham and Coventry, it is still
largely what it has always been, 'the green heart of
England'. It is that aspect of the county which these tours
will explore. Except for one very minor incursion into*

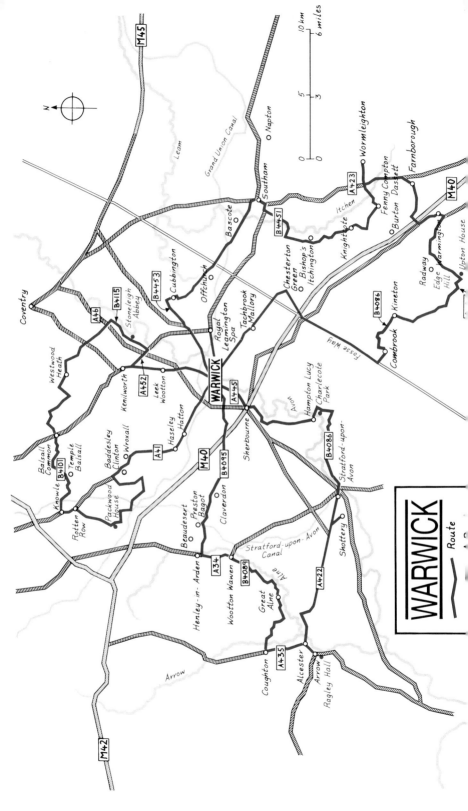

*Oxfordshire, the routes are all contained within the historic county of Warwickshire. The River Avon that flows through Warwick divides the county neatly in two, each part with a separate character and landscape: Feldon and Arden – field and forest. Great ancient roads, then great canals and railways, and now great roads again, have cut their way across the county. Warwickshire has always been a crossroads, a place where cultures met, clashed, and coalesced. The Romans established their rule here, the Saxons triumphed over the Danes, the Normans finally beat the Anglo-Saxons; battles and skirmishes in the civil wars of the Middle Ages were fought across the county, and here the first blows in the civil war of the 1640s were exchanged. One town, Stratford-upon-Avon, is inextricably linked with English culture through William Shakespeare.*

## 1. ROYAL LEAMINGTON SPA

Leamington, or in full Royal Leamington Spa, is Warwick's younger sister. It is considerably larger and has attracted the industry in the area, a factor which has preserved Warwick from the difficulties of rapid growth in the past 150 years. The essential dates in Leamington's history are few. In 1801 it was a village of 350 souls, with a small flow of visitors who came to take its spa waters. They were entranced by the rural tranquillity of the place; soon, with the opening of gushing new springs in 1806, the building of pump rooms and crescents, and the patronage of the Prince Regent (1762–1830, later George IV), Leamington became a rapidly burgeoning town with an appeal to newly wealthy Midlands industrialists. The conferring of the title Royal in 1839, and the far-from-disinterested exercise of patronage by the Duke of Bedford, saw Leamington Spa's population grow from 13,000 inhabitants in 1841 to 23,000 forty years later.

Warwick and Leamington merge into each other almost imperceptibly. The principal way from Warwick is down Coten End and Emscote Road. Across the Grand Union Canal – borne on a series of aqueducts – and the con-

fluence of the rivers Avon and Leam, Leamington Spa begins. Its particular delight lies in the sequences of stuccoed villas and terraces, set off by large public gardens. Some of the terraces, like those on the road from Warwick, have perhaps seen better days, but there is an undeniable sense of the grandeur of the 1820s and 1830s in Waterloo Place and Clarence Terrace. These lengthy terraces of houses, graced respectively by Ionic and Doric porches, face each other across Warwick Street. The crossroads of Warwick Street and Parade is the heart of the shopping and residential town: above it, the roads running east–west were built from 1815 to the mid 1830s, with pilastered stucco fronts and delicate ironwork balconies. Clarendon Avenue and, at its western end (above Waterloo Place), Clarendon Square, are fairly complete examples of the period around 1825.

Parade, the central road of the town, drops south to the river and the Pump Rooms, past the Regent Hotel which the playboy prince, who honoured Leamington with his presence in 1819, allowed to be named after himself. To the west of the gardens lining the river banks, the Pump Room was begun in 1813 (and restored in

1953). The spring inside was the last of the six spa waters to be discovered, and is the only one still in use.

Another spring bubbles up in front of All Saints' Church, across the balustraded late Georgian Victoria bridge. All Saints' is huge, 172 feet in length, and was begun in 1843 but only completed in 1902 when Sir Arthur Blomfield added the last two bays of the nave and the great south-west tower. This area was the original centre of Leamington Spa and contains a number of civic buildings including the *Royal Leamington Spa Art Gallery and Museum*. Many of the surrounding streets still have vestiges of the earliest stucco terraces, four storeys high with Grecian motifs in plaster and cast iron, deriving from examples at Brighton, that became characteristic of Leamington.

## 2. CASTLES, HOUSES, AND CANALS

The first of the more extensive tours circles to the north and west of Warwick, taking in a variety of fine houses, and industrial remains from the Middle Ages to the present day.

The first stopping place is on the banks of the Avon to the right of the A429 to Coventry, which runs up from St John's House Museum past the railway station and over the Grand Union Canal. The canal linked Birmingham with London in the 1790s, allowing easier transport of goods to and from the capital. Guy's Cliffe beside the Avon, approached down a little wooded lane on the right of the main road, is reputed to be the home of a much earlier resident. Guy of Warwick was one of the now-forgotten English folk tale heroes, who lived a life of daring before becoming a hermit— supposedly in the cave which is now incorporated into a little fifteenth-century chantry chapel (unfortunately, usually locked), adorned by the larger-than-life carved figure of a

knight. Guy's Cliffe is now rather melancholy, overlooked by the ruins of the once-great Georgian and High Victorian House on the river bluff. The old A429 (now declassified) through Leek Wootton leads to Kenilworth.

If Warwick is one of England's finest standing castles, Kenilworth Castle is one of its finest ruins. Its name has passed into romance, mainly through the ubiquitous novel by Sir Walter Scott (1771–1832). The Leek Wootton road joins the main road into town opposite the mid Victorian St John's church with its broach spire. Kenilworth's central axis is the High Street connecting the castle on the west to the abbey ruins and parish church on the east. This red sandstone church is mainly fifteenth-century, with an octagonal tower and spire, and incorporates a great Norman doorway that came from the abbey, the ruins of which lie to the south of the parish church. The abbey was founded in the early twelfth century by the de Clinton family who were also building the castle; only the gatehouse giving on to the High Street is still fairly intact.

At the western end of the tree-lined High Street lies the substantial turreted Elizabethan gatehouse into *Kenilworth Castle*. Most of the imposing red sandstone remains like the huge keep and the great hall were royal works, built under Henry II (1133–89) and King John (1167–1216), and then John of Gaunt (1340–99). In 1563 Elizabeth I gave it to Leicester, who added extensive new ranges, but the castle was wasted in 1649, and its great defensive lake was allowed to drain away leaving a wide open space on the far western side, terminated with the earthwork of the King's Pleasaunce, the hunting lodge built by Henry V (1387–1422).

The A452 Warwick Road out of Kenilworth crosses the dual carriageway of the A46, down into the Avon valley;

then follow the B4115 to *Stoneleigh Abbey* and the National Agricultural Centre. The village of Stoneleigh with its range of timber-framed and rust-red brick farmhouses and cottages stands on the west bank of the River Sowe. Closest to the river is the parish church, a substantial Norman building in the deep red local sandstone, a deeply caved chancel arch dominating its interior. Stoneleigh, with the spick-and-span air of an estate village, has belonged to the Leigh family of Stoneleigh Abbey since the mid sixteenth century. The core of their grand house is the Cistercian monastery that occupied the site before its dissolution.

To get to the Abbey, the road runs south crossing the Sowe by the elegant late Georgian bridge built by John Rennie (1761–1821), and then the Avon by the late medieval Stare Bridge with its nine stepped arches. The approach runs through the grounds of the National Agricultural Centre, where the Royal Show is held annually in the first week of July. Some of the monks' buildings were incorporated into the house the Leighs built from the late sixteenth century onwards. Its architectural showpiece is the south front, a fine piece of provincial baroque built by Francis Smith of Warwick in around 1720, with pediments (31 in all) crowding the grey stone façade. At the core of the house is the medieval cloister, while the grandest rooms, the Saloon and Staircase Hall, date from the mid eighteenth century, albeit restored after a disastrous fire in 1960.

Return via Stoneleigh village north-west over the A46 and A429 through the green belt that limits the growth of Coventry. The land rises and falls as the road cuts across the little river valleys, and past the hillside on which the University of Warwick is built. One of the new plateglass universities, Warwick was established in 1965.

Many of its earlier buildings were faced in white tiles that became notorious for falling off, endangering passers-by, but more recent designs like the prize-winning Arts Centre, opened in 1974, experimented much more boldly with external colour – in this case, bands of grey, orange, yellow, and black.

Forming the county boundary between Warwickshire and West Midlands, the road from the University continues west, past the little church at Westwood Heath, one of the earliest essays in 'correct' Gothic by the Victorian architect George Gilbert Scott (1811–78). At the T-junction a mile beyond, a left turn up the hill and then a right leads to the B4101 and Balsall Common. It is a large, modern village, but the surrounding area is studded with substantial timber-framed and brick-built farmhouses of the sixteenth and seventeenth centuries. More handsome still is the collection of buildings at Temple Balsall 1½ miles further along. This takes its name from the Knights Templars, the militant religious order disbanded in 1312, who founded a house at Balsall during the reign of Stephen (?1096–1154). Their chapel remains as the parish church, on a rise beside the river, a red sandstone building with huge windows, built in the late thirteenth century and rescued from ruin in 1662 by Lady Anne Holbourne. She made it into the chapel of the almshouses founded alongside by her sister, Lady Katherine Leveson, and it was thoroughly restored by George Gilbert Scott in 1849. The Hospital still stands east of the church, a long, quite plain courtyard building, designed by William Hurlbutt of Warwick in the late 1670s, together with a cupola-topped school and the original bailiff's house, all built of brick. A row of cottages, set in a little hollow on the other side of the church, contains a medieval hall within its structure, dating from soon after the Templars' suppression.

A mile further along you reach the Grand Union Canal. The towpath from the bridge leads to the Knowle flight of locks stepping down to Warwick and beyond. Knowle itself has become a dormitory village for Birmingham, yet it has, rather self-consciously, preserved its older character around the parish church. A large cedar tree and the closely timber-framed fifteenth-century Guild House beside the church form a beautiful picture from the south. The proud Perpendicular church is built in the two contrasting local sandstones, Arden grey and Kenilworth red. It was consecrated in 1402 as a chapel within the large parish of Hampton-in-Arden. But what a chapel, with the clerestory lighting the high, impressive nave, the tall rood screen, and the carved stalls, as well as the serene 1920s Arts and Crafts furnishings. The hourglass on the pulpit which dictated the length of the sermon was made in 1673; it runs 'a merciful' twenty minutes.

The proximity of Birmingham shows in the built-up area that runs south-west from Knowle, which developed with the advent of the railway and the speculative building of villadom in the 1870s. Yet the minor road south from Rotten Row on the A41 soon runs into open countryside again, and under the railway into Packwood. The church, seen across the fields to the right, has a proud battlemented tower paid for by Nicholas Brome (d. 1517) as penance for murdering the parish priest, whom he found 'chucking his wife under the chin'. The left-hand fork in the road continues to *Packwood House* which has one of the most curious gardens in England.

Packwood is basically a mid Tudor house, considerably enlarged and embellished in the 1920s and 1930s by Graham Baron Ash who incorporated

decoration from many English sources, before giving the property to the National Trust in 1941. Packwood's special interest comes from the gardens John Fetherston planted in the 1660s; a formal garden with gazebos and bee boles (niches for bee skeps) in one of the walls, and the celebrated yew garden, said to represent the Sermon on the Mount, with the great clipped yews as Christ, the evangelists, the apostles, and the multitude. (Possibly a fertile Victorian imagination and a vigorous pruning campaign turned a motley collection of outsized trees into a living parable.)

Another beautiful National Trust manor house, Baddesley Clinton Manor, lies a few miles to the east. The circuitous route is compensated for by the sight of the great flight of locks on the Stratford-upon-Avon Canal. At the junction with the B4439, a track leads to the head of the staircase of ten consecutive locks; another ten in the next few miles of canal brings the waterway up on to the Birmingham plateau. The Stratford-upon-Avon Canal was opened in 1816, and its canalside architecture is especially interesting and unusual: the barrel-vaulted lockkeepers' cottages and the cast-iron bridges with trellis parapets, split to allow the towing rope to pass through the centre. Another half-mile down the canal is the basin linking it with the Grand Union Canal.

Continue along the B4439, crossing the Grand Union Canal, left, and left again, past the expanse of Hay Wood to the turning into Baddesley Clinton. Its church tower was also paid for by Nicholas Brome in expiation for his sin. *Baddesley Clinton Manor* was his house, and it is one of the most beautiful examples in England of a moated manor house, its tall chimneys reflected in the dark waters. Brome built much of the grey stone entrance side. The Ferrers family added brick buildings ranged around a central court in the reigns of Elizabeth (1533–1603) and of Anne (1665–1714), to make this a very romantic setting.

From the modern village of Baddesley Clinton, almost a mile to the north, the A41 runs south-east, passing the avenue that leads down to Wroxall Abbey School and Wroxall church. The north aisle of the Benedictine convent church became the parish church after the Dissolution of the Monasteries, and retains much of its original stained glass. The estate was bought by Sir Christopher Wren in 1713, but the Elizabethan house was transformed for the Dugdale family into a harsh Victorian Tudor-style brick mansion (now the Abbey School). The heavy hand of the Dugdales can be seen all over the estate, in the form of polychrome brick cottages, the village school, and the smithy.

The A41 continues to Warwick, keeping to the ridge top. A pretty little Victorian Gothic school building at a crossroads marks the turning up a few hundred yards to the small, charming and little-touched church of Haseley, complete with box pews and a wagon roof. Almost beside, and rather out of keeping with the daintiness of these other buildings, it is another heavy Victorian Tudor-style manor house, built for a mining engineering family. Back on the A41 and just below the Haseley crossroads stands the parish church of Hatton, which was almost entirely rebuilt in 1880 for the Hewlett family of Haseley Manor. The church contains a memorial of 1825 to Samuel Parr, the eccentric rector who championed the unfortunate Queen Caroline (1683–1737), estranged wife of George IV. Stories about Parr abound, usually to do with his lengthy smoking breaks during divine service.

From here the A46 and the Grand Union Canal run side-by-side back to the outskirts of Warwick.

## 3. THE FOREST OF ARDEN

Of the two halves of Warwickshire, the Feldon was more intensively colonized until it began to experience depopulation in the Middle Ages. Arden, on the other hand, represented opportunities for new colonization in the rapid population growth of Tudor and Stuart England. It also offered the chance to establish industries. Shakespeare's Forest of Arden was not a dense wood, but a fast-growing and as yet under-exploited region. Woodland was cleared and settlements grew, and Birmingham's rising importance was to accentuate the differences between the country's two halves. This route explores the variety of the Avon valley and the Arden.

Leave Warwick on the A429 down West Street from the West Gate, with a few timbered buildings like the Tudor House Hotel (in reality seventeenth-century) to mark the way. Just across the M40 at junction 15, the first turning on the right leads into the little estate village of Sherbourne. Like the Dorset town, its name means clear river, and the Avon as it meanders to the south is usually exactly that. The parish church is one of the glories of George Gilbert Scott's Victorian church architecture, with its soaring spire and the marbles and mosaics that adorn the interior. The church and village were built in the 1860s by the Rylands family, with profits from their Birmingham wire-drawing fortune. Their house, the mid Georgian Sherbourne Park, lies behind the brick wall of the churchyard.

The road then runs south to Hampton Lucy, the village belonging to another estate, Charlecote. The estate is still in evidence, most spectacularly in the nineteenth-century parish church. With the exception of the chancel (again by George Gilbert Scott) the church was built in 1822 6 by Henry Hutchinson and Thomas

Rickman. It is the masterpiece of these early devotees of a fully Gothic style (it was Rickman who devised the sequence Norman–Early English–Decorated–Perpendicular to describe medieval church architecture which we still use). The church, in Decorated style, has a great pinnacled west tower, a splendid east window designed by Thomas Willements, while as an expression of the new age some of the tracery is in cast iron. The bridge over the Avon, carrying the road into *Charlecote Park*, is also of cast iron.

This was all the work of Revd John Hammond Lucy, who inherited Charlecote in 1786. The Lucy family have been at Charlecote since the thirteenth century. The estate as we see it today owes most to the sixteenth and nineteenth centuries. The church at Charlecote was rebuilt in 1851 by John Gibson, in a fussy Decorated style. The most interesting part of his interior is the Lucy family chapel, with three substantial tombs of the seventeenth-century family (all Sir Thomases). Gibson also did a great deal of the work at Charlecote House itself, although here in an Elizabethan style. Approaching the house through its Capability Brown parkland, the house looks entirely Tudor; in fact the only authentic parts are the great gatehouse with its angle turrets (and a family museum in the house above), some of the outbuildings, and the classical porch set between the wings of the front. Much remodelling and extension took place in the 1820s and 1850s, and the interior has a very sumptuous Victorian feel. The wealthy Hammond Lucys collected with great passion, notably in the purchase of items at the sale of William Beckford's effects, such as the massive Florentine table in the hall. According to tradition it was in this hall that William Shakespeare appeared before Sir Thomas Lucy in 1583 for poaching deer in the park, an event which precipitated his departure for London, and fame.

The B4086 below Charlecote Park runs westwards with the river as far as Stratford-upon-Avon, three miles away, a town inextricably linked with Shakespeare. The town has become one of the greatest of all tourist attractions – so it is better to come when visitors are few, or to wander around in the early evening before going to the theatre.

The approach to the town beside the river immediately reveals Stratford's two faces: late medieval prosperity, in the form of the fourteen-arch stone bridge across the Avon, and Shakespeare, in the Shakespeare Memorial Theatre further down on the opposite bank. At the top of Henley Street, forking right from Bridge Street, is *Shakespeare's Birthplace*, the half-timbered house in which Shakespeare is said to have been born in 1564, with the uncompromisingly modern Shakespeare Centre next door. Along High Street and Chapel Street, left from the top of Bridge Street, stands *New Place* where Shakespeare died in 1616 – or rather the foundations, since it was demolished by an eighteenth-century owner outraged at the intrusion of Bard-seeking visitors – and his son-in-law's home, *Nash's House*. Almost opposite are the fifteenth-century Guild Chapel, where the religious guild that ran the pre-Reformation town met beneath the great painting of the Day of Judgement, and the half-timbered complex of the Almshouses and *Stratford-upon-Avon Grammar School*, where the playwright is supposed to have been taught.

Close to the river, at the southern edge of the Old Town, stands Holy Trinity parish church, most of its fabric dating from the fifteenth century at the height of Stratford's prosperity from the cloth trade. The spire on the crossing tower was rebuilt in 1763, by Thomas Hiorn of Warwick. Inside, the main items of interest are in the chancel, the early Tudor misericords (where some of the carving borders on the obscene), and Shakespeare's memorial, his alabaster half-figure gazing out. 'Stay Passenger, why goest thou so fast', the inscription begins. Along the bank of the Avon up towards the bridge runs the sequence of gardens and theatres that constitute the Bard's national memorial. The first commemoration took place here in 1769. The neo-Gothic theatre of 1879, which largely burned down in 1926, has had an exciting modern theatre built onto it (opened in 1986), its timber interior echoing the theatres of Shakespeare's day. The main theatre was opened in 1932, an aggressively modern structure for its day in red brick, with a large square central block and terraces and balconies over the river.

Between the theatres and the bridge, the Stratford Canal empties into a broad basin with its wharf and a lock to the river. The extensive restoration of the nearby early Tudor Alveston Manor is a reminder of how thoroughly tidied up most of the centre of Stratford is – Georgian fronts have often been removed to reveal the timbering behind to make the buildings look more appropriately Shakespearean.

Alcester Road is the A422 west out of Stratford, and two miles out the left turn into Shottery leads to *Anne Hathaway's Cottage*. This timbered, thatched farmhouse with its cottage garden, which belonged to the family of Shakespeare's wife (and contains the fireside settle where the couple allegedly conducted their courtship), is one of the icons of Olde England. It should really be visited on a sunny day; unfortunately, everyone else will have had the same idea.

*Anne Hathaway's Cottage at Shottery.*

The A422 as it gently climbs west out of the Avon valley follows the line of one of the Roman roads that crisscrossed Warwickshire in the early centuries AD. It leads to Alcester – an important Roman market centre. The road swings round Oversley Hill to descend into Alcester, crossing the River Arrow just below its confluence with the Alne. The modern bridge stands close to its predecessor, a six-arched stone structure built in 1600; and the important Roman road Ryknield Street, running south from Redditch, crossed the Arrow here. Alcester's later importance, until the nineteenth century, was as a needle-making centre. Hundreds of people spent their days standing in their outhouses filing and eyeing needles, and many of these primitive small-scale industrial buildings are still to be seen in back yards and gardens. From the centre and the gently curving High Street, dignified by buildings like the part-plastered town hall, given in 1618 by Fulke Greville, small streets lead up to the parish church. Apart from the medieval west tower, the church is largely early Georgian. It was rebuilt in 1730, with Gothic decoration outside and classical inside. Alcester's most pleasing street is the curving Malt Mill Lane, which runs down from the churchyard to the river.

From the central roundabout in Alcester, the A422 continues for a little more than a mile south to Arrow and the entrance to *Ragley Hall*. On the site of Ragley Castle, the 1st Earl of Conway built a grand new baroque house here in 1690. Robert Hooke's monumental design, fifteen bays wide, was not completed and decorated internally until James Gibbs was engaged in 1750. The grandest room is the Great Hall, decorated with stucco work on a heroic scale. The Marquesses of Hertford, is the Conways became, were great art collectors, and

the Wallace Collection in London is the result. During the twentieth century the estate has been pulled back from the brink of ruin. The house has been thoroughly repaired, and huge modern wall paintings have been added to the South Staircase Hall as evidence of a continuing commitment to art. Capability Brown laid out the extensive grounds, which have been put to imaginative use with carefully sited adventure playgrounds and guided walks. The eye-catching Oversley Castle to the east is a Regency sham: the Prince Regent, a friend of the 3rd Marquess, recommended that a folly be built there to improve the view.

Back into Alcester, the course of Ryknield Street, the A435, follows the direction of the Arrow valley. Two miles further along the great tower gatehouse of *Coughton Court* rises to the east. Coughton was the principal residence of the Throckmorton family, who adhered to Roman Catholicism throughout the years of persecution. That gives the history of the house its colour: the early Tudor gatehouse with its defensive look was tested in the Civil War and again when a Protestant mob attacked in 1688. The subsequent rebuilding resulted in the pinky Georgian Gothic wings that flank the gate tower. The Tudor and early Stuart ranges are riddled with priest holes, while the drawing room with its oriel windows east and west is supposed to have been where the wives of the Gunpowder Plotters in 1605 waited to hear news of their husbands' success – or failure. When Catholic Emancipation came, the Throckmortons built a church in 1857, by the river, a short distance from the Anglican parish church their ancestor Sir Robert Throckmorton had built in around 1500. Most of the original furnishings remain in its light, plastered interior. Sir Robert died in the Holy Land in

1518, and his tomb in the nave remained empty until a later Sir Robert used it for himself in 1791.

From Coughton, the road crosses the River Arrow, beside the old ford, and up the valley side to join the B4089 above Alcester. The B4089 follows up the Alne valley, through the village of Great Alne, and on to Wootton Wawen with its variety of half-timbered and brick houses and inns. St Peter's parish church at the heart of the village was described by George Gilbert Scott as 'an epitome in stone of the history of the Church of England', starting with the eleventh-century Anglo-Danish church of which much of the central tower remains, and now ending with the abstract stained glass in the chancel windows. Examples of the work of almost every century are to be seen in the church fabric.

Water is one of the principal features of Wootton Wawen. The Alne and the Stratford Canal run almost side-by-side to the east, where the canal is carried across the road on an aqueduct built on tapering brick piers, while the sequence of weirs on the river survives from many former mills. One early nineteenth-century mill remains. Below it lies the serpentine lake dug to grace the grounds of Wootton Hall, the pedimented late Stuart house, just east of the church, which was the home of Mrs Fitz-Herbert (d. 1837), the irregular wife of the Prince Regent. Upstream, along the A34, lies Henley-in-Arden.

The occasional copses and woods on the further slopes above the Alne are the sole remnants of the forest in which Henley grew up, beneath the protection of the de Montforts' castle of Beaudesert. The market town is essentially one slightly curving street nearly a mile long with the parish church and market place at the mid-point. Many of the houses in the main street have fifteenth- or sixteenth-century timber frames, most notably the Guildhall beside the parish church. This also dates almost wholly from the fifteenth century, which was obviously the little town's heyday, until it became important again in the coaching age. Only a hundred yards east of Henley church, but over the river, stands the massive Norman church of Beaudesert. It served the de Montforts' castle, of which nothing remains but some raised humps in the ground to its north-east.

The lanes of Beaudesert drop down to the B4095 on its way east towards Warwick. A variety of once-fortified mounds and moated sites testify to the way in which the settlements in this part of the country were wrested from the woodland, occasional vestiges of which remain. This is a comparatively recent road, further evidence of the relative inaccessibility of the Arden until the last century. At Preston Bagot, a short way to the left at the bridge over the Stratford Canal, one of the first buildings is the Elizabethan manor house, timber-framed with brick infill. The hamlet clusters around the little Norman church set on a hill. At Claverdon, two miles further down the B4095, the stone building off to the left is an early seventeenth-century defensible tower house – a feature more common in Cumbria than in the West Midlands.

East of Claverdon, the road begins its descent towards Warwick and the Avon, with the views opening out across the town to the countryside and hills beyond. Crossing the M40 and then the A46 to skirt the race course, this road enters Warwick town centre at the West Gate beside the Leycester Hospital. The few urban staging posts along the way and the modern trunk roads and motorways only confirm the feeling which persists on some of these back roads of how enclosed and separate Arden was for so long.

## 4. THE HILLS OF FELDON

In contrast to the wooded enclaves of Arden, the other half of Warwickshire, the Feldon, is more open and, now, less densely settled. Until the Tudor period this was still the more populous part of the county, but aggressive land-ownership for animal farming and the legacy of medieval depopulation led to the shrinking and often the disappearance of many places. The wide undulating plain is terminated by the hills on the border with Oxfordshire and Northamptonshire, where there is a variety of substantial historic houses, many of them open to the public.

The route begins on the A445 to Leamington Spa, and continues along it, passing the site of the Lillington Oak, one of the candidates for the exact mid-point of England. From the second roundabout, the B4453 right-hand exit leads to the village of Cubbington, set among the hills above the Leam valley. Although some of the village has become a Leamington suburb, there are still some older black-and-white cottages. The parish church, down Church Lane to the right, is part Norman, part Victorian restoration, and contains a surprise for a place almost as far from the sea as you can get in England; the monument of 1703 to Captain Murcott, depicting a boat supported by a sailor and Neptune. The lane swings right below the church, where the village stops abruptly and the hills begin, to the Welsh Road running south-west in a fairly straight line. This was once a major cattle-droving route from Wales. This practice, which was at its height in the eighteenth and early nineteenth centuries, involved the movement on foot of hundreds of thousands of beasts from Wales and Scotland to feed the London market.

The Welsh Road crosses the Leam at Offchurch, a village set on a hill where Offa, the great Mercian king, is alleged to have been buried in AD 796. Two carved stones in the wall of the church are supposed to have come from his coffin lid. Whether you believe that or not, the views over the valley to the north and west are striking enough to make Offchurch a place worth stopping at. Much of the fabric of the church is Norman, while the fifteenth-century west tower is pock-marked with holes made (it is said) by Parliamentary troops in the Civil War. Half a mile east of Offchurch, the line of the Welsh Road crosses what is probably an equally ancient route, the Fosse Way – the great Roman road running from south Devon to Lincolnshire. Most of the Fosse Way is still in use as a road today, sometimes, as here, only a minor back road, elsewhere, as near Sherborne, as an important A road. Continue on the drove road, and cross the Grand Union Canal as it flows east of Warwick. The next crossroads is Bascote Heath, where in 1642 the very first skirmish of the English Civil War was fought; Lord Brooke, from Warwick Castle, routed a party of Royalists. Many important early actions of the war were played out in this area, culminating in the great battle of Edgehill. Now all is quiet among the woods at the crossroads and along the canalside walks just to the north. The Welsh Road continues into Southam, one of the market towns which prospered and then declined with the cattle trade.

The town's inns, like the Black Dog, must have refreshed many a passing cattle drover. Yet what dominates the town is the parish church, its red sandstone spire, 120 feet high, topping the silvery-grey building. The stream which flows past the church feeds a holy well half a mile to the west, which may be reached along the footpath through the fields. Georgian Gothick, cast-iron gates and pollarded lime trees make a fine setting in the churchyard, while the old market place and the town's houses lie below. The first Provident Dispensary in the country was opened in Southam in 1823, for which there is a commemorative urn outside the part-Gothic Stoneythorpe Hotel, its original premises. There are several handsome grey Georgian terraces on the Banbury Road, the A423, which is our route out of Southam south before turning west on the A425 and south again on the B4451. Shortly after Deppers Bridge across the little River Itchen, and then the railway bridge, the road turns very sharply back on itself, by the remains of the local cement works, a major local industry until their closure in 1969.

Bishop's Itchington is the first example of a common feature of this part of Warwickshire, the deserted village. Originally there were two settlements, Itchington Inferior, which expanded in the last century with the cement works, and Itchington Superior to its south, now occupied only by Old Town Farm. The farm lies on the lower road parallel to the river, leading through the hamlet of Knightcote where the long row of thatched cottages is built in a distinctive stone which make its first appearance, the brown stone of Edge Hill and north Oxfordshire. At the T-junction below Knightcote, the land ahead rises into the hills of the Burton Dassett Country Park, topped by an ancient beacon. The left turn reaches Fenny Compton after $1\frac{1}{2}$ miles, a village nestling below the hills, built in the yellow-brown Hornton stone and in brick. The best houses, like the brick-built early Georgian Red House, cluster around the church, which stands on a rise, its stout tower and spire reaching heavenwards.

On the road north-east of Fenny Compton, beyond the railway, there is a section of the Oxford Canal, with a marina and then, by the crossroads with the A423, a wharf. The canal winds its tortuous way north from here to join the Grand Union Canal above Napton, on the Warwickshire–Northamptonshire border. The village of Wormleighton, a little further along, is the rump of the much larger medieval settlement which was depopulated in the fifteenth century, when so many villages wasted away or, as in this case, were ruthlessly cleared by the landowner who wished to turn the fields into sheep-runs. Traces of the village, in the form of regular hummocks and hollows, may still be made out in the fields on the other side of the canal. In 1508, ten years after the clearance, John Spencer built his manor house, which later became part of the great animal-grazing empire that the Spencers developed, centred on Althorp in Northamptonshire. One range of brick buildings of the once-enormous Spencer manor house remains at Wormleighton, beside the church with its tall carved early Tudor screen that was probably a gift from the family.

Back down the A423, after it re-crosses the Oxford Canal at the highest point in its journey, the next village is Farnborough. It is a beautiful estate village, in the warm brown stone quarried in the hills, with church, reading room, and cottages huddled together. On the southern edge of the village the landscape gardens of *Farnborough Hall* swoop down to a sequence of lakes. The Holbech family acquired the estate in 1684, and their house has a west front of that period, and a north entrance front of 1750. The entrance hall and the dining room both have many rococo flourishes, and were designed to focus upon fine paintings the Holbeches acquired on the Grand Tour. The parkland is justly famous, with its temple and pavilion on the grassed terrace walk. Despite vigorous campaigns, the new M40 has been constructed through the valley below, destroying uninterrupted landscape views over to Edge Hill.

From Farnborough, the lane descends the steep hillside, and an unfenced road crosses the little valley bottom to Warmington. Warmington is one of the finest set-piece villages in Warwickshire, with Hornton stone houses clustering around the village green and pond and set on the hill, the late Elizabethan manor house on the western side, and the parish church standing above the village almost beside the A41. From here the B4086 runs up the escarpment, and a top road continues along the edge. The views across Warwickshire are extensive: Warwick itself is visible on a clear day, beyond the rolling hills, chequerboard fields and little villages. In the ground below, beyond the trees of the village of Radway, the first great battle of the English Civil War was fought on 23 October 1642. The result was a bloody and expensive draw, with heavy injuries and loss of life. The Castle public house on the escarpment edge itself was built by Sanderson Miller in 1750 as a Gothic eyecatcher, a memorial for the battle on the spot where Charles I's standard was raised. Miller's gentlemanly scholarship provided the basis for the earliest Gothic revival of the eighteenth century; he advised many of his neighbours, like the Holbeches at Farnborough, on embellishments to their houses and grounds.

Miller's own house, Radway Grange down at the foot of the escarpment, is not open to visitors, but many of his Gothick improvements to it are visible from the footpath which follows the slope down to the village, again where brown stone terraces cluster around a green. Unfortunately the parish church, where Miller and his family are buried, was rebuilt in particularly heavy Victorian Gothic in the 1860s. The delicacy of the design of the grey stone church of Ratley, on the

south-eastern side of Edge Hill, is often supposed to have been an important influence on Miller's work. At Ratley, terraces of stone houses are stepped down the hillside to a village green and the church. From here the lane passes through the hamlet of Edgehill to the A422 and the entrance to *Upton House*.

Upton, another National Trust property, is a house of many surprises. The essentially late Stuart, brown stone house, occupies the site of another late medieval deserted village. Sanderson Miller worked here, especially on the garden temple and its pool (which stand upon the county boundary with Oxfordshire), while the grounds are designed to spring surprise views on the visitor. The house is perhaps best known for its collection of English and Continental Old Master paintings and ceramics, assembled by Lord Bearstead in the earlier decades of this century, when most of the interiors were also remodelled. There are some famous works here, including William Hogarth's *Night*, Hieronymous Bosch's *Adoration of the Magi*, and an array of portraits that includes George Romney's *William Beckford*.

The A422 from Upton descends into the broader vale, skirting the battle site (which is now mainly, if ironically, in Ministry of Defence hands). This is still known as the Vale of the Red Horse, from the figure cut onto the hillside which was destroyed when the land was enclosed in 1798. From the height of Edge Hill and the hills of Oxfordshire, the route runs back into the undulating Feldon and the Midland Plain. North from the next crossroads (beyond the Radway turn) the lane leads gently down to Kineton. The cavalry under Prince Rupert (1619–92) killed and wounded many in the Parliamentary baggage train who were quartered in Kineton during Edgehill. Kineton's buildings are a mixture of brown and grey, as builders have access to both the Hornton stone and the grey lias of this part of Warwickshire. The market fell into disuse in 1840 (and a school was built on the site of the former market house), but the secluded market place is still there to the north of the parish church, with various late seventeenth-century cottages on its sides. St Peter's church, with its toffee-coloured late medieval tower, was otherwise rebuilt by Sanderson Miller in 1755 in his characteristic, slightly whimsical Gothick style, with ogee-headed windows – and his descendant, Revd Frank Miller, Gothicized it 'properly' in around 1880.

There is a network of footpaths to the west of Kineton, in the area below the B4086, running past the motte and bailey earthworks of King John's Castle (although whether it was his is a matter of conjecture) to the Victorian late Tudor-style estate village of Combrook and the grounds of Compton Verney. The road itself bridges the stream that connects the upper and lower lakes of the park landscape, and there is a circular public footpath around the lower lake taking in Combrook. Although Compton Verney house itself is not open to the public, there are glimpses of it from the road, with the great west range of 1714 built by Sir John Vanbrugh (1664–1726) or one of his pupils, other ranges added in 1760 by Robert Adam (1728–92), and the chapel by Capability Brown who also designed the magnificent park landscape. His cedar trees are a rare and successful addition to the grounds where graceful bridges cross the lakes and streams. A new opera house has been designed by the Danish architect Erik Larsen to rise beside the great lake, like the house superbly sited in the landscaped park.

The road crossing the B4086 just west of Compton Verney is the Fosse Way. Our route turns right to follow it through open rolling countryside, with surprisingly few houses, let alone villages, on its route. After some six miles, just across the A41, a right turn crossing the M40 leads to Chesterton Green set on its little hills, perhaps one of the most melancholy of the deserted villages. Where there were once seven separate settlements there are now only a few farm houses and cottages. Most of the desertion was well under way by the end of the fourteenth century, as population falls were compounded by the aftermath of the Black Death. Most prominent and eccentric of all the survivals in Chesterton is the windmill on the hill to the north-east, a domed tower set on an arcade of Tuscan columns. This curiosity was almost certainly designed by Sir Edward Peyto, the squire whose family lived in an early Stuart classical house beside the churchyard, until it was demolished in 1802. There are various Peyto family memorials (two of them by Nicholas Stone) in the long, low fourteenth-century parish church. It stands at the furthest end of the lane that peters out in the hills between the lakes and former fish ponds of the great house. Wide views from this point, down towards Warwick and up into the hillier part of the Feldon, emphasize how relatively unpopulated the area is.

The lane that passes below the windmill to its east connects with the road that runs back towards the Fosse Way, and continues beyond the ancient Roman route to Warwick, skirting the southern fringes of Leamington Spa. The cottages of Tachbrook Mallory alongside the road are the vestiges of another early Tudor village depopulated when the land was enclosed for grazing in 1505. The road descends into the Avon valley from Heathcote Hill, beside the newly-expanding light industrial estates to join the Banbury Road just to the south of the main bridge over the Avon.

# PRACTICAL INFORMATION

*The details which follow offer information on getting to the towns, places to eat and to stay when there, and admission details for the places mentioned in the town and touring sections. Constant changes have made it impractical to include hours of opening; if your time is limited, do phone ahead to confirm these. The listings for the towns themselves appear first, followed by the listings for the 'Round and About' sections. (NT) means that a property is owned by the National Trust, (EH) that it is in the care of English Heritage. The telephone numbers and addresses of Tourist Information Centres are also given; these are unfailingly helpful, and many supply lists, brochures and maps on request. The relevant pages in the 1991 Philip's Road Atlas of Britain are given, covering the town and the touring areas.*

## ——————— BAKEWELL ———————

Bakewell lies on the main A6, between Derby and Manchester. The nearest motorway is the M1 at junction 29, fifteen miles away. There is no railway station; the closest are at Buxton and Matlock, with a bus service connecting.

The best hotels are Milford House Hotel offering bed, breakfast and dinner in the former mill house: (0629) 812130; and, more expensive, the Rutland Arms Hotel built for the spa in the centre: (0629) 812812. Although it sits in the centre of the Peak District National Park, Bakewell itself is not over-endowed with bed and breakfast accommodation. The Bridge House can be recommended: (0629) 812867.

Eating out must involve a Bakewell Pudding. The Old Bakewell Pudding in Anchor Square is a small restaurant and cake shop. The best restaurant is the Green Apple on Diamond Court, off Water Street: (0629) 814404. There is also a number of very good butchers and cheesemongers.

*Philip's Road Atlas p. 45*

**Peak District Information Centre** Market Hall, Bridge Street; (0629) 813227. Daily.
**Old House Museum** Cunningham Place; (0629) 813647. Daily Apr–Oct, charge.

---

**Arkwright Mill** Cromford; (062982) 4297. Daily, charge. Also, Cromford Wharf Steam Museum and Leawood Pumphouse, and High

Peak Junction Workshop; (062982) 3727, 2831. Weekends in summer, charge.
**Blue John Cavern** Castleton; (0433) 20638. Daily, charge.
**Bolsover Castle (EH)** Bolsover; (0246) 823349. Daily, except Mon in winter, charge.
**Buxton Town Museum** (0298) 24658. Tue–Sat, free.
**Chatsworth House** nr Bakewell; (0246) 582204. Daily Mar–Oct, charge.

**Gulliver's Kingdom** Matlock Bath; (0629) 580540. Daily Easter–Sept, charge.

**Haddon Hall** nr Bakewell; (0629) 812855. Tue–Sun Apr–Sept, charge.

**Hardwick Hall (NT)** nr Chesterfield; (0246) 850430. Wed–Sun Apr–Oct, charge.

**Heights of Abraham** Matlock Bath; (0629) 582365. Daily Easter–Oct, charge.

**Ilam Park (NT)** nr Ashbourne; (033529) 245. Throughout year, visitor centre daily in summer, weekends Oct–Mar, free.

**Longshaw Estate Country Park (NT)** nr Sheffield; (0433) 31708. Throughout year, visitor centre weekends, free.

**National Tramway Museum** Crich; (0773) 852565. Daily except occasional Fridays Apr–Sept, weekends Oct, charge.

**Peacock Heritage Centre** Chesterfield; (0246) 207777. Mon–Sat, free.

**Peak Cavern** Castleton; (0433) 20285. Daily Apr–Sept, charge.

**Peak District Mining Museum and Temple Mine (fluorspar)** Matlock Bath; (0629) 583834. Daily, charge.

**Peveril Castle (EH)** Castleton; (0433) 20613. Daily, except Mon in winter, charge.

**Speedwell Cavern** Castleton; (0433) 20512. Daily, charge.

**Treak Cliff Cavern** Castleton; (0433) 20571. Daily, charge.

**Winster Market House (NT)** nr Matlock; (033529) 245. Weekends, summer, free.

# KENDAL

Kendal lies close to the M6 at junction 37 and the A6 passes through, while the main route across the southern Pennines is the A65 from Skipton and Leeds. The nearest mainline railway station is at Oxenholme on the London Euston–Glasgow line; the branch line to Windermere stops at Kendal. There are also buses from Lancaster.

Bed and breakfast accommodation is quite plentiful, and usually good value. Some accommodation is available in historic properties, like the Websters' 1812 house, now the Garden House Hotel on Fowling Lane; (0539) 731131. At lower prices, visitors might like the Hillside Guest House on Beast Banks: (0539) 722836; and the late Georgian no. 7 Thorny Hills, another Webster house: (0539) 720207.

Of the restaurants, the best is currently the Moon at 129 Highgate, open for dinner only: (0539) 729254. Many places serve lunch and tea, of which Farrer's Tea and Coffee House on Stricklandgate has probably the most interesting interior. The Old Brewery Restaurant, off Highgate, can also be recommended for the day and early evening: (0539) 725133. Some of the finest restaurants in the country are within reach of Kendal, further into the Lake District.

Other food items to look out for are Kendal Mint Cake, and Cumberland sausage.

*Philip's Road Atlas pp. 56–7*

**Abbot Hall Art Gallery and Museum of Lakeland Life and Industry** Kirkland; (0539) 722464. Daily, charge.

**Castle Dairy** Wildman Street; (0539) 721170. Tue–Sat, charge.

**Kendal Museum of Natural History and Archaeology** Station Road; (0539) 721374. Daily, charge.

**Tourist Information Centre** Town Hall, Highgate; (0539) 725758. Daily.

---

**Ancestral Research Centre** (Lady Anne Clifford Collection) Maulds Meaburn; (0930) 51458. Daily Apr–Sept, charge.

**Appleby Castle** Appleby; (0930) 51402. Daily May–Sept, charge.

**Beatrix Potter Gallery (NT)** Hawkshead; (09666) 355. Mon–Fri Apr–Nov, charge.

**Brantwood** nr Coniston; (0966) 41396. Daily Mar–Nov, Wed–Sun Dec–Feb, charge.

**Bridge House (NT)** Ambleside; (05394) 33883 (NT Information Centre).

**Brough Castle (EH)** Brough; (09304) 219. Daily, charge.

**Cartmel Priory Gatehouse (NT)** Cartmel; (05395) 36602. Tue–Sun Apr–Oct, charge.

**Dove Cottage and Wordsworth Museum** Grasmere; (09665) 544. Daily, charge.

**'Gondola' Steam Yacht (NT)** Coniston Water; (05394) 41288. Daily sailings in season from Coniston Pier and Park-A-Moor.

**Graythwaite Hall Gardens** nr Hawkshead; (0448) 31333. Daily Apr–Jun, charge.

**Grizedale Forest Park, Visitors' Centre** Grizedale; (022984) 373. Daily.

**Hawkshead Courthouse (NT)** Hawkshead; (05394) 33883. Daily Apr–Nov, free.

**Hawkshead Grammar School** Hawkshead. Daily Apr–Oct, charge.

**Hill Top (NT)** nr Sawrey; (09666) 269. Sat–Wed Apr–Nov, charge.

**Holker Hall and Lakeland Motor Museum** Cark-in-Cartmel; (05395) 58328, 58509. Sun–Fri, Apr–Oct, charge.

**Keld Chapel (NT)** Shap. Daily, free.

**Leighton Hall** Yealand Conyers; (0524) 734474. Sun, Tue–Fri May–Sept, charge.

**Levens Hall** nr Kendal; (05395) 60321. Daily, charge.

**National Park Visitors' Centre** Brockhole, nr Windermere; (09662) 2231. Daily, free.

**Rydal Mount** Ambleside; (05394) 33002. Daily Mar–Oct, Wed–Mon Nov-Feb, charge.

**Shap Abbey (EH)** Daily, free.

**Sizergh Castle (NT),** nr Kendal; (05395) 60070. Sun–Mon, Wed–Thu Apr–Oct, charge.

**Stagshaw Garden** nr Ambleside; (05394) 32109. Daily Apr–Jun, charge.

**Stott Park Bobbin Mill (EH)** Newby Bridge; (0448) 31087. Daily Apr–Oct, charge.

**Townend (NT)** Troutbeck; (05394) 32628. Tue–Fri, Sun Apr–Nov, charge.

# KING'S LYNN

King's Lynn is at the end of the line – of the A10 from Cambridge and London, and of the main railway from London Liverpool Street. The A47 connects with Peterborough, Wisbech and Norwich, and the A17 with Lincoln.

Of places to stay, the best in the historic centre is the Tudor Rose Hotel, a fifteenth- to seventeenth-century warren of buildings on St Nicholas St: (0553) 762824. The Stuart

House Hotel, 35 Goodwins Road, is a little to the east of the South Gate: (0553) 772169. There is a variety of reasonably-priced guest houses.

The most interesting place to eat, both for lunch and dinner, is the Riverside in the warehouses behind St George's Guildhall on King St: (0553) 773134. There are many pubs and small restaurants. Bank House, facing the Purfleet and Custom House on King's Staithe Square, offers accommodation as well as meals in this handsome mid-Stuart house: (0553) 765087.

*Philip's Road Atlas: pp. 38, 48*

**Guildhall of St George (NT) and Art Gallery** Fermoy Centre, King St; (0553) 774725. Mon–Sat, free.

**King's Lynn Museum** Old Market St; (0553) 775001. Mon–Sat, charge.

**Medieval Merchant's House** King St; (0553) 772454. By appointment, charge.

**Museum of Social History** King St; (0553) 775001. Tue–Sat, charge.

**Red Mount Chapel** The Walks; (0553) 763044. Open as part of guided tours.

**South Gate** Wed Jun–Sept, charge.

**Thoresby College** Queen St; King's Lynn Preservation Society (0553) 763871. Great Hall by appointment, donations welcome.

**Town Hall** and **Tourist Information** (Guildhall of the Holy Trinity and Regalia Room) Saturday Market; (0553) 763044. Mon–Sat Apr–Oct, charge.

**Castle Acre Castle (EH)** Daily, free.
**Castle Acre Priory (EH)** Castle Acre; (0760) 755394. Daily, charge.

**Castle Rising Castle (EH)** Castle Rising; (055387) 330. Daily, charge.

**Holkham Hall** nr Wells-next-the-Sea; (0328) 710227. Sun–Thu May–Sept, charge.

**Houghton Hall** New Houghton; (048522) 569. Sun, Thu Mar–Sept, charge.

**Leverington Hall** nr Wisbech. By written appointment.

**Oxburgh Hall (NT)** Oxborough; (036621) 258. Sat–Wed Mar–Oct, charge.

**Peckover House (NT)** Wisbech; (0945) 583463. Sat–Sun Mar–Oct, charge.

**Sandringham House** Sandringham; (0553) 772675. Sun–Thu Apr–Sept except when member of Royal Family in residence, charge.

**Trinity Hospital** Castle Rising. Tue, Thu, Sat, free.

**Wisbech and Fenland Museum** Wisbech; (0945) 583817. Tue–Sat, free.

**Wolferton Station Museum** nr Sandringham; (0485) 540674. Sun–Fri Apr–Sept, Sat–Sun Oct, charge.

# RICHMOND

Richmond sits very close to the A1 and the Scotch Corner junction with the trans-Pennine A66. The nearest railway station is some ten miles away at Darlington on the Edinburgh–London Kings Cross line; there is a fairly frequent bus service connecting Darlington and Richmond.

The grandest frontage of any of the Richmond hotels is that of the King's Head in the Market Place: (0748) 850220, and there is a number of other good town centre hotels: the Frenchgate, for example: (0748) 3596. A number of pubs offer decent basic accommodation, like the Bishop Blaise in the Market Place: (0748) 3065. The Culloden Tower is available for weekly lets from the Landmark Trust, but it is usually booked up well ahead: (062882) 5925.

Good accommodation is also offered at Richmond's best place to eat, Howe Villa at Whitcliffe Mill above the Swale on the outskirts, which serves dinner only, a fixed menu at a fixed time: (0748) 850055. The bakers, butchers, and cheese-mongers in and near the Market Place are among the glories of Richmond.

*Philip's Road Atlas, p. 58.*

**Culloden Tower** Bargate Green. By written appointment, Landmark Trust, Shottesbrooke, Berks, SL6 3SW.

**Easby Abbey (EH)** nr Richmond; (0748) 5224. Tues–Sun Oct–Mar, charge.

**Green Howards Regimental Museum** Trinity Church; (0748) 2133. Daily Apr–Oct, Mon–Sat Nov, Feb–Mar, charge.

**Richmond Castle (EH)** nr Market Square; (0748) 2493. Tue–Sun Oct–Mar, charge.

**Richmondshire Museum** Ryder's Wynd; (0748) 5611. Daily Mar–Oct, charge.

**Richmond Town Hall** Market Square. Visit by appointment.

**St Nicholas Gardens** Maison Dieu. Daily, charge.

**Theatre Royal and Theatre Museum** Friar's Wynd; (0748) 3021. Daily May–Oct, charge; also performances throughout year.

**Tourist Information** Friary Gardens; (0748) 850252.

---

**Aske Hall** nr Richmond. Exterior and garden, daily Aug, charge.

**Barnard Castle (EH)** Barnard Castle; (0833) 38212. Daily, charge.

**Bolton Castle** nr Leyburn; (0969) 23981. Daily Mar–Oct, charge.

**Bowes Museum** Barnard Castle; (0833) 690606. Daily, charge.

**Braithwaite Hall (NT)** nr Leyburn; (0969) 40287. By appointment, charge.

**Byland Abbey (EH)** nr Coxwold; (03476) 614. Daily, charge.

**Coach and Carriage Museum, Aysgarth** Daily Apr–Oct, charge.

**Duncombe Park** nr Helmsley; (0439) 70213. Sun–Thurs Apr–Sept, charge.

**Forcett Dovecote** nr Richmond; (0325) 718226. By appointment.

**Greta Bridge (and the buildings in The Square)** nr Barnard Castle. Written appointment, 1 The Square.

**Helmsley Castle (EH)** Helmsley; (0439) 70442. Daily, charge.

**Kirby Hill Grammar School** Kirby Hill. Written appointment, Landmark Trust, Shottesbrooke, Berks., SL6 3SW.

**Middleham Castle (EH)** Middleham; (0969) 23899. Daily, charge.

**Moulton Hall (NT)** nr Richmond. Written appointment.

**Mount Grace Priory (EH)** nr Northallerton; (0609) 83494. Daily, charge.

**National Park Information Centre** Old Railway Station, Hawes; (0969) 50456.

**Newburgh Priory** nr Coxwold; (03476) 435. Sun, Wed May–Aug, charge.

**Outhwaites' Ropeworks, Hawes**
Mon–Sat.
**Rievaulx Abbey (EH)** nr Helmsley;
(04396) 228. Daily, charge.
**Rievaulx Terrace (NT)** nr
Helmsley; (04396) 340. Daily Apr–
Oct, charge.
**Raby Castle** Staindrop;
(0833) 60202. Sun–Fri Apr–Sept,
charge.
**Rokeby Park** nr Barnard Castle.
Occasional days May–Sept,
charge.

**Shandy Hall** Coxwold;
(03476) 465. Wed, Sun May–Aug,
charge.
**Studley Royal** and **Fountains
Abbey (NT),** and church (EH) nr
Ripon; (076586) 333, 639. Daily,
charge.
**Swaledale Folk Museum** Reeth;
(0748) 84373. Daily Apr–Oct, charge.
**Thirsk Museum** Thirsk;
(0845) 22755. Daily Mar–Oct, charge.
**Upper Dales Folk Museum** Hawes;
(09697) 494. Daily Apr–Sept, charge.

# RYE

Rye sits on the A259 connecting Hastings with Folkestone,
and the A268 which joins the A21 to Sevenoaks and the M25.
The railway serves Ashford and Hastings, both connected to
London and, in Hastings' case, along the south coast.

There are two particularly handsome and well-appointed
guest house hotels in the prettiest part of the centre of Rye.
Jeake's House stands half-way up the steep cobbled Mermaid
Street: (0797) 222828. On Church Square close to the main
door of St Mary's, The Old Vicarage is painted a fetching
pink: (0797) 222119.

Landgate Bistro by the Landgate offers Rye's best cooking,
but at dinner only: (0797) 222829. There is a variety of other
restaurants, of which the Flushing Inn on East Street has the
most interesting setting: (0797) 223292. Rye offers a wide range
of good places to have tea.
*Philip's Road Atlas p. 13.*

**Lamb House (NT)** West St. Wed, Sat
Apr–Oct, charge.
**Rye Art Gallery** Ockman Lane, East
St; (0797) 223218. Daily, charge.
**Tourist Information** (with Rye
Heritage Centre and Town Model),
Strand Quay; (0797) 226696. Daily
Apr–Oct, weekends and mornings
Nov–Mar, charge.
**Ypres Tower and Rye Museum**
Church Square; (0797) 223254. Daily,
Apr–Oct, charge.

**Bateman's (NT)** Burwash;
(0435) 882302. Sat–Wed, Apr–Oct,
charge.

**Battle Abbey (EH)** Battle;
(04246) 3792. Daily, charge.
**Battle Museum** Battle;
(04246) 2439. Daily, Apr–Sept, charge
**Benenden Walled Garden**
Benenden; (0580) 240749. Daily
school holidays, charge
**Bodiam Castle (NT)** Bodiam;
(058083) 436. Daily Apr–Oct, Mon–
Sat Nov–Mar, charge.
**Brenzett Aeronautical Museum**
Brenzett; (0679) 20606. Sun and bank
holidays Apr–Jun and Oct, Tue–Thur
July–Oct.
**Brickwall House** Northiam;
(07974) 2494. Sat Apr–Sept, charge.
Court Hall Museum Winchelsea.
Daily May–Sept, charge.

**Dungeness Old Lighthouse**
Dungeness. Weekends, charge.

**Dymchurch Court Room**
Dymchurch. Occasional, charge.

**Fishermen's Museum** Hastings.
Sun–Fri May–Sept, charge.

**Greyfriars** Winchelsea. Daily, free.

**Great Dixter** Northiam;
(07974) 3160. Daily Apr–Oct, charge.

**Great Maytham** Rolvendon. Wed–
Thur May–Sept, charge.

**Haremere Hall** Etchingham;
(058081) 245. Daily Apr–Oct (shire
horses: Tue–Sun; house: bank
holiday weekends), charge.

**Lympne Castle** Lympne;
(0303) 67571. Daily May–Sept, charge.

**Martello Tower (EH)** Dymchurch;
(0303) 873684. Daily, Apr–Sept,
charge.

**Museum of Shopping** Battle. Fri–
Wed, charge.

**Pevensey Castle (EH)** Pevensey;
(0323) 762604. Tue–Sun, charge.

**Port Lympne, Zoo and Mansion**
Lympne; (0303) 264646. Daily,
charge.

**Romney, Hythe & Dymchurch
Railway;** (0679) 62353. Daily
Apr–Sept, occasional otherwise,
charge.

**Shipwreck Heritage Centre**
Hastings; (0424) 437452. Daily May–
Sept, Sat–Sun Oct–Mar, charge.

**Sissinghurst Castle Garden (NT)**
Sissinghurst; (0580) 712850. Tue–Sun
Apr–Oct, charge.

**Smallhythe Place (NT)** Smallhythe;
(05806) 2334. Sat–Wed Apr–Oct,
charge.

# SHERBORNE

The main A30 runs through Sherborne, and the A303 runs a
little to the north of it, both connecting the M3 from south-
west London with Devon and Cornwall. The A359 and A361
link Sherborne with the M4 thirty miles north. Sherborne
railway station is on the main London Waterloo–Exeter line.

Sherborne's premier place to stay is the Eastbury Hotel,
in its handsome Georgian building on Long Street: (0935)
813131. A number of town centre pubs offer accommodation,
notably the Britannia Inn on Westbury: (0935) 813300, and
the Half Moon Hotel on Half Moon Street: (0935) 812017.

The town's best restaurant is Pheasants on Greenhill,
offering an adventurous menu at both lunch and dinner:
(0935) 815252. There is a variety of small places for lunch and,
especially, tea: on Half Moon Street, the House of Steps
opposite the Abbey and the Church House Gallery in the
Tudor shops, and Oliver's on Cheap Street, as well as a
number of pubs like the Digby Tap on Cooks Lane.

*Philip's Road Atlas, p. 9.*

**Almshouse of Saints John the
Baptist and the Evangelist** Abbey
Close. Tue, Thu–Sat Apr–Sept, charge.

**Sherborne Old Castle (EH)** nr
Sherborne; (0935) 812730. Daily,
charge.

**Sherborne New Castle** nr Sherborne;
(0935) 813182. Thu, Sat–Sun Apr–
Sept, charge.

**Sherborne Town Museum** Church
Lane. Tue–Sat Apr–Oct, Tue, Sat
Nov–Mar, charge.

**Tourist Information Centre** off
Hound Street; (0935) 815341.

**Barrington Court (NT)** nr Ilminster;
(0460) 40601. Sat–Wed Apr–Oct,
charge.

**Brympton d'Evercy** nr Yeovil; (0935) 862528. Sat–Wed May–Sept, charge.

**Cerne Abbey** Daily Apr–Oct, charge.

**Compton House** nr Sherborne; (0935) 74608. Daily Apr–Oct, charge.

**Dorset County Museum** (incl. excavated Roman house and Old Shire Hall) Dorchester; (0305) 62735. Mon–Sat, charge.

**East Lambrook Manor Garden** nr South Petherton; (0460) 40328. Mon–Sat, charge.

**Fiddleford Manor Mill House (EH)** Sturminster Newton; (0258) 72597. Daily Apr–Sept, charge.

**Hardy's Cottage (NT)** Higher Bockhampton; (0305) 623666. Wed–Mon Apr–Nov, charge to view interior.

**King Alfred's Tower (NT)** Stourton, nr *Stourhead*; (0747) 840348. Sat–Sun, Tue–Thu, Mar–Nov, charge.

**Lytes Cary (NT)** nr Charlton Mackrell. Mon, Wed, Sat Apr–Nov, charge.

**Minterne House Gardens** Minterne Magna; (03003) 370. Daily Apr–Oct, charge.

**Montacute House (NT)** nr Yeovil; (0935) 823289. Wed–Mon Apr–Nov, charge.

**Purse Caundle Manor** nr Sherborne; (0963) 250400. Thu, Sun Apr–Sept, charge.

**Sandford Orcas Manor** Sandford Orcas; (096322) 206. Sun–Mon May–Sept, charge.

**Stoke-sub-Hamdon Priory (NT)** Daily, free.

**Stourhead (NT)** Stourton; (0747) 840348. Garden daily all year; house Sat–Wed Apr–Nov, charge.

**Tintinhull House Garden (NT)** nr Yeovil. Wed, Thu, Sat Apr–Sept, charge.

**Wolfeton House** nr Dorchester; (0305) 63500. Tue, Fri May–Sept, charge.

# WARWICK

The newly-completed section of the M40 London–Oxford–Birmingham motorway passes immediately by Warwick, crossed by the A46 connecting the Severn and the Cotswolds with Coventry and the M6. A branch railway line from Birmingham Moor Street runs through Warwick to Leamington Spa, which is also on the London Paddington–Birmingham line.

The Tudor House Hotel is in a seventeenth-century building on West Street with one of the grandest displays of black-and-white half-timbering in Warwick: (0926) 495447. The Lord Leycester Hotel on Jury Street is centrally placed, comfortable, and in another historic town building. A more inexpensive place to stay is the Cambridge Villa Hotel on Emscote Road, the way to Leamington Spa: (0926) 491169.

Fanshawes in the Market Place: (0926) 410590, and Randolph's on Coten End: (0926) 491292, offer the best restaurant menus in Warwick, while Pizza Piazza serves good pizzas in the medieval timbered interior of 33–35 Jury Street: (0926) 491641. The Aylesford restaurant at 1 High Street occupies one of the grand new houses erected after the Fire: (0926) 492799.

*Philip's Road Atlas, p. 35.*

**Tourist Information Centre** Jury Street; (0926) 492212.

**Lord Leycester's Hospital** Westgate; (0926) 492797. Mon–Sat, charge.

**Northgate House** Barrack St. Written appointment.

**Oken House Doll's Museum** Castle St; (0926) 495546. Daily May–Sept, charge.

**Shire Hall** Northgate St; (0926) 410410. By appointment.

**St John's House Museum** Coten End; (0926) 410410 ext. 2132. Tue–Sat Oct–Apr, daily May–Sept, free.

**Warwick Castle** (0926) 495241. Daily, charge.

**Warwickshire County Museum** Market Place; (0926) 410410 ext. 2500. Mon–Sat Oct–Apr, daily May–Sept, free.

---

**Anne Hathaway's Cottage** Shottery; (0789) 292100. Daily, charge.

**Baddesley Clinton Manor (NT)** nr Lapworth; (05643) 3294. Wed–Sun Mar–Sept, charge.

**Charlecote Park (NT)** Charlecote; (0789) 840277. Tue–Wed, Fri–Sun Mar–Oct, charge.

**Coughton Court (NT)** nr Alcester; (0789) 762435. Tue–Thu, Sat–Sun May–Sept, charge.

**Farnborough Hall (NT)** Farnborough, nr Banbury. Wed, Sat Apr–Sept, charge.

**Kenilworth Abbey** Daily, free.

**Kenilworth Castle (EH)** Kenilworth; (0926) 52078. Daily Apr–Sept, Tue–Sun Oct–Mar, charge.

**Kinwarton Dovecote (NT)** nr Alcester. Daily Apr–Oct, charge; key from farm.

**Packwood House (NT)** nr Lapworth; (05643) 2024. Wed–Sun Apr–Oct, charge.

**Ragley Hall** nr Alcester; (0789) 762090. Daily Apr–Sept, charge.

**Royal Leamington Spa Art Gallery and Museum** Leamington Spa; (0926) 26559. Mon–Sat, free.

**Shakespeare Birthplace Trust** Stratford-upon-Avon; (0789) 204016: Shakespeare's Birthplace, Hall's Croft, New Place and Nash's House. Daily, charge.

**Stoneleigh Abbey** nr Kenilworth; (0926) 52116. Occasional opening, charge.

**Stratford-upon-Avon Grammar School** (0789) 293759. Daily, Easter and summer holidays, charge.

**Upton House (NT)** nr Edgehill; (029587) 266. Sat–Sun Apr, Oct, Sat–Wed May–Sept, charge.

# INDEX